8,95

GROUP COUNSELING

F. E. PEACOCK PUBLISHERS, INC.
ITASCA, ILLINOIS 60143

GROUP COUNSELING
Theory and Practice

DON C. DINKMEYER
Communication & Motivation Training Institute
Coral Springs, Florida

JAMES J. MURO
University of Maine

To Jane and Pat our wives who taught us about caring, commitment, collaboration, cohesiveness, and IV E behavior.

Preface

COUNSELORS, psychologists, social workers, and educators are increasingly expected to be familiar with group dynamics, group forces, and procedures for organizing and maintaining a group. Too often specialists in these areas have been educated without specific training in group procedures. Thus, they are left without a basic skill in working with human beings.

There is a growing recognition that man is a social being, and his conflicts are typically interpersonal. It is becoming apparent that many concerns are best understood and resolved in the group setting. Persons who are expected to work with groups of people should have at least a basic knowledge of the complicated phenomena involved in group work.

Our original interest in writing in this area developed from our own search for materials and books when instructing courses in group counseling or group procedures. Although there were texts in group therapy, there was little available to assist both the beginning students and those who had some experience with group procedures. Instructors were forced to obtain several texts for a class in order to present all of the material necessary for those who would lead groups.

Our collaborative efforts began by comparing our individual course outlines and teaching materials and striving to develop a comprehensive outline. Once the outline was established, each chapter was exchanged, critiqued intensively, and rewritten. The chapters now are the product of intensive internal review by both authors. Upon completion of the first draft, the manuscript was mimeographed, distributed to several graduate classes and subjected to critical review by students. Their comments were utilized in assisting the authors to sharpen those ideas that were vague and unclear to readers.

The revised manuscript was then reviewed by William Fawcett Hill, editor of the *Comparative Group Studies Journal.* His detailed and intensive review supplied us with excellent feedback and provided direction for the final rewriting.

The book presently contains a comprehensive approach to group counseling. It includes detailed material on group dynamics, varied theories of group counseling, and an analysis of the forces which bring about change in groups. A detailed presentation of all the steps involved in group work is included. One is led through the skills necessary for leading groups, organizational procedures, methods of establishing and maintaining groups, and special problems in groups. A unique feature is a chapter on group counseling with children.

The final chapters present new and dynamic approaches to using group counseling with parents and teachers. Significant attention is also given to a discussion of the teacher as a leader of a classroom group. The last chapter provides an intensive overview of the research literature on groups.

The book is intended for all who would lead groups and who are concerned with improving their skills. It can be used in the education of counselors, psychologists, social workers, or any professional concerned with group procedures. We foresee that it will have value in teacher education—in acquainting teachers with this important but seldom-studied aspect of the teacher's role.

The book was a highly significant educational experience for the authors as they exchanged their thoughts, dialogued with students, and studied the review of Dr. Hill.

We hope it will be of equal value to those who work with persons in groups.

DON DINKMEYER
JAMES MURO

Contents

CHAPTER 1

Introduction to Group Counseling

THE LYRICS of a well-known song read, "People, people who need people, are the luckiest people in the world." The song might well be the theme for the growing national interest in group work. There is about the land a feeling of alienation and polarization. It exists between the generations, man and wife, teacher and child, administrator and teacher, and almost every describable facet of society. Truly, the lack of belonging, the failure to be identified as participating dynamically in the community and one's destiny are all symptomatic of the type of problem which is best treated in the group.

Hence, we see a growing interest in group procedures on the part of professionals and the general public. Human potential institutes are springing up and flourishing. Psychiatrists, psychologists, social workers, and educators are increasingly becoming involved in utilization of the group process.

There has also been a proliferation of books, articles, and related research studies. The *Review of Educational Research* devoted to Guidance and Counseling (1969) indicated that 240 articles were obtainable for review covering the period from the summer of 1965 to the fall of 1968. These were articles specifically related to research in group counseling.

Group process and group counseling mean different things to different people. At this point we would like to clarify what we mean when we refer to group counseling. Group counseling is an interpersonal process led by a professionally trained counselor and conducted with individuals who are coping with typical developmental problems. It

1

focuses on thoughts, feelings, attitudes, values, purposes, behavior, and goals of the individual and the total group. The group process permits the individual to examine and share self with others. Group transactions and group mechanisms facilitate increased understanding of self and others. Group counseling creates the conditions and climate for re-evaluating one's thoughts, feelings, and behavior. Through changing one's perceptual field, attitudes and feelings, or actions, one is better equipped to experience and cope with the tasks of life.

Content	Level I	Level II	Level III
		PROCESS	
A	Leader plans topics	Leader and group members collaborate in planning topics	Topics originate with group members
B	Lecture and recitation	Discussions, projects, panels, visits	Free discussion, role-playing
C	Facts and skills emphasized	Attitudes and opinions emphasized	Feelings and needs emphasized
	Units in regular classes	Separate guidance groups meet on schedule	Groups organized as needed, meet as needed
Type A Usual school subject matter mathematics, English, etc.	1	4	7
Type B School-related topics: the world of work, choosing a college, how to study, etc.	2	5	8
Type C Non-school topics: dating behavior, parent-child relations, handling frustrations, etc.	3	6	9

TABLE 1.
INTERACTION OF CONTENT AND PROCESS IN GROUP GUIDANCE,
GROUP COUNSELING, AND GROUP THERAPY[1]

[1]Leo Goldman, "Group Guidance: Content and Process," *Personnel and Guidance Journal,* Vol. 39, No. 6. (February, 1962). By permission.

A functioning group brings about a dynamic interrelationship between the members. There is a process of mutuality and identification with each other. Being in a group indicates acceptance of certain common purposes and the development of norms that are shared.

Since at present there is much confusion between the terms *group guidance, group counseling,* and *group therapy,* it may be important to look at the significance of the roles of content and process. This has been done very clearly by Goldman (1962). Goldman, in the accompanying diagram, shows how we move from an emphasis upon leader control and a focus on facts and skills to the originating of topics by group members with a real emphasis upon feelings, attitudes, and values. He makes it clear that the cells are not mutually exclusive but they do a comprehensive job of running the gambit from teaching through group guidance, group counseling, and might even in the final cell be considered to be involved with certain aspects of group therapy.

CHARACTERISTICS OF GROUPS

Groups that are developed for group counseling are particularly concerned with the interaction, verbal and nonverbal, which occurs in the group, and the achievement of individual and group goals. Interaction occurs whenever the behavior of a person directly affects the attitudes, feelings, and behavior of another. Individuals establish specific goals and agree to be willing to help others. Dynamic groups always contain considerable interdependence. The members identify with each other and develop common concerns, purposes, and attitudes.

As the group evolves, the people in it interact on the basis of certain patterns which have been established. When a group has progressed through the primary stages, then each member has some perceptions of all the other members that are distinct enough that he can clearly distinguish each member of the group. The best definition of a group for our purposes was developed by Cartwright and Zander:

> It seems likely, then, that when a set of people constitutes a group, one or more of the following statements will characterize them: (a) they engage in frequent interaction; (b) they define themselves as members; (c) they are defined by others as belonging to the group; (d) they share norms concerning matters of common interest; (e) they participate in a system of interlocking roles; (f) they identify with another as a result of having set up the same model-object or ideas in their superego; (g) they find the group to be rewarding; (h) they

pursue promotively interdependent goals; (i) they have a collective perception of their unity; (j) they tend to act in a unitary manner toward the environment. [Cartwright and Zander, 1968, p. 48]

RATIONALE FOR GROUP COUNSELING

It is important to be cognizant of the reason for working in groups. Awareness of the potential benefit of group counseling enlarges the perspectives and anticipations of the leader and the members.

Group counseling takes on added dimensions when seen from the perspective that man is an indivisible, social, decision-making being whose actions have a social purpose (Dreikurs and Sonstegard, 1968). Recognizing that human beings are social beings creates a new awareness of both verbal and nonverbal interactions and transactions. The individual's life-style is always expressed in his social transactions and psychological movement with others. His unique approach to the problems of life is always consistent with his concept of self and his assumptions about life. Thus, all the transactions that occur within the group take on added meaning insofar as they enable us to observe the personality of the individual as it is developed in the interaction patterns with others. Group counseling provides the counselor and the counselees with a very valuable social laboratory. The cohesive group becomes a small society or microcommunity.

The group process contains special values for both the diagnostic and therapeutic aspects of problem solving. There are certain behaviors which can only be observed in the group and there are certain therapeutic effects which can only be promoted and processed in the group setting.

The following group-interaction segment was recorded from a session with fifth-grade boys who were counseled by one of the authors. It illustrates the flavor of the interaction and the possible significance of group work.

John is very socially aggressive and hence antagonizes his peers. In individual counseling, he discusses solutions and new approaches, but does not seem to solve the problem. The counselor suggests group counseling.

Group excerpt:

BILL: I wish I was able to make friends.
JACK: Well, what do you do?
BILL: I have things I try to get them to do, but they won't.

JACK: Have you tried doing what they want?

JOHN: (interrupting loudly as Jack was continuing to be empathic) That's no fun. They should do what Bill wants.

JACK: That's what you think!

BILL: Yes, I can't force them.

JOHN: Then forget about them.

COUNSELOR: What do you think is happening here?

JOHN: Nothing! I was just telling him what to do. He worries too much about what others think.

JACK: Yes, and that's your problem. You never care what others think.

JOHN: Well ... Uh ... How?

CRAIG: When Jack tried to help Bill you blurted right in and didn't even hear Bill's problem.

JOHN: You mean I don't hear what's said?

CRAIG: Maybe you hear the words, but not a guy's feelings.

COUNSELOR: It seems Bill and John both have problems in being sensitive to others.

JOHN: I guess I do force my way in.

This brief excerpt from a group-counseling session enables the counselor as well as Bill and John to see their behavior and attitudes in a new light. They didn't merely discuss their problem but demonstrated to all concerned what caused their problem. Diagnosis is clarified by the insight which arises from the transactions. Craig's honest confrontation, and the counselor's ensuing sensitive support, can help John see his problem and become motivated to seek alternative actions.

The group-counseling process is always based on some theory about the nature of man and human relationships. The group is usually developed most effectively when the leader recognizes that most problems are primarily social and interpersonal. Problems arise because people must interact. Many developmental tasks are accomplished as an outgrowth of social interaction, and the attempt to meet our social needs. These tasks obviously are best solved in the social setting for a majority of individuals.

All behavior has social meaning, and is best understood in its social context. Our character is expressed through our social movements, interactions, and transactions. All psychological movement has a purpose, and the context of the behavior enables us to determine its social purpose. The group permits us not only to talk about the problem, but to engage in reality testing in a social laboratory. Observing the consequences of the interaction clarifies its purpose. Group counseling reveals individual and group convictions, purposes, and assumptions. It also provides the setting and mechanisms for changing one's purposes and behavior.

One of the most important components of normality and the ability to meet the tasks of life is involved in the capacity to give and take, defined by Adlerians as Social Interest (Dreikurs, 1958). The individual who matures socially desires to cooperate, and is interested in altruistically being of assistance. He must learn to interact effectively with his peers and the total group for the enhancement of self. It is only within the group that man can fulfill himself. Belonging is a basic need and man is not actualized unless he belongs. Thus, the individual's social interest is a measure of social maturity.

The significance of behavior lies in its social consequences. One can understand the real meaning of interaction and transaction when one looks closely at the consequences of the action. The individual who is aggressive causes others to counterattack or to shy away, developing social distance. He maintains his image by restricting positive social transactions. His purpose is achieved when these ineffective social relations are developed. They force people to deal with him on his terms. The individual who is socially passive, shy, and inactive may get others to serve him or pay special attention. He is ineffective and as a result is excluded or gets others to act for him.

Motivation is best understood in terms of comprehending how the individual finds his place. It is the way in which he seeks to be known and strives to be significant that enables us to understand the purpose of his behavior. Some find their place by being students, athletes, or social leaders. Others gain equal recognition, as they see it, from acting out, delinquency, rebellion, or passive withdrawal. The method of finding one's place in the group helps both the counselor and members to see the individual's motives and style of life.

The group provides the benefit of the corrective influences which can transpire in the group. It is one thing for the leader to disapprove of a behavior, but it usually has a more significant effect when a behavior is disapproved by peers who really count. The aggressive individual is often benefited by the natural and logical consequences of group interaction. On the positive side, peer encouragement is usually far more significant than that which comes from the counselor alone.

The group also provides the opportunity for individuals to make public group commitments to the leader. The commitment is verbal and the stating of a specific intention in the group may help the individual to focus on his goal. In certain instances behavioral counselors might help negotiate a behavior contract (Krumboltz and Thoresen, 1969). This is an agreement which specifies what each person will do for a specific time. The explicit nature of these contracts may sharpen focus on the desired behavior. In either instance the act of committing oneself to a course of action in the presence of peers and the ensuing reporting of progress are powerful forces in facilitating change. The opportunity to become more aware of the social purpose of behavior and to utilize the natural social consequences is a unique value made available in group counseling.

The group also presents a broader mirror of the individual's behavior than the counselor alone. It enables him to see himself both in others and in his own verbalizations. This leads to greater understanding of self and others.

Each individual has the need to feel that his problems are not completely unique, and that he is part of mankind. The opportunity to identify with others and to recognize that our problems as human beings are often universal, is provided in a unique way through the group experience. It is very therapeutic to learn that the problem which you have felt was yours alone is shared and that someone knows how you feel and will try to help. The group also provides the opportunity for spectator therapy—the opportunity to see others work out their problems and to profit from their experiences without revealing one's own problems.

The group, then, presents situations where one can consider alternative actions at his own pace. One may participate only when he is ready. There is no pressure to reveal what one is not ready to share.

Also, there is the opportunity for reality testing in a real social situation. One need not merely speculate or hypothesize about how he will act with others. He can try it out immediately. Concerns are not merely discussed, but the feedback from group members enables him to see his problems in a new light. More important, if he wants to change his interpersonal behavior, the group is available to provide support and instant feedback on how he is progressing.

The group provides another major contribution insofar as it is a value-forming element to the individual. He is helped to establish norms that are more reality based.

The group also can meet a very unique need of each human being —the need to give of one's self, to give love, not only receive it. This opportunity for mutual help which dissolves social isolation is found most readily in the group experience.

MEETING PUPIL NEEDS

Group counseling provides a unique leader-directed peer experience when the leader is aware of the personal–social–emotional needs of the individuals who are involved. Then he can utilize the group as an unusual opportunity to help meet the special needs of those who are in the group. Certain individuals have a greater need to belong, to be accepted, or to give affection. He can recognize this and help utilize the group as a unique setting for meeting these needs. The needs which can be potentially fulfilled in the group include:

1. The need to belong, to find a place, and to be accepted as one is.
2. Affection needs—to be loved and to be able to provide love; the opportunity to have a therapeutic effect on others.
3. The opportunity to engage in the give-and-take which is required for the maturing of social interest and altruistic feelings.
4. To help one see that his problem is not unique, but perhaps universally experienced in the group.
5. Provide the opportunity to develop feelings of equality, to be part of a group regardless of what one brings in terms of intellect, affect.
6. The need to work out one's identity and approach to the various social tasks of life.

THE SIGNIFICANCE OF THE SOCIAL PROCESS IN THE SCHOOL SETTING

The schools have always operated on a theoretical set of guidelines and objectives which indicate their concern for the whole child. This concern, of course, includes the social and emotional development of the individual. However, in practice, schools more frequently operate as if their primary concern is the cognitive development of the individual. Certainly the basic methods of evaluation which focus on mental ability and school achievement, the grading practices and reporting practices, are all evidences of an overconcern with the cognitive aspect of human development.

One of the primary values of group experiences in the schools relates to the personalization of the educational process. The group can help increase the communication processes which are vital for the development of real learning. These processes include communication across the generations—between teacher and student or parent and student —as well as communication between the varied age groups—primary and intermediate children, sophomores and seniors. Thus, properly utilized group approaches can add much to the total development and maximizing of the educational process. We recognize that the group process is crucial because human beings are social beings who grow and develop only through adequate and meaningful exposure to social situations.

The group has another benefit for the counseling and guidance department. It is apparent that children and adolescents are often more comfortable talking about their real feelings, attitudes, and beliefs in groups of peers than in one-to-one situations with adults. Thus, the avenue of the group permits us access to certain kinds of students and situations not possible in individual counseling.

The group procedure also recognizes that all human problems are primarily social. Problems exist because we must interact with others or because we are concerned with impressing people or controlling them in some manner. The group process provides the counselor with the opportunity to see the behavior of the child rather than having it described. It also presents a unique opportunity to deal with these central concerns and to provide the feeling of acceptance, belonging, and support that is necessary.

GOALS OF GROUP COUNSELING

The leader is concerned with establishing a relationship which is both accepting and permissive, and at the same time confronting and encountering insofar as it creates a setting in which the individual sees himself and receives genuine feedback. The leader becomes a congruent sender as well as a reflective listener (Randolph and Howe, 1966). It is only in this kind of environment that the goals and objectives of group counseling can be achieved.

The general goals of group counseling include:

1.   To help each member of the group know and understand himself. To assist with the identity-seeking process.

2.   As a result of coming to understand self, to develop increased self-acceptance and feelings of personal worth.

3.   To develop social skills and interpersonal abilities which enable one to cope with the developmental tasks in their personal–social areas.

4.   To develop increased self-direction, problem-solving, and decision-making abilities, and to transfer these abilities to use in regular classroom and social contacts.

5.   To develop sensitivity to the needs of others which results in increased recognition of responsibility for one's behavior. To become able to identify with the feelings of those significant others in our world as well as to develop a greater ability to be empathic.

6.   To learn to be an empathic listener who hears not only what is said but also the feelings which accompany what has been said.

7.   To be congruent with self, really able to offer accurately what one thinks and believes. To say what one means, to be a congruent sender.

8.   To help each member formulate specific goals for himself which can be measured and observed behaviorally, and to help him make a commitment to move toward those goals.

THE THERAPEUTIC VALUE OF GROUP PROCESS

The development of group work has a number of valuable by-products. As we learn to work with each other on the basis of group procedures which imply the development of mutual respect, we are bound to stimulate the formulation of a democratic environment. This environment would feature equality or the increased importance of each person's worth as an individual being. Each person then becomes equal as he contributes and participates in the give-and-take of the group. This increased freedom of self-expression usually results in a more productive community.

In the past, misbehavior and failure to function were often the result of mistaken methods of finding one's place in the peer group. The group and the democratic environment now provide the opportunity for the individual to make a new choice regarding how he wants to be known. He can now find his place of significance through contributing, and not merely through resistance. The group provides the opportunities to see the psychological movement and to correct it at the same time.

The group makes a unique contribution insofar as it meets certain psychological needs—to belong, to be accepted, to release negative feelings, and to participate in a supportive atmosphere which encourages self-exploration. This atmosphere, in which one feels free to express his feelings, thoughts, and ideas about self and others without any concern for adult censure, provides the opportunity for maximum human development. However, it is always done within the bounds of developing mutual respect and increased dialogue with each other. Confrontation is not done for catharsis or sensational effect, but with the goal of mirroring to the confronted his effect on others. It should be altruistically motivated.

The group provides an opportunity for the peers to make a unique contribution to each other. They can provide feedback at a point where it can be of maximal value, by giving it directly to the person who can benefit. They can also provide a kind of support, encouragement, and acceptance which cannot come strictly from the counselor.

Another unique value of the group is the freedom to be oneself, to test ideas and to get immediate, open, honest, and congruent benefit, too; this is the opportunity for spectator therapy. One can speak or be silent, but the opportunity for the choice is there. One is not forced to continue this dialogue, as it often may appear in individual counseling.

Thus, one of the great gains from the group process occurs insofar as each member becomes a therapeutic agent for every other individual (Moreno, 1957). This promotes integration of the individual with respect to himself while integrating the total group.

ASSUMPTIONS BASIC TO THE GROUP PROCESS

Group process has many of its roots in social psychology, sociology, and perceptual field theory. We always start by helping people to see their perception of the situation and to recognize that what they believe may not necessarily be common to what others believe. However, at the same time they come to recognize that what they think is unique to them may be a universal problem.

The group is concerned with the problem that immediately concerns the members and deals with the here and now. While certain analytic procedures may take an historical approach, we are not recommending them for group counseling. The group provides the settings where one can examine and explore the problem. There is a unique acceptance, support, and encouragement which exists within the group. As the individuals in the group become more secure and recognize the values which can be derived from this environment, they are now open to meeting their needs through the group. They can express their problems and see if others perceive the problem in the same manner. They find that because many of their problems are interpersonal, they can actually learn new approaches within this group. They come to see that they are not stuck with the problem but that there are options and choices and that it is up to them to evaluate these choices.

Group counseling actually involves a treatment which comes under the skillful guidance of a leader but which is really only possible through the group's presence. The peers are corrective influences in some instances and encouragers in others. Each member is able to see himself in the other members. He is able to see some of his faulty attitudes and assumptions. Sometimes he even recalls verbally or to himself, "I remember when I used to think that way, act that way, or believe that." He sees his social purposes and his characteristic style in finding his place. At the same time he receives feedback and disclosure from others. One of the greatest benefits comes from the opportunities to provide mutual help, love, affection, and assistance. These unique values and opportunities to be altruistic come only through the group. This is often accompanied by being able to experience the logical consequences of group action.

Walter Lifton lists eleven assumptions upon which he believes the group-centered approach is based:

    1.   Individuals and groups, when freed of threat, strive toward healthier, more adaptive kinds of behavior. There is a drive in everyone toward homeostasis.

    2.   Each individual lives in a world of his own, bound by the uniqueness of his perceptions and past experiences. No one can share past experiences of perceptions with another. We can only help people experience and clarify their own perceptions. Each group member checks his perceptions of reality by comparing them with significant "others." The most important "others" tend to be the member's peers.

    3.   Even when the individual is convinced of the correctness of his perceptions, if his behavior, based upon these perceptions, does not cause others to respond to him in the desired fashion, from a purely pragmatic point of view he will have to revise his behavior if he seeks a different response from others.

    4.   Because everyone needs ways of defending himself and avoiding unacceptable pressures, everyone has defenses which may cause behavior inconsistent with the verbalized goals he states to others. These defenses are necessary to existence and cannot be removed until a substitute is found.

    5.   People react to each other based upon what they feel the other person's behavior implies. Because of the incongruity between a person's communications to others (on a feeling versus a content level), breakdown in communication occurs. We assume people respond to what we say, rather than the feelings our words convey.

    6.   By providing acceptance and support to individuals and groups, they may be less constricted in their perceptions of their behavior, feeling safe enough to let themselves face feelings they know exist but could not before afford to acknowledge.

    7.   Since most people tend to move in their thinking from the concrete to the abstract, members dealing with their here-and-now problems in the group are more likely to see

the relevance of the group's activity and, given the security of the group, are likely to be able to generalize from their current experiences to past ones, which then have new meaning. Put in another way, by dealing with the here and now we also alter the meaning and import of the past.

8. The group leader, to be effective, must be able either to live out a variety of group roles or, at the very least, to ensure that other group members can serve as role models. Members then learn not only the many types of roles needed in our society, but they also can learn to emulate these roles and thereby increase their ability to cope with society.

9. Society is not something external to the lives of the group members. The group members by their behavior have a vital role in setting the limits and mores which individual members learn to understand and live with.

10. In a democratic society the ultimate source of authority is not vested in a single individual, but remains the responsibility of the entire group.

11. The group provides all the elements needed to assist change. It offers support, feedback of perceived behavior, information about alternatives which could be considered, reinforcement of positive behavior and rejection of unacceptable behavior, and new experiences designed to broaden the repertoire of experiences and skills needed to cope with society (the group). [Lifton, 1968]

PRINCIPLES OF GROUP WORK

Throughout this text we will provide specific help on various aspects of group counseling and group process. However, at this time we would like to provide an overview of certain principles which are basic to effective group counseling.

1. Group counseling will be most effective in a democratic environment where all concerned, and especially those with administrative responsibilities, recognize the value of group-based decisions. Thus, participants in the group will see evidences of group process at work in relationships between the significant members of the establishment, administrators, teachers, as well as members of their groups.

2. Group counseling can only work effectively when there has been adequate and intensive orientation of administration, staff, parents, and children. The purposes of group work must be clear to all concerned.

3. Groups are most effective when they are voluntary. The coun-

selor approaches the students who are potential members, explains the process, assesses their readiness, and develops some awareness of the kinds of experiences which may occur in the group. Before the group is formed, the counselor secures from each potential member a commitment to be willing to talk about their concerns as well as a willingness to help others who have concerns. It is vital that the client's anticipations and expectations of the group be realistic. They should come to the group with the expectation of making some changes.

4.   Since the initiation of the group is such a crucial factor, it is important that the group be attractive—that is, there should be more people who want to be in the group than there are places available. Thus, the group can utilize belonging and involvement to create a cohesiveness.

5.   It is important that each group assume its own responsibility for behavior in the group. It must establish, define, and enforce norms. The counselor is a member of the group but he helps the members to establish this personal and group responsibility for their values and behavior.

6.   The group is always aware that its long-range goals are the development of increased social interest, capacity to give and take, understanding of self and others, and as a result participation as a congruent sender and reflective listener.

7.   The group is based upon the premise of equality. This involves the willingness to understand and accept each other's deficiencies.

8.   Group procedures should never be confused with mass procedures. The leader recognizes that group processes in guidance occur along a continuum, and that it is the content, the technique, and the process that are interwoven. The leader is always alert to the most appropriate application of these three factors at a given moment.

THE PLACE OF GROUP PROCESS IN COUNSELING

Each counselor needs to establish some hierarchy in regard to the services he provides. He not only provides others with choices and alternatives, but by his very actions he is also a decision-making being. It is our contention that the skill of utilizing group process must be one of the primary skills of the school counselor. He places his skills in this area at the disposal of a vast range of clientele—teachers, parents, administrators, and children. While the primary target is the child, he recognizes that in many instances he will service more children more effectively through groups with the aforementioned significant adults. Thus, he may immediately establish some priority related to the attention he gives to direct and indirect services. While priorities will vary based on individual situations and counselor skills, we are suggesting that at this time counselors in the schools might work from the priorities of teacher, child, and parent groups in the following order:

1. Collaborating and consulting with groups of teachers. These teacher groups are focused primarily at the concept of working together in contrast to a consultant–teacher, or superior–inferior relationship. The concept of collaboration, working together, underlines all of this type of group work. This kind of a teacher group may focus on a specific child or group of children as a starting point. The groups are called C-Groups, and they start with a case (an external unit) but they also confront, encounter, and clarify the teacher's affective and cognitive domains to assess her perceptions, and to change beliefs, attitudes, and behavior. The group may be concerned with a specific child or with the effects of curriculum on the group. In all instances the C-Group is holistic in its treatment of the attitudes, beliefs, purposes, values, and behavior of both children and teachers.

This approach to work with teachers can be some of the most dynamic work that can occur in a school. It is most effectively utilized in schools where administrators develop schedules which permit team teaching, individualized approaches and flexible scheduling. In schools with less flexible schedules, physical education, art, music, recess, noon hour, or other special periods where specialists teach or assistants can be hired, provide time for the group. Groups can also meet before or after school.

Once the school administrator is convinced of the value of the group procedure with staff, then he is charged with the responsibility of developing time and schedules which permit and provide for meaningful and purposeful consultation. The group work with teachers hopes to change the teachers' feelings about self and others.

2. In counseling with groups of children, the group work is either developmental in nature or crisis oriented. In all instances it has the intent of attempting to work with as many children as are interested in the benefits of the group process.

3. Consultation with parents and groups may originally focus on parent education, child-study groups, and similar activities. However, the attempt is always to reach a large number of parents and help them understand more effective ways to relate with their children. These parent groups work with developmental problems with the same C-Group emphasis. The counselor attempts to identify problems and concerns, then he utilizes the group mechanism such as acceptance, universalization, feedback, and reality testing to develop a cohesive

group that looks at specific child-training situations, parent attitudes, and procedures. The group is focused on providing help with specific problems, parent attitudes and beliefs, and helping parents consider the alternatives and develop a commitment for change.

Group procedures, then, must occupy a most significant place in the training and competencies of the educator, counselor, and specialist in psychological approaches. Their rationale, relationship to pupil needs and objectives clearly point to the necessity of training professionals to utilize groups more effectively. The group and group forces will always exist. They will influence for good or bad. Our choice is whether we intend to be more aware of them and increase our skills so they can be used to benefit human development.

SUMMARY

Group counseling is an interpersonal process which permits the individual to examine and share self with others. It is differentiated from other group processes in terms of its process and content.

Group counseling has special value for both the diagnosis and the solving of the problem. There are certain behaviors which can best be observed in the group as well as certain therapeutic effects which can only be processed in the group. Behavior is best worked with in its social context.

Thus, groups have a unique rationale and can meet specific pupil needs which are often neglected. Groups can be used to personalize the educational process. Specific goals and therapeutic values of groups are detailed.

We view group procedures as the fundamental skill of the counselor, and they should be used in work with children, teachers, and parents.

REFERENCES

CARTWRIGHT, DORWIN, and ZANDER, ALVIN. *Group Dynamics: Research and Theory.* 3rd ed. New York: Harper and Row, Publishers, 1968.

DREIKURS, RUDOLF. *Fundamentals of Adlerian Psychology.* Chicago: Alfred Adler Institute, 1958.

DREIKURS, RUDOLF, and SONSTEGARD, MANFORD. "Rationale of Group Counseling," in *Guidance and Counseling in the Elementary School: Readings in Theory and Practice* (ed. DON C. DINKMEYER), p. 280. New York: Holt, Rinehart and Winston, Inc., 1968.

GOLDMAN, LEO. "Group Guidance: Content and Process," *Personnel and Guidance Journal,* Vol. 39, No. 6 (February, 1962).

KRUMBOLTZ, JOHN, and THORESEN, CARL. *Behavioral Counseling: Cases and Techniques.* New York: Holt, Rinehart and Winston, Inc., 1969.

LIFTON, WALTER. "Group-Centered Counseling," in *Basic Approaches to Group Psychotherapy and Group Counseling* (ed. GEORGE M. GAZDA), pp. 233–34. Springfield, Ill.: Charles C Thomas, Publisher, 1968.

MORENO, JACOB L. *First Book of Psychotherapy.* 3rd ed. New York: Beacon House, 1957.

RANDOLPH, NORMA, and HOWE, WILLIAM. *Self-Enhancing Education.* Palo Alto, Calif.: Sanford Press, 1966.

Review of Educational Research, "Guidance and Counseling," Vol. 30, No. 2 (April, 1969). Published by the American Educational Research Association, 1126 16th St. N.W., Washington, D.C., 20036.

CHAPTER 2

Group Dynamics and Group Process

ALTHOUGH THE TERM group dynamics is often associated with the current emphasis on group guidance and counseling in psychological literature, sociologists have been pondering concepts about groups for centuries (Durkin, 1964). The term, in essence, describes the complex and interacting forces within a common field or setting. Unfortunately, there is still no precise definition of the term that is universally accepted by various writers and researchers (Luft, 1963). In many instances, one may be forced to examine the particular context in which the term is used to determine any special meaning.

A study of some representative samples of attempts to define group dynamics, however, does reveal that if definitions are not always precise and concrete, a general tone of agreement does prevail. For example, Shertzer and Stone provided a brief but clear definition in a recent guidance text:

> Group dynamics is a term that refers to the interacting forces within groups as they operate to achieve objectives. [Shertzer and Stone, 1966, p. 169]

This definition closely approximates that presented by Bonner in his comprehensive text on group dynamics:

> We can now define group dynamics as that division of social psychology which investigates the formation and change of the structure and function of the psychological grouping of people into self-directing wholes. [Bonner, 1959, p. 5]

Cartwright and Zander elaborate and expand on the definitions offered by Shertzer, Stone and Bonner:

> In summary, then, we have proposed that group dynamics should be defined as a field of inquiry dedicated to advancing knowledge about the nature of groups, the laws of their development, and the interrelations with individuals, other groups, and larger institutions. It may be identified by four distinguishing characteristics: (a) an emphasis on the theoretically significant research; (b) an interest in dynamics and the interdependence among phenomena; (c) a broad relevance to all the social sciences; and (d) the potential applicability of its findings in efforts to improve the functioning of groups and their consequences in individuals and society. [Cartwright and Zander, 1960, p. 9]

Elsewhere, we have written (Muro and Freeman, 1968) that from a pragmatic sense it may be useful to conceive of the term within the context of the "why" of group functioning. Why do groups form? Why do individuals change in groups? Why are some groups cohesive and others not? The answers to such basic questions are vital to the group counselor who seeks to achieve counseling goals within the vehicle of the group.

ROOTS OF GROUP DYNAMICS

Bonner (1959) in reviewing the history of the group movement has noted that group dynamics, like most scientific ideas, have no single origin (p. 6). In fact, historical antecedents of group dynamics are found in sociology, anthropology, social psychology, field theory, and other areas of inquiry.

Early sociology, as represented by Comte and Herbert Spencer, was essentially philosophical and concerned largely with description and classification. It was not until the late 1800s that Ward in his two-volume *Dynamic Psychology* began to advance the concept of society as a self-directing whole (Bonner, 1959, pp. 6–7). At about the same period, Durkin theorized that human behavior, in reality, can only be understood by knowing the collective structure of the group, thus emphasizing the importance of the group in the life of the individual.

Interaction, a much-discussed group phenomenon, received heavy emphasis in the work of George Simmel in the early twentieth century. Simmel emphasized the centrality of interaction and the importance of group belongingness. Simmel's work is of particular interest to group counselors and group therapists in that it involves the concept of conflict. He conceived of conflict in terms of *opposition* or the high tension state involving the success or failure of a given group in its efforts to transcend the barriers to its freedom of movement (Durkin, 1964).

Among the most significant of the contributions of the sociologists to group dynamics was the work of Charles H. Cooley and his primary-group concept. According to Bonner (1959), when the modern dynamicists speak of the influence of the group on the individual's behavior in instances where individuals with divergent behavior personalities move toward a more common norm, they are, in reality, restating Cooley's basic and fruitful ideas. Group influence, cohesion, and the process of decision making may all be traced in some form to Cooley's early work (Bonner, 1959, pp. 12–13). "In summary, the primary group controls behavior, changes attitudes, and leads to common decisions" (Bonner, 1959, p. 13). If this last statement has a familiar ring to the reader, he, in all probability, saw it listed in the guidance literature under "advantages or rationale for group counseling."

SOCIAL PSYCHOLOGISTS' CONTRIBUTIONS

While Bonner (1959) notes that psychology had not concerned itself specifically with the study of groups until the end of the last century, Durkin (1964) contends that social psychologists have, in reality, contributed much in the areas of methodology and theory building. Early laboratory studies by Triplett (1897) and Molde (1920) were pioneer efforts in demonstrating that the influence of groups and individual behavior could be scientifically studied. In fact, these investigations were instrumental in providing early group-study techniques which were later developed and refined (Bonner, 1959). Contributors from this area include Triplett (1897) who initiated the first experimental investigation of social influence on group performance, Mayer (1903) who studied the work of children individually and in groups, and Molde (1914) who researched the role of the group in relation to its influence on the speed and vigor of individual performance (Bonner, 1959).

Later Allport (1924) evoked some controversy among those interested in groups with his challenge of McDougall's concept of the group mind. According to Allport, only the individual represents true reality while groups represent abstractions from collections of individuals. More recently, Schultz (1958) has suggested that "the individual be used as a model for the group and that in addition the reverse would be instructive" (Durkin, 1964, p. 14). What is significant from Allport's research is his conclusion that group influence improves the quantity but not the quality of group performance—a conclusion that was also reached by Burnham (1901) on the basis of a review of several studies (Bonner, 1959). Ohlsen (1970) notes that Hare also found that autocratic leadership seems to produce greater quantitative results whereas democratic leadership is more effective in producing better morale and qualitative results.

CONTEMPORARY GROUP DYNAMICS

Kurt Lewin, a prominent researcher and theorist, is generally recognized as the modern founder and promoter of group dynamics (Luft, 1963), although there appears to be an ongoing controversy as to whether or not Lewin's work should be considered as a priority over that of Moreno. Bonner (1959) writes that his survey leaves no doubt that neither one should be considered the founder of this discipline, although the Lewinians are more *directly* associated with this field both in their theoretical formulations and concrete applications than are Moreno and sociometry (p. 18).

Lewin (1940) labeled his approach *field theory* or the concept that behavior is derived from the totality of coexisting facts characterized by a dynamic field wherein one section of the field depends on every other segment of that field. Thus while Freudian psychology emphasizes the historical or past behavior of the individual and Adlerian psychology points to future or goal-directed behavior of the individual, Lewin theorized that behavior depends upon the present field. In this context, if one is to understand the behavior of a given individual, it is necessary to describe his present psychological environment. The impact of the here-and-now orientation is still a significant part of modern group psychology and continues to influence the theoretical and research efforts of numerous current writers and researchers.

While a complete review of Lewinian field theory is beyond the scope of this text, Shepherd (1964) traces his influence on modern group-dynamics theory to his early interest in phenomenology, his ingenuity in research design, and his theoretical system which he attempted to represent mathematically (p. 24). Basic to field theory, according to Bonner (1959), is the concept of action in a field. The human individual, who lives in groups, goes beyond the simple behavior of animals to one characterized by *symbolic interaction;* moreover, since group behavior is generally complicated by cultural demands, it is generally manifested in the form of "sanctioned forms of symbolic interaction" (Bonner, 1959, p. 19).

In order to make his theoretical constructs more accurate, Lewin developed a rather complex system of topology and vector analysis wherein behavior is explained in terms of what is perceived as attractive to the individual (positive valence) with reference to needs he may be experiencing at a given moment. The attraction is a psychological force or *vector* that directs one towards the attractive object. Conversely, if an object is unattractive to an individual (negative valence), he will be moved away from it or it may simply have no valence or not be in the perceived field. Regardless of whether or not an individual object has positive or negative valence for the individual, his movement in the field is termed *locomotion* or action in the perceived field. Barriers or constraints to locomotion may cause regressive or aggressive behavior (Harsh and Schrichel, 1959, pp. 351–360). In addition, Lewin advanced the concept that contrary to some earlier thinking the group is not the sum of its members but a "structure that emerges from the interaction of individuals, a structure which itself produces change in individuals" (Bonner, 1959, pp. 19–20). The modern counselor who is indeed attempting to produce change in individuals by promoting group interaction owes much to the early work of Kurt Lewin and his associates.

Cartwright and Zander (1968) reported that the mid-1930s provided ripe conditions for the rapid advance of empirical research on groups and that just prior to the Second World War much research activity did take place that displayed the characteristics now associated with group dynamics. Among the most influential contributors were Sherif, Newcomb, Whyte, Lewin, Lippitt, and White (Cartwright and Zander, 1968, p. 17). Each of these contributors will be discussed briefly here.

SHERIF'S EXPERIMENTAL CREATION OF THE SOCIAL NORM

The concept of a *social norm*—the general label Sherif applied to customs, traditions, standards, rules, values, and other criteria of conduct —was the basis for Sherif's rather ingenious laboratory study in the experimental creation of social norms (Cartwright and Zander, 1968, p. 14). Since social norms do indeed serve as behavioral guides, Sherif wondered what the individual would do when certain specific aspects of the external frame of reference were eliminated. Utilizing prior research in the area of the autokinetic effect (if a subject views a light in a darkened room, he will see it as moving), Sherif was able to demonstrate that the individual brings to a given situation a mental set which determines the range of movement he sees and that the individual is then influenced within his own range of judgments by the group itself

(Sherif, 1936). Although Sherif did not study social norms in a natural situation, his laboratory approach was indeed valuable to group-dynamics research. As Cartwright and Zander note:

> And his research helped establish among psychologists the view that certain properties of groups have reality for, as he concluded, the fact that the norm thus established is peculiar to the group suggests that there is a factual psychological basis in the contentions of social psychologists and sociologists who maintain that new and supra-individual qualities arise in group situations. [Cartwright and Zander, 1968, p. 16]

This phenomena is of particular interest to group counselors in that it serves to explain the creation of new norms within the small counseling group. For example, a group of four aggressive youngsters and a like group of shy and retiring ones might well develop a new norm of behavior after a period of interaction which could indeed be quite different than the social norm(s) that were their behavior guidelines prior to the counseling interaction.

NEWCOMB AND SOCIAL ANCHORAGE OF ATTITUDES

From 1935 to 1939, Newcomb completed a different if no less significant project in the field of group dynamics. Utilizing natural rather than laboratory methods, Newcomb investigated the effect of an individual's prior culture upon his reactions in a new group and later effect of the new group on his earlier perceptions. All of the students at Bennington College constituted his sample, and their attitudes toward political affairs provided the context for a study of social norms. Attitude scales, sociometric studies, and interviews were all used to control and check his observations (Durkin, 1964).

Since the campus attitude was designated as liberal and the entering students were essentially products of conservative homes and enrolled with political attitudes divergent from those on campus, Newcomb was able to show that the campus culture did indeed have an effect in changing student attitudes. Senior students each year were more liberal than freshmen.

More important, however, according to Cartwright and Zander was Newcomb's careful documentation of the way the college community rewarded students for their acceptance of approved values. Students, in turn, accommodated to social pressures of the community in several ways, although the situation did cause conflicting family–college loyalties. Of even more importance was the finding that individuals' attitudes are firmly "rooted in the groups to which they belong" (Cartwright and Zander, 1968, p. 17).

Thus, the counselor can be certain that if the group-counseling session becomes a significant event in the life of an individual, his attitudes may well take roots in the small-group life. The particular atmosphere or culture of the small group, then, is extremely important both to the counselor and the group. It raises some interesting and possibly ethical considerations for the counselor to consider in the formation of groups. Suppose, for example, ten college students elect to join a counseling group and the prevailing attitude is one of direct physical violence against the university administration. If seven of the ten individuals advocated violence and this became an acceptable group norm, the three in the group who hold attitudes of nonviolence could indeed be persuaded that violence is indeed right. While this example might be a bit farfetched, it does serve to illustrate the power of the group or culture in changing norms. The direction of change and the counselor's role in working for or against a prevailing small-group norm are not casual considerations!

WHYTE'S STREET-CORNER SOCIETY

The slums of Boston provided the social setting for W. F. Whyte's carefully documented research on the Norton Street Gang and the Italian Community Club. Closely following the participant-observer method developed in anthropological research, Whyte compiled careful notes in his investigation that covered three and one-half years (Cartwright and Zander, 1968).

Whyte carefully pointed out the importance of the primary group to the individual and noted how vital a pattern of satisfying human relations is to the individual's personal security. In the book, he notes that a member of the Norton Street Gang identified as Long John held membership within the group but had little influence over it. When a split in the gang occurred and several of Long John's associates joined a group called Spongi's Gang, Long John was excluded from the close association with a former group of friends. The condition so affected Long John that his bowling soon deteriorated, and this resulted in constant verbal attacks on him. As his personal relations with the group became ever poorer, Long John began to experience a long period of sleepless nights. The situation did not improve for Long John until Doc, one of his former close associates with the Norton Street Gang, managed to sponsor Long John into the newly formed Spongi group. Long John's bowling improved to the point that he was able to win a bowling championship in the 1939–40 season. In another incident, Whyte (1943) tells how Doc suffered a serious depression and dizzy spells as a result of behaviors that led to decreased interaction within a primary group structure.

As noted, Whyte was able to show how important the primary group is to the individual. Such security also goes beyond mere belonging, and involves belonging in more or less set social patterns in the group. When Long John lost his social rank as the Norton Street Gang broke up, he no longer enjoyed the relationships to which he was accustomed. The study also suggests that the group with potential for great help for the individual also has potential for producing great harm—in the case of Long John and Doc, a rather serious maladjustment took place as a result of changes within the social system. When Long John was able to move into a new social situation that was personally satisfying, he was able to function in an effective way.

Thus, when the counseling group becomes cohesive enough to be considered a primary group by its members it will also be a place where members exert great influence on each other. The group may not only dictate behavior within the counseling hour itself but may well influence members' behavior beyond the counseling hour. Member relationships to each other, the group leader, the rank each member holds in the group, and the ways in which individuals interact are of crucial importance to the counselor.

Although Whyte's study was not quantified, his respect for careful detail provides the counselor with some meaningful insights into the significance of interaction of group properties. Cartwright and Zander summarize the significance of his work in three major areas:

1. It dramatized and described in painstaking detail the significance of groups in the lives of individuals and in the functioning of larger social systems.
2. It generated a number of hypotheses concerning the relations among such variables as initiation of interaction, leadership, status, mutual obligations, and group cohesion.
3. It gave impetus to interaction of group properties and processes in terms of interaction among individuals. [Cartwright and Zander, 1968, p. 17]

EXPERIMENTAL MANIPULATION OF GROUP ATMOSPHERE

The now-classic experiments in the experimental manipulation of the group atmosphere were conducted by Lewin (1938) and Lewin, Lippitt and White (1939) and were instrumental in promoting an increased interest in a scientific study of group dynamics (Hare, 1962). In fact, one would encounter difficulty in discovering a group-guidance or counseling text where these investigations are not noted.

Suffice for the purposes of this text to note that the initial investigation of these researchers compared the group atmospheres created by authoritarian and democratic leaders and the second added the dimension of laissez-faire leadership. Members of authoritarian-led groups showed more leader dependency, more hostility, and more apathetic behavior among members. Members of laissez-faire groups, on the other hand, showed little leader dependency but greater anger, aggressiveness, and general dissatisfaction with the group activities. The members of the group that were democratically led showed less dependency on the leader and more friendliness and satisfaction with the club. In addition, autocratic groups surpassed the others in the quantity of group output, but the products of those in democratic groups were judged to be the best qualitatively (Hare, 1962, p. 321).

While it may be easy from the results of such research to jump quickly to the conclusion that the group counselor or group leader should indeed be democratic, such is not necessarily the case. Counseling groups, like other groups, are generally formed for specific purposes, and the counselor may not necessarily be concerned with either more or better group output. A counselor, for example, who believes that an individual's present level of functioning has deep historical antecedents might lead a group in a very autocratic manner since member satisfaction and good group productivity may not be his or the group's goal.

SOME THEORETICAL CONSIDERATIONS

Like other areas of the social sciences, the field of group dynamics has been guided by theoretical as well as research efforts. One of the more significant contributors to both theory and research in group dynamics, Kurt Lewin, was discussed earlier in this chapter because of his prominence and place in the group-dynamics movement. Other individuals, however, have also made contributions that are worthy of note, and while it is in a sense unfair to present some significant efforts in what may appear to be a cursory approach, the reader who wishes to go more deeply into the works discussed here should consult original sources.

INTERACTION THEORY—BALES'S INTERACTION PROCESS ANALYSIS

In the early 1950s, Robert F. Bales and his colleagues devised a unique and useful system for classifying group communication that is still

widely utilized by group workers today. In essence, Bales provides a
system wherein what group members say to each other may be classified into twelve basic categories. Group communications are either
questions or answers or positive or negative reactions. Within this context, the following chart shows how member reactions may be grouped
into the following categories:

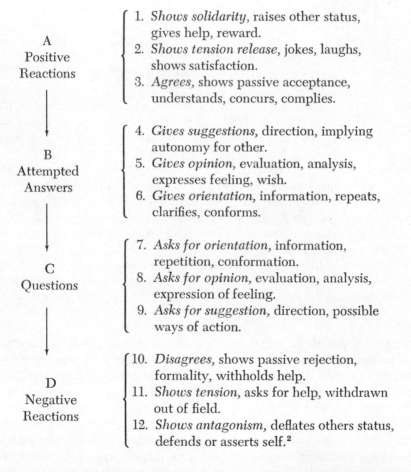

A
Positive
Reactions

1. *Shows solidarity,* raises other status,
   gives help, reward.
2. *Shows tension release,* jokes, laughs,
   shows satisfaction.
3. *Agrees,* shows passive acceptance,
   understands, concurs, complies.

B
Attempted
Answers

4. *Gives suggestions,* direction, implying
   autonomy for other.
5. *Gives opinion,* evaluation, analysis,
   expresses feeling, wish.
6. *Gives orientation,* information, repeats,
   clarifies, conforms.

C
Questions

7. *Asks for orientation,* information,
   repetition, conformation.
8. *Asks for opinion,* evaluation, analysis,
   expression of feeling.
9. *Asks for suggestion,* direction, possible
   ways of action.

D
Negative
Reactions

10. *Disagrees,* shows passive rejection,
    formality, withholds help.
11. *Shows tension,* asks for help, withdrawn
    out of field.
12. *Shows antagonism,* deflates others status,
    defends or asserts self.[2]

The counselor who wishes to study the communication of groups can
use the Bales system to determine the number of positive and negative
reactions and the frequency of attempted questions and answers as well

[2]Reproduced from Robert F. Bales's *Interaction Process Analysis* (Cambridge, Mass.:
Addison-Wesley Publishing Company, 1950), Chart 1, p. 9. Used by permission of author.

as other facets of group communication. Although the counselor may not be able to utilize this approach while he is actually leading the group, the use of trained observers and audio and video tapes can make Bales's approach a viable possibility for group-counseling research.

HOMANS'S SYSTEM THEORY

Unlike Lewin who was primarily concerned with developing abstract concepts to apply to an individual's or a group's situation, or Bales who was interested in the classification of communication, Homans's work was closely related to everyday life (Shepherd, 1964). Using everyday life as his base, Homans developed a system wherein human interaction could be described in terms of activities or things people do with objects, sentiments or individual inner feelings, and interaction when movement toward someone is directed in a way that the individual's reaction will be taken into account. These elementary forms of human behavior lead to a large number of hypotheses suggested by Homans (1950), but according to Shepherd, the

> basic point Homans is seeking to make in this analysis is that interaction, sentiment, and activity are dramatically related so that a change in one will lead to a change in others. Thus the behavior of members of a group must be considered as a system of behavior and not as discrete behaviors unrelated to each other. [Shepherd, 1964, p. 38]

Of interest to the group counselor is the possibility of viewing counseling interaction within the context suggested by Homans in that members of groups frequently engage in setup operations or activities wherein a member or members of a group will say something in order to obtain a particular desired response from another group member. Thus individuals will say things to bring about group or individual anger, love, piety, hostility, or attention.

Homans further relates that a given social system is composed of the "character and state of relations among interaction, activity, and sentiment among a collection of two or more persons who are identifiable as a unity" (work group, family group, or clique) (Shepherd, 1964, pp. 38–39). In the social system, one may discover an *external system* or the forces imposed on a unit by an outside force, and an *internal system* characterized by the relations among interaction, activity, and sentiment within the group. For example, a graduate student studying for a doctor's degree in guidance is invariably subjected to certain external forces from the university, graduate school, and the department of which he is a member. His work at this level can and often does change his pattern of living within the family structure because of long hours of study and other factors. In such cases, the university structure becomes the external system of forces acting on the individual, and the family structure is the internal system that influences him. Both forces may affect a group, and Homans has also developed interesting concepts of role, rank, and norms to help explain his social system. Like all good theories, Homans's work has generated a large number of hypotheses (Shepherd, 1964).

SYSTEMS THEORY

Newcomb has developed a system of understanding interpersonal relationships which notes that since social psychologists must depend upon their observation of what people do in interpersonal relations as their source of raw information, it is necessary for them to be able to distinguish between enduring and transitory aspects of behavior. It is, therefore, necessary for the social scientist to be able to codify that which creates stability in human interaction if he is to be able to make meaningful interpretations of human interaction (Newcomb, 1961, p. 4).

From this base, Newcomb presents the concept of *orientation* or that "property of an individual inferred from his behaviors that have to do with the specified object of orientation" (Newcomb, 1961, p. 5). An orientation of attitude is persistent in the sense that it is the result of persisting residuals of experience with previous experiences (p. 5). Included in the concept of orientation are *sign,* or the positive–negative, approach–avoidance property, and *intensity,* or the strong–weak, external-moderate property. One can label orientations and distinguish them from one another by calling them either specific or general, or concrete or abstract, but always expressed or implied. Orientations may also be categorized in terms of attraction, attitude, and perceived orientations of others. From these concepts, Newcomb has outlined a *systems theory* of interpersonal orientations. With regard to the general nature of systems, he writes:

> We shall define a system as any set of entities so related to one another that changes in certain states of any one of them (regardless of the source of that change) induces specifiable kinds of changes in one or more of the others. Since a system so defined is of little interest if such relationships of interdependency are only short lived, we shall apply the term only when it can be shown that under specified conditions, such interrelationships persist through time. [Newcomb, 1961, p. 9]

Newcomb sets forth individual and collective (group) systems of orientation, and his book should be read in its entirety for a complete understanding. Briefly, however, under the general title, *The Acquaintance Process,* he presents the premise that in almost any face-to-face encounter of two or more humans, certain processes occur that are acquaintance-like. As individuals, we gather information about each other, assess one another's attitudes, and either reinforce our existing orientations toward each other or develop new ones. Such processes in systems theory are interdependent and governed by principles of balance in the individual or the collective system. The human condition is such that individuals constantly face a three-pronged adaptation problem wherein they must simultaneously come to grips with other individuals and groups with the world they have in common and with their own intrapersonal autistic demands (Newcomb, 1961, p. 259).

Applied to the group-counseling situation, Newcomb's work is of interest. As individuals interact (are becoming acquainted, in Newcomb's language), there is some scanning of the "area of mutually shared orientations" (p. 261). For example, a brief account of interaction in a beginning group might show how scanning takes place.

> JOE: I like the new mass (Catholic). I feel so much more a part of the Church now than I did when I was in high school.
> MARY: Me, too. I like it much better.
> SALLY: I didn't know you were Catholics. I guess I haven't seen you at Newman.

Interacting opportunities for reciprocal scanning allow the group members to determine the areas upon which they agree and disagree—they come to know each other's orientations rather well. Mutually shared orientations are the basis for understanding the development of stable interpersonal relationships. Although collective systems may be in balance without mutually shared orientations of importance if the attraction is not high, it is the high-attractions systems that are most stable in time and space (Newcomb, 1961, p. 26). Thus, it is possible to view the cohesive, stable counseling group as one wherein the collective system is in balance with members sharing areas of mutually important orientations.

SOCIOMETRIC THEORY

J. L. Moreno's work in sociometry, though well known, has not been widely recognized within the context of group dynamics (Bonner,

1959). Although Moreno is perhaps best known for his work in psycho-drama, Warters (1960) notes that the word itself is a generic term that encompasses psychodrama, sociodrama, and role playing.

In Moreno's thinking, the individual personality is seen as the totality of social and private roles that the individual plays in his contacts with others. The individual thus achieves effective human relations through his efforts to understand and evaluate his own roles and those of others (Warters, 1960).

Since man is by nature a spontaneous individual, Moreno has developed his psychodramatic and sociodramatic techniques around spontaneity. Psychodrama is the technique devised by Moreno for working with an individual and in a group setting. Using a stage, director, and auxiliary egos, an individual who is the focal point of a psychodramatic production may enact problems, events, and scenes from his past or project himself into the future. The director is the coordinator of the production and may call for audience responses. Auxiliary egos may function as counselors and play significant other roles in the process of psychodrama. Through group discussion following the enactment of a personal experience, members gain new insights into their behavior and that of others (Muro and Freeman, 1968).

In sociodrama, the focus shifts from individual problems to those of a group nature. While the techniques employed are similar, the concerns of the members are groupwide—for example, a sociodramatic production could involve a country club that for the first time is concerning itself with whether or not to allow minority group members to enter its ranks.

One of Moreno's major contributions is the concept of *Tele,* or the desire to belong and the feeling of belonging. It is this factor which permits close relationships between individuals and hence the establishment of cohesiveness in the group. *Tele* is, in effect, a cohesive force at work that serves to stimulate relationships.

Of particular interest to counselors and teachers is the widespread adaptation of Moreno's sociometric concepts for assessing the attractiveness or lack of it in human relations. Labeled *sociometry* by Moreno, it has been used within situations ranging from kindergarten groups to therapy groups. Sociograms or diagrams of human relations allow one to learn who is accepted and rejected in given groups; they are also valuable in leadership studies as Jennings's (1950) work illustrates.

PSYCHOANALYSIS AND GROUP THERAPY

Probably there are numerous views on psychoanalysis and the group situation, but as a representative viewpoint, we shall present here in abbreviated form the concepts advanced by Scheidlinger:

> Furthermore, . . . the group leader represents to each group member a parental figure, while the other group members come to have the emotional significance of siblings. It is in this way that the emotional attitudes evolved in the course of family living are subject to transfer in various degrees to subsequent group relationships. [Scheidlinger, 1952, p. 60]

After discussing the importance of transference in both individual and group approaches to treatment, Spotnitz describes the process of therapy in analytic groups:

> When the treatment process is carried on in the group setting, many changes take place. One of the more obvious ones is in the form and spirit of communications. In individual treatment, the personal history flows along as an autobiographical narrative. Feelings bound up in the patient's images of childhood figures are transferred to the analyst in a sustained and consistent way. Generally, he does not fit himself into more than one image at a time, since the same emotional tone is held throughout a treatment session. The members of a therapy group relive their experiences more dynamically through their spontaneous interchanges as well as through their memories. They can strike many different feeling tones during a session, covering the whole scale of human emotions in their fantasies. (Spotnitz, 1961, pp. 58–59)

With respect to the position of group dynamics in group therapy, Scheidlinger perhaps summarizes the thinking of the majority of those who practice psychoanalysis in groups:

> It is not surprising that, in general, Lewin's experimental findings in group dynamics not only do not contradict but at times even seem to support Freudian assumptions. Difficulty arises, however, with the interpretation of the finding because, as was seen above, these are geared to the momentary dynamic action only. [Scheidlinger, 1952, p. 172]

Scheidlinger, like others who practice psychoanalysis, objects to the idea that one's behavior can be explored in terms of his reaction to the field as perceived at the moment. Genetic factors and individual differences in perceiving, according to Scheidlinger, are related to the history of the individual.

In another vein, Bach (1954), who also holds a psychoanalytic view, notes that not all studies of group dynamics are interesting to psychotherapists in that a large measure of group-dynamics studies do not clarify the process most relevant to group therapy. Cartwright has noted that for the group to be an effective medium of change:

> (1) all members must feel a sense of belonging; (2) that the more attractive the group is, the more influence it will exert on its members; (3) that values, attitudes, and behavior are more amenable to change if they are relevant to members; (4) the group member with the most prestige will exert the most influence in the group; (5) that efforts to change individuals or group subparts if successful would result in having such individuals deviate from group norms and encounter strong resistance; (6) that pressure for change in the group is created by a shared perception of a need for change; (7) that information related to the need, plans, and consequences of change must be shared by all relevant group members; and (8) changes in one part of a group will produce strain in other parts of the group. Such strains can only be reduced through elimination of the change or by readjustment of related parts. [Cartwright, 1951, pp. 381–92]

Although Bach discusses Cartwright's principles in some detail, he states that cohesiveness is essential to therapy groups, that member-to-member congeniality is important, and that the therapy group because of its potential for the improvement of mental health is a basis for attraction of members (Cartwright Principles 1, 2, 3). He encourages a careful study of the prestige roles that a group gives to a leader or a member (Cartwright Principle 4); cautions the therapist against allowing too rigid a norm structure to develop (Cartwright Principle 5); and calls for the therapist and group members to share perceptions about communication blocks (Cartwright Principles 6 and 7). Finally, he acknowledges Cartwright's Eighth Principle—that a change in subgrouping increases the tension level of the whole group (Bach, 1954, pp. 347–61). His position with regard to group dynamics as it relates to group therapy is made explicit in the following statement:

> As research in group dynamics proceeds, it is becoming more and more evident that more effective methods for changing

individual behavior, the very thing that the psychotherapeutic clinician is vitally interested in, can be obtained
through a better understanding of the group's influence on
behavior change in its members. [Bach, 1954, p. 347]

ASCH'S CONFORMITY STUDY

The social psychologist, Asch (1956), provides the group counselor with
some interesting data on the susceptibility of people to suggestion. He
utilized a set of twenty cards with four lines on each card—one line was
designated the criterion line and the other three lines were different
in length, with one line more closely approximating the length of the
criterion line. A single subject along with three *plants* or individuals
who were aware of the nature of the experiment was used each time.
After an explanation of the nature of the task at hand, the four individuals were seated around a table and shown one card at a time. They were
asked to indicate which line was closest to the criterion line. Initially,
the plants responded differently, but toward the end of the experiment,
all selected the same line. The object of this research was to determine
if the group norm, in this case the selection of a single line, would
influence the uninitiated subject. In most cases, Asch found that individuals would indeed conform to the group norm, although a few did
report their private judgments.

The implication of this research for group counseling is noteworthy.
As groups interact and become more cohesive, new norms tend to arise.
Such norms may then hold profound influence over a given individual,
and if Asch's study is any indication, this result could produce both good
and bad effects according to one's personal value system and the purposes of the counseling group. A group of overly aggressive boys, for
example, could influence a nonaggressive youngster to their way of
thinking and acting so that he, too, became aggressive and perhaps
overly aggressive. On the other hand, a group norm of *moderation*
evolving from an interacting group could assist some aggressive individuals to modify their behavior to the point where they are less
aggressive. A key question is, of course, the extent to which an individual is or should be guided by the counseling-group norms and
whether or not such conformity is beneficial to him in terms of his
individuality. The counselor needs to be aware that groups produce
norms, and these norms influence behavior. He helps the group to
clarify the norms that are being accepted, to become aware, and to
remain free to determine their values with full awareness of the social
consequences.

FESTINGER'S SOCIAL COMPARISON PROCESS AND COGNITIVE DISSONANCE

Festinger, in two separate publications, (1954 and 1957) advances two theories of interest to the group counselor. In his earlier effort, he proposes that individuals in a small group are motivated to evaluate their opinions and abilities in terms of the reactions of other individuals as opposed to some external standard, although people will use an objective standard of evaluation when one is available. In addition, individuals tend to compare themselves to those who are similar to them as opposed to those who are different (Shepherd, 1964).

Even the neophyte group counselor has probably observed individuals in their attempts to seek out and speculate on some aspects of their personalities as they interact with others whom they perceive to be similar. The gap that exists seems to stimulate self-evaluation among individual members.

In his widely quoted theory of cognitive dissonance, Festinger advances a theory to explain the reasons for an individual holding a certain opinion, expressing a certain behavior, or in some way changing his behavior. As conceptualized by Festinger, there is a drive to maintain or hold together one's attitudes and opinions in a consistent and meaningful way. When one aspect of an individual's collection of thoughts and ideas seems awry (becomes dissonant) from his total mental functioning, the individual is motivated to reduce the gap. He may do this by ignoring some things, reinterpreting observations, or by modifying previously held ideas and attitudes (Shepherd, 1964, pp. 47–48).

Suppose, for example, that in a given group the individual who viewed himself as essentially unliked begins to receive feedback that other members of the group really care for him. If he firmly holds a perception of himself as unloved, the incorporation of warm thoughts may temporarily create a gap (or dissonance) in his overall image of not being liked. He may then choose to ignore the feedback, perhaps reinterpret his feelings about himself, or change his behavior by perhaps becoming more social now that he knows he can be liked. In situations like this, group members created dissonance in the individual that may have helped him meet a basic need. The group can, of course, create negative types of dissonance by verbally lashing out at the individual and making him feel worthless when his self-concept was essentially positive.

HEIDER'S THEORY OF BALANCE

Heider (1958) advances the theory that individuals tend to want the same positive or negative relationship to an attitude, idea, object, or value that is held by another individual with whom they have a positive relationship. Conversely, people want the opposite positive or negative relationship as those held by individuals with whom they are negatively related (dislike). For example, the professor who sees himself as negatively related to a campus group like the Students for a Democratic Society will want to hold views opposite from those expressed by this group, while a professor who agrees with SDS principles may want to agree with its members. Thus, in counseling groups, much of the early negative comment or disagreement in a group may be directed by some members toward those with whom they have a negative relationship. Positive comments and arguments, on the other hand, will be directed toward those with whom positive relationships are established. If group members or the counselor wish others in the group to change attitudes, then they must create a positive feeling toward themselves on the part of other members (Gage, 1963).

PRESSURES TO UNIFORMITY IN COUNSELING AND OTHER SMALL GROUPS

There can be little doubt that under certain conditions small groups, including counseling groups, will apply pressure toward individuals regarding conformity of behavior. It is for this reason, among others, that some group therapists reject the premise that the group leader should focus on the dynamics of the group. Luchins (1954) notes that a focus on the dynamics of the group tends to cause one to concentrate on theoretical constructs rather than on actual behavior on a phenomenal level. For example, he is referring here to the group leader who is so busy trying to figure out how the members are ranking each other that he ignores the individual for the sake of the construct. Nevertheless, whether or not he chooses to focus on the dynamics or the individual, the group leader can be assured that group forces will be at work. The question is not so much one of group-dynamics forces or not as it is one of ways to utilize group-dynamics principles for optimal individual benefit. Cartwright and Zander note that while group pressures to uniformity are colored by value judgments, the basic problem for social policy is determining how to strike a desirable balance between the benefits and costs of pressures to uniformity (Cartwright and Zander, 1968, p. 141).

While such pressures to conformity do exist, they are useful from a group standpoint for helping a group reach its goals, helping a group maintain itself, creating a social reality where objective standards for such creation are absent, and defining relations to social surroundings.

The relative impact of the group's ability to exert group pressures is related to the importance of the task that requires uniformity to complete, the cohesiveness of the group, the rewards the group can offer, and the types of punishment it can inflict for deviant behavior. Groups do, however, require different standards of behavior from different individuals. Group norms, once established, have a strong degree of consistency and are resistant to change. New members who are added to existing groups will tend to conform to group standards but will exert some minimal effects on these standards themselves. Group decisions are also more effective in the process of evoking behavioral change than are group decisions or discussions where no decision has been reached (Cartwright and Zander, 1968, pp. 143–49).

What, then, does this suggest to the group counselor? Obviously, the formation of a counseling group, whether it is initiated by the counselor or a number of individuals, is built on some values and assumptions. We assume, for example, that groups have potential for great good, that the individual will indeed gain from the experience, and that the directional change that results from the group experience is in a positive direction. Without attempting to define good positive change, the counselor should be aware of the fact that the group, as interaction increases and cohesiveness grows, will increasingly exert greater influence on the individual to conform to the new and evolving norms produced by the interaction. The extent of the power to force conformity will depend upon how significant the counseling group is in the life of the individual —how much he values this group in comparison to the others of which he is a member. Awareness of these concepts will enable the counselor to determine his leadership role in terms of his philosophical position and desired group and individual goals. He might, for example, wish to support a member who deviates from group norms if the deviation is, in some way or another, beneficial to the individual.

THE PROCESS OF MOTIVATION IN GROUPS

Cartwright and Zander's position on the motivational properties of groups makes explicit the fact that members who are clearly aware and acceptant of group goals are more likely to cooperate in attaining group objectives. On the other hand, the individual who either dimly perceives the group goal or is not in agreement with it will tend to be motivated by personal needs. If we are seeking to elicit change, group members must be aware of the purposes of the group, see clearly the expectations, accept some responsibility to change and help others change, and be working at the mutually aligned goal of personal–social growth. If one can accept this premise as advanced by two of America's most notable group-dynamics experts, then he may, if he is a counselor, find himself on the horns of a dilemma. More specifically, one finds scattered throughout literature such statements as "group counseling is characterized by lack of a common group goal" or "the counselor, though he works in a group setting, is concerned mainly with individual needs." In reality, such statements really should not be too disturbing because all counseling groups have some goal even if it is for members to meet and talk about anything that comes to mind. The problem with many counseling groups, in the opinion of the authors, is that (for research purposes or whatever) the goals of the counselor and the goals of the group members do not seem to be in agreement. For example, professional guidance literature is replete with studies that attempted to study the effect of such a process on academic achievement. One must wonder if the purposes of the group (as defined by the counselor) were ever really explained or more importantly, were accepted and internalized by prospective group members. One might hypothesize that many groups have been founded to "talk about anything you want" in the vague hope that some magical effect on school achievement would occur.

"A person with a particular motive will engage in a certain activity if he believes it will bring about satisfying consequences" (Cartwright and Zander, 1968, p. 403). Thus individual performance in a counseling group will be in direct relation to the degree he finds it satisfying on a personal level or on a broader group level.

Enduring groups also have certain relationships with other groups and agencies that have an influence on the setting of group goals. Outside influence on group goals can be considered an aspect of goal setting that is related to the group's attempt to establish a relationship between the group itself and the external, social environment (Cartwright and Zander, 1968, p. 405).

Counselors who form groups must be concerned with the conversion of the various goals individual members might hold into a group goal that will be influential enough to start group activity. For example, a counselor might hypothesize that self-understanding via member-to-member confrontation and speculation is a desirable group goal. Members, however, might have individual goals of obtaining information from the counselor or perhaps discussing the relative merits of a college education at the University of Maine or DePaul. Such counselor–group dissonance will probably create an ineffective work group and perhaps one that will never become cohesive and possibly disband.

Another factor that influences group motivation is the aspirational level or the selected goal of a group in terms of how difficult the goal is to reach. A group of potato pickers at harvest time in northern Maine may set a group goal of forty barrels for the day, anything below which would be group failure. Aspirational levels for individuals and groups are quite similar in that successful performances by individuals and groups tend to raise group aspirational levels while poor performances cause a lowering of the level. Forces outside the group, such as a similar group competing for the same goal, tend to cause movement within a group to the point where goals are raised or lowered by what is happening in other groups as opposed to the one to which members themselves belong (Cartwright and Zander, 1968, pp. 407–8).

Group goals are also inducing agents and serve to steer group action. Once a goal has been set, belonging members are expected to work toward that goal even when the goal may not have been the one selected by an individual member. Moreover, movement toward a group goal necessitates appropriate individual behaviors, although the behavioral pathways toward these goals may be different for different members (Cartwright and Zander, 1968, pp. 407–10). In essence, the goal of a group, once selected, is a group-motivating factor with varying degrees of intensity and influence for different members. The goal of self-understanding in counseling groups may indeed influence members and guide the course of action within the group; however, the behaviors of individuals in process toward this goal could range from indirect topic-centered discussions to direct member-to-member confrontation. As Olmsted noted with regard to motivation: ". . . behavior depends on the nature of the task and on the nature of the individual's perception of his relation to the group" (Olmsted, 1959, p. 68). For example, a member may fully agree that the purpose of a given group is to gain better self-understanding by each member actively seeking feedback from others. If, however, he does not feel secure and accepted in the group or value the group very much, he may remain a silent, nonverbal member. It is not enough for the counselor to say "everyone belongs here"—the individual must feel accepted prior to taking any risks in the group.

Luft notes that "structure refers to the internal organization and procedures of a group" (Luft, 1963, p. 21). Olmsted (1959) in talking about social structure notes "that it may be thought of as the patterns of relationship among members of society or a group" (p. 94). Structure originates in order to make group performance more proficient because of the abilities and motivations of individual members and because of the physical and social environment of the group. It is difficult to characterize the structure of a given group, although some approaches to conceptualizing group structure—including those of (1) office, position, status, and subgrouping; (2) interpersonal relations (Moreno's sociometric procedures); (3) ranking of members; and (4) mathematical approaches like those of Glanzer and Glaser (1959) and Forsyth and Katz (1946)—are reported in the literature (Cartwright and Zander, 1968, pp. 489–93).

Structure is a problem for all groups (Luft, 1963) and counseling groups are no exception. Like other groups, those formed for counseling purposes can be structured according to communications flow, work flow, mobility, authority relations, and ranking along such dimensions as importance, prestige, and popularity (Cartwright and Zander, 1968, p. 464).

When counseling groups meet initially and throughout the life of the group, members will tend to rank other members along various dimensions. In general, the counselor or group leader may receive high ranking because of his perceived status and potential influence on the group. Communication will also tend to be directed from the high-ranking members in a group to those of lower status, and it is not unusual in early sessions for members to direct verbalizations to the counselor or other members who hold high group status. The counselor, however, can break the dependency-on-the-leader syndrome by turning the queries addressed to him back to the group, or if a member asks the counselor why four members are silent, he may simply say: "Would you like to ask them—or some other members of the group?"

The effects of structure, according to Cartwright and Zander are related to the different types of structure that may occur in groups, the opportunities, demands, and experiences he may have for locomotion or movement within a group, the performance of the group, and the changing properties associated with the size of the group (1968, pp. 464–99). For example, French and Roven (1968) assume a relationship between the sociometric structure and the power structure of a group.

With regard to group performance, Shaw (1964) reports that groups without a central person (or those in circular arrangements) tend to solve problems faster than groups with a central person in a chain pattern. Group size, a key concern to the counselor, was a subject of a critical review of the literature by Thomas and Fink (1963). Among their findings was the conclusion that group size did influence the dependent variables of group performance, distribution of participation, nature of interaction, group organization, member performance, conformity, consensus, and member satisfaction. They do, however, note that methodological shortcomings of some of the research reviewed prevents broad generalizations. In terms of counseling groups,

however, the larger the group the greater the demands on the counselor and the necessarily decreased participation time of individual
members. Group size is discussed further in Chapter 6.

While the topic of structural properties is still one of much speculation and research, the group counselor should at least be aware of the
potential effects of structure on group process and outcomes.

ROETHLISBERGER AND DICKSON'S HAWTHORNE EFFECT

Of interest to the group counselor is the work of Roethlisberger and
Dickson in the Hawthorne Plant of the Western Electric Company.
Although this study is widely quoted in literature dealing with psychological and educational research, it is noted here because the *Hawthorne Effect* or the phenomenon that the individual who receives
special attention will in some way improve is the concern of the group
counselor.

In the series of studies carried out at the Hawthorne Plant (hence the
name *Hawthorne Effect*), researchers gradually increased the illumination in three departments where workers were inspecting certain elec-
trical equipment. As the intensity of the light increased, the efficiency
of the workers gradually increased also. However, further experimentation involving a gradual *decrease* in the intensity of illumination also
increased group efficiency. Additional studies involving rest periods
and varied work days also increased worker efficiency even when the
work conditions became somewhat less desirable. Of major importance
from the study is the fact that the attention paid to the workers, *not*
the experimental conditions *per se,* was the significant factor in producing change.

What might this research say to the group counselor? Perhaps an
example will illustrate one possible meaning. Suppose the counselor
wants to work with a group of behavior problems from an eighth-period
study hall. As the group progresses from week to week, several teachers
note improved behavior from those in the counseling group. While the
counselor might readily conclude that the change and progress were
due to his skillful counseling, he must also be aware that his removing
the individuals from a dull, late afternoon study could have been the
significant factor in producing the change. Like the workers at the
Hawthorne Plant, these children may be reacting to the fact that they,
of all those in the study hall, were selected for special attention. He may
not be able to conclude that his counseling skill and the influence of the
group were instrumental in producing change. If, for example, the
group became as dull and boring to the members as had the study hall,
it is conceivable that a regression to former behavior could take place.

It is interesting to note that many group-counseling studies involved relatively short periods of time and have generally hit at a special group (i.e., poor self-image, underachievers). It is possible, of course, that the *Hawthorne Effect* is operating at least in part with those groups who have somehow changed in a short period of time.

GROUP DYNAMICS AND GROUP COUNSELING

Throughout this chapter, the authors have discussed group dynamics from several viewpoints, and when appropriate, they have attempted to provide a relationship between group-dynamics theory and the operational work of the group counselor. In summary, then, it is perhaps appropriate to review the status of group dynamics from the views of those who have concerned themselves with the problems of how, if at all, the counselor might utilize group-dynamics concepts in his role as group leader.

First of all, the position one takes regarding group dynamics is likely to be contingent on the assumptions one is willing to make about the nature of counseling (Whitaker and Lieberman, 1964). Such therapists as Bion, Foulkes, Bach, and Frank are essentially positive toward the use of the group dynamics in their work. As Bion notes:

> The point is critical; if the psychiatrist can manage boldly to use the group instead of spending his time more or less unconsciously apologizing for its presence, he will find the immediate difficulties produced are more than neutralized by the advantages of a proper use of the medium. [Bion, 1961, pp. 80-81]

Those who have spoken favorably about group dynamics point out that the developments in group dynamics have been influential in paving the way for better communication among psychologists of the several disciplines (Durkin, 1964). Whitaker and Lieberman also note that the group is the center of civilized values and the source of central overdestructive impulses. In addition, there is evidence that solutions and successful ones at that do emerge from group interaction (1964, pp. 290–92).

Not all group-dynamics research and theory, however, in the minds of some writers is applicable to group work, group counseling, or group therapy. Durkin notes that although the construction of theories applicable to all types of groups is a legitimate concern of the group-dynamics researches, any *particular* finding may not be applicable to all groups in all conceivable settings (1964, p. 27). Perhaps the most outspoken critic of group dynamics regarding its relation to therapy groups is Slavson. He writes:

Thus, even the most common group dynamics described here are not permitted to operate for it is the task of the therapist ... to uncover the underlying, most often the hostile feelings from which reactions follow. Thus, dynamics in therapy groups are nipped in the bud, as it were, for just as soon as responses are analyzed and related to their emotional sources, they no longer operate. [Slavson, 1957, p. 145]

In fact, Whitaker and Lieberman have voiced the concern of some experienced group leaders about the potential harm of the power of the interacting group. They note, for example, that the individual may become the victim of group forces, that groups tend to make individuals anxious, force pressures of uniformity, and engage in scapegoating wherein the first individual who acts is guilty and the others blameless. In addition, hostility by members may not be directed toward its appropriate target, and the majority (consensus of opinion) view may not be always right. Finally, there is group pressure for the individual to accept solutions if his deviation threatens group existence (Whitaker and Lieberman, 1964, pp. 285–89).

Durkin (1964) also questions some other aspects of group-dynamics research as it applies to counseling and therapy groups. More specifically, she notes among other things that the "family atmosphere that develops in groups makes the individual too comfortable and prevents him from 'moving out' beyond the group to new relationships" (p. 33). In addition, group decisions, the preferred path in many groups, are inappropriate for therapy; and cooperation, a product of interaction, stresses conflict avoidance and members must feel free to express socially unavoidable feelings (pp. 29–30).

Others have questioned certain group-dynamics principles with regard to group (counselor) leadership. Durkin (1964) notes that an exaggerated democratic reaction on the part of the leader could be a reaction formation against unconscious power needs (p. 32). Bonner (1959), a recognized group-dynamics expert, contends that people do not object to strong leadership if they know they can participate when they want.

In light of these samples of opinion from the field, it would appear that the use of group dynamics in therapy groups is indeed an issue. Whitaker and Lieberman (1964) describe what may perhaps be a workable approach to conceptualizing the problem in their discussion of group dynamics. They note that the issue is no longer one of whether or not the group can be described in terms of group-dynamics constructs, but rather one of whether or not the use of these constructs is valuable to the primary goal of assisting individual growth.

The authors are essentially in agreement with this view. Regardless of whether or not the counselor tends to utilize group—dynamics principles or oppose them is contingent upon how he views the group-counseling process. It is possible, for example, that some of the cautions listed earlier in this section have merit, and the natural forces of group life could, indeed, contribute to individual harm. The key point, however, and the reason for including an introduction to group dynamics in this text is that in order for the counselor to make decisions regarding the potential worth or harm of group dynamics, he must at least be familiar with and aware of fundamentals in this field of study. Group dynamics and forces will be occurring in the group, and it is critical that the leader be aware of them so they can be utilized to foster growth.

SUMMARY

The term *group dynamics* is often associated with group guidance and group counseling. At times, writers have used the terms *group guidance, group counseling,* and *group dynamics* synonymously, although these terms generally have quite different meanings. Group dynamics refer to the "forces interacting in groups as they operate to achieve objectives" (Shertzer and Stone, 1966, p. 169).

The roots of group dynamics are to be found in sociology, anthropology, social psychology, and field theory (Bonner, 1959). The most rapid advance of the study of group dynamics has taken place since the mid-1930s and key contributions to the area have been made by Sherif, Newcomb, Whyte, Lewin, Lippitt, White, Bales, Homans, Moreno, Asch, Festinger, Heider, Bonner, Cartwright, Zander, Roethlisberger, and Dickson.

The group counselor must be aware of the research and writing of these individuals. He must know what forces affect a group, what forces tend to destroy it, and how these same forces promote or retard individual growth. How one chooses to regard group dynamics, both as a field of inquiry and as guidelines for his personal counseling behavior, is probably related to his personal philosophy and how he views counseling (Whitaker and Lieberman, 1964). One thing is certain—the counselor cannot ignore the dynamics of a group or pretend that they exist only as theoretical constructs. All groups have forces that affect their growth and development. The counselor's job is to understand and use these in constructive ways.

REFERENCES

ALLPORT, F. H. *Social Psychology.* Boston: Houghton Mifflin Company, 1924.

ASCH, S. E. "Studies of Independence and Conformity: A Minority of One against a Unanimous Majority," *Psychological Monographs,* Vol. 70, No. 9 (1956), (Whole No. 416).

BACH, GEORGE R. *Intensive Group Psychotherapy.* New York: The Ronald Press Company, 1954.

BALES, R. F. *Interaction Process Analysis.* Cambridge, Mass.: Addison-Wesley Publishing Company, Inc., 1950.

BION, W. R. *Experiences in Groups and Other Papers.* London: Tavistock Publications, 1961.

BONNER, H. *Group Dynamics: Principles and Applications.* New York: The Ronald Press Company, 1959.

CARTWRIGHT, DORWIN. "Achieving Change in People: Some Applications of Group-Dynamics Theory," *Human Relations,* Vol. 4 (1951), pp. 381–92.

CARTWRIGHT, DORWIN, and ZANDER, ALVIN (eds.). *Group Dynamics: Research and Theory.* New York: Harper and Row, Publishers, 1960.

——. (eds.). *Group Dynamics: Research and Theory.* 3rd ed. New York: Harper and Row, Publishers, 1968.

DURKIN, HELEN E. *The Group in Depth.* New York: International Universities Press, 1964.

FESTINGER, L. A. "A Theory of Social-Comparison Process," *Human Relations,* Vol. 7 (1954), pp. 117–40.

——. *A Theory of Cognitive Dissonance.* Evanston, Ill.: Row, Peterson, 1957.

FORSYTH, E., and KATZ, L. "A Matrix Approach to the Analysis of Sociometric Data: Preliminary Report," *Sociometry,* Vol. 9 (1946), pp. 340–47.

FOULKES, S. H., and ANTHONY, E. J. *Group Psychotherapy.* Penguin Books, Inc., 1965.

FRANK, J. D. "Some Determinants, Manifestations, and Effects of Cohesiveness in Therapy Groups," *International Journal of Group Psychotherapy,* Vol. 7 (1957), pp. 53–63.

FRENCH, J. R. P., and ROVEN, B. "The Basis of Social Power," in *Group Dynamics: Research and Theory.* 3rd ed. (eds. DORWIN CARTWRIGHT, and ALVIN ZANDER). New York: Harper and Row, Publishers, 1968.

GAGE, N. L. *Handbook of Research in Teaching.* Chicago: Rand McNally and Company, 1963.

GLANZER, M., and GLASER, R. "Techniques for the Study of Group Structure and Behavior: I, Analysis of Structure," *Psychological Bulletin,* Vol. 56 (1959), pp. 317–22.

HARE, P. A. *Handbook of Small-Group Research.* New York: The Free Press, 1962.

HARSH, C. M., and SCHRICHEL, H. G. *Personality Development and Assessment.* New York: The Ronald Press Company, 1959.

HEIDER, F. *The Psychology of Interpersonal Relations.* New York: John Wiley and Sons, Inc., 1958.

HOMANS, G. C. *The Human Group.* New York: Harcourt Brace Jovanovich, Inc., 1950.

JENNINGS, HELEN H. *Leadership and Isolation.* New York: Longmans, Green, 1950.

LEWIN, K. "Formulation and Progress in Psychology. University of Iowa Studies," *Child Welfare,* Vol. 16 (1940), pp. 9–42.

LEWIN, K., and LIPPITT, R. "An Experimental Approach to the Study of Autocracy and Democracy: A Preliminary Note," *Sociometry,* Vol. 1 (1938), pp. 292–300.

LEWIN, K., LIPPITT, R., and WHITE, R. "Patterns of Aggressive Behavior in Experimentally Created Social Climates," *Journal of Social Psychology,* Vol. 10 (1939), pp. 271–99.

LUCHINS, A. S. *Group Therapy: A Guide.* New York: Random House, Inc., 1954.

LUFT, J. *Group Process: An Introduction to Group Dynamics.* Palo Alto, Calif.: National Press Books, 1963.

MURO, JAMES J., and FREEMAN, S. L. *Readings in Group Counseling.* Scranton, Pa.: International Textbook Company, 1968.

NEWCOMB, T. M. *Personality and Social Change.* New York: Dryden, 1943.

———. *The Acquaintance Process.* New York: Holt, Rinehart and Winston, Inc., 1961.

OHLSEN, MERLE M. *Group Counseling.* New York: Holt, Rinehart and Winston, Inc., 1970.

ROETHLISBERGER, F. J., and DICKSON, W. J. *Management and the Worker.* Cambridge, Mass.: Harvard University Press, 1940.

SCHEIDLINGER, SAUL. *Psychoanalysis and Group Behavior.* New York: W. W. Norton and Company, Inc., 1952.

SHAW, M. "Communications Networks," in *Advances in Experimental Social Psychology.* Vol. 1 (ed. L. BERKOWITZ). New York: Academic Press, Inc. 1964.

SHEPHERD, C. R. *Small Groups: Some Sociological Perspectives.* San Francisco, Calif.: Chandler Publishing Company, 1964.

SHERIF, M. *The Psychology of Social Norms.* New York: Harper and Row, Publishers, 1936.

SHERTZER, B., and STONE, S. C. *Fundamentals of Guidance.* Boston: Houghton Mifflin Company, 1966.

SLAVSON, S. R. "Are There Group Dynamics in Therapy Groups?" *International Journal of Group Psychotherapy,* Vol. 7 (1957), pp. 144–45.

SPOTNITZ, HYMAN. *The Couch and the Circle.* New York: Alfred A. Knopf, Inc., 1961.

THOMAS, E. J., and FINK, F. C. "Effects of Group Size," *Psychological Bulletin,* Vol. 60 (1963), pp. 371–84.

WARTERS, JANE. *Group Guidance: Principles and Practices.* New York: McGraw-Hill Book Company, 1960.

WHITAKER, D. S., and LIEBERMAN, M. A. *Psychotherapy through the Group Process.* New York: Atherton Press, Inc., 1964.

WHYTE, W. F. *Street-Corner Society.* Chicago: University of Chicago Press, 1943.

CHAPTER 3

Theoretical Approaches to Group Counseling

GROUP APPROACHES to counseling and psychotherapy are generally considered to have originated in the United States, even though there were a number of predecessors in Europe. Alfred Adler used collective counseling perhaps as early as 1922 in his child-guidance clinics in Vienna. Jacob L. Moreno indicates he did some group work prior to his coming to the United States. However, the type of group work which precedes group counseling was really first developed in the United States.

The term *group therapy* was introduced by Jacob L. Moreno in 1931 and in 1932 he presented the term *group psychotherapy* (Moreno, 1966). Slavson, another pioneer in group work, suggests that the criteria in modern groups, such as permissive discussions, small size and spontaneity were not met in groups before 1930 (Slavson, 1959).

The more immediate precursors of group counseling can perhaps best be found by investigating class presentations which were titled "Group Guidance." This format was present in the schools in 1931 (Allen, 1931). Credit for the actual development of the term *group counseling* must go to Allen. "A technique that combined the technique of 'counseling in groups' and 'group counseling' was used by Allen and practiced in the public schools of Providence, Rhode Island more than twenty-five years ago" (Jones, 1963). This would give some indication that group counseling or its earlier equivalent in certain forms was being practiced in the schools as early as 1937.

There have been many forms of group procedures used in the past, and Goldman (1968) has provided our most accurate definition of the group procedures as they relate to the schools. He suggests that one understands group methods only by clarifying the roles of content and process. Goldman then discusses a variety of processes from leader-directed procedures to groups which are organized to meet the perceived needs of members. It is suggested that both group guidance and counseling have often been inadequate in the schools because the leader did all the planning and focused the discussion on his own concerns and not on the priorities of the members.

Coffey has distinguished groups in terms of their goals. He indicates that the psyche group is concerned with satisfying the emotional needs of its members, while the socio group is concerned with completing specified goals of the group (Coffey, 1952). The socio group is very task oriented. However, close inspection would indicate that groups are seldom merely psyche or socio groups, but tend to overlap on a continuum. Currently group counseling is distinguished by being more growth centered than task centered in its emphasis. Each member comes to the group with a personal commitment related to self and his participation in the group.

There is a variety of theoretical orientations to group therapy and group counseling. It is to the group counselor's advantage to be aware of the unique procedures which certain approaches afford. His exposure to these approaches helps expand his perceptual field and enables him to participate in a more meaningful manner. Our purpose in this chapter is not to train the counselor in any specific approach, but to develop acquaintance with some of the basic constructs which underlie the group process. It will be the counselor's task to integrate these concepts into his personal approach to the group process.

THE SOCIOTELEOLOGICAL APPROACH

This approach is based upon the Adlerian understanding of human behavior. While Adler was not a group counselor in a technical sense, he certainly provided much stimulation for group approaches in his writings and family-counseling demonstrations. His leading exponent has been Rudolf Dreikurs who has written extensively on group psychotherapy and group counseling (Dreikurs, 1957, 1960; Dreikurs and Sonstegard, 1967).

Dreikurs's students have made extensive application of the group approach in the schools and other settings. Some of these students include: Christensen (1969), Corsini (1957), Dinkmeyer (1969), Grunwald (1955), Rosenberg (Corsini and Rosenberg, 1955), Sonstegard (Dreikurs and Sonstegard, 1967), and Stormer (1967). The Adlerian approach stems from the assumption that man is an indivisible, social, decision-making being whose actions have a social purpose (Dreikurs and Sonstegard, 1968). Basic to this approach are certain conceptual foundations related to the nature of man:

1. All behavior has social meaning. Man is understood as a social being and his behavior is always understood in terms of its social context. The interaction and the transactions between people help to clarify the meaning of behavior. Man can only fulfill himself and become significant in the group. The group provides a basic ingredient for his personal development.

The significance of all behavior also lies in its social consequences. Social striving is basic to understanding behavior, not secondary, as it is postulated in the psychoanalytic model. Since behavior is influenced by the reactions of others, the group provides an excellent setting for understanding the meaning of all behavior.

2. Behavior is best understood on a holistic basis, in terms of its unity or pattern. This holistic approach enables one to focus on the pattern of behavior in contrast to the specific unit or detail of an action. In this sense, psychological movement portrays the relationships between men and their intentions and the effect of these intentions on others.

3. Behavior is goal directed and purposive. All psychological movement has a purpose, and the goals then become the psychic stimuli that motivate the individual's behavior. The goals are clarified more accurately in group interaction.

4. Motivation is understood by observing how the individual seeks to become significant. This striving for significance receives its direction from the individual's subjectively conceived self-ideal. The striving emerges as the individual experiences the subjective feeling of being less than others, and thereby engages in attempts to compensate. Thus, primary attention is given to determining the individual's central purpose or master motive. The group provides the opportunity for us to observe how the individual seeks to be accepted and how he seeks to be known—i.e., to get our attention, to show he is in control, or to require special service. Group interaction helps us understand some of the forces which may be directing his behavior.

5. Belonging is a basic requisite for adequate development. The individual has the need to belong to someone or something. His significance stems from how he is accepted, and where he belongs. Man cannot become self-actualized without belonging. In many instances his basic anxieties arise from the fear of not being acceptable. The group provides the opportunity to be accepted despite his deficiencies, and to become significant and interdependent with mankind.

6. The individual is understood in terms of his phenomenological

field. The group permits us to see how he perceives life and the meaning that certain transactions have for him. His anticipation of success or failure, acceptance or rejection, often provokes responses from others which will reinforce his interpretation of life. The group, then, is concerned with helping each individual to move from his private logic to a more rational or commonsense assessment of life. The group works to help the individual explore his phenomenological field. The group accomplishes this insofar as it introduces new data in terms of feelings, attitudes, and values which cause one to reevaluate and change perceptions.

7.   The development of social interest is vital for mental health. Social interest is more than a feeling of belonging. It reflects our attitudes toward others. An individual with an adequately developed social interest will accept responsibility. He is concerned for others, and he wants to participate in the give-and-take of life. Dreikurs has perhaps defined it best. "The social interest has no fixed objective. Much more truly it can be said to create an attitude towards life, a desire to cooperate with others in some way and to master the situations of life. Social interest is the expression of our capacity for give and take" (Dreikurs, 1958, p. 9). The development of social interest, from this point of view, is one of the objectives of group counseling. Dreikurs traditionally dealt with all counseling including group counseling in terms of its structure. The group process is discussed in terms of four phases: (1) The relationship, (2) Exploration, (3) Revealing goals, and (4) Reorientation. Obviously, because Adlerians deal with the here and now, the process is not one which must occur in sequence, but is always related to the here-and-now interaction between group members.

1.   THE RELATIONSHIP.   The relationship is based upon mutual trust and respect. The counselor is both firm and kind. He seeks a cooperative relationship because it is only through the active participation of the group members that progress can occur. He recognizes that the group has an advantage insofar as it stimulates cooperation. It is his task to develop in the group members an anticipation of success from their experience. Thus, he works to utilize forces such as informality, frequent meetings, cooperative relationships, mutual responsibility, and social interest, to bring about a cohesive group. The group then provides a unique kind of social-stimulus situation not to be found in typical interpersonal relations. Papanek (1961) has identified some of the factors which make a group therapeutic. They are:

a.   The group must be cohesive and flexible, possessing a resiliency that helps the group members communicate in a friendly manner with each other.

b.   There should be shared social norms which provide equality for the members and responsible leadership.

c.   There should be open communication and mutual helpfulness, a desire to give assistance altruistically to others.

d.   The patients need to make realistic observations of one another that are spontaneous but that provide corrective and meaningful feedback. The clarity and correctness of these perceptions make the relationships in the group more satisfying.

e.   Social feeling, the pleasure that one has in being of assistance to others, must exist in the group.

2.   EXPLORATION.   The group provides unique opportunities insofar as the interactions and social behavior of the individual are more obvious in group than individual counseling. One doesn't only listen to how one says he will behave, but has the opportunity to observe his social and psychological movement.

The group, then, begins by exploring the here and now of the social situation. The members are interested in how their present transactions may reveal their immediate goals and involvement in their social field. Since the significance of behavior lies in its consequences, the consequences are revealed most clearly in the interaction between members of the group. Thus, a focus is always on the purpose of the behavior. The leader may originally confront individuals with their purposes, and in this manner he serves as a model so that group members may later assist in the exploration of purpose. This confrontation is never immediate nor charged with negative emotion or a psychological sophistication, i.e., "I know why you are doing what you are doing." Instead, it is done with real concern and interest for helping the individual explore self. The tentative hypothesis of a purpose is presented; i.e., Could it be? Is it possible? This alludes to an individual goal or purpose which may be conscious or unconscious. It has been determined that this type of confrontation, which also shows that one really cares, assists in developing the confidence that occurs in a relationship when one feels that he is truly understood.

3.   REVEALING GOALS.   The psychological-disclosure phase is obviously an overlap of the exploration phase. It is important to recognize that teleological interpretations are always made tentatively and in relationship to the individual's unique goal. They may be confirmed by a recognition reflex (a smile, grin, or twinkle of the eyes) on the part of the client which enables one to see that the client does understand. The group members can also develop an understanding of themselves as they see their behavior in the behavior of others. This indicates that at

times a group is benefited by having a number of members who portray the same mechanisms, thus enabling one to develop the mirror effect.

4. REORIENTATION. Some of the greatest advantages of group counseling occur during the reorientation phase. The group permits genuine feedback and corrective influence from the peers. This is often more efficacious than the suggestion of the counselor. This opportunity to confront the client with his goals and intentions, while providing him with the opportunity to consider alternatives, and try them out in this setting, is a unique contribution of the group process. Another advantage is inherent in the possibilities for spectator therapy, the opportunity to see someone else talk about a problem similar to yours and work through it in the group. This enables one to experience some of the benefits of problem solving without necessarily revealing oneself.

Group counseling can provide some unique contributions, in terms of status, responsibility, choice, acceptance, self-understanding, and social interest. It is the counselor's responsibility to keep these factors in balance. They do not occur spontaneously without some well-structured leadership. Thus, we see that the opportunity to test oneself in a real social situation, see oneself in others, and perhaps be more open to the redirective and corrective efforts of peers, are all special benefits of the group.

The teleological approach has been advocated in the schools for a number of years. Experiences have indicated that the group approach is most effective when it is comprehensive. "To be effective, the program must be instituted simultaneously on four levels with the peer group, the teacher group, the family group, and the child himself" (Dreikurs and Sonstegard, 1967, p. 12). The emphasis is on a coordinated and innovative effort with the child, the teacher, and the parents. It is obvious that some of the benefits already described are valuable to adult as well as child groups. Counseling groups in this frame of reference believe that the child has become dysfunctioning as a result of faulty approaches to finding his place in the group. Therefore, they hypothesize that interpersonal problems are best solved by creating new social-interaction patterns and procedures. This opportunity to experience a new social transaction helps one become aware of the way he functions in the life tasks.

THE BEHAVIORAL APPROACH

Behavioral theory states that most human behavior is learned. It is unique in its application of learning principles and processes to counseling procedures for changing behavior.

Behavior modification involves the development of procedures which utilize systematic environmental contingencies to alter the subject's response to the stimuli about him (Ullman and Krasner, 1969). Behaviorists operate on the principle that in order to change a feeling, you begin by changing the behavior. If one is to feel better about the situation, he must begin by becoming involved in the behavior that he may not desire immediately, but which would help him feel better. He must be encouraged to engage in behaviors that are incompatible with his current feelings. For example, if he feels isolated he must move towards people; if he feels inadequate at a specific skill, he must be willing to try. The approach to a new or unfamiliar situation is always arranged in simple, easy, sequential stages. This behavior is developed in such a way that it is self-reinforcing, and hence maintains itself.

While early behavioral studies were directed towards problems related to individual counseling, behaviorists have increasingly recognized that many of our problems stem from ineffective interactions with persons and the total social environment. If the situation is to be corrected, one must become involved in a new way with the interpersonal process. They have also recognized that peers are among the most important sources for influencing behavior. The behaviorists have maintained that the use of learning principles in group process makes the group even more efficient because:

1. There are greater numbers of varieties of models within a group;

2. There are greater numbers of sources of reinforcement within the group;

3. There are more opportunities for creating realistic social enactments whereby role rehearsal can be practiced, changed, and strengthened;

4. There is an immediate situation in which generalization as well as discrimination can be learned with greater efficiency; and

5. Membership in the group itself can be utilized as a powerful reinforcing agency. [Varenhorst, 1969, p. 131]

Behavioral group counseling is characterized by its systematic approach to the group. There is no ambiguity about what the group is to accomplish. It is expected that each member will communicate to the group his concerns and solicit feedback about himself. He is expected to formulate goals regarding the kind of person he desires to become. It is the group task to help him accomplish his goals. The procedure suggests a mutual reinforcing community that works on a specific problem to help him see more clearly his goals and alternatives.

A clear statement of the contrast between behavioral approaches to group counseling and the more traditional has been presented by Varenhorst in describing unique aspects of behavioral group counseling:

> 1. The goals for group counseling are distinctly specified and agreed upon in advance by each member individually and the group collectively.
> 2. The goals are specified according to behavioral terminology so that the outcome of the goal may be observed and evaluated at the conclusion of the group sessions.
> 3. Only one unit of behavior is dealt with at one time. Successive behaviors may be considered in turn which may lead to the performing of more complex units of behavior.
> 4. A systematic plan for achieving the goal is developed by the counselor, before the group counseling begins, involving a choice of techniques that will be used for counseling.
> 5. Both verbal and nonverbal techniques may be used.
> 6. The counselor takes an active and important role in the process, frequently taking the lead in directing the discussions. [Varenhorst, 1969, pp. 137–38]

The group counselor who takes a behavioral approach meets with each member in advance of the group meeting. He establishes specific behavioral goals with each person. The similarities, attitudes, and purposes in the persons who desire to be members of the group are investigated. Possible methods that the group might use are considered. The counselor must mobilize the group to work together toward common purposes, so that they become sincerely interested in helping each individual accomplish his goals. The behaviorists suggest that persons who are in the group need to perform certain specific behaviors:

1. Share feelings openly.
2. Suggest ideas and actions.
3. Reinforce others as the need occurs.
4. Give feedback.
5. Participate in demonstrations or role playing of alternative actions.
6. Be willing to accompany group members on assignments outside the group.
7. Make a commitment to one's goal and the purposes of the group.

The importance that some in the behavioral school of thought placed upon group work is best portrayed by Varenhorst:

> Kurt Lewin (1947) observed, following several of his studies, that the behavior of individuals is usually easier to change when they are formed into a group than to change any one of them separately. This has been supported to a degree by the experimental work done on behavioral group counseling. It has been found that the variety of sources for reinforcement and modeling contained within a group offers a rich field for behavior modification. The prestige of group membership itself can be utilized as a reinforcing stimulus. [Varenhorst, 1969, pp. 152–53]

TRANSACTIONAL GROUPS

Transactional theory originates with the work of Eric Berne (1966). Transactional theory is concerned with determining which ego state is active at a particular time in transactions. The leader and members of the group are concerned with which ego state is active in sending messages and which ego state responds to messages. The transactional theorist refers to three ego states: Parent, Adult, and Child. Parent is the vestige which remains in the individual from the messages which have been sent by the parents. The Parent is a sum of the shoulds and oughts. Berne has suggested it is almost as if they were "tape-recorded parent messages." The Parent talks about the ways in which one must behave in order to survive. The Adult is the data-processing center, less involved with affect and feeling. It serves as a computer which assesses the parental messages and the childish ego state. The Child is the pleasure-seeking part of the ego. It is concerned with its personal desires and effective means of getting what it wants.

The transactional leader focuses on the transactions that are before him and the interactions between members of the group. He doesn't ask why; he has hunches about why people are behaving this way in the here and now. The advantage of the group process is that it provides members with a variety of ego states which require their Adult to respond in various ways.

The leader takes an active directive role. In transactional terms he holds onto his Adult role. He does not become a member of the group. He does not seek to obtain their acceptance and affection. He uses simple language. He becomes concerned with the happenings which provide him with clues about the behavior of members.

The transactional leader prefers to have one interview session with each person before the individual enters the group. He prefers a heterogeneous group. The group time is used to help make members aware of how they use certain approaches to the problems of life.

Contracts are an important part of the transactional approach. The leader asks, "What is it you want to work on now?" It is important to get agreement from each member of the group about the thing on which he is willing to work. It is important to recognize that contracts should be very attainable. They are stated and made in the presence of the group.

The leader is concerned with existentially working with the contract that a person has for a specific meeting. He is less interested in focusing on what has happened between meetings, and more concerned with what is going on in the present. The purpose is to maximize the choice of individuals. Thus, his focus and talk are usually to individuals and not to the group in general.

The leader is concerned with speaking to the patient's Adult and confronting the Adult with what is happening at this time. He tries to make him aware of the varied positions in life, such as:

I am OK—You're OK

I'm not OK—You're OK

I'm OK—You're not OK

I'm not OK—You're not OK

He tries to have him see how he is functioning with people and how his behavior tends to bring certain predictable responses. Thus, the therapist would be engaged in behaviors such as:

1. Clarifying the purpose of the meeting.
2. Establishing contracts.
3. Confronting individuals with what is happening now.
4. Identifying ego states.
5. Clarifying vagueness and the attempt on the part of the patient to talk about "it," "they," "them."
6. Determining what it is that the patient is feeling right now and what he wants to do about the feeling.
7. Making the patient aware that he is responsible for how he feels.
8. Facilitating patient talk between each other.

The counselor is also involved in seeking out any legitimate opportunity to give strokes to members of the group. Strokes are classified as positive, negative, or conditional. A positive stroke can be a positive verbal contact, verbal comment, or physical touch. A negative stroke involves any negative handling of the individual. Conditional strokes are positive strokes which are dependent upon the individual meeting certain conditions. The leader helps the individual to see how they get their strokes to determine if they are getting enough strokes, and to decide whether they are using appropriate alternatives in obtaining strokes.

In transactional analysis the leader calls to the attention of the individuals which ego state is in control at a particular moment—one's Parent, Adult, or Child. He helps the member to determine if that is the part that he wants turned on at a specific time. He helps the members assess the Parent messages that they have, and to find ways of dropping some of them so that they can become more free and spontaneous. He makes us aware of certain rituals and games that we play. Games are transactional maneuvers which are played over and over again. Berne has described this most extensively in his book, *Games People Play.* The goal of transactional analysis is to help the individual toward awareness of what is going on in other persons so that he can become completely open and spontaneous, more comfortable, and hence, more intimate with his fellowman. This is an experience which most people seldom achieve with many of their fellowmen and in some instances, they never achieve intimacy. The advanced transactional group also helps the individual become aware of his unconscious life plan.

GROUP-CENTERED COUNSELING

The group-centered approach emerged from the client-centered work of Carl Rogers. Its philosophical origins are found in the writings of Rank (1945), Taft (1933), and Rogers (1951). Combs and Snygg (1959) have also made a significant contribution with their phenomenological approach. One of the leading proponents of this approach is Walter Lifton. He indicates that this approach insofar as he formulates it, includes "some of the concepts found in ego psychology (emphasis on strengths), reality therapy (need to be honest and share feelings), and existential thinking." [Lifton, 1968, p. 261]

While a number of Rogers's students might be considered representative of the group-centered approach, we have selected Lifton as our example because of his more extensive and explicit writing on applications of group-centered approaches. Lifton makes the following assumptions regarding group counseling:

1. To help people we need to start with their perception of a situation.

2.   Help is most useful if it is initially directed toward the problem causing an individual (or group) the most immediate concern.

3.   Individuals (groups) have an innate capacity to heal themselves, if they are provided a setting where they can feel secure enough to examine their problems.

4.   As an individual (group) is helped to feel more secure, his need to shut out unwanted bits of information decreases. As he broadens his perception of the problem, he must by necessity include the values and attitudes expressed by society . . .

5.   A change in any part of an individual's life affects all other aspects of his being. A new perception today can cause all past experiences to have a new and different meaning. [Lifton, 1966, p. 28]

This approach to the counseling process will be an acceptable one to those who have become familiar with and accepting of the phenomenological approach as it has been developed by Combs and the writings of Carl Rogers.

Lifton has summarized his position by stating,

Group-centered counseling is a humanistic, existential approach where the source of support for the individual rests upon each person's perceived dependence on his fellowman and his willingness to help others, since in the process he helps himself. The leader's role is basically one of facilitating group interaction, so that the group develops ways of functioning which will increase communication between group members, while providing a setting for ongoing reality testing. [Lifton, 1968, 234–35]

The process, then, is seen as a reeducative one. The concern is with facilitating the change of an individual's perceptions or helping the individual change his own perceptions based on the assumption that this will then alter his attitude, behavior, and eventually, his personality. This suggests that the group should reflect, insofar as possible, a microcosm of real life—a reflection of society as a whole. This suggests the importance of heterogeneity in the selection of group members. The functions of the leader involve setting and establishing an atmosphere which provides support and acceptance. His skills include the ability to link the thoughts of group members, enabling them to see how they agree or disagree, and thus helping them clarify their own perceptions of the world. He must also be skillful in the capacity to reflect not only the individual's stated and unstated feelings, but the group atmosphere as well. These observations are always brought to the group in terms of his hypotheses and hunches about what is happening between individuals and in the group. He helps them keep their focus on the problems and issues which are central, but at the same time is aware of what is happening in the group in the here and now. In this manner the group becomes a resource for each member. It is facilitated insofar as it is concerned with topics which develop personal involvement and meaning and deal with the intragroup relations.

Insofar as the group should focus on central concerns and contents, the leader must also develop and utilize skills in confrontation. This involves his enabling the members in the group to view clearly the content and behavior which they are presenting and projecting and either accept, avoid, deny, or evade that content and behavior. This procedure is consistent with Rogers's theoretical concept regarding the importance of being truly congruent, saying what one means, and reflecting what one hears. The leader facilitates the group's growth towards independence in the capacity to see its own needs. This is done insofar as he provides a mirror which helps the group see the group process.

A group-centered counselor might be distinguished from other theoretical approaches in his emphasis upon the process in contrast to the product. He is more concerned with what is happening to the people and between the members, and in developing an awareness of that for all in the group, than he is with goals of the group which may change. As a member of the group, the leader serves as a model of ways in which group members may also learn to provide support, acceptance, to link, clarify, and reflect. His sensitivity to the group becomes a trait which as it is modeled, can be learned by members of the group.

This sensitivity involves not only verbal cues but awareness of non-verbal cues in the areas of avoidance behavior—cues that signify tension or emotion, and cues that have symbolic meaning within a particular and cultural context (Lifton, 1968, p. 242).

Lifton summarizes the role when he states:

> The major role of the group leader is to facilitate group awareness of the interaction between group members or their need to cope with a problem which is affecting the group climate, nonverbal behavior will be reflected when it affects either of these two situations. [Lifton, 1968, p. 244]

To be most effective, the group-centered counselor needs to help the members see their strengths. A primary focus is placed on enabling them to become aware of their own strengths and the strengths of the other members so that they can cope with their tasks of life. An effective group is one in which the positive strengths of the members are always made evident and are valued.

The approach suggests, then, that the leader is concerned with helping the members become aware that they must never assume what is meant, but that they need to help the individual clarify what he is saying and what he thinks he is hearing. It involves developing clarification in the communication process.

While there are many procedures involved in the group-counseling process, it is vital that the leader indicate to members his genuine concern and care.

In the technique area, Lifton divides procedures as follows:

> *Clarifying Operations*—include reflection, illustration, the pointing out of inconsistencies, the noting of similarities and differences, the questioning of meaning, and the evaluation of individual purposes.
>
> *Show-how Operations*—involve the utilization of demonstrations, resource persons, and the evaluation of alternative procedures.
>
> *Security-giving Operations*—involve the meaning of certain basic emotional needs such as: the need for belonging, the need for achievement and personal growth, the need for economic security, the need to be free from fear, the need for love and affection, the need to be free from guilt, the need for acceptance of others. [Lifton, 1966, chapter 3]

THE T-GROUP APPROACH OF THE NATIONAL TRAINING LABORATORIES

Developed by the National Training Laboratories, the T-Group (T stands for training) is a specialized approach to group work used to develop sensitivity in others (Glanz and Hayes, 1967). Although T-Group concepts and methodology are not an outgrowth of any formal personality theory, they have important implications for group counseling, especially to those counselors who prefer a here-and-now as opposed to an historical approach to working with groups.

Bradford, *et al.,* define the T-Group in the following manner:

> A T-Group is a relatively unstructured group in which

individuals participate as learners. The data for learning are not outside these individuals or remote from their immediate experience within the T-Group. The data are the transactions among members, their own behavior in the group, as they struggle to create a productive and viable organization, a miniature society. [Bradford, *et al.,* 1964, p. 1]

Since these groups are formed with the purpose of assisting members to grow in sensitivity in human relations, the T-Group approach is frequently labeled *sensitivity training.* Unfortunately this term has been adopted by a large number of group leaders, and it is generally beneficial to note carefully what an individual author means when he refers to a training group or sensitivity training. Not all sensitivity training involves T-Group procedures.

In T-Group approaches, members meet together for a period of time, ranging from ten to forty hours, either in a solid block or marathon approach, or for periods as long as two or three weeks. The emphasis in the experience is on the process of the group—that members learn through an analysis of their own experiences. The data for group study include feelings, reactions, perceptions, and behavior (Seashore, n.d.). Members are deliberately placed into an ambiguous situation with no organizational structure or planned agenda.

The role of the group leader is one of helping the group learn from its own experiences, but no attempt is made to organize or structure the proceedings. The leader at the outset explains to the members that he will not be a typical structuring leader, and that the group must proceed on its own. The members must then move into this vacuum, and they do so in various ways. Some will attempt group organization, others will withdraw, and still others will attempt to suggest group topics. By a study of the process within the groups, members gain an understanding of the impact that they make on other members, an understanding of group forces—such as climate, cohesion, and power—and a grasp of the organizational point of view or the relationship between such factors as competitiveness, communications, and stereotyping (Seashore, n.d.).

The elements that characterize the T-Group approach include:

1. Lack of formal approaches to group study
2. A seminar as opposed to classroom arrangement
3. The group generally does not meet in the usual situations (school, office)
4. The usual symbols of status (dress, titles) are not a part of the proceedings

5.   The leader is a participating group member
6.   The content of the discussions is minimized, and the
process or ways in which the group handles communications
is distinguished and clarified
7.   The atmosphere is permissive. [Luft, 1963, pp. 7–8]

By an inspection of these elements, one can see that the T-Group approach is closely related to group counseling in that it is a special type of growth experience. In the process of growing personally, the members also learn about group life itself and gain a better understanding of the more formal groups in business, education, and other areas of society.

As with other growth experiences, T-Group training is based on certain underlying assumptions. It is, as noted in the definition by Bradford, *et al.* (1964) a learning experience, and individuals who enroll in the workshops are assumed to be responsible for their own learning. What one learns is a product of his personal approach to the group and the relationships he develops with others. T-Group theory is based on the premise that learning is a combination of conceptualization and experience, and that an individual is most free to learn when he establishes authentic relationships with people. The group leader then is a teacher only in the sense that he facilitates the examination of the group's experiences. An examination of an individual's value structure formed within the context of feedback from others is an important aspect of this process (Seashore, n.d.).

Since its formation at Bethel, Maine in 1947, the National Training Laboratory has worked with individuals from many professions and many walks of life. The work of the National Training Laboratory has had an impact on the fields of psychology, education, religion, and sociology as well as numerous other aspects of society. According to Seashore (n.d.), research evidence gathered from those who attend NTL workshops shows that while all people do not obtain equal benefits from the experience, many report significant changes and impacts on their lives as citizens, members of families, and workers.

THE HILL INTERACTION APPROACH TO GROUP COUNSELING

In this chapter, the reader has been provided with an introduction to several theoretical approaches to group counseling. While each of these has value and merit for the counselor, there are those who believe that the adaptation of individual theories of personality and individual approaches to working with clients are inappropriate for group purposes.

Certainly, some of the theoretical positions covered in this chapter are particularly relevant in terms of the significance of individual behavior in the group; most notable is the socioteleological position of the Adlerian school.

Hill, however, contends that the small group is the intervening variable between personality and culture—that it both shapes the individual and transmits the culture. It is, therefore, necessary to understand group dynamics, group process, and group development in order to exploit adequately the potential of the small group (Hill, 1965a). Hill further notes that while many beginning therapists and counselors are receptive to the group approach as a vehicle for self-understanding, they have few group concepts at their disposal; and while they attempt to think group, they are unable to exploit its unique potential.

VALUE SYSTEM OF THE HILL INTERACTION MATRIX

While not a full-blown theory of personality, the Hill Interaction Matrix (HIM) provides the counselor with a unique approach for conceptualizing group phenomena as well as providing him with counseling guidelines and a vehicle for both process and outcome research.

As can be seen in Figure 1, the HIM is a matrix of twenty cells that represents a particular type of group interaction. The matrix has a dual dimension—that of work-style and content-style categories—that assures a wide variety of behavioral phenomena and verbal content (Hill, 1965b), and was derived from an intensive study of many groups. Complete details of Hill's developmental procedure may be found in his monograph, *The Hill Interaction Matrix.* These categories were arranged or ranked in terms of presumed therapeutic effectiveness and included the assumptions that member centeredness or the desirability of having a topic person much of the time, interpersonal risk taking or the abandonment of personal security operations, and the phenomena of both client and counselor role taking (or acting as both giver and receiver of help) are valuable in the group situation.

Included in this system are the inferred goals that the objectives of group psychotherapy and group counseling are a change from maladaptive, antisocial behavior to that which allows the individual to assume a more productive life. This is accomplished by assuring the individual that by developing self-understanding he will be able to modify and change in a desired direction.

As you view the matrix (*See* Figure 1), you will note that across the top there are four content style categories which are, broadly speaking,

HILL INTERACTION MATRIX

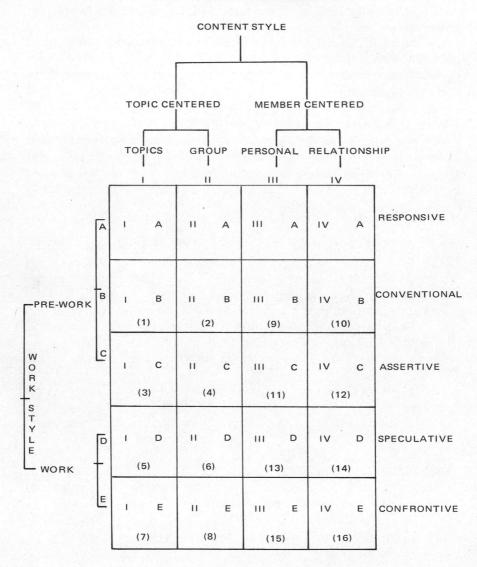

FIGURE 1.
HILL INTERACTION MATRIX

Reprinted by permission of Dr. Wm. Fawcett Hill. From W. F. Hill, *Hill Interaction Matrix,* Youth Studies Center, University of Southern California, 1965.

the four possible content areas for group topics: I—General topics; II—The group itself; III—Personal or problems of the individual; and IV—Relationship or the here and now effect of one member's actions on another.

Note that categories I and II (topic and group) are topic centered and present a rather indirect approach to self-understanding, while topics III and IV (personal and relationship) are member centered and present a direct approach to the therapeutic goal of understanding self. While the HIM may be conceived as either a nominal or ordinal scale, it would seem that more group action in categories III and IV would be the more direct and perhaps more advantageous procedure for groups. Stated another way, the more efficient group is likely to spend a greater amount of time in categories III and IV.

Along the left-hand side of the matrix, the reader will note the work-style categories of group life. By the concept *work,* Hill means that someone in the group is taking the role of the client and actively seeking self-understanding. Thus, categories A (responsive), B (conventional) and C (assertive) are labeled *pre-work* in that individuals responding in these categories are not in the process of actively seeking self-understanding. It is not until individuals begin to operate in category D (speculative) and E (confrontive) that work, by Hill's definition, takes place. To explain further the work-style aspects of the matrix, Hill discusses how individuals may act in one of five levels:

1. RESPONSIVE (Category A). At this level, the individual merely reponds to questions directed to him. The group leader or other members promote the interaction and direct it toward some individual in the group.

2. CONVENTIONAL (Category B). Here the group interaction is characterized by coffee-klatch discussion. The interaction is conventional and stereotyped but does have some therapeutic potential.

3. ASSERTIVE (Category C). This, the last of the pre-work levels, is used to describe those interactions in which the individual talks about a problem but is unwilling to get help with it. In effect, he denies the group as a source of help. He is not in the process of obtaining self-understanding; thus, he is at an assertive or nonwork level.

4. SPECULATIVE (Category D). This is the first category of the work level and was labeled *speculative* by Hill since the interaction has to do with the individual asking questions and formulating hypotheses about presented problems. At this level, the verbalizations are often intellectual in nature and are rated lower in the matrix value system because the individual or topic person controls the data and can shut off or distort the discussion.

5.   CONFRONTIVE (Category E).   At this level, individuals confront each other with their behavior at a point that goes beyond superficial human contacts. It is a major part of reality testing (*See* Chapter 2) and is always accompanied by group tension (Hill, 1967).

Thus, it is now possible to visualize and categorize all group interactions in terms of the matrix. A group, for example, could be operating on a I C level or one where the statements are about general-interest topics on a pre-work level. The approach to self-understanding is indirect, and the style of interaction is assertive. An example might be: "No one with any sense would enroll in the courses they have in this diploma factory." At the IV E level (relationship–confrontive), the group interaction is characterized when the speaker makes a direct bid for self-understanding by specifying the behavior which has caused his reactions. Thus, the stance is work and the style of interaction becomes confrontive. The content of the discussion is derived from relationships within the group. For example, an individual operating in category IV E might say: "I don't know why you jump on me—I get the feeling you wish I'd split (leave the group)." Other interactions, of course, may be placed in each of the twenty cells, and Hill has two publications—the *Hill Interaction Matrix* (1965) and the *Hill Scoring Manual* (1965c)— which should be consulted for a full discussion of his approach.

The HIM concepts, as can be readily seen, offer tremendous research potential. Of perhaps more importance to the practitioner, however, is Hill's contention that the unique aspects provided by the group situation can be maximized through use of his matrix. Also through use of the HIM, one can, if he accepts Hill's value system, determine how efficiently the group is moving toward the stated goals of self-understanding.

The group leader will recognize that this chapter serves as an introduction to varied theoretical approaches to group work. As he develops his leadership skills and self-awareness, he will want to do more reading to determine which approaches are congruent with his personal lifestyle. One's theory and practice of group work should evolve from wide reading, the development of an understanding of how his personality influences his personal theory preference, and opportunities to observe varied styles of leadership. The leader's opportunity to serve as a cofacilitator and eventually to be supervised in the conduct of his own groups, enables him to integrate theory and practice.

SUMMARY

Currently, a variety of theoretical orientations to group counseling is available. In this chapter we have focused on acquainting the counselor with varied assumptions and procedures utilized in group counseling.

The socioteleological approach views man as a decision-making being whose actions have a social purpose. The group process is discussed in terms of: (1) The Relationship, (2) Exploration, (3) Revealing Goals, and (4) Reorientation.

The behavioral approach operates on the premise that most human behavior is learned. Unlike many other formats for group counseling, it operates on the principle that in order to change a feeling, you first change the behavior. The behavioral approach is very systematic and usually requires that each member formulate specific goals. Varenhorst clearly contrasts the behavioral and more traditional approaches to group counseling.

Transactional groups are concerned with three ego states: Parent, Adult, and Child. The leader focuses on the transactions and is active in analysis of the interactions and ego states. Contracts—the securing of an agreement from each member of the group about a thing on which he is willing to work on—are basic to this approach. More emphasis is placed by the leader on dialogue with individuals than with the group, and greater concern is shown for the here and now than the there and then.

Group-centered counseling is tied philosophically to the work of Carl Rogers. It emphasizes a humanistic and existential approach, and the leader is primarily concerned with facilitating group interaction. The leader serves as a model for ways in which group members may learn to provide support, acceptance, to link, clarify, and reflect.

The T-Group approach is a specialized procedure used to develop sensitivity by the National Training Laboratories. The group leader helps the group to learn from the transactions between the members of the group.

William Hill has developed a unique approach for conceptualizing group phenomena. His matrix enables the group leader to analyze group transactions and group development.

The purpose of this chapter is to acquaint the counselor with a variety of theoretical approaches, but it is the counselor's responsiblity to select the style which is most productive for his clientele and which fits his personal life-style.

REFERENCES

ALLEN, R. D. "A Group-Guidance Curriculum in the Senior High School," *The Educator,* Vol. 52 (1931), p. 189.

BERNE, ERIC. *Games People Play*. New York: Grove Press, Inc., 1964.

————. *Principles of Group Treatment*. New York: Oxford University Press, Inc., 1966.

BRADFORD, L. P., GIBB, J., and BENNE, K. *T-Group Theory and Laboratory Method*. New York: John Wiley and Sons, Inc., 1964.

CHRISTENSEN, OSCAR C. "Education: A Model for Counseling in the Elementary School," *Elementary School Guidance and Counseling*, Vol. 4, No. 1 (October, 1969).

COFFEY, H. S. "Socio and Psyche Group Process: Integrated Concepts," *Journal of Social Issues*, No. 8 (1952), pp. 65–74.

COMBS, ARTHUR, and SNYGG, D. *Individual Behavior*. Rev. ed. New York: Harper and Row, Publishers, 1959.

CORSINI, RAYMOND. *Methods of Group Psychotherapy*. New York: McGraw-Hill Book Company, 1957.

CORSINI, RAYMOND, and ROSENBERG, BINA. "Mechanisms of Group Psychotherapy," *Journal of Abnormal and Social Psychology*, Vol. 51 (1955), pp. 406–11.

DINKMEYER, DON C. "Group Counseling: Theory and Techniques," *School Counselor*, Vol. 17, No. 2 (November, 1969).

DREIKURS, RUDOLF. "Group Psychotherapy from the Point of View of Adlerian Psychology," *The International Journal of Group Psychotherapy*, Vol. 7 (1957), p. 363.

————. *Fundamentals of Adlerian Psychology*. Jamaica, B.W.I.: Knox Publications, 1958.

————. *Group Psychotherapy and Group Approaches*. Chicago: Alfred Adler Institute, 1960.

DREIKURS, RUDOLF, and SONSTEGARD, MANFORD. *The Teleoanalytic Approach to Group Counseling*. Chicago: Alfred Adler Institute, 1967.

————. "Rationale of Group Counseling," in *Guidance and Counseling in the Elementary School: Readings in Theory and Practice* (ed. DON C. DINKMEYER). New York: Holt, Rinehart and Winston, Inc., 1968.

GLANZ, E. C., and HAYES, R. W. *Groups in Guidance*. 2nd ed. Boston: Allyn and Bacon, Inc., 1967.

GOLDMAN, LEO. "Group Guidance: Content and Process," in *Guidance and Counseling in the Elementary School: Readings in Theory and Practice* (ed. DON C. DINKMEYER). New York: Holt, Rinehart and Winston, Inc., 1968.

GRUNWALD, B. "The Application of Adlerian Principles in a Classroom," *The American Journal of Individual Psychology*, Vol. 11, No. 2 (1955). Copyright, The American Society of Adlerian Psychology, Inc.

HILL, WILLIAM F. *Group-Counseling Training Syllabus*. Los Angeles, Calif.: University of Southern California, Youth Studies Center, 1965*a*.

————. *HIM, Hill Interaction Matrix*. Los Angeles, Calif.: University of Southern California, Youth Studies Center, 1965*b*.

————. *HIM, Hill Interaction Matrix Scoring Manual*. Los Angeles, Calif.: University of Southern California, Youth Studies Center, 1965*c*.

————. "Group Therapy for Social Impact: Innovation in Leadership Training," *American Behavioral Scientist,* Vol. 11, No. 1 (September–October, 1967).

JONES, A. J. *Principles of Guidance.* 5th ed. New York: McGraw-Hill Book Company, 1963.

LEWIN, K. "Group Decision and Social Change," in *Readings in Social Psychology* (eds. T. M. NEWCOMB, and B. L. HARTLEY), pp. 330–44. New York: Holt, Rinehart and Winston, Inc., 1947.

LIFTON, WALTER. *Working with Groups.* 2nd ed. New York: John Wiley and Sons, Inc., 1966.

————. "Group-Centered Counseling," in *Basic Approaches to Group Psychotherapy and Group Counseling* (ed. GEORGE M. GAZDA). Springfield, Ill.: Charles C Thomas, Publisher, 1968.

LUFT, J. *Group Process: An Introduction to Group Dynamics.* Palo Alto, Calif.: National Press Books, 1963.

MORENO, ZERKA. "Evolution and Dynamics of the Group-Psychotherapy Movement," in *The International Handbook of Group Psychotherapy* (eds. JACOB L. MORENO, *et al.*). New York: Philosophical Library, Inc., 1966.

PAPANEK, HELENE. "Psychotherapy without Insight: Group Therapy as Milieu Therapy," *Journal of Individual Psychology,* Vol. 17 (November, 1961), pp. 184–92.

RANK, OTTO. *Will Therapy; and Truth and Reality.* New York: Alfred A. Knopf, Inc., 1945.

ROGERS, CARL. *Client-Centered Therapy.* Boston: Houghton Mifflin Company, 1951.

SEASHORE, C. *What is Sensitivity Training?* Washington, D.C.: Series 6306 (no date).

SLAVSON, S. R. "Parallelisms in the Development of Group Psychotherapy," *International Journal of Group Psychotherapy,* Vol. 9 (1959), pp. 44–51.

STORMER, G. EDWARD. "Milieu-Group Counseling in Elementary School Guidance," *Elementary School Guidance and Counseling,* Vol. 1, No. 3 (June, 1967).

TAFT, JESSIE. *The Dynamics of Therapy in a Controlled Relationship.* New York: The Macmillan Company, 1933.

ULLMAN, L. T., and KRASNER, L. (eds.). *Case Studies in Behavior Modification.* New York: Holt, Rinehart and Winston, Inc., 1969.

VARENHORST, BARBARA. "Behavioral Group Counseling," in *Theories and Methods of Group Counseling in the Schools* (ed. GEORGE M. GAZDA). Springfield, Ill.: Charles C Thomas, Publisher, 1969.

CHAPTER 4

Therapeutic Forces in the Group

Gᴿᴼᵁᴾ ᴾᴿᴼᶜᴱˢˢ ᴬᴺᴰ Gᴿᴼᵁᴾ ᶜᴼᵁᴺˢᴱᴸᴵᴺᴳ still are without a comprehensive theory which attempts to explain the behavioral, attitudinal, and emotional changes which occur in the group therapeutic process. Until recently, there have been few who have even attempted to develop a specific theory directed only to group therapy and group counseling.

Fullmer has attempted to deal with group-theory development. In a personal communication he indicated that he believes "behavior forms to express a meaning for the experiences which are created in a life event, and that as a result each person creates a new experience in each life event" (1970). This suggests to the authors that Fullmer's theory, which focuses on the fact that each person creates his life experiences and that his patterns of behavior are a choice, is crucial to understanding the group process. In the group, the person still creates his experiences and projects his life-style and pattern of behavior. However, it is through the group experience and process that he becomes aware of what he is doing. It is through group dynamics that feedback from group members enables him to see the meaning of his idiosyncratic transactions.

The group counselor must learn to read human behavior. All messages are transmitted through a personal verbal and nonverbal message system. The individual's behavior is always programmed in a sense by his culture—the behavior expected by others in his life arena (Hall, 1959).

In order to understand the language of behavior, one begins by noting if the person's basic organic, emotional, and safety needs are being met. One becomes aware of the individual's psychological needs for identity and the social needs to belong by noting the system of beliefs that the individual brings with him to the group. His set of assumptions about self and others is constantly being confirmed and occasionally rejected through reality testing in the group. The counselor helps the group members become aware of the language of behavior.

In Fullmer's terms, the individual tests his beliefs against a social (other person) response (behavior). The results confirm or deny his identity. He then assesses how his beliefs and those of the cultural system are either congruent or in conflict (Fullmer, 1970).

The basic task of the group is to deal with the communications between members and to work on the resolution of conflict that is interpersonal (between people) and intrapersonal (between the real and ideal self or the adequate and inadequate self). The group process hence involves risk in being real, genuine, and open. It is only as the participants become congruent (saying what they truly feel and experience) and process authentic feedback that the group can be of mutual assistance. Each individual can choose to be committed, involved, or to change.

Each individual must decide if he is in the group to deal with others in terms of mutual respect or exploitation, personal and self-references, or in terms of impersonal, conversational references. Is he willing to be concerned and care enough to deal with both the past and present? Can he deal with the here and now? Will he utilize his altruistic tendencies to help others? The group is completely dependent upon the decision and capacity of each person to share his self-perceptions and to encourage others to do the same. The sharing of perceptions, known as feedback, permits the group mechanisms and the positive therapeutic forces to operate.

Bach believes that it is impossible for the individual to grow psychologically without a concomitant change in the growth of the group towards therapeutically significant communication (Bach, 1954, p. 268).

Group interaction is best understood when we recognize that behavior has a purpose and whatever happens in the group, the group as a dynamic whole permits to happen. The group dynamics and forces reveal the purposes and psychological movement. The content and the process reveal the public and private agendas in the group and hence the purposes. The leader and group members must learn to confront purposes both in the here and now and there and then.

W. Penfield (1952), a neurosurgeon, conducted experiments with electrodes during brain surgery. He concluded that past events and the feelings associated with them are recorded in detail. An event and the feeling produced by the event are inextricably locked together in the brain so that one cannot be evoked without the other. We are truly feeling and thinking beings at once. The group experience provides the opportunity to deal with the whole person.

GROUP MECHANISMS

In this chapter we will investigate the forces which develop in the group setting and which are responsible for bringing a change in human behavior. The leader must be cognizant of the mechanisms which can occur in the group and their effect upon the members. He must recognize his responsibility for creating a climate and interaction which promote growth, self-understanding, and change. His knowledge of the therapeutic forces in the group and his ability to utilize these forces are the essential competencies for effective leadership (Corsini and Rosenberg, 1955, p. 4.)

The group mechanisms provide the climate which facilitates effective communication. The mechanisms enable the client to participate in a meaningful therapeutic experience.

Group mechanisms are really dynamic processes that occur within a therapeutic group. It is critical that the leader be aware of the potential that exists through full utilization of the mechanisms. However, they do not occur automatically just because the group is formed. The mechanisms can provide the catalyst for the development of the individual as well as the total group.

Group counseling provides the setting which may facilitate the occurrence of the mechanisms. For many it is only in the group that they have the opportunity to experience these mechanisms and the process.

The mechanisms that particularly concern us are taken from the order developed by Corsini and Rosenberg (1955).

1. ACCEPTANCE. This involves respect and empathy with each individual in the group who is received as a person of value without discrimination. He might even be valuable to the group because of his problem, his concern, his capacity to listen. In many instances his deviancy qualifies him for acceptance in contrast to secluding him from membership. Acceptance involves the development of group identification, a strong communal feeling, a belief that this is where I belong, and a climate of trust. It works against alienation and anomie.

The development of strong feelings of belonging is crucial to the healing process. Each individual has the need to belong. The group provides the unique opportunity to find one's place. There are more opportunities for acceptance in the group than in one-to-one counseling. It is almost certain that either the leader or one of the members will provide the necessary basic acceptance.

The value of the group for developing acceptance is demonstrated by the following example: an individual who feels individual counseling carries a stigma, or who cannot relate easily to the available counselors, may find he can make a unique contribution to his group. His capacity for empathic listening or ability to clarify for some members, enables him to become not only accepted, but a valued member. Thus, his feelings of belonging and self-esteem are enhanced by the opportunity to be accepted as he is.

However, this acceptance is *not* an unconditional regard in the sense that it inhibits forces which facilitate change. Matthes, Kranzler, and Mayer (1968) found that unconditional regard might impede change in children. The counselor, instead, will be active and use the full range of both empathic and confrontive skills once he has established the relationship and basic acceptance.

2.   VENTILATION.   The group provides an opportunity for the members to express those feelings and concerns which have been internalized. "Expressions such as emotional release, expression of repressed drives, release of unconscious material, etc. convey the idea that one of the essential processes in successful therapy is catharsis or ventilation" (Corsini, 1957, p. 45).

The group with therapeutic intent is one which permits the individual the opportunity to expose his inner self, his feelings, thoughts, values and attitudes whether they be self-condemning and hostile, or positive and accepting. The ventilation mechanism and its acceptance and discussion allow the individual to learn that being honest and open can be accepted, tolerated; and that it also helps him not only to reduce internal pressures but to become more rational and grow psychologically. The opportunity to express anger and to deal with it helps the group member to mature. His verbalizing of repressed anger may develop new personal insight and may process feedback to members of the group, as in the following example.

John has strong feelings about group members who talk disparagingly and with a gossip type of approach about people not in the group. He feels uncomfortable when this is done and he does not feel it benefits the group. However, he lacks the courage to ventilate and reveal his feelings. After several group meetings and shortly after Joe has been very critical, John says:

> JOHN: It really makes me very angry when Joe talks negatively about his friends, teachers, and parents. I'd like to hear their side. There must be some good things about them. I feel I'd be negative if I had to live with Joe all the time. He's . . .

he's always pessimistic, hostile, and self-centered. I guess I shouldn't have said that, but I'm glad.

COUNSELOR: You're mad about those who complain and can't see the positive side.

JOHN: Yes, they really bug me; but I usually take it. I don't think it helps to say anything.

JOE: I imagine you feel I should be mad, John. Well, I feel you've really helped me. I never realized how I must sound and come over to people. Thanks for being honest!

3. REALITY TESTING. This opportunity to experience a field of social relationships in which one can test his attitudes, values, actions, and relationship skills, work through his anger, his defenses, frustrations, and find outlets, provides the method for the client to see his behavior more accurately, and to experiment with new procedures for relating with members of the group. In simple terms, the group provides an opportunity to practice the new life-style in a social setting, a phenomenological field that is nonthreatening and accepting, which permits him to get direct feedback on his new behavior and attitudes.

For example, John is afraid to relate with girls. In the heterogeneous group he is able to see what is keeping him from functioning. The opportunity is presented not merely to talk about ways to relate but actually to test these approaches in the group.

4. TRANSFERENCE. This involves the development of a strong emotional attachment, often to the leader originally, frequently to other members of the group, and perhaps eventually to the group as a whole. Transference can involve either positive or negative feelings. It may be expressed in forms of positive and normal warmth and is a strong therapeutic agent. The group setting provides an opportunity to help others, both to give and receive love. Some have said about transference that "The cement that makes a group . . . is the identification with each other through the common attachment to the leader" (Sternbach, 1947).

Transference is best defined by Corsini when he refers to "a strong bond of relationships between members of the group . . . a 'continued flow of emotional support' " (Corsini, 1957, p. 41). It refers to the mutual attraction, the liking and love that develop within the group. This strong affect becomes the force that stimulates personal growth. It provides the unique opportunity actually to give love in a culturally approved manner, and is a powerful force in promoting emotional maturity.

Our culture provides few opportunities to give emotional support. It

is a frequent observation that the structured and approved opportunity
to become concerned about another is growth producing for the one
who gives love. The chance to be of real assistance to another, to understand how he feels and become emotionally involved with another
person, can be therapeutic.

In an elementary school group, the boys have all been attacking
Jimmy and trying to force him to speak, urging and cajoling:

> COUNSELOR: Do any of you have any ideas about why Jimmy
> doesn't talk much in our group?
> SAM: Yes, because we don't give him a chance. We just talk
> about what he can't do and tease him. He talks a lot to me
> on the playground. (Sam had been concerned about what the
> group was doing to Jimmy and came to his rescue, also show-
> ing another side of Jimmy. He understood how Jimmy felt
> and cared enough to say so. Later in the group the boys are
> attacking Sam for not trying in reading.)
> JIMMY: I know Sam would like to read, but some of the words
> are just too hard. He likes books on airplanes, but can't get
> the words. (Jimmy has an opportunity to reciprocate and
> show he cares and is. concerned.)

5. INTELLECTUALIZATION AND FEEDBACK. These concepts refer to
the learning that goes on in the group. The group process is not only
emotional (affective) but it is also cognitive and intellectual. It is directed at supplying feedback information and eventually insight. The
group member becomes aware of the interpersonal relations and experiences and has the opportunity to explain his behavior and that of
others. He can explore and learn about his feelings, purposes, values,
perceptions, and attitudes. He is able to reevaluate all of his concepts,
assumptions, faulty attitudes and mistaken perceptions. It is through
learning the thoughts that one has that are in common with others and
by understanding the defenses that are utilized that one develops some
understanding and awareness of interpersonal relations.

In a group session, there has been some discussion of getting along
better with teachers. Bill has complained that teachers are all unfair.
Jeff interjects, "You seem always to feel that not doing things your way
is being unfair." The feedback starts some honest exploration of how
Bill sees things. He becomes aware of how he impresses Jeff and perhaps
other group members. Feedback then is a form of learning about self.

6. INTERACTION or relationships that occur within the group permits the counselor and the group members to recognize the individual's
goals and purposes. As they become more evident, the counselor does

not have to depend only on what the counselee states he does. He can clearly see in the group interaction what is happening. Corsini has stated, "If a group meets in which every member intends to enter into a communication network and if the discussions are such as to permit maximal relationships, regardless of method used, benefits will accrue" (Corsini, 1957, p. 46). Interaction creates awareness, reveals psychological purposes, and permits the group to grow and progress.

7. UNIVERSALIZATION is the realization that one is not unique and that others have similar problems. In other words, "my thoughts are common to many in the group." This realization reduces alienation and loneliness. The client becomes a member of the group and mankind in general. This mechanism breaks down isolation and stimulates communication. The leader stimulates universalization by creating a climate that facilitates open, congruent communication; then he seeks to underline similarities in thoughts, feelings, and actions by pointing them out as they occur.

Sue is talking about her problem making new friends and dealing with fluctuating friendships. She says, "I just can't count on the kids to go to a show or come over to my house." As the counselor explores to see if others have the same problem, it may become apparent to Sue that her problem is common in her group. Recognizing that one is not alone may stimulate the courage to learn ways to become more effective socially. The leader must be alert to ways in which problems, feelings, and thoughts are similar and link these similarities. Universalization is a crucial factor in developing a cohesive group.

8. ALTRUISM suggests that there is a positive desire in man to help others, actually to lose oneself in service and mutual assistance. The group provides the opportunity for the members to be of service to others. The leader obviously needs to model and demonstrate altruism if it is to be emulated. Social interest involves the capacity to participate in the give-and-take of life. The stimulation of social interest permits the person to mature socially. Attempts at expressing altruistic feelings by group members should be encouraged by the leader. More important, the opportunity actually to help one another should be encouraged.

9. SPECTATOR THERAPY permits one to achieve understanding of self by hearing of the concerns of others. This puts his own concerns in focus. While it is a passive type of participation, the very virtue of proceeding at one's own pace and learning almost vicariously has great therapeutic potential.

While some leaders and groups are very annoyed by members who are silent, most counselors feel that the individual can and does learn from the actions of others.

For example, Fred has many problems relating with his parents. However, he does not feel it is safe to discuss this with the group. As he listens to Sue and George present similar problems, and as the group explores new ways to relate to adults, he is able to learn even though it appears that he is not involved.

ADDITIONAL GROUP FORCES

Cartwright (1951) summarized some basic implications of group dynamics which are relevant for changing individual behavior:

1.   Those people who are to be changed and those who are to exert influence for change must have a strong sense of belonging to the same group—a cohesiveness. There is a cotherapeutic influence of the peers. Participation in the group's self-regulation process will reinforce a feeling of togetherness, and the participation underlines the psychological interdependence.

2.   The more attractive the group is to its members, the greater is the influence that the group can exert on its members. This emphasizes the importance of selection for a group.

3.   Only values that are relevant to the goal of the group have an effect on members of the group. There is usually a rejection of anti-therapeutic tendencies.

4.   The greater the prestige of a group member in the eyes of the other members, the greater the influence he can exert.

5.   Individuals will change basic attitudes and their whole personality to maintain membership in a group that is of vital importance to them. Thus, groups should avoid rigid norms of conformity in order to stimulate personal meaningfulness and a feeling of belonging.

6.   Everyone in the group should share a perception of the need for change if the source of pressure for change is to lie within the group.

7.   Everyone in the group should be explicitly aware of the psychological processes in the group such as the need for change, plans for change, and the consequences of change.

8.   Changes in one part of a group produce strain in other related parts which can be eliminated only by eliminating the change or readjusting the related parts. Changes in substructures such as friendship coalitions or fighting pairs will create a heightened tension in the whole group.

Thelen believes the group exists as a whole and that every member represents the whole and participates in it. Thelen provides us with the following principles:

PRINCIPLES UNDERLYING THE CONTROL OF THE GROUP

1.   Each individual statement, as soon as it is made, becomes the property of the group, and it is up to the group to test it, using the individual as a resource to clarify his thought.

2.   Emotional expression by individuals expresses the needs of the group, i.e. conflict may express the needs of the group at that time to fight.

3.   In all but extreme cases, problem people are to be considered group problems. In the NTL group the group works only on group problems, not problems of individuals.

4.   The question is "To what problem is this behavior relevant?"

5.   A problem is what everybody feels to be a problem.

6.   The group moves by consensus and agreement, not by taking sides in disputes.

7.   A decision has been reached whenever people feel sufficiently confident to act.

8.   Voting is never used to determine the right alternative.

9.   Whenever the group does not know what it is doing, it ought to stop and find out—clarify member roles.

10.   All seriously intended contributions are responded to.

11.   No individual can speak for the group; the group speaks for itself.

12.   There are individual differences and people play different roles in each situation.

13.   Every change in activity alters the prestige system and the opportunities for reward in the group. [Thelen, 1954, pp. 285–89]

Bach believes that participation in the group helps the individual grow through a process called *theragnosis*. "Theragnosis refers to a variety of communications which aim, by the conscious purpose of those participating in the communications, (1) to diagnose an individual's personal idiosyncrasies in interpersonal contact and traffic; and (2) therapeutically to help the individual patient to a better understanding of how his repeatedly observable behavior patterns affect others in the therapy group" (Bach, 1954, p. 192). Theragnosis thus involves processing feedback about the individual's pattern and life-style to him in order to help him become aware of the impact of his behavior on others. This increases awareness, insight and sensitivity.

Bach describes the member-to-member exchange of their analysis of the impact of others on them in terms of seven phases of the group's theragnostic work:

1. Sensing a behavior problem—The group determines that a unique pattern of behavior exists in an individual.
2. Acknowledgment of the behavior problem and conflict—After group consensus no further work is done until the member can acknowledge his full awareness of it.
3. Reactive avoidance or suppression of the recognized behavior problem—The member may recognize the problem and begins to rid himself of it.
4. Pinning down the instigation for the behavior problem—If the behavior does not change, the group may turn its attention to the nature of the conflicts that evoke this pattern. They seek to have the member become aware of the social-stimulus response pattern.
5. Recognition of unconscious needs—The group may now speculate on the nature of the needs met by the behavior pattern.
6. Demonstration of the unreality of defensive needs—The group and the member investigate the lack of necessity of maintaining these defenses.
7. Discovery of ways of utilizing the environment.—Once the member gains ego strength, he works through to remove the need for the maintenance of defensive, disjunctive patterns."They are encouraged to expand the response repertoire of the self." [Bach, 1954, p. 200]

In searching for a theory of group counseling, the authors have attempted to draw upon some of the best thinking that is currently available. This also involves consideration of the socioteleological approach of Dreikurs and Sonstegard. The socioteleological principles really provide a very broad base for understanding the meaning and purpose of group counseling (Sonstegard and Dreikurs, 1967). This approach understands man as an indivisible, social, decision-making being whose actions have a social purpose. All that occurs in the group also has a purpose. The significance of behavior lies in its social consequences.

The individual's life-style is expressed in his social transactions within the group. It is through the group interaction that his personality is revealed, character expressed, and eventually personality changed.

The group is a social laboratory. The psychological movement in the group provides diagnostic opportunities. The leader and the members attempt to clarify the purpose of the behavior both inside and outside the group. The group provides a set of therapeutic effects which occur only in the group.

The socioteleological approach believes that because most problems are interpersonal, they are best solved in the group setting. All behavior has social meaning and is best understood by comprehending its social context. It is within the group that man can be most adequately diagnosed, and the group provides the opportunity for man to fulfill himself. There are specific corrective influences and peer effects which can only occur within the group.

Another theorist of the Adlerian school who has contributed to the development of theory is Raymond Corsini. Corsini was perhaps the first to go into any detailed explanation of group psychotherapy and theory. He indicated that theory can be simple, it may be derived from work experiences, but that theory always serves as a guideline for practice.

Corsini describes how theory may rise from practical experience. He discusses the development of a procedure sometimes called the *behind-the-back technique.* The practice developed by Corsini suggested that the member talk about himself and then withdraw from the group psychologically. The member's back is turned to the group and he does nothing but listen. Corsini suggests that a theory then emerged to explain this procedure which did not appear to be a part of existing theories.

Thus, there developed a theory for the release of inhibition and freedom of emotional reaction to information when it is not presented in a face-to-face manner. The theory is then stated—that in group therapy the discrepancy between what a person thinks he would like to be and what he is, and between what others think of him and how they treat him, is often incongruent. The behind-the-back technique is a therapeutic process which brings these concepts into adjustment (Corsini, 1957).

Moreno's theoretical framework is group centered. It is interactional group psychotherapy. It involves the simultaneous treatment of several individuals in interaction within the group. It treats not only the individual but the entire group. The aim is to promote the integration of the individual with respect to the uncontrolled forces surrounding him through sociometric analysis. Every individual is a therapeutic agent of every other individual, so that every group is a therapeutic agent of every other group. It is based upon reciprocal integration and spontaneous and free interaction (Moreno, 1966). Groups grow according to sociogenetic laws, which state that higher forms of group organization always proceed from simpler forms. Every group has a distinct cohesion. The sharing of experiences increases group cohesiveness. Moreno referred to the force that ties people together and makes for cohesiveness as *Tele.*

Corsini intensively reviews the theories of Adler, Freud, Moreno, and Rogers. Those interested in theories of group process will want to acquaint themselves with this overview (Corsini, 1957).

Bennis investigated the actual process of group movement. The first session involves attempts to ward off anxiety and to search for structure or a common goal. There is also some dependency on the leader which may result in either seeking to please or resentment and rebellion. The next phase involves more open rebellion against the leader involving hostility and suspicion of the leader's motives. This is followed by a resolution of the conflict and the nonconflicted members help the group to become responsible for itself. Affectional relationships between members develop after the feelings of dependence toward authority are resolved (Bennis and Shepard, 1956).

Gibb and Gibb have described the TORI processes in the book edited by George Gazda, *Innovations to Group Psychotherapy* (1968). They state,

> In normal interaction there is movement, in individuals and in groups, toward trust and away from fear, toward open and away from closed behavior, toward self-realization and away from imposition, toward interdependence and away from dependence. For communicative ease these processes of growth have been called the TORI processes, representing movement toward trust, openness, realization, and interdependence. These processes are therapeutic—define therapy—are independent of the presence of a therapist, regenerative in character, and intrinsic to all normal life processes in human organisms.

William Schutz (1966) has provided us with FIRO, a three-dimensional theory of interpersonal behavior. He says, "people need people." They need people to receive from and give to. He calls this "wanted behavior and expressed behavior" and talks about the interpersonal needs as having properties which are close and analogous to those of biological types of needs. He then postulates that every individual has three interpersonal needs: inclusion, control, and affection. These constitute a sufficient set of areas of interpersonal behavior to enable us to predict and explain the interpersonal phenomenon. Schutz's postulate of Group Development states

> The formation and development of two or more people into an interpersonal relation (i.e. a group) always follows the same sequence. Under this postulate fall two principles: (1) For the time period starting with the group's beginning . . . the predominant area of interaction begins with inclusion, is followed by control, and finally by affection. (2) This cycle may recur. [Durkin, 1964, p. 53]

Ohlsen has dealt more directly with the therapeutic forces in a counseling group. He suggests that both the counselor and the clients must recognize and use these forces. Ohlsen identifies nine major therapeutic forces:

> 1. *Commitment.* To profit from group counseling they must recognize the need for assistance and be willing to talk about their problems, solve them, and change their behavior.
>
> 2. *Expectations.* To benefit most they must understand what is expected before they decide to join.
>
> 3. *Responsibility.* Clients must take responsibility for themselves and for modifying their perceptions of the world.
>
> 4. *Acceptance.* This enhances self-esteem and encourages a client to change his behavior.
>
> 5. *Attractiveness.* If the group meets members' needs, has goals that are perceived as important, and includes prestigious members, it will exert a greater influence on its members.
>
> 6. *Belonging.* All must sense a strong feeling of belonging.
>
> 7. *Security.* When the clients feel reasonably safe in the group it is easier to be open and express genuine feelings.
>
> 8. *Tension.* Growth involves productive tension.
>
> 9. *Group Norms.* When the member accepts the necessary conditions for a therapeutic group he then is influenced by the group norms. [Ohlsen, 1970]

Herbert Otto (1967) has been concerned with stimulating human potential. His groups focus on fostering self-realization and self-actualization. Considerable emphasis is placed upon methods and techniques. The methods can be used as separate units. They focus on and emphasize strengths, assets, and positive approaches to goal establishment.

One of the methods which the authors believe has great potential for producing growth is:

MULTIPLE-STRENGTH PERCEPTION METHOD

Multiple-strength perception must also be voluntary.

STEP I.   Those willing to participate write their names on a folded slip of paper which will be drawn from a receptacle. As soon as the slip is drawn the leader asks for a volunteer who takes notes of the strengths and blocks which keep the person from using his strengths.

STEP II.   The target person lists out loud (spontaneously without reading) all of his strengths as he sees them.

STEP III.   When he has finished listing his strengths as he perceives them, he turns to the group and asks "What other strengths or potentialities do you see me as having, and what do you see is keeping me from using these strengths?"

STEP IV.   The group bombards the target person with their perceptions of his strengths and the forces which keep him from utilizing his strengths and potentialities. They may also ask questions to solicit clues of strengths or to clarify those forces which keep him from using his strengths. It is important that they focus on strengths and assets in analysis of blocks.

STEP V.   When the leader senses that the group is running out of material he will ask if there are any other strengths they see in the target person.

STEP VI.   The leader then asks, "Now that we have seen the range of strengths and potentialities in John (or Mary) what sort of group fantasy or dream do we have for him (her) if he uses all these strengths?" In closing the exercise the leader asks the target person, "How did you feel while this process was going on?"

The methods are effective exercises for stimulating interaction and the creativity and spontaneity of group members. Another of Otto's procedures, the DUE method, is discussed in Chapter Five.

Virginia Satir has developed a communication theory which is helpful in explaining the forces in the group. Communication refers to interaction or transaction and can be nonverbal as well as verbal within a social context. This includes all the clues we use to give and receive meaning. In the group the members find out about others, the nature of relationships, and become aware of self so they can let others know what is going on inside of them. The focus is on developing functional communication.

Satir indicates a functional communicator is one who can:

a. Firmly state his case.
b. Yet at the same time clarify and qualify what he says.
c. As well as ask for feedback.
d. And be receptive to feedback when he gets it.
   [Satir, 1967]

Satir points out that both the sender and the receiver of the message have the responsibility to make the communication clear.

THE FORCES THAT BRING ABOUT CHANGE IN HUMAN BEHAVIOR

As one attempts to analyze the forces that bring about change in human behavior, it is apparent that one must take a close look at what it is that actually happens in the group. A dichotomy might be developed between:

Negative	vs.	Positive forces
anxiety	vs.	security
fear	vs.	positive expectations
distrust	vs.	openness
anger	vs.	love, warmth
misunderstanding	vs.	understanding
rejection	vs.	acceptance
incongruence	vs.	congruence
failure to accept and understand feelings	vs.	empathy
lack of respect	vs.	mutual respect
confusion	vs.	goal directedness

It thus appears that each group begins by dealing with a set of forces that we temporarily will define as negative. In simple terms:

1. The group is anxious. They are expecting something of the leader.

2. They are resistant to personal expression and personal exploration. Most of their expectations are composed of confused ideas about what is expected, what they might accomplish, how they can work together.

3. They have many fears of the unknown; fear they will be hurt. Whenever one is fearful his participation is limited.

4. There is considerable distrust of sharing with each other.
5. Certainly underneath the surface there is much hidden anger.
6. Feelings in many instances are of alienation and rejection.

At this stage the members need the healing power of the group. It seems that the forces that are within the group are the forces that bring about change. These forces come through all the therapeutic mechanisms which have already been described. As soon as one is able to:

. Make a commitment
. Feel that he belongs
. Utilize his social interest

he is well on the way to self-actualization and personal-social growth. The forces that exist in the group, that bring this about, involve the development of security—the security that enables one to move from the description of past feelings to the expression of genuine current feelings, from the exploration of surface, casual (almost social) material to the expression and exploration of meanings that are personal. The individual begins to reveal himself and personally meaningful material. This tends to bring immediate feelings into the open and free the spontaneous and creative capacity which we have to deal with the pain and suffering we and others experience. The capacity to deal with the here and now, and to work from self-acceptance—that "I am okay" and "I can try"—leads to the cracking of poor communication and the destruction of facades. It is through this type of interpersonal communication and reception of feedback that the individual begins to care, the group begins to accept, belongingness and identification emerge, and behavior beings to change.

Through genuine communication and confrontation and a direct leveling with each other, feedback produces what many have called the *basic encounter* in which an individual is truly in contact with his feelings and the feelings of others. This closeness and personal interaction enable the individual to change.

It is in the group that the leader utilizes the very unique factors or therapeutic experiences insofar as he:

1. Develops cohesiveness or the sense of belonging.
2. Defines reality for the individual.
3. Both induces and releases powerful feelings which process change.
4. Enables one to consider his position and significance as a person.
5. Enables one to consider the personal meanings in life.
6. Provides a contact in which one can attempt to change, develop social comparisons, and process feedback.

THE LEADER AS FACILITATOR

We need to look at what the facilitating individual in the group actually does. The facilitator is one who is concerned about having contact with the total person—his thoughts, feelings, purposes, and actions. He does this by enabling the person to participate not only verbally but in terms of his feelings and even in terms of his actions and interactions. He starts at the level where the group is ready to function, he listens closely not only to what is said but to what is not said. He regards each person as important, and he values personal meanings. He works in such a way as to create psychological safety. He does this by having people recognize that it is safe to ventilate anger, pain, fear, suspicion, and hurt. He provides an area where one can move at his own speed, while considering his feelings and his effect and impact on others. This basic acceptance for the participant as well as the silent individual who may participate primarily in terms of spectator therapy facilitate the development of courage.

Thus, it is the leader's empathic understanding which eventually becomes part of the function of the group members and which enables personal meaning to become clear to the sender as well as the receiver. In this setting and contact both verbal and nonverbal messages are clarified. This suggests that all within the group must be aware of and sensitive to their own feelings, attitudes, purposes, and goals. They must be "with themselves" and aware of their own feelings. It is only through this type of communication in which members can express positive and good feelings as well as angry and negative feelings. It is only through this process that they may truly develop trust, and as a result, clear communication.

The leader utilizes all of his own sensory modalities including hearing and visual cues. He also utilizes procedures such as those mentioned in Chapter 5. He may confront specific behaviors, or he may talk about his feelings. He certainly reflects, clarifies, and collaborates. It is through his awareness not only of the process which at times he may clarify, but of the fact that he values the whole person and any genuine contact which may occur as being of value, that the forces work and the group grows. The role of the leader is explored in greater detail in Chapter 5.

SUMMARY

It is crucial that the group counselor understand the forces which bring about behavioral and emotional changes in the group setting. The group mechanisms of acceptance, ventilation, reality testing, transference, intellectualization, interaction, universalization, altruism, and spectator therapy are discussed in detail. Consideration is given to group forces as they have been conceptualized by Cartwright, Thelen, Bach, Moreno, Bennis, Gibb, Schutz, and Ohlsen.

The chapter presents the Multiple-Strength Perception Method of Henry Otto. Attention is given to the group forces that bring change in human behavior. The leader then is described as a facilitator who enables the individual and the group to develop.

REFERENCES

BACH, GEORGE R. *Intensive Group Psychotherapy.* New York: The Ronald Press Company, copyright, 1954.

BENNIS, W. G., and SHEPARD, H. "A Theory of Group Development," *Human Relations,* Vol. 9 (1956), pp. 415–37.

CARTWRIGHT, DORWIN. "Achieving Change in People: Some Applications of Group-Dynamics Theory," *Human Relations,* Vol. 4 (1951), pp. 381–92.

CORSINI, RAYMOND. *Methods of Group Psychotherapy.* New York: McGraw-Hill Book Company, 1957.

CORSINI, RAYMOND, and ROSENBERG, BINA. "Mechanisms of Group Psychotherapy," *Journal of Abnormal and Social Psychology,* Vol. 51 (1955), pp. 406–11.

DURKIN, HELEN E. *The Group in Depth.* New York: International Universities Press, 1964.

FULLMER, DANIEL. Personal Communication. Honolulu, Hawaii: Department of Educational Psychology, University of Hawaii, 1970.

GIBB, JACK R., and GIBB, LORRAINE M. "Emergence Therapy: The TORI Process in an Emergent Group," in *Innovations to Group Psychotherapy* (ed. GEORGE M. GAZDA, p. 96. Springfield, Ill.: Charles C Thomas, Publisher, 1968.

HALL, E. T. *The Silent Language.* New York: Doubleday and Company, Inc., 1959.

MATTHES, WILLIAM A., KRANZLER, GERALD D., and MAYER, G. ROY. "The Relationship between the Client's Perceptions of Counselor Behavior and Change in the Client's Behavior," *Elementary School Guidance and Counseling,* Vol. 2, No. 3 (March, 1968).

MORENO, JACOB L. *The International Handbook of Group Psychotherapy.* New York: Philosophical Library, Inc., 1966.

OHLSEN, MERLE M. *Group Counseling.* New York: Holt, Rinehart and Winston, Inc., 1970.

OTTO, HERBERT A. *Group Methods to Actualize Human Potential, A Handbook.* Beverly Hills, Calif.: Holistic Press, 1970, pp. 56–104.

PENFIELD, W. "Memory Mechanisms," *A.M.A. Archives of Neurology and Psychiatry,* Vol. 67 (1952), pp. 178–98.

SATIR, VIRGINIA. *Conjoint Family Therapy.* Rev. ed. Palo Alto, Calif.: Science and Behavior Books, 1967.

SCHUTZ, WILLIAM C. *The Interpersonal Underworld.* A Reprint Edition of *FIRO: A Three-Dimensional Theory of Interpersonal Behavior.* Palo Alto, Calif.: Science and Behavior Books, 1966.

SONSTEGARD, MANFORD, and DREIKURS, RUDOLF. *The Teleoanalytic Approach to Group Counseling.* Chicago: Alfred Adler Institute, 1967.

STERNBACH, O. "The Dynamics of Psychotherapy in the Group," *Child Psychiatry,* Vol. 1 (1947), pp. 91–112.

THELEN, HERBERT A. *Dynamics of Groups at Work.* Chicago: University of Chicago Press, 1954.

CHAPTER 5

Group Leadership

Perhaps more has been written and less agreed upon regarding leadership than any other subject being studied in the social sciences.

GORDON L. LIPPITT

THE COUNSELOR AS A PERSON

So much has been written about the qualities and traits needed by the successful counselor that one must wonder why the topic must be again approached in this text. Researchers have long sought to identify the ideal counselor and in the process have compiled long lists of traits and factors needed to comprise an effective helping relationship. When one pauses a moment to consider even a few representative lists, he soon discovers that any given counselor who possessed all the qualities necessary and sufficient for the helping relationship would indeed be the atypical individual.

In addition to those who would identify traits and factors of successful counselors, there are others who regularly enter the classic debate of what prior experience the counselor must have to enter the field of guidance. More specifically, this needless and frequently useless debate seems to center on the teaching-experience or no-teaching-experience issue. One must wonder why a field as sophisticated as guidance and counseling should direct so much of its energy to this discussion, as if teaching experience or lack of it were polarized concepts separated by miles of something else on the good counselor–poor counselor continuum. While most guidance personnel object to labels as a way of describing a child, we have persisted in utilizing the label *teacher* as if it described a given, single, readily identifiable personality. Then depending on what end of the continuum one chooses to operate, we have advanced persuasive arguments to prove why one should or should not teach children prior to counseling them. The term *teaching* is, in the final analysis, more descriptive of a profession than it is of an individual. After all judgments have been made as to whether or not an individual will be a successful counselor, the probability is that his prior occupation will have little effect on his counseling performance.

If one could venture a guess, most counselor educators and others responsible for the selection and education of the neophyte counselor would probably admit that we are not at all certain about the best way to select prospective counselors. In spite of the expressions of opinion and the research that is done on this topic, the most common selection of the prospective counselor still follows the guidelines of a university graduate school. Generally, these call for some acceptable grade-point average, and a Graduate Record Exam or Miller Analogies score that is acceptable to a majority of a selection committee. In some cases, a personal interview may be required. Some institutions also ask for personality data gathered through the Minnesota Multiphasic Personality Inventory (MMPI), the Edwards Personal Preference Scale, or some other such instrument. Yet, in spite of our efforts to screen, we have not been as good at selection as we might like. Also, if one could trace the history of selection procedures at various universities, it would be interesting to discover who selected the *original* counselor educators, who in turn developed the criteria we now use. What seems most striking to the authors is the fact that we are constantly amazed by how well some students seem to do after they were accepted on probation because they somehow seemed to lack some or all of what selectors seemed to deem valuable for counseling success. It also is somewhat amazing to note that some of those who seem to carry a *can't miss* label fail to live up to a projected expectation. The history and current level of functioning of a given individual—whether gathered through interviews, tests, or inventories—may well tell us how an individual *might* perform but are less accurate in telling us how he *will* perform. Like the professional horseplayer, selectors of counselors gather data, make a bet, and start the race. We have won with long shots and failed with favorites and vice versa.

With the current active interest in group counseling, it is probable that we shall view in the future at least minimal interest in the selection and professional preparation of the group counselor as a specialized entity. There are some in the field who now contend that selection of the student for individual counseling is a simpler task in that the skills and attitudes needed by the group counselor exceed those required for individual counseling. In this context, the process of counselor selection for group work presents the counselor educator with an additional professional concern. After this discussion on what appears to be limited evidence for counselor selection, it may be risky indeed to attempt to identify the "person" of the group counselor. Like other counselor educators, the counselors by the nature of their work have been engaged in the educational process for a number of years. Various systems have been employed—ranging from the open-door policy of allowing everyone who wishes to prepare for group work to do so, to the more rigorous prerequisite system combined with identified individual skills. Although little new light can be shed on the topic of who the effective group counselor is, it may be of worth to note some of the elements that seem to be inherent in those who have been (in the authors' judgment) effective group counselors. Unfortunately, no accurate yardstick is available for use by others in that there are degrees of the following counselor traits. In terms of such factors as client satisfaction, smooth group operation, and in some cases positive client change, the following characteristics appear in those who are good group counselors.

1. THE EFFECTIVE GROUP COUNSELOR IS ONE WHO IS PERCEIVED BY GROUP MEMBERS AS BEING WITH THEM AND FOR THEM AS INDIVIDUALS. While this statement will startle practically no one, our experience has taught us that the successful group counselor as opposed to his unsuccessful counterpart is able to convey or at least is perceived as conveying an attitude of care and concern for each group member. While groups constantly engage in a ranking process of various members, the successful counselor is able to recognize and deal with this group dynamic to the extent that the group members do not see him ranking them as better or worse along any given dimension. No individual is sacrificed for a theory, no participant is required to respond to a given group technique, and no group member is in any way made to respond to queries that the counselor himself would not care to have asked of him.

Perhaps more than one counselor will recall a supervisor or group leader who verbalized that the counselor had complete freedom to operate as himself in counseling, provided, of course, that he expressed the theoretical and operational guidelines of the supervisor! In a like manner, the client in a group cannot be told he has complete freedom to discuss whatever he wishes and then find that the counselor is more interested in Helen's sex problems than he is in Joe's inability to obtain a B grade in biology. Effective group counselors also answer honestly and refrain from using a reflection or summarization for the sake of the reflection or summarization. Success in group counseling, regardless of how one chooses to define it, is a product of strong and mutual liking and respect between the counselor and the group members and among the clients themselves. No counselor will gain either the respect or care from his group if he cares little for them.

2.   GROUP COUNSELORS ARE ABLE TO OPERATE WITHIN THE AFFECTIVE AND DEVELOPMENTAL PHASES OF THE GROUP.   Bach (1954) and Martin and Hill (1957), among others, have described the process of group development. For example, Martin and Hill propose a six-phase group theory of development wherein the group members initiate counseling by engaging in individual, unshared attitudes and gradually move into phases of reactivation of fixed attitudes, exploration of interpersonal potential, awareness of interrelationship, consciousness of group dynamics, and finally develop into an integrative–creative social instrument. Not only does the effective group counselor have knowledge of the concept of group development, he also is able to guide his individual behavior so that what he says and does are not antithetical to effective group functioning. For example, in phase one of Martin and Hill's classification system, the counselor is aware of minimal groupness or cohesiveness. He must, in this phase, expect to develop a climate of acceptance, be prepared to function as the one to whom the majority of verbalizations are addressed, and expect and be prepared to handle rather extensive individual and group ventilation.

Some highly successful individual counselors have encountered difficulty in thinking group and in recognizing that the group does indeed go through developmental stages. Others who intellectually accept and recognize the concept of group development do not seem to grasp the necessary skills to handle the group in the various phases. Moreover, the good group counselor is one who appears able to sense the emotional climate of the group in a manner similar to the skilled individual counselor who recognizes the underlying affect in verbalizations of clients. Group counselors who constantly miss the affective levels of the group as a whole continually lead individual members and the group as a whole into tangents and channels that delay the group development. In some cases, such counselors destroy counselor–group rapport, hinder group morale, and eventually cause members to discontinue group counseling. More than one graduate student has seen a well-planned group project fall apart because, among other things, he failed to operate within the developmental level of the group and misread or misinterpreted the emotional climate present in the group. For example, in an early session wherein a member's response could be directed to the counselor, it could be a mistake for him to attempt a confrontation of that individual even though he had made a correct interpretation of his intentions.

> GROUP MEMBER (to counselor):   You've been sitting back saying nothing for almost half an hour; aren't you supposed to be part of this group?
> COUNSELOR: I understand how you feel, John, but I've noticed you're not really angry with me. What you really want is greater participation from Sue and Jane who have been ignoring you.

In this instance where the counselor should have been prepared for little interpersonal group-relevant behavior, he is pushing for a rather sharp confrontation prior to the development of good group cohesion. In the early stages of group development, there is generally perception of the counselor as the acknowledged leader of the group, and the counselor might have more appropriately responded to the member in terms of the effect the verbalization had on him.

3.   GROUP COUNSELORS ARE ESSENTIALLY POSITIVE INDIVIDUALS.   The effective group counselor, from our experience, is the individual who views others in essentially positive ways. He tends to view his group members as normal, possessing great potential, and sees his job as a counselor as essentially one of helping people build on what is already a good formation. He is one who is not disturbed by the group's small talk, is not overly anxious to focus on problems of individuals. His thinking would be more patterned after the developmental principles advanced by Dinkmeyer (1967), Blocher (1966), Peters and Farwell (1959), and Glasser (1965) than that of Freud or the Philosopher Nietzsche who hold a more negative view of man. In addition, the effective group counselor possesses the attitudes so brilliantly outlined by Combs who has devoted years to the study of effective counselors. Combs provides seven criteria as guidelines for good counselors and much of what he says appears applicable to those who would counsel groups. Foremost among the attitudes of an effective counselor are:

1.   Effective and noneffective counseling is not a question of method, but a question of beliefs on the part of the counselor. Counseling is a question of having understanding, belief in, and relationship with a counselee.
2.   Good counselors are more concerned with people than with things.

3. Good group counselors see people as those who can. They are individuals who believe that people are able, friendly, and who possess dignity and worth. In addition, the good counselor sees people as dependable and able to make their own decisions.

4. Good counselors see themselves as being with people; poor ones set themselves apart in one way or another.

5. Good counselors tend to view the counselee with the question: "What does this mean to him?" Good counselors also feel that they're enough; poor ones are always trying to keep others from finding out.

6. Good counselors see their job as one of freeing people, not fencing them in or controlling them.

7. Good counselors can reveal themselves to people—that is, to be what he is. In addition, the good counselor is able to get involved in the process; the poor one does not enter into the process. [Combs, 1969]

Regardless of whether or not one wishes to accept the phenomenological views of Combs, it is difficult to take issue with his positive view of man. In our experience, the good group counselor might, at times, deviate from strict phenomenological psychology, but he does indeed view his clients in the ways that Combs suggests.

4. EFFECTIVE GROUP COUNSELORS ARE THOSE INDIVIDUALS WHO ARE ABLE TO AFFIX A STATUS ROLE TO GROUP MEMBERS. Regardless of the degree of acceptance and positive attitudes inherent in the personality of the counselor, many clients enter into the group situation with a feeling of inferior status. In some cases, the feelings of inferiority are present in relation to the counselor, in others they are felt in relation to other members of the group, and in some cases an individual may feel inferior to both the counselor and the group. Heilbrun, who identified this phenomenon in individual counseling relationships, suggests that two lines of counselor action be initiated early:

1. Actions intended to increase the status of the client's role (encouragement of client initiative and responsibility) in counseling and avoidance of authoritative–directive counseling behavior.

2. Actions intended to acknowledge and clarify the client's feelings about his perceived status role. [Heilbrun, 1962]

To increase the status of a group member, the counselor should closely observe the group-interaction patterns to determine the ranking system in the group. Most groups will develop a rough ranking system of individuals and generally those with the most status will both initiate and receive the greatest number of verbalizations. In such cases, the counselor may have to sponsor a group member by supporting and encouraging him in an effort to raise his status in the group.

> COUNSELOR: I've noticed that John hasn't been saying much, yet he seems to agree readily that Harry is indeed angry with Mary much of the time.
>
> JOHN (low status member): Yes, I think you're right. Everytime Mary says something, Harry is at her! I feel kinda bad for Mary, but you know me; I always hesitate to say something.
>
> COUNSELOR: I'm glad you said that John, that's an observation that I, too, have made, and I'm glad you picked it up! Is it possible that John and I are on the right track, Mary? (Counselor supports and sponsors John.)
>
> *or*
>
> COUNSELOR: John, you've been very quiet for about two weeks. I have a hunch you want to tell us something.
>
> JOHN: Well, I do, but nobody pays much attention to what I say anyhow!
>
> COUNSELOR: I may be way off base, John, but is it possible that you think the rest of the group is really putting you down?

5.   SUCCESSFUL GROUP COUNSELORS ARE AN INTEGRATED BLEND OF SPECIALISTS AND ARTISTS. While it would not be difficult to find supporters among practicing group counselors who would testify that group counseling is indeed an art, the experience of the authors in working with practicum students over the years is that really good group counseling is more than insight, sensitivity, and charisma. While the effective group counselor seems to possess the attitudes and traits noted earlier in this chapter, the effective group counselor needs to be familiar with the professional literature in the field of group counseling as well as the contributions from the group therapists, sociologists, and other supporting sciences.

Hill (1967), who has long been an advocate of a scientifically oriented approach to group therapy, notes that in most fields of professional endeavor one man emerged as leader and formed groups of others in the master–apprentice mode of teaching others the skills of a given profession. "At this stage in the development of group therapy, we are no longer in the business of populating Mt. Olympus with demigods but are more concerned with preparing certain people with a calling for the priesthood" (Hill, 1967, p. 26). Hill further notes that although those who have received training with some of the leaders of the group-therapy movement would probably not accept training in university courses as a substitute for close work with outstanding men, the course approach is necessary if we are to move toward a more scientific approach to group work:

> I suspect that there are many who have received their training through association with Berne, Bach, Beukenkamp, Moreno, Slavson, Scheidlinger, Stein, or whatever gods there may be, and they feel certain that this training cannot be substituted for by some core courses at the university. This is, of course, true if group therapy is to remain exclusively an art, but if it is to become more and more of a science, it is to become more and more untrue. [Hill, 1967, pp. 28–29]

Hill's views regarding group therapists can also be considered within the context of group counseling. Certainly, those who learned to counsel groups under the direction of Ohlsen, Lifton, Driver, Kemp, and Glanz would probably not substitute course work at a given university for their experiences with these individuals. Yet, in spite of the number of effective teachers of group counseling these men have prepared, the demand for an ever-increasing number of group counselors is such to require that group counseling become more and more of a science.

Our observations for this view are predicated upon our experience in the preparation of group counselors. Formerly, a single course—generally entitled *Group Guidance*—was deemed sufficient to enable counselors to work with groups. While numerous fine artists moved through this course and became effective group counselors, the view held by the authors is that such individuals become more complete group counselors when they are knowledgeable about the fundamentals of group work. In this context, the good group counselor is a good scholar and a scientist as well as an artist. He possesses more than a gut-level feeling for what he does and possesses a model (or models) to guide his practice. As Hill notes:

> In group therapy we should someday be able to specify the style or type of group therapy indicated for a kind of client

and what mix of clients will optimize the condition and what kind of therapist can best administer the specific therapeutic treatment. [Hill, 1967, p. 32]

The implications of this statement for group counseling are obvious.

6. THE EFFECTIVE GROUP COUNSELOR MAY BE RELATIVELY FIELD DEPENDENT; HIS PERCEPTION IS INFLUENCED BY THE GESTALT OF THE FIELD. In recent years, considerable attention has been given to research on the stylistic dimension in the performance of cognitive tasks (Witkin, *et al.,* 1954, 1962). In essence, these dimensions are conceived as cognitive styles that characterize an individual's way of thinking, perceiving, and problem solving. This mode of personal functioning Witkin and his associates have labeled *field independence–dependence:*

> In a field dependent mode of perceiving, perception is strongly dominated by the overall organization of the field and parts of the field are experienced as fused. In a field independent mode of perceiving, parts of the field are experienced as discrete from organized background. There is now considerable evidence that a tendency toward one or the other ways of perceiving is a consistent pervasive characteristic of an individual's perception. [Witkin, 1965, p. 318]

Several ways to assess the dimension of field independence—dependence are currently available—including a body-adjustment test, a rod-and-frame test, and an embedded-figures test. Over the past year, the authors became interested in the concepts advanced by Witkin and his associates largely because the research of Pollack and Kiev (1963) found that psychiatrists who tested extremely field independent on the Witkin tests seemed to favor either a directive and instructional or a passive observational approach to their patients in therapy. Relatively field-dependent therapists favored personal and interdependent relations with their patients. Working on the hypothesis that an effective group counselor would be one who is able to work with clients on a more personal as opposed to an instructional way, we administered the embedded-figures test to a small number (nine) of group counselors enrolled in a group practicum. Since our only criterion for judging effective group counseling was supervisor ratings and client self-reports (indicating satisfaction with counseling or lack of it), our results must be considered highly tentative. In addition, the smallness of our sample makes generalizations to other samples difficult. Nevertheless, of the nine tested, three were found to be relatively field dependent and six relatively field independent on the embedded-figures test. At the end of the semester, all supervisors and clients alike rated the field-dependent counselor as more effective. Obviously, much more work needs to be done in this area, and the statement at the head of this section indicating that the counselor is relatively field dependent must be open to question. Yet, the authors are intrigued by the possibilities of the concepts of cognitive style as they relate to group-counseling success. In addition to some of the factors listed for an effective group counselor earlier in this chapter, the counselor educator is still in need of ways to assess effective group leaders in a more scientific way. We are currently gathering further data to decide if we can assess group counseling success in terms of cognitive style.

7.   THE EFFECTIVE GROUP COUNSELOR IS ONE WHO ALLOWS GROUP MEMBERS AUTONOMY.   The final outcome of all counseling is to allow the individual to function more freely without unnecessary dependence on others. In both individual and group sessions, neophyte counselors sometimes consciously or unconsciously must allow the group to move from dependence upon him to a state wherein each member, including the group leader, is both a giver and receiver of help. The counselor who controls too long and who does not allow for the natural psychological weaning that will eventually happen in group work is much like the possessive mother who refuses to allow her son to wear long trousers. Group members can and do become dependent upon the group and the group leader, especially after a cohesive unit has been formed. As the group develops, the effective counselor seems to be one who can let go and allow members to move toward increasing independence. Poor group counselors are those who seem to foster leader dependence throughout the group life.

8.   ALL GROUP COUNSELORS SEEM TO BE MORE EFFECTIVE WHEN THEY ARE MATCHED WITH THE CONTROL STYLE AND WORK LEVEL OF THE GROUP MEMBERS. This premise concerning the effective group leader stems directly from the work of William Fawcett Hill and his rather significant research in the development of the Hill Interaction Matrix. As noted earlier in this text, Hill proposes a twenty-cell matrix to explain the content-style categories and work-style categories of group interaction by both group leaders and members. The reader will recall (See Chapter 3) that Hill has shown that group members discuss one of four content categories (topic, group, personal, and relationship) and five work-style categories (responsive, conventional, assertive, speculative, confrontive). Additional research by Hill and his associates resulted in the development and standardization of the HIM-B—an instrument designed to select members for a group, categorize group therapists, and diagnose prob-

lems stemming from conflicts in group composition. In essence, the instrument is designed to determine the amount of acceptance an individual has for operating in the various HIM cells. In other words, utilization of the HIM-B provides the counselor with the prospective group members' expressed preference for working in one of the four content categories and at one of the five work-style categories. Obviously, no counselor and no group member remains exclusively within the confines of a particular work-style/content-style category for the total amount of time that he is in the group. As an experimental instrument, however, the HIM-B seems to provide a good basis for determining the individual's modal way of responding when he is involved in group situations. Through use of norms provided by Hill (1965), the authors have conducted some preliminary research to determine if group counseling was likely to be more successful if counselors and group members were matched as closely as possible on the work and content styles of the HIM-B. Thus, we have matched counselors who expressed a preference for a conventional mode of operation with counselees who have indicated a similar operational performance and paired other group leaders and members on the various other work/content-style categories of the HIM. To date, one study (Muro and Apostal, 1970) and other subjective data (client self-reports, counselor holding power) lead us to believe that the group counselor is much more likely to be effective when he is counseling a group who prefers to operate in a work/content style that closely approximates his own. In fact, the authors are also of the opinion that the matching of content/work-style categories may be one of the most crucial variables to determine good group counseling. A confrontive counselor, for example, when paired with a conventional group may find his task a difficult one indeed. Even though he possesses many of the qualities that we have suggested for the good counselor, he may discover that his group will not function. Much more research needs to be done on the HIM-B as a selection instrument, but even at this date there is some indication that a good group counselor is one who closely approaches the way his group prefers to operate. In children's groups, when the child has little choice of counselor or little knowledge of counseling style, the counselor will need to adapt his personal method of operation to meet the needs of a given group.

Obviously, numerous other qualities could be attributed to the good group counselor. As Dinkmeyer has suggested, the counselor needs to communicate to each individual that he cares about him, he must be able to develop free and spontaneous interaction in the here and now, be able to develop cohesion, be flexible, and be perceptive of the needs of members (Dinkmeyer, 1970). Other writers have presented other important traits and qualities needed by those who are group leaders. The list presented here is by no means exhaustive nor is it intended to be. Our search for effective group counselors is a combination of judgment and preliminary trials at measuring what traits a good counselor possesses. Rather than report finalized data, our suggestions should perhaps be considered hypotheses that await further testing. Perhaps one day we may be able to say with some assurance what one is or should be to be an effective counselor of groups.

THE EDUCATION OF THE GROUP COUNSELOR

It is perhaps safe to hypothesize that the majority of the school counselors who are now practicing group counselors have had little formal preparation in group work. Although universities seem to be increasing their course offerings (Gazda, Duncan, and Meadows, 1966), numerous graduate schools still list a single course—generally entitled *Group Guidance*—as their only offering in the area of group work. Either this particular course is broad enough to include group counseling as a separate entity from group guidance or else some counselor educators feel that a single course in group work is sufficient to prepare the neophyte to handle all group situations in counseling and guidance. Scattered throughout the literature of group counseling and group therapy are numerous cautions that the group counselor does indeed need specialized training. Beukenkamp, *et al.* (1958) point out that group therapy is much more difficult than individual therapy and that the differences between the two are pronounced enough to dictate that the counselor who is prepared to work with individuals is not properly prepared to work with groups. Similar recommendations are issued by Moreno (1947) and Slavson (1947).

In individual counseling, the counselor focuses on one individual and his full attention can be given to the psychodynamics of that individual. When four or more people are gathered in a group, the individual dynamics of a member as well as complex group dynamics begin to operate. The counselor may have to decide, for example, if any verbalization by an individual is really harmful to other members even though such ventilation may provide emotional release for the speaker. Other group skills such as moderating, linking, group interpretations, and consensus taking also seem to require specialized skills that are not needed in individual counseling.

Among the prerequisites most commonly listed for those who wish to become group counselors is that the prospective group leader have

acquired competence in individual counseling, have at least one supervised individual practicum experience, a number of graduate courses
in psychology, sensitivity in interpersonal relationships, a high degree
of self-awareness, and the ability to command the attention of the group
(Beukenkamp *et al.,* 1958; Slavson, 1947; Taggart and Scheidlinger,
1953).

Ideally, it would appear that only counselors with substantial experience in one-to-one counseling should be prepared in group procedures
(Beukenkamp *et al.,* 1958; Knopka, 1949; Slavson, 1947). The rationale
for this concept stems from the fact that the experienced counselor
would possess a backing of supervised experiences upon which to draw
which beginning counselors would not—in fact, could not—have. Pragmatically, however, such prerequisites would present counselor educators with obvious problems, such as the length of time required to
prepare the counselor, supervisory loads, and state certification demands. While it is not always possible nor perhaps even desirable to
hold to rigorous qualifications for the selection of the prospective group
counselor, certain minimal requirements seem to receive support from
those who have concerned themselves with this view. The candidate for
preparation in group counseling should have:

1.   Satisfactorily completed courses in three of the following areas:
personality and learning theory, developmental psychology, abnormal
psychology, group dynamics, and group guidance. In addition, he
should be well grounded in counseling theory and, if possible, should
have experience as a member of a counseling group.

2.   Successful counseling experience and/or demonstrated outstanding counseling qualities in a supervised practicum.

3.   The necessary qualities as estimated by counselor educators and
standardized personality assessment for working with groups.

4.   A stated desire to receive preparation in group work.

For further information on the above qualifications, see Beukenkamp
et al., 1958; Moreno, 1947; Slavson, 1947; and Taggart and Scheidlinger, 1953.

Since training programs vary from institution to institution, a standard procedure for the preparation of the group counselor may not be
possible; however, a description of one approach to group-counselor
preparation may serve to illustrate how the group counselor may be
prepared. The following sequence represents the preparation format at
a university where one of the authors is employed:

1.   All prospective group counselors must first have completed a
basic course in counseling theory. In addition, each prospective group
counselor must have demonstrated satisfactory skill in an individual

practicum consisting of thirty hours of supervised one-to-one interaction. Candidates also should demonstrate knowledge of personality theory, abnormal psychology, and social psychology.

2.   Prospective group counselors are screened and interviewed and some staff judgment is made of their personal qualifications along the dimensions suggested in this chapter. All prospective group counselors are also administered the ETS experimental form of the group embedded-figures test (little memory, no color) and the HIM-B. These instruments are now primarily administered for research purposes and no selection or rejection of the candidate is made on these alone.

3.   The actual sequence of training is a three-step process consisting of related learning experiences. The first of these is enrollment in a course entitled *Group Guidance* wherein the group candidate studies the nature of groups, reviews some pragmatic approaches to group-guidance activities, and investigates the findings of significant small-group research. The group-guidance course also contains a laboratory experience wherein the class members are placed in leaderless groups and instructed to (a.) develop a group topic and (b.) analyze the process of the weekly group meetings.

The rationale for this course stems from our belief that the prospective counselor can best learn about small groups by actually experiencing small-group life. Individuals are asked to record the "what" of group functioning, identify member roles, and analyze the group movement or lack of it. Thus, the first group experience serves as a screening ground in that some counselors discover that they are not comfortable with groups and prefer to operate as individual counselors. On the other hand, some counselors learn that the group can be very rewarding and the group-guidance experience seems to stimulate their interest in further group training.

After completing the group-guidance experience, potential group counselors may choose to enroll in *Group Procedures in Counseling* which is a combination didactic–experiential course that focuses on the art and science of group counseling. Members discuss group-counseling theory, examine process and outcome studies related to group counseling and therapy, and role play as counselors and group members.*

The final and perhaps most important experience in the preparation of the group counselor is his work in the group-counseling practicum, for it is in this aspect of his preparation that the counselor candidate is actually able to merge the intellectual concepts gathered in the

---

*Some forms the authors have found useful in the supervision of the group counseling courses are included in Appendices III, IV and V.

theoretical courses with the more effective approach of the live group. The beginning counselor is likely to approach his initial group-counseling venture with a marked degree of apprehension (Stein, 1962; Berger, 1963). In light of this, small-group meetings between counselor educators and counselor candidates are held prior to the counselor's actual counseling experience. The mechanics of group counseling are reviewed and students role play group situations that may be of concern to them (i.e. the silent group, the domineering group member). Other useful tools include the *Encounter Tapes* developed by Berzon and Reisel at the Western Behavioral Science Institute and the recent *How to Use Encounter Group Concepts* by Carl Rogers, published by Instructional Dynamics Inc. Once the group member actually begins his experience, he is periodically observed by an experienced counselor educator and asked to submit reports of the various aspects of group life including his observations of nonverbal data, group development, goals, norms, structure, and the client roles (Muro, 1968). Students are asked to tape-record all sessions; and video taping of at least one session whenever possible is a cumbersome but useful approach. Since group life, at times, can become extremely complex, counselors encounter difficulty in reconstructing all that occurred in a given session from memory. Audio and video recordings allow both counselor and supervisor to analyze the group process as it actually happens. Video taping, of course, provides the added dimension of allowing an analysis of nonverbal cues. Some counselors elect to enroll in advanced group practicum to refine further their skills and techniques. While this system is not flawless, the three-step sequence suggested here seems to be adequate for the preparation of the beginning counselor.

THE COUNSELOR IN THE GROUP

Although some writers, including Bennett (1955), have attempted to describe group leaders as essentially didactic, permissive or a combination of the two, such a classification seems to be artificial. It is not entirely possible or even desirable to label the group leader as fitting neatly into one of these because he simply does not do so. Even counselors who espouse what could be called a pure client-centered philosophy seem to engage in more confrontation, interpretation, and questioning than might be expected of one with this persuasion, and the recent work of Rogers with groups (1969) is a strong indication that he is an active, even confrontive group member. The very nature of group life seems to call for more active, dynamic counselor participation in spite of the call for generally passive leadership by Hobbs (1948) and others who advocate a more passive counselor approach.

Regardless of where the counselor rests on the active–passive continuum of group leadership, he can be assured that he will have some effect on the group's output by his selection of group members, his personal philosophy, his level of operation, his articulation of the purposes of the group, and the degree to which he enters the group process. Whatever happens in the group will depend largely on him for as Durkin noted at an early date "the problems that come up in the course of group therapy can, like most others, be traced to the therapist himself" (Durkin, 1939, p. 594). For example, the overly directive counselor who constantly controls and directs group interaction to himself should not be surprised to find low group morale and poor group cohesion.

FUNCTIONS OF GROUP LEADERSHIP

While certain functions of group leadership will be detailed here, it is obvious that any or all of these procedures assume the necessity of a helping relationship. It is, of course, a relationship based upon mutual respect, and while the counselor demonstrates his concern and kindness, he actively works within the structure that allows the group to achieve its purpose. Therefore, the following procedures must be considered selected avenues which the counselor and the group utilize to reach agreed upon goals and in no way represent a bag of tricks the counselor uses on the group members. No one technique or series of them should be emphasized unless they move the group toward a set of obtainable goals.

1. PROMOTING COHESIVENESS. Although the process that must operate between the counselor and his group is perhaps easier to define than to attain, the counselor will discover that he must consciously seek to establish rapport and cohesiveness within the group. Members must feel comfortable in the presence of the counselor and other group members, and members must trust each other to the extent that each is willing to venture considerable psychological risk if growth is to occur. Group cohesiveness is not given; it must be attained, and the counselor himself must be willing to take personal risks if the group is to become cohesive.

This may be especially true during early sessions where group cohesion is minimal and the counselor is attempting to work toward member-to-member interaction. For example:

> COUNSELOR: Is it possible that all of us are a little uneasy
> since this is our first meeting? I know that I always feel a little
> uneasy with each new group that I'm in. In fact, that last
> silence made me quite uncomfortable.
> C^1: Gee, I'm glad you said that because that's just the way
> I feel. I could hardly look at anybody!
> C^2: Me too! I almost wanted to scream out—I wanted some-
> body to say something, anything.

Group members will not blend into a single cohesive unit unless they
perceive each group member to possess equality in the group. This does
not mean that group members will not engage in a ranking system, for
group-dynamics research tells us that all group members consciously or
unconsciously assign a rank to other members of the group. What it does
mean is that the counselor, although he may be an active group leader,
is also a functioning group member in the sense that he, too, is vulner-
able to group interaction. The counselor must be perceived as an equal;
he cannot talk down or constantly draw the group's attention away
from him simply because he is the counselor and initial group leader.
*Groups will not become cohesive unless all members interact on an
equal basis,* and the counselor who overly directs or stands behind age,
experience, title, or other cover will soon discover that his group will
not become cohesive. To become cohesive, group members must
gradually grow to like one another, and this process is not possible in
counseling groups where the group leader is an expert who merely
observes the interaction from an aloof position. In fact, an effective
technique for the group leader to promote interaction is to share his
feelings early in the life of the group. He should perhaps admit his
anxiety, uneasiness, or joy and display an open and honest approach to
the members. Only in this way will he be able to initiate a solid group
climate. This does not mean, however, that the counselor should utilize
the group to solve his own personal concerns unless his concerns closely
coincide with those of the total group. While the counselor may be
more active in early group meetings than he would in later sessions, the
needs of the members, not the counselor's, are of primary concern.

In the early life of a group, the counselor should be aware of and
carefully note the patterns of interaction to determine the subgroup
patterns that seem to be forming. *The larger the group, the greater the
possibility for one, two, or even three members to gravitate to small
cliques or subgroups that seem to share common values and perceptions.* For example, if a counselor was working with a group containing
a number of acting-out boys, he could discover that these individuals

would begin to support, protect, and reinforce each other on a number of topics. If the counselor is unaware of this phenomenon or chooses to ignore it, the group will gradually develop into two or three subunits that may work at cross purposes with each other. Therefore, the counselor must promote interaction between members who may not share the same values. The verbalization of an aggressive boy, for example, should be tested within the context of the perceptions of a shy one, or a girl who violently states that she dislikes school should hear directly from one who is fond of school. For example:

> COUNSELOR: Ted thinks the teachers are all against him. What do you think of that? (If no general reply is given, the counselor might find it necessary to ask a specific member.)

At times, the exchange will be a natural one, and in cohesive groups this is often the case. Early in group life, however, the counselor should promote interaction among those who *may not* share values in order to prevent rigid subgroup formation.

Group cohesiveness is also promoted by the frequency of interaction; *hence, the more often members speak to each other, the more rapidly cohesion will develop.* The leader must be sensitive to opportunities to link ideas and feelings. "Mary is saying she feels all alone, and this seems to be similar to Ruth's concern that no one cares" or "John didn't come to school because he was afraid he'd fail the exam; this is something like Mary's worry of forgetting her speech in front of the class." Thus, the frequency of meetings has some direct bearing upon cohesiveness and a group that meets three times a week is more likely to be cohesive than a group that meets once a week, if other factors are equal.

When individuals are in some way forced or referred to group counseling by either a teacher or parent or other adult, the counselor's work becomes increasingly difficult. The group member must be willing to share in the interaction, he must have a desire to participate, and he needs to know what is probably going to happen in the group sessions. Those referred to counseling may have little or no knowledge of what is expected of them, have no desire to change or participate, and may be shocked by the new and different type of interaction. The counselor of the nonvolunteer client would have to accomplish within the group life what should have been accomplished in orientation sessions.

In a similar view, the counselor who works with volunteers for group counseling is also more likely to develop group cohesion than one who works with those who are assigned to counseling groups. In this respect, the counselor must create a readiness for the group experience and select, if possible, volunteers for counseling.

As one might expect, cohesion is more likely to develop in groups where members remain intact for long periods of time. If the essence of cohesion is the promotion of interaction under conditions of equality, the counselor should strive, whenever possible, to work with closed as opposed to open groups. Some counselors and numerous therapists utilize the practice of adding new members after a given group has been under way for a number of weeks or months. While there are philosophical and pragmatic values to open groups, the presence of a new group member can and does affect group cohesion. New members may not share group values or group norms and frequently tend to cover old ground. Therefore, the new group member may have to be actively sponsored in the group by the counselor for a period of time. He may have to direct questions to her, ask for her perceptions, and perhaps deal with group resistance to her presence. Failure to do so is almost certain to delay, if not destroy, movement toward group cohesion.

2. SUMMARIZING. As early as 1953, Powdermaker and Frank noted that in spite of the varied backgrounds, symptoms, and complaints of group members certain themes persisted over a number of sessions. The concept of group theme has also been studied with reference to group counseling, and Bates (1966) and Muro and Denton (1968) have identified recognizable themes in separate investigations of high school and college students. In essence, a theme in group counseling or therapy is a topic and point of focus in the group's interaction with a clear beginning and stopping point. A given session may contain one or several themes. In most cases, a group meeting of an hour or more will contain a number of themes (Hobbs, 1951).

It is important for the counselor to recognize the prevailing group theme in order to help the individual and the group as a whole to develop meaning from the discussion. Requiring the group to think about what has been happening may accelerate and facilitate the group process (Dinkmeyer, 1970). A statement such as "What do you think we learned today?" or "What has been happening in here for the past half hour?" will suffice to have the group members reflect on the essential elements of the session.

The counselor may choose to cap all major themes and subthemes in individual sessions and occasionally summarize what has been happening in the group over several sessions. He should not only report what has been said but should attempt to identify and feed back to the group the emotional level of the discussion. The job of the counselor and the

skill required are those of tying together numerous thoughts and feelings in a brief and coherent way. Early summary statements by the
counselor should be made cautiously lest he misinterpret the group's
feeling or misread the group's consensus. Thus, summary statements
early in the life of the group are best presented in a tentative fashion.
The counselor might well preface his summary with statements like: "If
I read the group correctly, you seem to be saying . . ." or "Although I'm
not completely certain about what you seem to be saying, it seems to
be that . . ." By soft-pedaling early group summaries, the counselor runs
less of a risk of damaging rapport and destroying cohesiveness. An
example of such interaction might be as follows:

> COUNSELOR: If I understand what the group has been saying
> for the past half hour, it seems that John, Joe, and Mary are
> quite upset about the lack of fairness in the grading system,
> but Helen, Ann, and Sue are pretty sure most teachers grade
> fairly. I guess I'm not quite sure how Robbie feels about this.
> JOHN: She complains a lot about grades.
> ROBBIE: I know I do, and I guess I see it like you (to John)
> and Joe and Mary. Yet I can't say all grade unfairly.
> COUNSELOR: I gather then Mary that you have a number of
> teachers who seem fair to you and a few who do not!

In summarizing, the counselor must also be aware that complete
group consensus on a given topic will not always be reached. In fact,
groups who have not been in session for long periods of time will
probably have at least one minority opinion or several subgroup opinions. The counselor, therefore, must try to summarize all member opinions. Suppose, for example, the group were discussing Judy's impact on
the other group members, and the group opinion was divided on Judy's
aggressive characteristics. The counselor might summarize by stating:
"As I see it Joe, John, Jim, and Mary seem to feel Judy is a bit overly
aggressive, and Steve, Sue, Joel, and Helen feel that Judy's behavior is
not at all aggressive. Does it seem this way to anyone else?" By recognizing both sides of a given discussion, the counselor not only leaves the
group open for further discussion or disagreement, he also requires
each member and the total group to reassess what they have said.
Group members may, for example, be unaware of what they are communicating to another individual over a period of time, and the counselor's efforts at helping them clarify their verbalizations will foster
group interaction and development.

As with other leadership functions, the counselor may find that group members may gradually take over the role of summarizer from time to time without a true awareness that they are engaging in this process. One of the paradoxes of the group situation is the fact that those who are in need of help are often the helpers. Often the group members' perceptions of what is happening in the group are as accurate as the counselor's, and in some cases young children and adolescents are even more attune to the perceptions of their peers than the counselor may be. The counselor must be ready, however, to fill in gaps and pick up perceptions that a less experienced group member could miss.

PROMOTING INTERACTION

More than one group counselor has been puzzled by the lack of interaction within his group—and this condition seems to prevail in most groups as they get under way. The lack of interaction in a beginning counseling group should not surprise the counselor since he can almost expect that group members placed in a novel and relatively unstructured situation will interact on a rather minimal and superficial level. In some ways, the beginning group presents the counselor with a paradox since the interaction will increase as the group becomes more cohesive, but the interaction is the very force that promotes such cohesion.

In the early stages of any group life, the interaction will be primarily addressed to the counselor since, in most cases, he is the perceived group leader. Members will question him, ask his opinion on topics, look to him to resolve conflicts, and, in some cases, seek his protection. This is what Bach calls the *leader-dependence phase* in the life of the group wherein the group will unconsciously assign the counselor as leader even when he attempts to move away from overt leadership behaviors (Bach, 1954, p. 75).

It is, therefore, the contention of the authors that the counselor should take an active part in the early life of the group and perhaps even program some of the early sessions by introducing topics for discussion.

It is important for the counselor to utilize linking as much as possible in early sessions since the promotion of member-to-member interactions is crucial at this juncture of group life:

> COUNSELOR: You're saying that I should decide what we should talk about.
>
> or
>
> You feel I should get us going.

JOE: Well, yes, you're the leader—I guess I expected you to
tell us something about ourselves.

COUNSELOR: I think I know what you're saying—that we
seem to be going nowhere, yet I kind of have the feeling
others here like the way we've been operating; (to group) am
I right, Jane and Bill?

Gradually, however, the counselor should begin to reflect statements
addressed to him and encourage other members to summarize. He
should look for nonverbal cues of the way members are reacting to
verbalizations directed to him and risk a soft-pedaled tentative hypothesis designed to get member-to-member interaction. Questions directed to him, though some may be answered directly, should be
gradually turned back to the group as a whole. It is important for the
counselor to turn back some questions to the total group if he is to
develop group cohesion and involve the members in the group process.
Failure to do so will perpetuate leader dependency and hinder the
member-to-member interaction that is so vital to effective group counseling. In some instances, the counselor may reflect individual and
group feelings, and in others he may choose to interpret what is not said
but implied by nonverbal cues:

COUNSELOR (to group):   If I sense what you seem to be saying,
it appears as if most of you are quite unhappy about the way
things are going. Am I right?

(Or after noting symptoms of anger on Mary's face)

COUNSELOR: Mary, I've noticed that you seem a little upset
with what John and Jane have been saying. Is it possible that
you're angry with them?

In other words, the counselor must gradually relinquish the expert role
in the group if he desires to promote interaction for much of the communication in groups is a function of ranking. Members of less status
typically address themselves to members of higher status, and as previously noted, the counselor is initially at least a high status individual.

Group interaction is also closely related to the physical arrangements
utilized for counseling, and it is interesting to note that the use of a
square or rectangular table hinders member-to-member interaction,
while a round table is a definite aid to the promotion of member-to-
member verbalization. For a number of years, one of the authors taught
a class in group counseling where the only available room had a square

table. By plotting the interaction patterns from recordings of the sessions, a general outline of the communication patterns would closely resemble those in Figure 2.

All patterns are not shown in this diagram, but one can see that much counselor–client interaction takes place in this arrangement because of the facility and ranking phenomenon, but the client-to-client patterns —other factors being equal—are related to physical proximity. Obviously, this arrangement also has an effect on subgrouping and group cohesion.

A round table, however, eliminates some of these patterns since members are more or less face-to-face and in better proximity to one another. McCann and Almada (1950) have utilized a round table as part of an effective group procedure with hospitalized individuals. Sommer in a study of 182 adults and teenagers reported that individuals prefer to face each other when they interact. Leavitt's investigation, however, provides the counselor with good reasons for utilizing a circular arrangement. In studying the effects of communication patterns on group performance, he presents strong evidence that communication patterns do effect group behavior. With regard to circular arrangments, he notes that an individual seated in a circle "gets information from both sides; sometimes he gets the answer, sometimes he sends it. He has two channels of communication. He is exclusively dependent upon no one" (Leavitt, 1951, p. 48). Since the essence of group work lies in the member's ability to give and receive feedback, it would appear that counseling groups arranged in circles would help to maximize member-to-member interaction.

RESOLVING CONFLICTS

Even in cohesive groups, the potential for conflict is generally present. Conflict may result from frustrated individual needs, conflicting goals, hidden agendas, disappointment in leader function, groping for structure, and anxiety over a new and novel situation (Bach, 1954 and Warters, 1960). In many cases, group conflict arises out of divergent value systems wherein some group members share common or closely aligned perceptions about a given topic and discover that other members do not share similar views. For example, a majority of group members may feel that no two group members should be speaking at one time and that no one member should interrupt another while he is speaking. A few members, however, while perhaps consenting to this principle, may continually disrupt other members with laughs, giggles, or other behaviors that tend to hinder group movement. Such situations

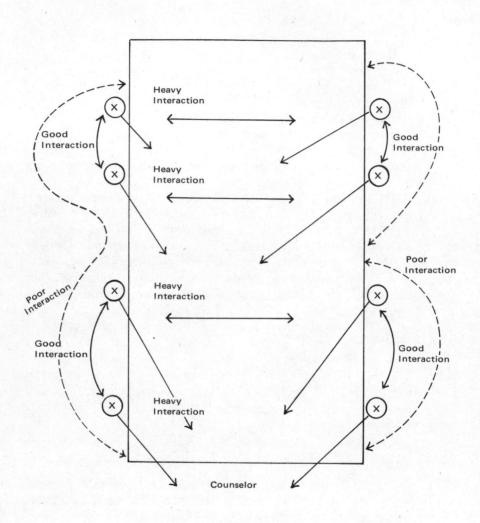

Heavy Interaction
Good Interaction
Heavy Interaction
Good Interaction
Heavy Interaction
Poor Interaction
Poor Interaction
Good Interaction
Good Interaction
Heavy Interaction
Counselor

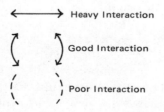

Heavy Interaction

Good Interaction

Poor Interaction

FIGURE 2.

tend to be particularly common in groups of young adolescents who use laughter and horseplay as a way to gain group recognition and keep the group's focus away from touchy topics. The counselor can if he chooses elect to employ a well-timed confrontation to assist the group to become aware of the purpose of such behavior.

As noted previously, the cohesive group is more likely to police itself with regard to conflict than a noncohesive one. The group tends to influence behavior of the members when members are attracted to it, have a voice in determining its goals, and value the support and encouragement of the members more than that of other reference groups that may influence individual behaviors.

The counselor's first role in keeping conflict to a minimum then is one of promoting group cohesion so that points of conflict are minimized. In addition, he must be certain that each member and perhaps the various subgroups are provided with opportunities to express opinions. Like other group members, the counselor may unconsciously develop a ranking system and provide some members with greater status than others. In so doing, he may also provide unequal opportunities for all views to be expressed and unwittingly promote subgrouping and chances of conflict.

In some cases, group conflict can reach the point where the climate of the group disintegrates into a series of small verbal wars. Empathic understanding of others, which is a key counselor trait, is also highly desirable in group members if they are to be able to share the perceptions of others. When conflict reaches heated proportions, however, empathy seems to give way to a series of attacks and defenses and members frequently are unwilling or unable to empathize with another member. In such cases, the counselor may wish to introduce a modified psychodramatic or role-playing technique in order to assist individuals to understand another point of view. In a group counseled by one of the authors, three rather aggressive teen-aged boys launched a somewhat prolonged attack on what they called the *varsity* group. Utilizing shower-room talk and engaging in some rather sharp name calling, the three soon had five other individuals quite defensive and heatedly reactive. By simply asking the three aggressive boys and the other group members to shift roles for a ten-minute period and argue as if they supported the opposite point of view, both sides gained insight into their own behavior and the behavior of others.

While role playing is not a magical solution to the reduction of conflict, it can provide the counselor and the group with a vehicle for moving the group forward. Perceptions which may have been perceived and dichotomized in either-or and black-and-white situations may gradually give way to individual and group perceptions that allow for shades of grey and a willingness to consider another's views.

In addition, the counselor may wish to test constantly for group consensus during an impasse, being careful to note both majority and minority opinions. He should also be alert for shifts of opinion—no matter how small—which may be indications of changing perceptions. For example, he might note: "John, you were quite certain that all athletes were basically show-offs, and Joe agreed with you. Yet, I believe you just noted that basketball can be fun even if you don't want to train to get on the team. Do you mean that Jack and Harry may get some kicks from the game?" The objective of this consensus taking is to provide each group member with a chance to share in the experiences that can lead to a change of perceptions. Only when group members are satisfied that they have a share in the process will conflict be resolved.

GUIDING

In group counseling, the term *guiding* should not be taken to mean that the counselor directs the group to certain courses of action or pushes for the verbalization of certain accepted values. Rather, guiding refers to a number of techniques that assist the group to move toward its accepted goals. Viewed in this context, resolution of conflicts, summarizing, and consensus taking are all part of the counselor's work as a group guide. In a broad sense, guiding is the sum total of the counselor's efforts to utilize effectively the unique benefits of the group situation for personal growth. Several avenues for guiding group interaction are available to the counselor:

1.   TONE SETTING. Many neophyte group counselors naïvely expect the group to react to the counseling situation much as a client might react to an individual counseling session. Such is not the case, and the counselor who deliberately remains aloof from the group process as a type of high-level observer will soon discover that members of the group are unwilling to share significant perceptions of self and others within the group.

Risk taking may be minimal and discussion topics may be conventional and external to the group life. Therefore, the counselor may wish to guide the tone of the group by sharing some significant aspects of his own life with the group. He may choose to relate his feelings in the here and now perhaps indicating his anxiety over a beginning group or giving his first impressions of group members and asking for their views of him. In this vein, Otto has suggested that the counselor utilize an egg timer and take six minutes of group time to share those experiences that have contributed to the development of his (the counselor's) personality. The last minute of time is utilized to relate the happiest moment in his life. Upon completion, the group is allowed to ask questions, and then other group members follow the same procedure (Otto, 1967, pp. 2–10). While this depth-unfoldment method tends to lead group members to an historical as opposed to a here-and-now orientation, it is extremely effective in moving groups to a work level of operation very rapidly.

Dinkmeyer has also described a technique to develop good group climates that he has labeled the *inner–outer circle* game. In this technique, five or six children are grouped in an inner circle and an equal number are grouped in a larger circle in a concentric pattern. Each member of the inner circle has a partner on the outside circle who, after a period of inner-circle interaction, provides feedback on what he liked about what his partner said and did. Following this feedback process, members of the inner circle move to the outside and the outside members move in to become the interacting group. The feedback process is then repeated. While this technique might not be too effective in early grades of elementary school, it is a valuable counselor tool for use with students who are ten years of age or older.

2. STRUCTURING AND LIMIT SETTING (Dinkmeyer, 1970). Even those groups which have had a thorough orientation to group counseling may require further structure by the counselor while the group is in process. The leader's task in such situations is essentially one of assisting the group to understand the importance of being ready to share concerns and helping those with problems. The contract of group work necessitates that members are both willing to discuss their concerns and listen closely to others for the purposes of providing feedback. Early in the session, the leader establishes the importance of social interest and a willingness to give and take. When a member refuses to cooperate with the purpose of a group, the leader allows that person to choose to leave or stay and participate within established guidelines. The counselor, however, must be careful to have the group help build the values and norms that set structure since member feelings of safety are necessary if each is to develop a committment to the group.

3. BLOCKING. While it may seem improbable that the counselor will actually desire to impede group progress, there may be times when he might choose to hinder the efforts of a majority of the group or of a subgroup to enhance total group movement. As an example, a noisy clique of two might prove to be quite disturbing to other group members, and the majority of the group might attempt to get the counselor

to admonish or expel the deviant members. The counselor who falls
victim to this trap is letting the group use him to express their own
hostility. Since group members must deal with their own feelings and
behavior and since eventual confrontation is desirable in group life, the
counselor may wish to block the efforts of the majority to use him by
encouraging them to express their own hostilities.

4.   LINKING (Dinkmeyer, 1970). Linking refers to the counselor's
efforts to point out the similarities and differences in the feelings and
verbalizations of group members. Gordon (1964) describes the linking
function as the effort of the leader to perceive the linkage between
separate comments and convey this relationship to the group. Frequently, this may be accomplished by linking the meaning of the member's comment which may be observed from the content. For example:

> C^1:   Billy tries to make teacher think he is dumb.
> C^2:   Yes, he doesn't even try at his reading. (After a space of
> the other comments in the protocol.)
> C^3:   I do it sometimes, but other guys do too.
> C^4:   I sometimes get out of math by telling Miss Fairfax this
> is too much. I just can't do it.
> COUNSELOR: It seems Billy and Dave are doing the same
> thing—getting the teacher to give up. What do you think
> about that?

Here the counselor attempts to link the thoughts and behavior of
C^3 and C^4 for the purpose of having them recognize a common problem.

5.   PROVIDING SUPPORT. At times, separate individuals and the group
as a whole may need to have the support of the counselor. The counselor may choose to back the thoughts of members or lend encouragement to a general topic under discussion. Support may have to be
utilized rather frequently when the counselor is working with open
groups and finds it necessary to sponsor a new member into the group
interaction. The counselor may also wish to assist members to develop
an ability to search out and identify individual strengths in individuals
since group feedback can slip into a constant pattern of individuals
seeking out liabilities in others to the exclusion of their strengths.

6.   REFLECTION. The counselor will guide the group interaction by his
use of reflection with individuals and at times the reflection of the
feelings of several members. He is not only a parrot of group feeling,
but he is constantly alert to detect feelings not expressed but implied.
He facilitates awareness occasionally by being ahead of the counselee.

This is accomplished by guessing at the feeling or offering a tentative analysis (Dinkmeyer, 1970):

> C: The teacher expects too much!
> COUNSELOR: They treat you unfairly.

7. PROTECTING. Although the very essence of group life is free and open communication on an interpersonal level, individuals do not reach risk levels or readiness to disclose self simultaneously. While some group members seem to be able to verbalize their feelings easily, confront others, and in turn be confronted, others may find this more difficult. Occasionally, an entire group or subgroup will attempt to force interaction from a given member when an individual may not be ready to share his concerns with the group. In such cases, the counselor may wish to intervene and perhaps inquire why the group finds it necessary to discuss the concerns of one member. He could, for example, allude to the purposes of the group in dealing with one member only:

> COUNSELOR: I wonder why we seem to be concerned only with John and his concerns? Is it possible that perhaps we feel a little superior to him?
>
> or
>
> COUNSELOR: I wonder why we seem to be focusing so much on John? Is it possible that talking only about John saves us from having to talk about ourselves?

Generally, the counselor's intervention in this fashion will serve to relieve the group pressure on an individual. While the authors believe that some benefit can be obtained through spectator therapy on the part of the continually silent group member, direct interpretation and feedback are less available to him. In this sense, the counselor might actively seek member participation, but he must sense when individuals are ready to enter the group and may have to intervene and protect when they are not.

8. QUESTIONS. As in individual counseling, the group counselor will at times question the individual and the group as a whole. He may ask overhead questions—such as: "What is happening in the group right now?"—designed to energize and motivate the group, or he may simply be asking for expressions of opinion or a clarification of an interaction. Beginning group counselors tend to guide interaction by extensive questioning in early sessions and often actually hinder the group development by introducing material that may not be relevant to the group.

As with other techniques, questions are only appropriate when the response is likely to contribute to group and individual goals.

9. REGULATING. While no group counselor should envision his role as that of an air-traffic controller, he will frequently be cast in the role of moderator if he wishes to insure maximum individual participation. For example, a dominant, highly verbal member may find that the sounding board provided by the other members is a golden opportunity for him to exercise control. Left to his own devices, he may completely monopolize group proceedings and while this may be beneficial to him, it probably does little for his fellow participants. The counselor, therefore, may want to exert a degree of control and pave the way for less vocal members to join in the interaction. In addition, the counselor may from time to time remind the group of the limits and ground rules under which it is operating (Brammer and Shostrum, 1960).

PROGRAMMING VERSUS FREE DISCUSSION

"To have or not have programs is a controversial point of technique in group therapy" (Bach, 1954, p. 73), and while little has been written on this topic with respect to group counseling, one could probably safely surmise that group counselors might also tend to line up on either side of the spontaneous and programmatic categories. To program a group simply means that the group counselor, the official group leader, chooses to initiate specific group behaviors of his choosing at some time in the group's life. Spontaneous interaction, of course, refers to behaviors that originate within the context of group life itself.

Much of whether a counselor chooses to program or not is closely related to his personal philosophy. Bach (1954) reports that Foulkes with his leadership-defaulting approach and Hobbs with his group-centered therapy are among those who exclude therapist-instigated activities, while Moreno is among those who attempt to develop spontaneity with programs through psychodrama.

No estimate of where group counselors stand on this issue is currently available. Yet from the large number of studies described in the literature as client centered, one might hazard a guess that large numbers of practicing group counselors (at least those who publish) are not in favor of programs. Some, however, such as Gazda[3] who has had extensive group experience, describe themselves as eclectic and include the utilization of programs.

In general, the authors take the position that to program or not to

---

[3]Personal communication.

program should not be an either-or controversy, but rather one of *why program* and *when* and *for what purposes*. Bach notes that programmed activity with its drawbacks has as its chief values the enhancement of group cohesiveness in early group life, the provision of structure with a corresponding decrease in anxiety over what to do by both new members and new therapists (Bach, 1954, pp. 74–75).

Most group counselors would probably agree that the most difficult aspect of their role is getting the group under way. While the advocates of free discussion could state that programs destroy spontaneity, reflect the counselor's needs, and set him up as an authority figure, the fact remains that the novel unstructured situation of the group life can be tremendously anxiety provoking and the use of programs at least in the initial phases of group life can get the group moving. The group counselor can and does later relinquish much of his leadership role as the group develops, but like or not, he will be largely responsible for leadership in initial group meetings. Leadership here can mean that he assumes temporary responsibility for group movement. In addition to promoting initial cohesiveness, additional clinical advantages of organized programs are reported by Bach. In his view, programs have the advantages of: (1) enlarging weak minority participation; (2) contrasting individual performance against the background of group activities; (3) externalizing defenses; (4) differentiating group life from the outside world culture; and (5) reducing emotional anxiety over free expression without altering the therapist's role (Bach, 1954, pp. 72–80).

Programs may range from role playing to discussion of sociometric relationships in the group and include any number of the specialized techniques listed in Chapter 8. In fact, Malamud and Machover (1965), Schutz (1967) and Otto (1967) among others have suggested group techniques that are essentially leader initiated and in this sense programmatic.

EFFECTS OF COUNSELOR STYLE ON GROUP

The studies of Lippitt (1939, 1940) and Lippitt and White (1952) in the areas of group atmospheres and authoritarian, democratic and laissez faire leadership have been reviewed so often in other texts that little mention of them need be made here. Suffice for the group counselor to note that members of authoritarian-led groups showed more leader dependency and more hostile and apathetic behavior among members. In laissez faire groups, there was little dependency on the leader, but greater irritability and aggressiveness among members to include dissatisfaction with the task at hand. The democratic groups, on the other hand, showed less leader dependency, more friendliness and satisfaction with the activities of the club.

What may be of more interest to the group counselor is the probable effect of his style on the members of the group. Therapist or counselor style is defined by Hill as "the characteristic behavior of a therapist in his approach to clients either in individual or group treatment" (Hill, 1965, mimeographed). As previously noted, there are, of course, individual differences in style. There appears to be a modal or typical way in which one responds to a group as a result of the counselor's experience, training, and personality (Hill, 1965, mimeographed).

Liebroder (1962), in a study reviewed by Hill (1965), studied the impact of three classic approaches to group therapy on interaction in matched-therapy groups. Utilizing psychoanalytic, group-analytic, and relationship (nondirective) approaches to working with groups, he found that a psychoanalytic approach by the therapist was characterized by a high group-participation rate in personal discussions, while the group-analytic approach was characterized by a high participation rate in relationship-type topics. In the nondirective group, the therapist spent the majority of his time on topics external to the group. As might be expected, when the therapist behaved in a manner consistant with the psychoanalytic-group style, members engaged in more behavior of a personal nature; when he behaved in a group-analytic style, members produced more relationship-type behaviors; and when he behaved in a nondirective style, members produced significantly less personal and relationship behaviors than did the members of the psychoanalytic and group-analytic approaches.

While it might appear from this investigation that a nondirective style of group leadership was least effective if one considers personal and relationship discussions to be more beneficial to members, one cannot automatically jump to that conclusion. In another investigation of therapist style, Ends and Page (1957) found that members in a client-centered group showed a more healthy self-concept following group therapy than did members of psychoanalytic, learning-theory, and social-discussion groups.

These studies seem to hold several important implications for the group counselor. While it would appear that one counselor style insofar as it can be identified is not necessarily superior to another in terms of producing some desired outcome, the counselor may be reasonably assured that his style will indeed have a great deal to do with the group process. More research is needed to provide further data on the influence of counselor style on outcomes, but the set or expectation the counselor brings into the group will be an extremely important influence on what he does, how he does it, when he does it and why. In a very pragmatic sense, the counselor who believes groups should discuss problems will probably consciously and unconsciously steer the group into problem discussion, and the counselor who chooses to seek out individual and group strengths will discover that group members will follow suit. For example:

> MARY: I've had trouble with my father for a long time. He won't let me date; he grounds me (i.e. keeps her at home) at least once a month, and he makes me miserable!
> COUNSELOR: I think I know how you feel; you're quite angry and hurt with the way things are going between you and your dad! Would you like to tell us a little more about it?

The same counselor with a strength orientation would obviously listen and allow the individual to discuss her concerns. Yet while he accepts this ventilation, he looks for opportunities to discover what Mary's strengths are and uses the group to help her use these strengths in decision-making and problem-solving encounters. Obviously, even the most permissive, laissez faire counselor will influence the group even if he influences it by allowing it to move in any direction that it chooses.

VARIATIONS IN LEADER ROLE AS A RESULT OF GROUP PURPOSES

Not all groups form or are formed for the same reasons, and the group counselor may find that he is also a leader in group-guidance sessions, task-oriented groups, teacher groups, class groups, and parent groups. When the purposes and goals of the groups are different, the group leader's approach may also have to be varied to be appropriate to the particular situation. For example, confrontation on a personal level may be a quite desirable bit of counselor behavior in a cohesive counseling group, but quite inappropriate for a group of parents in a child-study class. Although this text is primarily concerned with group counseling, a brief description of group-leader behavior in other group situations will be considered.

TASK-ORIENTED GROUP LEADERS

The dichotomy between a task-oriented group and the counseling group is perhaps a false one, for as Glanz and Hayes note "whether the goal of the group is building a bridge or developing better personal insight, if the members of a group perceive the goal, then that becomes their task" (Glanz and Hayes, 1967, p. 8). For our purposes here, however, we shall define a task group as one whose goals are primarily concerned with the accomplishment of a specific bit of behavior external to the group itself. While members may indeed gain insight or change behavior as a result of participation, the intent of the group and its specific reason for being are not primarily the self-improvement of the members.

Making a task an external one does not imply that the leader make drastic changes from his personal philosophy and *modus operandi* as a group counselor to something entirely different. While the task-group leader may engage in more programming behavior, he does not initiate all action, make all plans, provide for complete structure, and conduct group evaluations.

The most effective group task leader is likely to be the individual who sees his role as essentially one of sharing his leadership functions, his designated or group-given authority and responsibility with the other members of the group. Rather than operate as an authoritarian external force, he encourages leadership on the part of others and encourages member interaction and personal contribution while still retaining his role as a group member with special responsibilities. Such group leadership was sufficiently described by Hopkins as early as 1941.

> Each individual voluntarily accepts special responsibilities for executing some part of the plan, yet he carries full responsibility for the success of the entire enterprise. While one or a few persons will probably be designated to coordinate the efforts of individuals and smaller groups, such persons are not leaders but service agencies. Leadership and intelligent followership reside in each individual, and the success or failure of the group purpose will be determined by how well each person performs these functions. [Hopkins, 1941, p. 217]

In most cases, what the group task leader actually does within the group will closely conform to what the members of the group expect of him. For example, the counselor who finds himself the head of a teacher's association salary committee might be expected to draw up certain guidelines, present these to the teachers, and perhaps represent them when the salary guide goes before the board of education. The effective task leader, therefore, must be cognizant of the group needs and expectations of the group as he goes about pursuing his task. Moreover, he must be perceived by the group he represents as one who has particular skill or competencies in the task at hand, and he should also be one who shares the group's norms and goals. Thus, in many cases, the principal of the school may not be the designated leader of the teachers in matters with the board since he may possess the necessary skill for the task at hand but may not share the norms of the group.

In task-oriented groups, the leader must also deal with individual goals along with the goals of the group. In the example just cited, a given group member may, for example, want to enhance his personal prestige by playing a vital role on the salary committee. The leader must be able to recognize this very private and individual goal as a vital part of the total group structure and provide possible channels for this individual need to be met as the total group moves toward its goals.

The type of leadership mentioned by Hopkins is obviously the ideal approach for the group leader because the democratic principles that guide the group leader are more than a function of his humanistic views toward the group members; it is also the most efficient way to meet group and individual goals and to increase member satisfaction, independence, and productivity. Members who share in the leadership of the group are better motivated, their decisions are more realistic, hostility is decreased, and personal relationships are vastly improved.

The actual functions of a leader in a task-oriented group vary with the occasion, nature of the group, and personality of the leader, but a list of the typical types of duties he performs at some time or another has been compiled by Gibb, *et al.* Some of his key duties are:

1. Makes pre-meeting preparations, prepares agenda, collects materials, makes appointments to duties, arranges place for meeting, gets programs or speakers.
2. Presides or acts as chairman during meetings, rules on debates, recognizes speakers in discussions, interprets Roberts' Rules, conducts elections.
3. Acts as standard setter, plays father role or chaperone on group conscience, interprets etiquette rules for group, feels responsibility for group and its duties.
4. Allocates responsibilities to others, appoints committees or officers.
5. Helps members, gives training, aid, suggestions, protection, or advice to members needing it or requesting it.
6. Finds out information, acts as keeper of the information, gives out information.
7. Exercises direct or indirect control by subtle suggestion, use of prestige, picking chairman, arranging agenda.
8. Coordinates activities of the group, harmonizes actions.

9. Initiates action, gets activity started, makes suggestions for new activities.
10. Energizes, expedites, and sustains action, keeps interest up, encourages action, directs action by centering group effort on one specific proposal or task. [GIBB, *et al.,* 1951]

GROUP GUIDANCE

Elsewhere, we have defined group guidance as "those aspects of the guidance program that are content centered and involve such counselor activities as dispensing educational and occupational information, planning and conducting orientation programs, group follow-up meetings, and group testing" (Muro and Freeman, 1968, p. 44). Like the somewhat artificial dichotomy between task groups and counseling groups, the differences between guidance groups, counseling groups, and task groups merge into a semantic quagmire in that a guidance group may also be a task group and the content of a guidance group may be that of improving interpersonal relations. Like the task-group leader, the group-guidance leader is concerned with dispensing facts and information, but he is also vitally interested in the interpersonal relationships that are part of this process. The traditional conception of group guidance seems to be one wherein the counselor and/or teacher select certain materials they deem important to youngsters and proceed to teach this segment of knowledge to them. Group guidance then is more akin to the typical classroom process than it is to the more affective counseling activities.

Perhaps the close tie-up with the classroom in activities labeled *homeroom guidance* has been one major cause of the classical failures associated with group guidance. And failures indeed we have had. The authors once surveyed five schools in three different states to determine student perceptions of group guidance and to the surprise of practically no one, we discovered that group guidance was about on a popularity par with the student discipline code handed down by the vice-principal. Yet, we do not have to conduct extensive research to determine why this is so. Teachers, for example, had little loyalty to group guidance and viewed the homeroom period as one more nasty chore. Counselors spent relatively little time in group activities and much of the material had little relevance or personal meaning to the students. Moreover, most of the students had little say in determining the goals of the group, what would be discussed, for how long or why. Group guidance was scheduled as one more class period, sometimes involving a grade, and usually quite deadly. Fortunately, much of this has disappeared from the public schools, and from our viewpoint, the demise was a welcome one. Guidance groups, like other small-or medium-sized groups, are effective only when the group leader is sensitive to the dynamics of group interaction and utilizes leadership style and the principles of group formation, influence, and interaction to meet group goals. In this sense, the typical group-guidance class, where the counselor or teacher selects the topic, dispenses the information, and hopes for a change of student attitude or behavior, is an exercise in futility as well as a waste of counselor and student time.

For group guidance to be effective, the program or units to be discussed must come from the needs of the students, not the needs of the instructor or some curriculum committee. While the counselor or group leader must have an intellectual understanding of personal and social needs of a given age group or class, his job as guidance leader is one of assisting the class to translate these needs into appropriate classroom or small group learning situations wherein the process within the group is equally as important as the content.

Such a guidance leader has been described by Kemp (1966) as one who sees his basic function as improving the quality of behavior instead of merely imparting information. The counselor, in turn, receives his satisfaction from the growth of the group members rather than from the fact that he has developed a well-organized body of knowledge.

The guidance leader then is a counselor in the true sense of the word. He creates an effective climate for learning, and while he has knowledge of sources of material that could be useful and valuable to young people, he realizes that such materials are only vehicles for meeting group needs. He plans cooperatively with the guidance group, allows the members to have an important say in establishing the goals, and assists them to determine pathways to these goals. Like the group counselor, he is concerned with developing personal growth of the members and utilizes his counseling skill and knowledge of group dynamics to promote interaction and cohesion among members. He is not an external judge or evaluator, does not assign term papers or grades for participation, or force the group into areas of study that may be meaningful only to him.

SUMMARY

The personality of the group counselor is probably closely associated with productive group counseling, although the individual traits one must possess to become a good group leader are still a matter of speculation. In general, effective group counselors: (1) are able to care for others; (2) operate within the context of group development; (3) are essentially positive individuals; (4) are able to provide status to members in the group; (5) allow the group autonomy; (6) are a special blend of scientist and artist; and (7) are most effective when they are matched with the expressed content style and work level of the group. As an interesting hypothesis, group counselors may be relatively field dependent.

The education of the group counselor includes substantial one-to-one counseling experience integrated with a solid theoretical base. He should be further prepared in group theory and practice and have some experience as a member of a counseling group. A suggested sequence includes a course in counseling theory, and individual-counseling practicum, a course in group guidance, another in group counseling, and a supervised group practicum.

The role of the counselor in the group involves: (1) promoting cohesiveness; (2) summarizing; (3) promoting interaction; (4) resolving conflicts; (5) guiding; (6) providing support; (7) reflection; (8) protecting; (9) questioning; and (10) regulating and perhaps providing specialized programming.

At times, all counselors may have to serve as leaders of task-oriented groups. When called upon to do so, the counselor does not make a radical departure from his counseling approach but instead sees himself as one who shares the leadership role. His actual behavior will be related to what the group expects of him and to the individual and group goals. The role of the counselor as a group-guidance leader is also closely related to his counseling approach but is somewhat broader in scope, including duties related to the providing certain types of information.

REFERENCES

BACH, GEORGE R. *Intensive Group Psychotherapy.* New York: The Ronald Press Company, 1954.

BATES, MARILYN. "Themes in Group Counseling with Adolescents," *Personnel and Guidance Journal,* Vol. 44 (1966), pp. 568–75.

BENNETT, MARGARET E. *Guidance in Groups.* New York: McGraw-Hill Book Company, 1955.

BERELSON, B. and STEINER, G. *Human Behavior, An Inventory of Scientific Findings.* New York: Harcourt, Brace & World, 1964.

BERGER, M. M. "Problems of Anxiety in Group-Psychotherapy Trainees," in *Group Psychotherapy and Group Function* (eds. M. E. ROSENBAUM, and M. M. BERGER). New York: Basic Books, Inc., Publishers, 1963.

BEUKENKAMP, G., MULLAN, H.,PAPANEK,H., TATE, F., and BURGER, M. M. "Training in Group Psychotherapy: A Symposium," *American Journal of Psychotherapy,* Vol. 12 (1958), pp. 463–507.

BLOCHER, D. H. *Developmental Counseling.* New York: The Ronald Press Company, 1966.

BRAMMER, L. M., and SHOSTRUM, E. L. *Therapeutic Psychology.* Englewood Cliffs, N.J.: Prentice-Hall, Inc., 1960.

COMBS, ARTHUR W. *Florida Studies in the Helping Professions.* Gainesville, Fla.: University of Florida Press, 1969.

DINKMEYER, DON C. "Counseling Theory and Practice in the Elementary School," *Elementary School Guidance and Counseling,* Vol. 1 (1967), pp. 196–207.

———. "Group Counseling: Leadership Functions." Mimeographed. 1970.

DOWING, B. C. *4-H Junior Leader's Advisor's Manual.* Berkeley, Calif.: University of California Press, Agricultural Extension Service, 1964.

DURKIN, HELEN E. "Dr. John Levy's Relationship Therapy as Applied to a Play Group," *American Journal of Orthospsychiatry,* Vol. 9 (1939), pp. 583–98.

ENDS, E. J., and PAGE, C. W. "A Study of Three Types of Group Psychotherapy with Hospitalized Male Inebriates," *Quarterly Journal of Studies of Alcoholism,* Vol. 10 (1957), p. 2.

GAZDA, GEORGE M., DUNCAN, J. A., and MEADOWS, M. E. "Surveys of Group or Multiple Counseling: Report of Findings." Paper read at APGA Convention, Washington, D.C., April, 1966.

GIBB, JACK R., GRACE, N., and MILLER, LORRAINE F. *Dynamics of Participating Groups.* St. Louis, Mo.: John Swift Company, 1951.

GLANZ, E. C., and HAYES, R. W. *Groups in Guidance.* 2nd ed. Boston: Allyn and Bacon, Inc., 1967.

GLASSER, WILLIAM. *Reality Therapy.* New York: Harper and Row, Publishers, 1965.

GORDON, THOMAS. "The Functioning of the Group Leader," in *Perspectives on the Group Process* (ed. GRATTON KEMP), p. 240. Boston: Houghton Mifflin Company, 1964.

HEILBRUN, A. B. "Psychological Factors Related to Counseling Readiness and Implications for Counselor Behavior," *Journal of Counseling Psychology* (1962), Vol. 9, pp. 353–58.

HEINZELMAN, WILMA B. *The Club Member and the Leader.* Corvalles, Ore.: Oregon State College, Cooperative Extension Service, 1957.

HILL, WILLIAM F. *Group-Counseling Training Syllabus.* Los Angeles, Calif.: University of Southern California, Youth Studies Center, 1965.

———. *HIM, Hill Interaction Matrix.* Los Angeles, Calif.: University of Southern California, Youth Studies Center, 1965.

———. *Bulletin on Group-Counseling Supervision and Psychotherapy.* Los Angeles, Calif.: University of Southern California, Youth Studies Center, 1967.

HOBBS, N. "Group Psychotherapy in Preventive Mental Hygiene," *Teachers College Record* (1948), pp. 50, 170–78.

––––––. "Group-Centered Psychotherapy," in *Client-Centered Therapy* (ed. C. R. ROGERS). Boston: Houghton Mifflin Company, 1951.

HOPKINS, L. T. *Interaction: The Democratic Process.* Boston: D. C. Heath and Company, 1941.

KEMP, C. G. "A Program for Counselors Going into Group Guidance." Paper read at APGA Convention, Washington, D.C., April, 1966.

KNOPKA, GESELA. "Knowledge and Skill of the Group Psychotherapist," *American Journal of Group Psychotherapy,* Vol. 19 (1949), pp. 56–60.

LEAVITT, H. J. "Some Effects of Certain Communication Patterns on Group Performance," *Journal of Abnormal and Social Psychology* (1951), pp. 38–50.

LIEBRODER, M. N. "Effects of Therapist Style on Interaction in Psychotherapy Groups." Ph.D. dissertation, University of Utah, 1962.

LIPPITT, R. A. "An Experimental Study of the Effect of Democratic and Authoritarian Group Atmospheres," *American Journal of Sociology* (1939), Vol. 45, pp. 26–49.

––––––. "Field Theory and Experiment in Social Psychology: Autocratic and Democratic Group Atmospheres," *American Journal of Sociology,* Vol. 15 (1939), pp. 26–49.

––––––. "An Experimental Study of the Effect of Democratic and Authoritarian Group Atmospheres." University of Iowa Studies in Child Welfare (1940), Vol. 16, pp. 43–195.

LIPPITT, R. A., and WHITE, R. K. "An Experimental Study of Leadership and Group Life," in *Readings in Social Psychology.* Rev. ed. (eds. G. E. SWANSON, T. M. NEWCOMB, and E. L. HARTLEY), pp. 340–55. New York: Holt, Rinehart and Winston, Inc., 1952.

McCANN, and ALMADA, A. A. "Round-Table Psychotherapy: A Technique in Group Psychotherapy," *Journal of Consulting and Clinical Psychology,* Vol. 14 (1950), pp. 431–35.

MALAMUD, D. I., and MACHOVER, S. *Toward Self-Understanding.* Springfield, Ill.: Charles C Thomas, Publisher, 1965.

MARTIN, E. A., and HILL, WILLIAM F. "Toward a Theory of Group Development," *International Journal of Group Psychotherapy,* Vol. 7, No. 1 (1957).

MORENO, JACOB L. "Open Letter to Group Psychotherapists," *Sociatry* Vol. 1 (1947), pp. 16–30.

MURO, JAMES J. "Some Aspects of the Group-Counseling Practicum," *Counselor Education and Supervision* Vol. 7 (1968), pp. 371–86.

MURO, JAMES J., and APOSTAL, R. A. "Effects of Group Counseling on Self Reports and Self Recognition of Counselors in Training," *Counselor Education and Supervision* (1970) Vol. 10, 56–63.

MURO, JAMES J., and DENTON, G. "Expressed Concerns of Teacher-Education Students in Counseling Groups," *Journal of Teacher Education,* Vol. 19 (1968), pp. 465–70.

Muro, James J., and Freeman, S. L. (eds.) *Readings in Group Counseling.* Scranton, Pa.: International Textbook Company, 1968.

Otto, Herbert A. *Group Methods Designed to Actualize Human Potential.* Chicago: Stone-Brandel Center, 1967.

Peters, H. J., and Farwell, G. F. *Guidance: A Developmental Approach.* Chicago: Rand McNally and Company, 1959.

Pollack, I. W., and Kiev, A. "Spatial Orientation and Psychotherapy: An Experimental Study of Perception," *Journal of Nervous and Mental Disease,* Vol. 1 (1963), pp. 137, 93–97.

Powdermaker, Florence, and Frank, J. *Group Psychotherapy: Studies in Methodology of Research and Therapy.* Cambridge, Mass.: Harvard University Press, 1953.

Rogers, C. R. *The Basic Encounter Group.* Big Sur, Calif.: Esalem Institute, 1969.

Schutz, William C. *Joy: Expanding Human Awareness.* New York: Grove Press, Inc., 1967.

Slavson, S. R. "Qualifications and Training of the Group Therapist," *Mental Hygiene,* Vol. 31 (1947), pp. 386–96.

Sommer, R. "Studies in Personal Space," *Sociometry* (1959), pp. 22, 247–60.

———. "The Distance for Comfortable Conversation: A Further Study," *Sociometry,* Vol. 25 (1962), pp. 111–16.

Stein, C. "Emotional Needs of Professional Personnel in the Training of Psychodramatists and Group Therapists," *Group Psychotherapy* (1962), pp. 15, 118–22.

Taggart, Alice D., and Scheidlinger, S. "Group Therapy in a Family-Service Program," *Social Casework,* Vol. 24 (1953), pp. 378–85.

Warters, Jane. *Group Guidance: Principles and Practices.* New York: McGraw-Hill Book Company, 1960.

Witkin, H. A. "Psychological Differentiation and Forms of Pathology," *Journal of Abnormal Psychology,* Vol. 70 (1965), pp. 317–36.

Witkin, H. A., et al. *Personality through Perception.* New York: Harper and Row, Publishers, 1954.

———. *Psychological Differentiation.* New York: John Wiley and Sons, Inc., 1962.

CHAPTER 6

Group Organization

GROUP GOALS AND VALUES

Group goals have been discussed in several different contexts in Chapters 2 and 3. We have shown, for example, that a counselor with a behavioristic orientation would perhaps perceive the goals of a group quite differently than one schooled in transactional analysis. Glanz (1962) in an early edition of his book *Groups in Guidance* notes that groups exist for one of three purposes: (1) to accomplish a task; (2) to develop or change the participants; and (3) to provide a structured learning situation (p. 10). In a broad sense, a counseling group is formed for all three of these purposes. Counseling groups do have a task, even if that task is defined as the development of self-understanding. Counselors do seek to work with group members to facilitate their development toward mutually accepted and internalized directions. If one can accept the contention that most aspects of what one has labeled *personality* are learned then the small group is indeed a structured learning situation.

The question of group goals and values is one that has stimulated much controversy and discussion in the professional literature. Slavson (1955), for example, does not consider the development of group goals and norms as crucial for therapy groups, while others such as Luchins, *et al.* (1960), hold an opposite point of view. Whether a group has external goals or not, it is clear that all counselors who form groups do so with some goal in mind. Bonney writes that the counselor could decide to adopt one of three possible goals or directions:

1. *The adjustment approach.* Through group discussion, help the members realize that there is not much one can do about the environment and the intelligent thing to do is to accept and adjust to it.
2. *Openness approach.* The counselor stimulates the members to relate to each other at a deep emotional level with total openness.
3. An approach that falls somewhere in between the two extremes just described in terms of group structure and context of discussion. [Bonney, 1969, p. 159]

Within the three approaches listed by Bonney are a number of assumptions, goals, and values. Mahler (1969) has identified some of these goals, which in a sense constitute a theoretical rationale for group counseling. He notes that: 1. A major goal of group counseling is that of helping students meet developmental needs, 2. Students counseled in groups learn to examine their feelings and attitudes, deepen their understanding of behavior, and become more confident about their own skills and abilities (p. 14).

These are, in effect, rather concrete external goals the counselor has in mind when forming the group, and the authors contend that most counselors hold goals similar to these when they initiate counseling groups, in spite of Durkin's (1964) contention that a group formed for the purposes of therapy does not have fixed external objectives. In fact, a review of the readings in Muro and Freeman's (1968) book on group counseling will reveal that numerous counseling groups are formed to see if the process affects achievement, class behavior, and a host of other objectives—on the assumption that these external goals are in fact good or desirable outcomes for the individuals in the group. Hill (1965) notes that any value system infers goals and that the goal of group psychotherapy is a change on the part of individual members from maladaptive or self-destructive behavior to that which allows them to live a more useful, rewarding life. This objective, in Hill's thinking, is accomplished through the process of self-understanding. Counseling groups, of course, can and are formed on the premise that the group situation with its objective of self-understanding is also appropriate for those whose behavior is not maladaptive or self-destructive. In fact, many counseling groups are formed on the assumption that self-understanding is also a valuable asset to assist one to reach his full potential. Related to this concept is the excellent work developed by Otto (1967) and his concept of the use of groups to maximize human potential. The developmental as opposed to remedial concept of groups is an innovative conceptual scheme of interest to all counselors.

Broad group goals, regardless of how they are expressed, are generic in the sense that private or individual goals are also possible within the context of the group situation. Maximizing human potential—a goal listed by Blocher (1966) in his text on developmental counseling— might assume smaller, more concrete goals for different individuals. A shy adolescent may wish to overcome his fear of speaking in front of a group. While he fully agrees to the expressed group goal of self-under- standing, it must also be possible for him to deal with that specific behavioral change within the group process. Another individual may discover that the therapeutic mechanism of ventilation is useful in relieving pent-up emotions, and that while the group may not have been organized for this purpose, this private, concrete goal is possible as the group moves forward to self-understanding. Muro and Freeman describe individual growth as the core of counseling:

> Yet the core of group counseling is the effort, through group interaction, to help each individual gain different perspec- tives on the many experiences he has in coping with a world of change and to find, through these new perspectives, a personal meaning and a set of values which will guide his decision making and problem solving outside the group. [Muro and Freeman, 1968, p. 10]

Thus while group interaction promotes cohesion and aids and pro- motes the development of new norms, the object of group counseling is not to stress conformity at the expense of individuality. Within the broad group goals and values assured by any group or counselor, there must be enough freedom and flexibility for the individual to grow, develop, and work on matters of concern to him even if his personal objectives may at times be in opposition with those of the group as a whole.

The goals of a counseling group should provide the counselor with an appropriate yardstick to assess the value of the group experience. If a group is formed for the specific purpose of increasing self-understand- ing, then this objective for evaluation purposes can be formulated into a question that lends itself to research. Does group counseling help one understand himself better? If so, how? Does self-understanding modify perceptions, lead to greater acceptance of self and others? If so, in what ways? Can an individual gain new insights into his own behavior? Are there measurable personality and behavioral changes evident in an individual after he has engaged in a counseling group? Group and more concrete individual goals are the criteria that guide practice and provide a vehicle for appraising outcomes. Unfortunately, some of the goals frequently set by counselors (such as improved grade-point average) have not always been useful for assessing the individual changes that may have transpired during the life of a counseling group. Research in group counseling is discussed more fully in Chapter 13, but the objectives of counseling must also be conceptualized as questions that can be answered through objective, and perhaps subjective, research procedures.

Goals, especially concrete individual ones, are also useful for the counselor and the group members to obtain feedback and stimulate interaction. It is useful to conceptualize the goals of the individual within the context of set-up operations or the process wherein a member—or members—of a group expresses himself for the purpose of obtaining a desired reaction from the other members of a group. At times, individuals will do this unconsciously, and at other times, they are fully aware of the potential impact of what they say or do on the other group members. In fact, Bach (1954) notes that resistance in a group is frequently the result of the group's refusal to provide the individual with the response he had hoped to obtain.

The Adlerian school of thought has provided the counselor with a useful model for understanding the individual, and Dinkmeyer and Dreikurs (1963) and Dreikurs and Soltz (1964) have shown how the counselor may assist the individual to obtain insight by alluding to those goals (belonging, for example, is a basic need and, therefore, an individual goal) that motivate human behavior. The child in a group might choose to relate to others how he bugs the teacher. The counselor who is aware of individual goals might help the child gain new insights and promote interaction and feedback by stating: "Johnny, is it possible that you often want the teacher to be busy with you?" Elsewhere, Muro and Dinkmeyer (1971) have shown how the technique of alluding to goals and other verbalizations can affect the directions that counseling will take. For example, suppose several members of a children's group were discussing how they bugged the teacher by sassing her orders.

JOE: I got her good today; she was real mad.
MIKE: Me, too—boy she got on us, didn't she?
COUNSELOR: Would you like to know why you're sassing the
            teacher?
JOE: I guess so.
MIKE: Yeh.

COUNSELOR: Is it possible that you just want her to be busy
with you (tentative analysis)?

The tentative analysis described here is an attempt to help the individuals develop insight into their own behavior. Following this, of
course, the counselor might utilize other leads for the purposes of reorientation. Among these the utilization of encouragement (Dinkmeyer and Dreikurs, 1963) is most important.

Ohlsen (1970) also calls the counselor's attention to the fact that there
is a tendency to use vague general goals for group counseling and
ignore the unique goals of the individual. Group counseling like individual counseling is still concerned with the promotion of individual
growth and development—the end is more effective people, not more
cohesive groups. In this context, an individual may join a group because
he desires a better understanding of himself. Yet, he may be seeking
assistance with a concern or perhaps a problem that is unique to him
and perhaps unrelated to self-understanding, at least in a direct way.
The group counselor and the group must be flexible enough to allow
individuals to work on personal concerns, and the broad general goals
of the group must not be so rigid that the individual is sacrificed to some
theoretical construct. Krumboltz (1966b) also makes a strong case for
the concept that the wishes of clients, insofar as this is possible in terms
of competencies, ethics, and professional interests, be a determining
factor in evaluating all counseling. For example, an individual may
participate in a group formed for the purpose of self-understanding and
show little change on a post-test measure. He may, however, have had
an opportunity to become less lonely as a result of the group interaction
—thus realizing a unique individual goal.

ORIENTING STAFF AND STUDENTS TO GROUP COUNSELING

Group counseling, even with its present level of popularity, is not always readily understood by the counselor's coprofessionals in a school
and by parents and other adults in the community. In fact, there is some
evidence that counselors themselves are not fully aware of the nature
of group counseling. Several years ago, the authors conducted an informal survey in northern New England designed to determine the extent
of group counseling in public school settings. While almost all respon-
dents reported that they were doing group counseling, most indicated
that counseling consisted of such things as dispensing college information, interpreting SAT scores, and vocational group discussions. While
these activities could be conceived as coming under the generic term
guidance, most authorities would probably agree that information dis-

pensing and the like are essentially not counseling. As with other areas of guidance, we in the field who supposedly specialize in communication have been negligent in communicating what we do with adults and with children under the label of *counseling*. Too often, we have donned our clinical robes within the safe confines of a remote office and waited for the world to beat a path to our door. The counselor who would work with groups cannot afford the luxury of solitude—it is he who must make contact with the teaching staff and possible clientele.

Perhaps the initial step the counselor should take even prior to talking with students about groups is an orientation of the school staff. It is not uncommon for teachers to fear counseling in that they wonder if the child is spending time talking to counselors about them! Most counselors who have spent any time at all in public schools will recall incidents when teachers will ask: "What did he say about me?" While this could be dismissed as mild educational paranoia, the counselor needs good staff relations to be effective; hence, an orientation is necessary.

The purposes of counseling—its expected goals—must be explained to the staff in nontechnical terminology in order for teachers and administrators to grasp what group counseling really is. The counselor must be careful not to promise miracles or make claims beyond what he could hope to achieve. He must honestly state that in the course of counseling, a teacher's name could be mentioned but that the goal of a group session is not the mass character assassination of the staff. He must explain and demonstrate to teachers that he is not the referee or field judge who mediates the differences that may exist between children and educators, but he must also show that in order for child growth to take place, the child may have to vent pent-up, albeit misdirected, anger and hostility. By relating to staff members how even they as adults must deal with frustrations and anger in order to grow, he should be able to show that the process of counseling must be an experience where freedom of expression is a vital vehicle for growth.

Pragmatically, we have found that the utilization of a recorded prior session is helpful in assisting teachers to understand what happens in counseling. Such tapes, of course, must be employed with member permission and full protection of member identity as prescribed by the APGA Code of Ethics. Professional usage of such tapes is very effective with teacher groups. The counselor can stop the action, explain the group movement, and show how the members are interacting toward agreed goals. This process serves to remove group counseling from the cloud of mysticism that surrounds it and also shows that the counselor is simply human and not a faith healer with magical solutions.

If a recorded session is not available, the counselor may choose to role play a group meeting with the teachers serving as group members. In the authors' experience, this practice has not only served to assist teachers to understand group counseling, it has also promoted teacher referrals. In addition, teachers frequently become interested enough in the process to initiate action to form counseling groups themselves. In one particular school the authors were able to involve about 80 percent of a staff in counseling groups and improve teacher communication and school climate.

Orientation, however, does not stop with the school staff for the major purpose of the counselor's presence in the school is his assistance to youth. While it may be argued with some validity that the counselor is really helping *more* students by working with teachers in counseling groups, most counselors would agree that some direct involvement with children is necessary. Some suggestions for orientation of teachers regarding group counseling are as follows:

1.   Teachers should be aware of the nature of groups—of why and how students are selected. They should have some understanding of the proposed goals—both for the group as a whole and for specific individuals.

2.   Faculty members should be aware of the necessity for confidentiality—both in terms of ethical considerations and as a vital precondition for self-disclosure.

3.   Teachers need to understand that the primary purpose of the group is not to promote a systematic attack on the school, the staff, or society at large. Too often, staff members seem to feel that the counselor sides with the kids in attacking the school. All staff members must be aware that while a discussion of a teacher may come up in the course of group interaction that such ventilation is part of the process and is useful only in helping the individual understand himself—and perhaps *his* part in contributing to any deteriorating relationships that may prevail between a child and a teacher.

4.   The organizational and mechanical steps of group organization should be explained to the faculty. They should know when and where groups will meet and what students are involved. This is especially true for teachers who may be supervising large study halls and have to keep attendance records. If a child is going to be removed from any academic or cocurricular activity, the teacher in charge of such groups should be notified.

5.   The counselor should make his point of view known to the staff, especially in terms of group composition. Does he want teacher referrals for groups? If so, what types of individuals does he prefer—the shy, the acting-out, the underachiever or what?

6. Whenever possible, the counselor should report back to the faculty on the groups. This does not mean that he disclose the confidential interaction of the group, but rather make a general statement such as: "The group meeting in my office from the cafeteria study is going well; several students have been helped to make important decisions about their educational plans." In this way, the faculty members feel that they are more a part of the process, are more inclined to suggest students for referral, and gain a better understanding of why the groups have been formed.

7. If the school provides for in-service sessions, the counselor might consider presenting a brief, uncomplicated report on the rationale for group counseling, its possible benefits, and an example of how groups work. In addition to providing teachers with a basic factual knowledge of group counseling, it may suggest some group leadership skills that would be useful to them as classroom teachers.

Whether the counselor chooses to work with children individually or in groups, there are likely to be certain obstacles he must overcome if he is to create an effective climate for counseling within the school setting. First, there appears to be a resistance to self-disclosure—especially to groups of peers—that stems from a lack of knowledge about counseling, his level of insight into his own concerns, and his expectations of the role the counselor will play (Brammer and Shostrom, 1968, p. 133). Children, for example, are often taught to keep family concerns to themselves—"What goes on at home is our business." Even children who may wish to seek out the counselor tend to have a distorted picture of what he does. For example, in a recent investigation, Muro and Revello (1970) found that a selected sample of high school seniors tended to view the high school counselor as primarily a college placement officer and not one who dealt with personal concerns—a finding supported by several earlier investigations. Other factors such as the physical setting for group counseling, prior unpleasant experiences with the process, a lack of understanding of the client role, and an institutional climate of readiness are other factors that hinder the counselor in his efforts to develop groups (Brammer and Shostrom, 1968, pp. 135–36).

Such factors need to be recognized and handled. Two of these deserve special mention in passing—that of poor physical settings and the prior unpleasant experiences in counseling. With regard to prior unpleasant experiences, the authors have encountered numerous youngsters who for one reason or another had experienced group situations where the total atmosphere must have been one of psychological destruction. There seems to be a rather common, if unfounded, attitude among those who participate in groups that the purpose is to "dump on each other." Surprisingly enough, even some counselors feel this way, though the recent efforts of Otto (1967), Glasser (1965), and Blocher (1966) have been important contributions to offset this notion. This negative set—the belief that groups are harmful—has done more to promote a fear of group involvement than any other single factor, and the time is past due when professional guidance people need to do something about it—both in their personal approaches to counseling and in their orientation to those who will be group members.

Secondly, many school guidance complexes were not designed to house group-counseling activities and the make-do rooms have in some cases hindered the interaction. Rooms where the group may be observed or where the participants can possibly be heard are poor counseling settings. Counseling settings will be discussed more fully later in this chapter.

The importance of careful preparation of students for group sessions cannot be overstressed. Writing to this point, Mahler notes that:

> Careful attention should be given to how the leader can inform students that he is beginning a group counseling program. If at all possible, he should arrange individual interviews with each potential member. This approach gives the counselor a head start in knowing the members of his group and provides him with the opportunity to balance the composition of the group. [Mahler, 1969, p. 59]

We would agree with Mahler that the counselor should indeed inform students of what is to take place and then hold an initial interview with each student. Bach (1954) has outlined this procedure for therapy groups in some detail, and Gazda (1968) calls for a screening interview to explain ground rules and ascertain an individual's readiness to participate. Prior to the initial interview, however, certain steps are necessary. Muro and Freeman have suggested the following guidelines starting with the counselor's appearance in each grade in those subject-matter classes (English, social studies) attended by all students as *one* approach to the orientation of students:

1. Students should be told in simple terms about the nature of group counseling. It may be helpful to inform prospective counselees that participants will be given an opportunity to learn more about themselves, their plans, and the ways that other students see them.

2. Prospective group members should know that group meetings are confidential and the topics discussed in groups are not for general discussion outside the group meetings.
3. Students should be informed that they are not joining a "therapy" group. Students frequently associate any type of counseling activity for those who are in some way "unhealthy."
4. The counselor should prepare a schedule of the time he has available for working with groups. Within this limitation, the number of meetings a week and the duration of counseling should be a topic to be decided after the groups have been formed.
5. The counselor should emphasize that a group counseling session is not a "class" and grades are not given for group participation.
6. Students should know whether or not volunteering to participate would mean that they would be selected as group members. It is best to inform class size groups of the number of students the counselor wishes to have in a group and how the final selection will be made if the number of volunteers is too large.
7. It is beneficial to inform the class size groups that students who wish to participate may be interviewed individually. This will give the counselor an additional opportunity to make decisions about placing the student in a group. In addition, students may wish to ask the counselor personal questions about group participation that may be embarrassing to ask in a class size group.
8. A "sign-up" sheet should be passed around following each presentation in order for interested students to place their names on a list for possible group participation. An additional "sign-up sheet" should be maintained in the counselor's office or with his secretary. [Muro and Freeman, 1968, pp. 314–15]

This procedure must be modified for young elementary school children who may not comprehend the impact of verbal communication as well as adolescents. The authors have found it useful to present the counseling story by means of a puppet show wherein the orientation is done through the use of simple hand puppets from a small stage. Each student is also provided with a coloring book that tells what happens in the groups. Small group demonstrations in the classroom or audio and video tapes of what happens in groups have also proved to be useful.

WHEN SHOULD A GROUP MEET?

What is the appropriate length of a group meeting? Should groups meet once a week for an hour, twice a week for several hours, or in some other arrangement? How long should counseling be continued—for a semester, a year, or just a few sessions? Can one weekend marathon be as effective as hourly sessions spread out over a number of months?

The fact of the matter is that although these questions seem to be of concern to many counselors, very little research data is available to serve as guidelines. Studies are often reported descriptively under *short-term group counseling* or *sessions of an hour's duration once a week.* A vast number of research projects also seem to run for a period of fifteen weeks—just about the length of one school semester with a little time saved for pre- and post-testing! Perhaps this is not surprising in light of the fact that many studies reported are those done for doctoral and master's theses where the goals of group counseling, among other things, focus upon the collection of data for testing various hypotheses.

On the other hand, there is little supporting evidence for the theory that a particular number of sessions or a predetermined weekly meeting schedule for an hour or two hours is any more beneficial for obtaining desired results than any other time schedule. In a word, most counseling groups are formed, of necessity perhaps, with an eye to the administrative framework wherein the counseling is to take place—not for reasons based on the findings of controlled research. In a way, this is unfortunate and much work needs to be done to determine the effects of these variables. Until such evidence is available, however, the rather tenuous armchair-philosophy approach becomes the basis for our guiding tenets.

With regard to the frequency of meetings, the authors generally support the contention that the more often a group meets, the greater the cohesion of the group (Berelson and Steiner, 1964). Cohesion, as we have noted elsewhere, is a function of interaction, and the more interaction the greater the cohesion will be. With group cohesion, more exploration, ventilation, confrontation, spectator therapy, and other mechanisms are possible. Since most counseling groups seem to meet either once or twice a week, the authors prefer twice-weekly meetings for the reasons just given. In addition, the authors concur with Luchins' (1964) suggestion that the frequency of meetings should reflect the pace at which the group is proceeding. In general terms, it has been the authors' experience that a group of normals, once established, will initiate action for more frequent meetings on their own. Apparently, the benefits of the group and the desire to move and grow are two driving forces for increased meetings. The reverse, of course, could also be true, but in most cases, we have found that starting with meetings once a week and increasing the frequency as the tempo picks up are generally workable.

The length of a particular session can also vary. We have run children's groups for as brief a time as half an hour and have had adolescent and adult groups in modified marathons of four hours or more. As with the frequency of meetings, no concrete evidence supports a given time block as being necessarily superior. One thought, however, comes to mind. Groups of adolescents and adults seem to require a warm-up period of ten to twenty minutes prior to settling into a work mood. Generally, this period is characterized by laughter, jokes, nongroup topics, and informal member-to-member sessions. This can be explained in part by the individual and group anxiety over anticipated proceedings and in a sense represents group fear and tension. This period is sometimes frustrating to group counselors, especially beginning ones, to see the hour slipping away without anything significant happening. Actually, this period is significant, and while the counselor may call for a group opinion of "what's happening in here now," there is nothing inherently wrong in allowing even the experienced group to settle down into a work atmosphere. This is discussed here for the simple reason that the authors wish to express the opinion that perhaps group sessions should be extended for slightly longer than a single clock hour. While no definite time limits can be set, sessions of an hour and a half to two hours are preferable to those of an hour's duration. Counselors, however, should not be discouraged or be reluctant to initiate groups if a block of one and a half to two hours time is impossible because of school schedules. Each counselor should feel free to experiment with whatever time he has available and perhaps be flexible in his meeting periods. For example, if a group can meet for two hours on Monday and only one hour on Friday, the counselor should adapt to this schedule. In a similar vein, one must also decide about termination of an individual meeting. Groups sometimes just seem to get going when the agreed-upon time for termination is at hand. While it may be desirable at times to let the meeting continue, we have generally held to time limits since group members seem to reach work levels of interaction more rapidly when they know they must do so within a given period. The counselor can, if he chooses, refer to this limit as a session approaches closure with such comments as: "We have about a half an hour remaining; is there something we should concern ourselves with?" The group then is reminded that termination is close at hand and that the time is appropriate for new and perhaps previously uninitiated actions.

Final termination of a counseling group, as we have noted, seems to be an administratively related decision in many cases. Unlike the clinician in a mental hospital who may have rather specific goals (personality change sufficient to release the individual to society), the counselor usually does not exert such strong external controls. Rather he is concerned with an abstract more-or-less philosophy on a behavioral or attitudinal continuum. For example, the group goals might be those of allowing people to become more open-minded, more self-accepting, or whatever. The counselor's general clientele, then, are those that are already functioning in society to some degree and he strives to help them become more effective. Unfortunately, we do not know just how or under what conditions such changes occur. Some studies report positive change after as few as eight weeks, while others show no change after a semester or longer. Part of the problem lies in our inability to agree on goals and to determine really what group counseling can and cannot do. An additional problem is that of the inability, in many cases, to measure just what we have done. How, for example, does one measure just when an individual has reached maximum potential or complete self-understanding? Most frequently, we have gone to paper-and-pencil inventions that allow us to sum up some score and make an inferential jump—in other words, we define a construct like self-understanding operationally and fervently hope for change. Since many of these instruments are rather weak, measurable change is not always evident; hence, the current shot-gun approach to group-counseling studies is common. In these investigations, the researcher employs a host of instruments and attempts to see if the group-counseling process affected any of the scales on any of a number of instruments.

The ultimate number of sessions, then, is a judgmental matter—one that perhaps should be decided by the counselor and the group. Flexibility is again the byword and group members who have met for ten weeks may wish to continue. If the counselor and group decide that continuation is beneficial, the group may continue. There is a point, however, when the authors feel the group should disband, although it would not be possible to tell one just when that should be. As a guiding tenet, the counselor should always be working to help each member eventually become independent of the group—to meet his needs in society as a whole. The warmness and acceptance of many groups are powerful lures to keep members involved indefinitely since they count on this interaction as the sole source of support. Therefore, members must be encouraged to take group learnings beyond the confines of the group and move toward more healthy interactions in society at large.

GROUP MOBILITY

Group mobility, for the purposes of this text, refers to the issue of whether or not one should use open or closed group approaches in counseling. A closed group is one that is formed with a specific number of counselees and thereafter no new individuals are brought into the sessions. The open-group concept, on the other hand, calls for a flexible and perhaps changing membership where a core of counselees with some experience in an ongoing group work with new arrivals as others depart. In this arrangement, an old member may terminate counseling and someone new may be selected either by the counselor or the group itself to take his place.

Various writers and researchers have addressed themselves to the issue of the possible benefits and limitations of each approach. Mahler (1969) notes that the closed group has many advantages for the group counselor since the interaction of new members requires that he attend to new and different behavior patterns. The introduction of more experienced members to a group has the advantage of providing a more sophisticated model for less experienced members (p. 205). Bach (1954) apparently makes a common practice of admitting new patients to his therapy groups, but he allows the group to make decisions and selections from one of several possible new members. Luchins (1964) in noting certain disadvantages to both approaches, notes that the weaknesses in both approaches may provide material for group discussion. Thus in his thinking, a group may be open or closed depending on whether or not a group is working on a problem that is specific to the members.

From a pragmatic standpoint with adolescent and adult counseling groups, the authors have found from experience that closed groups seem preferable for several reasons. Primarily, a group must develop, it must move or pass through certain phases for optimal effectiveness. Such movement requires time, continual interaction, and a sense of cohesiveness. These are not given; they must develop. Introduction of new members, though such individuals bring with them new perceptions and patterns of relating, tend to cover old ground, and if such individuals are inexperienced in groups, they tend to move the group away from here-and-now work to topics that hinder group movement. Older members almost always feel superior to new ones, and the assimilation process is generally difficult. While this might provide as Luchins

(1964) notes fodder for the counselor, he may have to spend large blocks of time sponsoring a new individual to work him into the mainstream of group life. Most important, however, is at least a temporary period of lack of group cohesiveness. In several informal studies of open groups which failed to function, the authors described that a real feeling of we-ness never materialized in relatively short-term counseling groups which changed membership fairly often. Perhaps one reason for this was the newcomer's tendency to dominate a session or completely withdraw because of his anxiety in the rather novel world of the group.

The reader should note that the authors are expressing a preference and not attempting to set a rule that open groups are better since this is simply not so. Like other aspects of group life, open and closed groups must be viewed within the context of open or closed for what purposes. However, in verbal counseling groups of short duration, the authors have obtained better results with the closed-group concept.

In what may seem a contradiction, the authors have found that open groups with young children have proven to be quite satisfactory. We refer here to those groups where play media has been utilized as at least one important aspect of children's communication. A major reason for self-referrals of young children is their expressed desire to get along better with age mates. Sociometric isolates have functioned very well in play-media groups where the balance for the group composition was the inclusion of a different number of stars in weekly sessions. Since the group goal was that of assisting these children to form better relationships with a greater number of children, the changing group structure seemed ideal for this purpose. Obviously, it could be argued that the same rationale could hold for verbal counseling groups, and this is quite possibly accurate. Play, however, is an important aspect of a young child's life, and some young children who fare poorly in their relationships with more popular peers find that this media gives them (and some counselors) a smooth road of communication in the group.

PHYSICAL ARRANGEMENTS FOR GROUPS

While the physical arrangements for group counseling have probably not provoked as much discussion as the physical arrangements for the Paris Peace Talks in 1969, the location of group-counseling sessions is of some interest. In schools, counselors may have little choice as to where they will meet. Muro (1968) has noted that few university counseling centers lend themselves well to group activities, and in most public schools, the problem is even more acute. Most schools were built with class-sized groups of twenty-five to forty, and most counseling areas were built for one-to-one interactions. It must be remembered that group counseling in the form discussed in this text was not as popular in the 1950s and early 1960s when NDEA funds helped promote guidance throughout the land. As a result, the counselor is indeed lucky to find a conference room or other small-group discussion areas for use with groups.

In an earlier text, Muro and Freeman (1968) recommended that the room utilized for group counseling be: (1) relatively free of distractions and (2) the same for each session in that roaming seems to hinder group work because of possible distractions. Luchins (1964) notes that one cannot deny that the location of a group in a common area is a solidifying force in a group.

The number of members present obviously has some effect on the location of a counseling group, but beyond the size factor some group therapists feel that the very dimensions of a room have an effect on what may transpire in the group. Foulkes and Anthony, for example, call for a small-table technique with kindergarten children and for the small-room technique for latency-age children. With regard to the latter, they write:

> The disadvantage of working with children of this age in a large room gradually became clearer over the years. The large room allowed the children to scatter, to get away from the therapist, to become inaccessible to interpretations, and to become caught up in fragmented group activities and sub-group formations. The idea of a small room evolved from the need to keep the members in close therapeutic contact with the therapist. [Foulkes and Anthony, 1965, p. 209]

In addition to the room itself, the furnishings may be of some significance. Bach (1954) for his outpatient therapy groups employs a modern circular sofa, coffee table, and easy chairs to create an informal living room atmosphere. McCann and Almada (1950) employ a round table as an aid to their particular approach to therapy, and Luchins (1964) has noted that some therapists have discussed the use of hard and soft chairs. While some of these issues may seem of little importance to the counselor who must counsel with whatever furniture the school provides, he should strive to employ the best possible conditions within the framework of what he has available. Thus, a circular arrangement is generally preferable to the use of a square table for the purposes of good communication (See Chapter 5). Muro and Freeman (1968) write that the lack of a table was a hindrance in at least one group because several of the female members indicated that they could not sit comfortably and still concentrate on what was going on. This seems to be a problem, however, only when the participants are not properly attired for an informal atmosphere. During the past year, the authors have been engaged in numerous mini-marathons where participants sat on pillows on a floor, and the lack of a table did not seem to curtail interaction. In fact, the relative ease with which individuals could physically and psychologically move in and out of the interaction was used as an important part of the process. Other types of groups where various nonverbal techniques are used also function in settings where physical barriers that separate members are removed.

Of importance to the counselor are the ways in which individuals select their spot in the group. Who, for example, sits close to the counselor? Who avoids him? Do certain members always sit together? Are they a pair? Do subgroups tend to use one portion of the physical arrangement? Has there been a shift in the pattern of seating arrangements? By carefully noting the seating patterns from session to session, the counselor may well be able to formulate certain hypotheses about the sociometric structure of the group, and if he chooses, utilize such observations as a basis for group discussion. Of course, too much can be made of this type of data, and the counselor must be careful not to make gross interpretations about why an individual selects a certain chair. As Luchins (1964) has observed, the furnishing and seating arrangement will neither foster nor destroy a group, but they can serve to foster certain social atmospheres. For example, a counseling arrangement that is set up in a manner similar to the typical classroom would seem to be a poor practice. The authors have found that a positional chart, modified from that suggested by Foulkes (1965), is a useful tool for plotting the seating arrangements of members.

CONFORMITY AND GROUP BEHAVIOR

In other areas of this text, we have discussed the concern of some counselors that the group will tend to force individuals to conform to some standard norm or value when the true job of counseling is that of freeing the individual to capitalize on his strengths and abilities. There can be little doubt that such a concern is to some extent justified. Studies in the area of group dynamics (See Chapter 2) show that under certain conditions individuals will conform to group consensus even when their individual judgments are in opposition to group opinion. Hence exists the warning of some group therapists that the dynamics of the group be opposed at least insofar as these dynamics are in opposition to certain therapeutic goals.

Group _____ .
Session Number _____ .

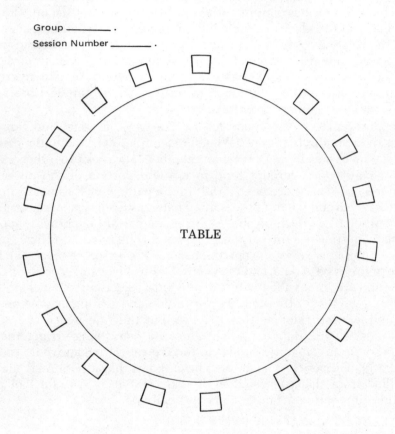

TABLE

Leave empty chairs blank.

Cross out missing chairs.

Change in seating arrangement from previous session.

Change in seating arrangement from beginning of group _____ .

Position of new members _____ .

FIGURE 3.

On the other hand, as Sherif (1961) has noted, conformity is not good or bad in and of itself. Rather the key question is conformity for what. In this context, the counselor and the group never force any value or behavior on a given individual. He is always free to choose, free to respond, and free to leave the group. In fact, in the view of the authors, it is the job of the counselor to protect the individual from the possible harmful effects of group dynamics. In the same way he utilizes group forces to promote cohesion, he must also be aware of group forces that hurt and punish an individual.

Most group counselors, at one time or another, will struggle with the issue of group conformity and its effects on individual behavior. For the authors, the Glasserian concept of responsibility (Glasser, 1965) is as useful as any in coming to grips with this issue. In Glasser's conceptual approach to counseling, he contends that the individual is free to meet his individual needs through any behavioral pathway he chooses—as long as he does not interfere with the right of others to meet their needs in a similar fashion. The individual selects his values and methods of living within them and so it must be in the group. The group is often a testing ground, a type of sophisticated mass-media arrangement that provides data called *feedback* to the individual. The recipient of such feedback must retain the right to reject or ignore advice and suggestions inappropriate to him. Perhaps it is in this area that the art of counseling comes to fore—when the counselor must make decisions because of his knowledge of group dynamics as to whether or not he should intervene when the group pushes for conformity.

GROUP COMPOSITION

Who belongs in a counseling group? How does one determine what combinations of individuals produce optimal conditions for maximum effectiveness? On the one hand, one might take the position that counseling involves people, and since the counselor deals essentially with normal individuals, the composition of the group makes very little difference. On the other hand, there are those who feel that the composition of a group along certain specified dimensions such as sex and age are key variables and may well determine the eventual success or failure of the counseling process.

Mahler and Caldwell (1961) have suggested that the purposes of counseling set the limits for determining group counseling and recommend that school counselors start with groups of students who have similar concerns or with those who are in trouble for minor misconduct problems. In a recent text, Mahler suggests that the counselor give careful attention to balancing the factors of sex, age, prior acquaintance, and personality factors. In addition, for some purposes, equal numbers of males and females should be included with students who have reached junior high age, although all boy and all girl groups are recommended for elementary school children (Mahler, 1969, pp. 52–53). Gazda recommends preliminary or trial grouping if the counselor cannot predict the behavior of a given individual group. In the approach, the counselor either starts with a specific number and excludes those who appear to be ill-suited for group counseling or selects twice as many members as needed for a permanent group (fourteen to sixteen members) and subsequently divides this original gathering into two permanent groups of seven or eight. In the former approach, individuals who are excluded are offered individual counseling. He also recommends a diagnostic interview for each prospective client in order for the counselor to inform the individual of the ground rules, responsibilities, and make some judgment of the individual's readiness for group counseling (1968, pp. 276–77). Ohlsen suggests that no individual should be assigned to a group until he can be placed in one that is appropriate. Thus, the counselor must ask: "How will the group effect each individual? How will each individual effect other individuals and the group process itself?" (1964, p. 155).

Most writers in discussing group composition have limited their discussions to selection methods where the final selection is left solely in the hands of the counselor. Yet, some other possibilities exist, at least if the counselor and group are functioning within the concept of open groups. In some cases, it is possible for the individual himself to select the group. This is not an infrequent occurrence in schools where groups are functioning and the word gets out that group counseling is indeed helpful. In such cases, individuals can and do approach the counselor and ask to become members. Since the individual may or may not fit into the counselor's preconceived beliefs about group composition, the counselor and the group may have to make judgments as to whether or not that specific group is appropriate for the individual who seeks admission.

Secondly, it is possible for the group to suggest that a new member be added. Elementary school children sometimes ask to bring a friend and adolescents and college students who find the group beneficial will more often than not ask if an acquaintance can be admitted. Both approaches are important from the standpoint of how the new member might effect cohesion and other dynamic factors. The authors agree with Luchins (1964) that these methods of selection can be useful if they are employed to give members an understanding of their actions, the reasons for their actions, and the consequences of their actions.

SOME SPECIFIC APPROACHES TO GROUP COMPOSITION

We have, in general terms, noted some of the thinking of numerous group counselors with regard to group composition. Some rather specific factors, however, have been utilized in forming groups, and it would perhaps be beneficial to note some of the common approaches here in order for counselors to make some determination of how they wish to form groups.

1. EXCLUSION LISTS. In general terms, the concept of exclusion lists refers to an "anyone but" approach to group composition. Perhaps the reason for developing such lists is a result of the thinking of some therapists and counselors that the group with its potential for growth also has a potential for harm and that some individuals could in fact be hurt by participation in a group. Thus, group leaders were warned by such experienced group leaders as Bach (1954) and Hinkley and Herman (1951) against allowing psychotics or prepsychotics in a group. Others such as Warters (1960) called for the counselor to be aware of the chronic monopolist. In fact, Wolberg as early as 1954 developed a representative list in which he indicated that psychopathic personalities, depressives, homosexuals, paranoids, and those who act out too readily be excluded from participation.

The major problem with exclusion lists from the standpoint of group counseling at least is that the counselor in dealing with essentially normal individuals finds such lists next to useless in his work in public schools. With the possible exception of the chronic monopolist, the counselor is not likely to encounter large numbers of psychopaths, paranoids, and the like. In addition, the authors in informal discussions with those who are responsible for group therapy in clinical sessions have found rather general agreement that diagnostic categories are not utilized for grouping persons nearly as much as one might believe. Therefore, the counselor who wishes to employ the concept of exclusion may have to utilize either trial grouping as suggested by Gazda (1968) or make a careful and rather global assessment of the prospective group member from a screening interview. He may well wish to use certain personality measures as a criterion for grouping, but usually these are insufficient as predictors of behaviors within a group. The authors have found that basic honesty on the part of the counselor in explaining what will happen in the group and commitment on the part of the members are at least as useful as approaches to grouping as exclusion lists.

2. GROUP-REACTION APPROACH. The essence of this approach is best summed up by Ohlsen's (1964) questions: What effect will the in-

dividual have on the group as a whole? Will he disrupt the group? Will
he attempt to dominate it, become overly aggressive, or will he completely withdraw? The reader will note, of course, that the group-
reaction viewpoint is in one sense a type of exclusion list viewed from
another vantage point. Instead of attempting to make a diagnosis of a
certain category, the counselor surveys his group, takes account of the
potential members, and makes a professional judgment of the impact
each will have in the group. In some cases, he may wish to include
members who by their prior group experience and global personality
may well foster the group process. Hill (1965) summarizes the group-
reaction viewpoint by suggesting that the leader be guided by the
principles that those individuals who either are always disruptive or are
not able to profit from the experience should be excluded. These factors
are also noted in exclusion lists and once again call for a judgment of
just what is too disruptive and who indeed can and cannot profit from
the group experience.

3. HOMOGENEITY–HETEROGENEITY GROUPING. Those who have
served time in the classroom and are new to counseling may feel that
the homogeneous versus heterogeneous groupings are debates best left
to principals and curriculum directors. Such, however, is not the case.
Counselors and therapists alike have discussed and argued about the
relative merits of having a homogeneous as opposed to a heterogeneous
counseling group.

In a strict sense, of course, it is never possible to have a completely
homogeneous group when one works with people as any neophyte
student teacher soon learns. Individuals who are alike in IQ may vary
in background, temperament, patterns of relating, and a host of other
factors. Thus, when the concept of homogeneity is discussed in terms
of group counseling and therapy, writers generally mean that they are
attempting to control or reduce the differences among group members
on certain specified factors. Heterogeneous grouping for counseling
purposes refers to the concept of forming groups of people who are
essentially dissimilar in certain traits (age, sex, IQ). Like all trait and
factor approaches to human personality, this approach suffers from the
reduction of the total personality to a list of factors that in someone's
judgment represent good criteria for grouping. In addition, as Hill
(1965) notes, the argument of homogeneity and heterogeneity is frequently presented in either-or terms when it might be more appropriate to conceptualize groups in terms of being homogeneous for some
things and heterogeneous for others. *Homogeneity for what* is better
than *homogeneity is good.*

In spite of the difficulties one encounters in attempting to group along these dimensions, for some reasons counselors do and perhaps should consider the possible effects and limitations of narrowing or broadening the range of differences in a group. To illustrate an improbable absurdity, no counselor would want to mix play-media first grade groups with twenty-year-old college juniors unless he had some rather narrow and specific purpose.

Defining a homogeneous group as "one in which a reasonable similarity in psychodynamics and pathology is known to exist among the members of a group," Furst presents an enlightening review of the relative merits and disadvantages of both approaches. Of homogeneous groups, he notes that:

1. Group identification takes place rapidly and transferences are rapidly formed.
2. Re-education takes place rapidly and insight develops quickly.
3. Psychodynamics are more rapidly laid bare.
4. Duration of treatment is lessened.
5. Attendance is more regular.
6. Interferences, resistances, and interactions of a destructive nature are lessened.
7. Intramural cliques are uncommon.
8. Recovery from symptoms is more rapid. [Furst, 1953, p. 120]

The negative aspects of such grouping include: the difficulty in forming such groups, possible decreased interaction, untouched character structure, lessened reality testing, and lack of multiple and shifting transferences (pp. 120–21).

In discussing heterogeneity, Furst notes the following advantages to such grouping:

1. Heterogeneous groups by their very nature tend to take the therapist whether or not he so desires into deeper levels of therapy.
2. Character structure as well as symptom formation is influenced by the process of therapy.
3. Reality testing is more adequate and thorough.
4. Intra-group transference of a diverse and shifting nature can be formed readily in the heterogeneous group in accordance with individual needs.
5. Heterogeneous groups are easy to assemble and screening need not be as thorough. [Furst, 1953, pp. 121–22]

Furst also notes that negative aspects of heterogeneous groups include: slower recovery of patients, magnified tensions, slow group identification, delayed therapist transference, slow insight, and irregular attendance.

The use of the approaches depends upon the nature and type of therapy, and Furst calls for homogeneous groups for therapy (1) when the interview type is utilized; (2) when less profound and intensive therapy is indicated; (3) when the therapist is not prepared to handle deep levels of therapy; and (4) when the factors of time and expense are important. Heterogeneous groups should be used (1) when deep levels of therapy are required; (2) when modification of character structure is necessary; (3) when the training and experience of the therapist are adequate; and (4) when time and expense are less important (Furst, 1953, p. 127).

When one reviews the opinions of Furst, it would seem that counselors and counseling insofar as these two can be differentiated from therapists and therapy might well lean toward the composition of relatively homogeneous groups along certain dimensions. Counseling may well be less profound than therapy; the counselor usually does not have the training of the therapist nor is he generally interested in deep therapy, transference, and character reorganization. In addition, time is a crucial variable to most counselors. Thus, the authors feel that for most, if not all, counseling, a certain type of homogeneity is workable. To clarify this, we would not advocate combining several *severe* acting-out boys or several severely withdrawn youngsters in a single group. The question remains *homogeneous for what?* Each counselor, of course, must seek his own answers, but the authors, who prefer an interaction type of approach to counseling, have found that the key variable is that of homogeneity as it refers to the expressed way that individuals prefer to behave in groups. Thus, homogeneity for us is determined by Hill's HIM-B, an instrument we shall now discuss in greater detail. In spite of Furst's contention that heterogeneous groups are necessary for interaction approaches, the authors have found that using Hill's constructs of homogeneity in the matching for topic and work-style categories on the Hill Matrix actually *fosters* interaction (See Chapter 3 for a discussion of the Hill Matrix).

4. THE HIM-B.   The reader will recall that in Chapter 3 of this book a discussion of the Hill Interaction Matrix was presented. Utilizing empirically derived categories to illustrate the two basic dimensions that characterize group interaction, Hill has presented the researcher and group practitioner with a pragmatic scheme for use in group therapy and counseling. Though a quick review of the section on the

Hill Matrix would be helpful in understanding the HIM-B, it will suffice for the moment to recall that Hill's dimensions are along four content-style categories (topic, group, personal, and relationship) and five work-style categories (responsive, conventional, assertive, speculative, and confrontive). Thus, the complete matrix contains twenty cells, each of which represents a type of group behavior.

From the matrix just described, Hill developed a psychometric test for group members which he labeled the HIM-B (See Appendix B). The major purpose of the instrument is to determine the amount of acceptance that an individual has for operating in the various HIM cells (Hill, 1965, p. 88). Stated another way, the counselor by administering the HIM-B prior to forming groups is provided with information about each individual's preferred mode of group behavior. One can learn, for example, what content-style category the individual prefers. Does he prefer to discuss topics, the group itself, personal concerns, or relationships? In a similar manner, the counselor is also able to note the preferred work mode of the individual. Does he prefer to operate in a conventional fashion, in an assertive or speculative way? Does he describe himself as essentially confrontive?

The test contains sixty-four items, and there are four items keyed to each cell on the Hill Matrix. (The responsive level is excluded since this usually is applicable to severely regressed, hospitalized individuals.) An individual's response on each of the sixty-four items provides a two-dimensional description of his preferred content-style and work-style modes of group behavior. Scores for each cell are converted into percents and then compared to norms provided by Hill (1967). This allows comparisons with groups of male and female California probationers, California minimum-security people, industrial school, prison, hospital, public school and college groups, school counselors, and group therapists. The HIM-B also yields a TAS or total acceptance score which is a good indication of the overall mode of group operation by a prospective member. Completed instruments allow for group composition along the dimensions of the Hill categories. For example, those who prefer to operate on a relationship-confrontive mode could be placed in one group, those who prefer a topic-conventional method of operation may be placed in another, and so on. All types of group combinations are thus possible; and as one can see, the HIM-B provides an excellent research tool. While counselor judgments are not eliminated entirely, the HIM-B is one of the few scientific approaches to group composition currently available.

Extensive use of the HIM-B and HIM-A (an identical instrument to the HIM-B with simpler language and slightly different norms) has been

made at the University of Maine during the past few years. Our experience has shown that the HIM-B is an excellent indicator of how individuals will probably operate in a group—at least in the initial stages
of group development. The HIM-B has also been used with elementary
school children as low as the fifth grade, and our preliminary evidence
suggests that this approach to grouping may be extremely valuable with
younger children. For example, in a recent practicum experience with
bright fifth grade students, each prospective group member was administered the HIM-B. Although the counselor had to assist several children
with the meanings of several of the items on the inventory, most had
no trouble completing it. Children were then grouped as either conventional or confrontive according to their scores on the HIM-B. An analysis of tapes from both groups indicates that children who listed
themselves as confrontive did indeed engage in more confrontive-type
behavior than did their conventional counterparts. Such evidence,
however, is far from conclusive since the experiment was uncontrolled.
Nevertheless, the use of the HIM-B as an approach to grouping with
elementary school children is at least an interesting hypothesis.

In a prior section of this chapter, the authors noted that they preferred essentially homogeneous groups, and by this we mean homogeneous according to the Hill category system. We have found, for
example, that a mixture of conventional and confrontive individuals (as
measured by the HIM-B) poses numerous difficult problems for the
counselor and the group. Individuals who do not like confrontive interaction seem to shy away to a topic level when they are confronted,
and those who prefer a confrontive approach seem to resist topical
discussions. For some years, the authors and perhaps other group counselors have noticed the phenomenon in groups wherein several members never seemed to move into work levels of operation. At best, such
groups moved slowly, had trouble in becoming cohesive, and were
frequently beset with almost unreachable subgroups. At worst, attendance seemed to fall off and the groups disbanded. While the HIM-B
may not be the final answer to group composition, the authors feel that
the counselor's choices of an effective group are greatly enhanced
through utilization of Hill's concepts. Full information on the matrix
may be found in the *Hill Interaction Matrix Monograph* (1965) and the
September–October issue of the journal *American Behavioral Scientist*.
The former may be obtained from the Youth Studies Center at the
University of Southern California, and the latter is a production of the
Sage Publications of Beverly Hills, California.

5.   BALANCED GROUPS AND HETEROGENEITY.   No instrument known to
the authors will completely eliminate counselor judgments. While the

authors have noted that they prefer homogeneous groups with regard to the Hill dimensions, individual members may still vary on a wide range of other traits. Confrontive individuals, for example, may vary on age, sex, verbal ability, and so on. Thus, obtaining homogeneity along the Hill dimensions does not eliminate heterogeneity along any one of numerous others. Counselor judgment and perhaps other assessment devices may still be utilized for specific purposes.

Another dimension the counselor may wish to consider is that of group balance or the concept that any one individual in the group should exert some sort of remedial effect on the other (Ginott, 1968). In order to set up balanced conditions, the counselor must consider what traits and factors he wishes to balance and organize his group along these dimensions. An aggressive individual might be paired with one who is passive, a shy child with one who is more outgoing, a dogmatic person with an open-minded one, and so on. Ginott, a strong advocate of balance with children's groups, notes that the selection of a play-therapy group is never a random matter (p. 177). If one is indeed able to determine what factors or what global personality types can be optimally balanced, the concept seems logical. We can be fairly certain that good group interaction does indeed produce new attitudinal and behavioral norms, and in forming groups, no new norm is likely to emerge if the interactions are more or less reinforcements of attitudes and behaviors already held. For example, more than one unsuspecting counselor has grouped aggressive, acting-out adolescents in a single group with the expressed (or perhaps hidden) wish that somehow a change could take place. Such grouping is frequently followed by little or no behavioral change and perhaps soured many a group counselor on the group approach. If an interaction approach is used and if a change is to take place, the group must be balanced. Poor students reinforce poor students in groups; acting-out boys provide other acting-out boys with support of their behaviors. In this context, then, the balance of a group must be considered. If it seems to the reader that we are advocating homogeneous groups on the one hand and diverse heterogeneous grouping on the other, you are right! We prefer homogeneous groups for interaction purposes as Hill suggests, but the concept of balance like other factors must also be considered. We agree with Ginott (1961) that grouping is never random. In fact, it may be the single most crucial variable in counseling success.

6. AGE AND MATURITY FACTORS. The factor of age in grouping is given at least passing reference by numerous writers. Driver (1954), Patterson et al. (1956) and Van Hoose et al. (1967), for example, note that latency-age children can function successfully in groups whose

members are within two years of each other. Ginott (1968) in discussing play-therapy groups suggests that the shorter the age span the better and that groupmates should never differ in age by more than a year (p. 177). Mahler (1969) writes that college students are generally more comfortable meeting with people their own age, while Joel and Shapiro (1950) feel that mixed-age groups are more natural in that older persons offer more significant transference and identification opportunities for younger members while more youthful participants serve in a similar capacity for older members.

With junior high and high school groups, the composition with respect to age is generally rather well determined by the administrative arrangement of the school. Even so, wide differences of age at the high school level may pose a problem if rather mature seniors are grouped with younger ninth grade adolescents. The factors of experience and maturity and status levels create a general domination syndrome in school groups wherein the more worldly senior controls and sometimes excludes his younger counterpart. The counselor can intervene and control this situation to a degree if he chooses, but he will generally find group counseling more productive when the age range does not vary a great deal.

With college and adult groups, the authors are in general agreement with the contention of Joel *et al.* (1950) that mixed-age groups are a rather natural approach. While Mahler (1969) may be essentially correct in his view that college students prefer to be with others similar in age, the authors have not found that a mixture of college-age students and older adults is a great hindrance. In fact, insofar as the group can be conceived as a slice of life or a microcommunity, the perceptions of older members are a valuable addition. The group is a testing ground for new behaviors, and the arena should, when possible, contain the crucial elements of the larger society. Few will contest the fact that the college student of today is inevitably entwined with the perceptions of oldsters in a host of day-to-day situations.

With respect to elementary school children, the authors are of the opinion that more attention needs to be given to the developmental factors in grouping rather than to the chronological ones. At least two writers, Foulkes (1965) and Redl (1966), have suggested this concept, yet scant attention has been given to developmental grouping for counseling purposes. Of particular interest to the authors has been the *Developmental Examination*[4] developed at the Gesell Institute in New Haven, Connecticut.

---

[4]See Frances L. Ilg and Louise Bates Ames, *School Readiness* (New York: Harper and Row, Publishers, 1965).

In essence, the Gesell Institute suggests that chronological age is not an ideal criterion for determining placement in schools. They propose instead that a behavioral age obtained from a fairly simple behavior examination provides greater clues to a child's developmental level. The chief areas of the examination include: (1) an initial interview; (2) copy forms and the completion of an incomplete-man form; (3) adjustment to right and left commands; (4) Monroe Visual Tests One and Three—an examination designed to determine the child's readiness to match and memorize designs; (5) the naming of animals for a period of one minute; and (6) a final interview on interests. An additional exam, the mosaic test, is sometimes included in the screening. From this screening, the examiner is able to get a behavioral range for a given child. For example, a child's behavior on the exam may range from five to seven years of age. An experienced examiner, however, is able to determine a modal score or cluster of behavior for a given child. In the example just given, a child may range behaviorally from five to seven years of age, but most of his behavior may fall at a six-year level. In Gesell terms, the child is a developmental six-year old even though his actual chronological age may be six and a half, seven, or perhaps five and a half or younger. To date, the battery has been standardized at seven different age levels from five to ten years of age.

Use of these materials will convince most counselors that there are indeed wide differences in child development, and if he desires a relatively homogeneous developmental group, this instrument can be of great value. Unfortunately, the Gesell approach requires at least a brief training period coupled with extensive practice since the exam requires some subjective interpretation. To date, the authors have organized three counseling groups based upon Gesell developmental practices, and our judgment at this point is at least suggestive that this approach holds promise. While the Gesell examination is not flawless, it provides excellent data to assist the counselor in forming developmental groups.

7. SEX GROUPING. The question of whether or not counseling groups should comprise members of a single sex or whether mixed-sex groups are preferred is a frequent topic in group-counseling and therapy literature. As one might expect, opinions on this subject range from the it-makes-no-difference approach to rather specific positions favoring either sex homogeneity or heterogeneity.

Glanz and Hayes (1967) note that sex homogeneity may hamper or help a group in the discussion of particular problems, but they present no opinions or data on what problems would be hindered or helped. Ohlsen (1964) favors a mixed-group concept since issues may be discussed on a higher plane and members will speak out with greater frankness, although there seems to be little evidence to support this contention. In fact, in some cases, one might well agree with Glanz and Hayes that some problems might well be hindered by mixed-sex groups. Mahler (1969) suggests mixed-sex groups for certain purposes, but he, too, does not indicate what these purposes might be.

Johnson (1963) in discussing the sex composition of groups writes that the segregated hospital wards naturally result in groups of the same sex, but he also notes that mixed-sexed groups are likely to produce anxiety levels too high for group therapy. Bach (1954), however, in dealing with outpatient groups prefers a mixed-sex grouping because he feels it is beneficial to broaden the experiential horizon of his patients (p. 26). Whitaker and Lieberman (1964) see the problem of sex along with age and race as less important than an individual's capacity for tolerating anxiety in that problems evolving from one type of grouping or another may be handled in the group process.

With respect to children's groups, Ginott (1968) suggests mixed-sex grouping with preschool groups but advocates some sex grouping for school-age boys and girls. The rationale for this contention stems from Ginott's view that there are no compelling reasons for separating groups of preschool children but that school-age boys and girls are in the process of seeking a masculine or feminine identity. Support for this view is provided by Churchill (1965) whose experiments with diagnostic groups were more functional and productive with children who were of the same sex.

Since no final unbending reasons for the sex composition of a group can be provided, the authors generally follow the guidelines suggested by other writers. For preschool groups (kindergarten), the mixed-sex concept seems appropriate since the child is reaching out perhaps for the first time in an organized way to others around him. We also agree that, for most purposes, the use of single-sexed groups is appropriate for children enrolled in grades one through six. From junior high on, the mixed-sex concept is preferable in that this seems to be a natural type of environment. We hasten to point out, however, that like many other aspects of counseling the purposes may delimit the composition. For example, there may be times when a short-term mixed-sex group is beneficial for fourth grade boys and girls for the purpose of working out some particular concern that is of importance to both sexes. The counselor must remember that his population is essentially normal and the purposes of a group leader in a hospital are likely to be quite different than those of the counselor in a modern elementary school.

8. SOCIOMETRIC GROUPING. The sociometric test, a common guidance instrument in many schools, was developed by Moreno and

adapted for research purposes by Jennings (Warters, 1960). Members are asked to respond to questions with the names of those members that they prefer or reject in certain situations. In schools, such questions generally take the form of: "With whom would you prefer to work on our science project?" or "We are going to form a Christmas committee; select two people with whom you enjoy working most." Of course, the questions and the purposes of sociometric tests vary with different groups and at different age levels.

Bach (1954) has even devised a rather extensive instrument to assess the structure of therapy groups. Moreno and Kipper describe the sociometric test in the following manner:

> The sociometric test requires an individual to choose his associates for any group of which he is or might become a member. He is expected to make his choices without restraint ... [Moreno and Kipper, 1968, p. 52]

Since the purposes of sociometric grouping are to discover the organization of the group, the social status of each member, and the patterns and quality of interpersonal relations in a group, the basis for the choice should be real as opposed to hypothetical (Warters, 1960, pp. 93–94). Leaders and isolates may thus be identified and data are provided for teacher or counselor action in organizing group activities.

Warters emphasizes that data gathered via a sociometric device be utilized only in the situation for which the choices were expressed and that an individual be allowed to be placed in a group with his highest degree of choice or with the highest degree of reciprocated choice (p. 145). Warters further notes that the unchosen and much-rejected members be given their first choice in that such individuals may need assistance in feeling emotionally comfortable in the group situation and in expanding socially. Rejected persons should be placed apart from those who reject them, and cleavages can be reduced by placing members of different segments into an existing subgroup. Warters feels that restricting the group on the basis of sociometric findings aids social learning, and Jennings (1953) and Zeleny (1956) have provided experimental evidence that those who interact with those they choose are more ingenious, productive, and creative.

Sociometric grouping as a basis for formulating counseling groups offers the counselor several intriguing opportunities, but he should consider several factors. The most obvious, of course, is that the unchosen child may not necessarily be the most poorly adjusted, and the fact that he is unchosen in a given group is not always an indication that he has not obtained acceptance elsewhere. In addition, if we follow Warter's suggestion that mutual choices or high-degree choices be placed together, we would only have counseling groups of people acceptable to each other. If one can conceive of counseling as at least in part a process of expanding relations with those who are not compatible, we might well group high-degree isolates with stars. One function of counseling is to help the child to expand—to become more acceptant of self and others. Such mutual acceptance, to the best of the authors' knowledge, is best promoted through interaction under conditions of equality; hence, instead of placing the child with those whom he accepts, we might do the opposite. By this, we mean that the counselor should create the conditions where opposites meet, interact, and change rather than the opposite. The purposes and processes of counseling can be and often are different from those of the classroom which is frequently task oriented. Therefore, though the child may be more productive with those whom he likes, we must judge what type of productivity we desire. Production in a counseling group where increased acceptance of others is the goal is something quite different from planning a sixth grade science project.

Some rather recent research in group counseling with elementary school children is an indication that some investigators view a rise in social acceptance as a desirable outcome of the group process (Biasco, 1965; Kranzler et al., 1966; Mayer, 1966; Mayer et al., 1967; Hansen et al., 1969; Thombs, 1970), and the authors have no quarrel with this procedure. One must wonder, however, if this approach can really be a valid criterion of counseling success with young children whose patterns of social relationships are in a state of constant flux. One does not have to work with young children long to discover that today's best friend is tomorrow's worst enemy.

GROUP SIZE

Counseling groups in various organizational patterns have ranged from as few as two people to fifty or more. Sociologists—and it would be presumed most counselors—consider group size an important variable. Thomas and Fink have reviewed thirty-one empirical studies of small groups and conclude that the size of a group is an important variable in any theory of group behavior. They write:

> On the basis of this review, it is apparent that group size has significant effects on aspects of individual and group performance, on the nature of interaction and distribution of

participation of group members, on conformity and consensus, and on member satisfaction. [Thomas and Fink, 1968, p. 343]

At least one writer, Geller (1951), has approached the problem of group size within the context of depth and aims and goals. For example, the psychoanalytic approach to group therapy with its depth approach requires a minimum of three to four people and a maximum of six to ten. Other approaches that would hope to provide greater symptom control could have as many as fifty individuals involved. Johnson (1963) considers group size in terms of its effect on the emotional climate, noting that the larger the group the less the emotional involvement. He does, however, think that group therapists recommend eight or fewer as optimal for their purposes. Those who have written specifically for counseling as opposed to therapy groups seem to agree with the group therapists. Glanz and Hayes (1967) note that groups in excess of ten could not have the necessary degree of interaction for good group counseling; Gazda (1968) writes that a sufficient number is five to ten; and Warters (1960) proposes a somewhat more liberal range of ten to fifteen. While not specifically noted, each writer here is presumably advocating group size for adolescent and adult groups.

With respect to preadolescent groups, Ginott (1961) believes that for therapy no group should exceed five members. After a careful review of group studies, Mayer and Baker write:

> The size of the counseling group must vary with the age or maturity level, or both, of the counselees. It appears that optimal size for effective group counseling with elementary school children should probably not exceed five or six. Furthermore, in consideration of children's personal–social development, group sizes of less than five or six would seem more appropriate for younger or more immature elementary school students. [Mayer and Baker, 1967, p. 143]

As with other areas of group composition, the question of size is often a factor that must also be considered with the purposes of the group. The authors have no empirical evidence that would allow us to state that a specific size is right for groups. From an experiential background, however, we generally support the notion that a group of eight members is optimum for adolescents and adults and a group of ten is maximum for most interacting groups. With children up to junior high, five seems to be the maximum number for efficient operation. Our rationale for advocating relatively small groups stems from the fact that group counseling is and must be a very personal experience. As group size grows, the group must become more impersonal, less intimate, and less satisfying to members (Berelson and Steiner, 1964). A passing note to those who do group-counseling research for doctoral dissertations is in order at this point. The authors suggest that if a minimal number of students (perhaps eight) is needed for the purposes of equal N's in statistical treatment, select more members than needed (perhaps ten or twelve). For any number of reasons, a member or members may choose to terminate counseling, and more than one aspiring doctoral candidate has found himself facing the dilemma of "come back little data."

VOLUNTARY OR REQUIRED PARTICIPATION

Gazda (1968) in discussing voluntariness writes that an individual must either have or be capable of developing a desire to change at the time he enters a group. Involuntary clients can be assisted, however, if they remain in counseling long enough to experience the beneficial effects of the process (pp. 268–69). He further notes that one way to handle the involuntary client is to permit him to leave if he so desires after five or six sessions. Mahler (1969) advocates required participation for certain people (i.e., acting-out boys), but recommends that in most cases the decision of whether or not to participate be left to the individual. Like Gazda (1968), he feels that resistance may be overcome if the individual is offered a trial period.

The authors are in strong support of volunteers for group counseling. An individual must both see the need and value of participation if he is to commit valuable time and energy to attendance at group sessions. Much can be accomplished through orientation programs, but perhaps the most effective way for students to learn of the benefits of the group is through word of mouth. During the current school year, weekend minimarathons or abbreviated five-to six-hour sessions were conducted by one of the authors in conjunction with a campus church. After a rather slow start with twelve volunteers, an additional eighty-six members volunteered to participate in a forthcoming group. Once individuals learn that the group is helpful, the counselor's main job may be that of trying to meet the demand.

We have no quarrel with the view that the involuntary client may be helped, but the problems encountered here are obvious. The client may neither want nor feel he needs the group as a source of help, his perceptions of the counselor may be negative, and he may not value the group experience. The authors feel that the issue of involuntariness should be approached directly. The counselor should state that some members may or may not wish to participate but that since they are required to spend the hour (or whatever) in the group, he is willing to help. This will not produce magic and resistance will be high. However, a warm individual who shows he cares may skillfully help the members grow to value the group. The progress may be slower, and the counselor may have to handle much anxiety and anger. Hopefully, he will be able to provide benefit for those who are in some way forced into counseling to gain from the experience. Obviously, it is much less satisfying than groups who of their own volition have made a contract to participate.

SUMMARY

Group organization is a pragmatic concern of most counselors. In this context, the counselor must deal with broad group goals in addition to very specific individual goals. The use of tentative interpretation in which the counselor alludes to the tentative goals of individuals is a useful technique in helping group members develop insight.

Since group counseling is poorly understood by teachers and lay people, the counselor has the specific responsibility to provide a thorough orientation to these individuals as well as to prospective group members. Such factors as the nature of groups, the need for confidentiality, the purpose of groups, and the mechanical steps involved in forming groups are vital to a successful program of group counseling.

Once a group has been organized, the counselor must pay attention to such pragmatic concerns as: (1) when a group should meet; (2) group mobility; (3) physical arrangements for groups; (4) conformity and group behavior ; (5) group composition; (6) group size; and (7) voluntary or required participation.

REFERENCES

BACH, GEORGE R. *Intensive Group Psychotherapy.* New York: The Ronald Press Company, 1954.

BERELSON, B., and STEINER, G. A. *Human Behavior.* New York: Harcourt Brace Jovanovich, Inc., 1964.

BIASCO, F. "The Effects of Individual Counseling, Multiple Counseling, and Teacher Guidance upon the Sociometric Status of Children Enrolled in Grades Four, Five, and Six." Ph.D. dissertation, University of Indiana, 1965.

BLOCHER, D. H. *Developmental Counseling.* New York: The Ronald Press Company, 1966.

BONNEY, W. C. "Group Counseling and Developmental Process," in *Theories and Methods of Group Counseling in the Schools* (ed. GEORGE M. GAZDA). Springfield, Ill.: Charles C Thomas, Publisher, 1969.

BRAMMER, L. M., and SHOSTROM, E. L. *Therapeutic Psychology.* Englewood Cliffs, N.J.: Prentice-Hall, Inc., 1968.

CHURCHILL S. R. "Social Group Work: A Diagnostic Tool in Child Guidance," *American Journal of Orthopsychiatry,* Vol. 35 (1965), pp. 581–88.

DINKMEYER, DON C., and DREIKURS, RUDOLF. *Encouraging Children to Learn: The Encouragement Process.* Englewood Cliffs, N.J.: Prentice-Hall, Inc., 1963.

DREIKURS, RUDOLF, and SOLTZ, VICKI. *Children: The Challenge.* New York: Duell, Sloan and Pearce, 1964.

DRIVER, H. I. *Multiple Counseling: A Small-Group Discussion Method for Personal Growth.* Madison, Wis.: Mona Publications, 1954.

DURKIN, HELEN E. *The Group in Depth.* New York: International Universities Press, 1964.

FOULKES, S. H. *Therapeutic Group Analysis.* New York: International Universities Press, 1965. Overseas publisher: George Allen and Unwin Ltd.

FOULKES, S. H., and ANTHONY, E. J. *Group Psychotherapy.* Baltimore, Md.: Penguin Books, Inc., 1965.

FURST, W. "Homogeneous versus Heterogeneous Groups," *International Journal of Group Psychotherapy,* Vol. 3 (1953), pp. 59–66.

GAZDA, GEORGE M. "A Functional Approach to Group Counseling," in *Basic Approaches to Group Psychotherapy and Group Counseling* (ed. GEORGE M. GAZDA. Springfield, Ill.: Charles C Thomas, Publisher, 1968.

———. *Basic Approaches to Group Psychotherapy and Group Counseling.* Springfield, Ill.: Charles C Thomas, Publisher, 1968.

GELLER, J. J. "Concerning the Size of Therapy Groups," *International Journal of Group Psychotherapy,* Vol. 1 (1951), pp. 118–20.

GINOTT, H. G. *Group Psychotherapy with Children.* New York: McGraw-Hill Book Company, 1961.

———. "Group Therapy with Children," in *Basic Approaches to Group Psychotherapy and Group Counseling* (ed. GEORGE M. GAZDA). Springfield, Ill.: Charles C Thomas, Publisher, 1968.

GLANZ, E. C. *Groups in Guidance.* Boston: Allyn and Bacon, Inc., 1962.

GLANZ, E. C., and HAYES, R. W. *Groups in Guidance.* 2nd ed. Boston: Allyn and Bacon, Inc., 1967.

GLASSER, WILLIAM. *Reality Therapy.* New York: Harper and Row, Publishers, 1965.

HANSEN, J. C., NILAND, T. M., and ZANI, L. P. "Model Reinforcement in Group Counseling with Elementary School Children," *Personnel and Guidance Journal,* Vol. 47 (1969), pp. 741–44.

HILL, WILLIAM F. *Group-Counseling Training Syllabus.* Los Angeles, Calif.: University of Southern California, Youth Studies Center, 1965.

——— (ed.). "Group Therapy for Social Impact: Innovation in Leadership Training," *American Behavioral Scientist* (1967), pp. 1–48.

HINKLEY, R. G., and HERMAN, L. *Group Treatment in Psychotherapy.* Minneapolis, Minn.: University of Minnesota Press, 1951.

JENNINGS, HELEN H. "Sociometric Structure in Personality and Group Formation," in *Group Relations at the Crossroads* (eds. M. SHERIF, and M. OHL-SEN). New York: Harper and Row, Publishers, 1953.

JOEL, W., and SHAPIRO, D. "Some Principles and Procedures for Group Psychotherapy," *Journal of Psychology,* Vol. 29 (1950), pp. 77–88.

JOHNSON, J. A. *Group Therapy: A Practical Approach.* New York: McGraw-Hill Book Company, 1963.

KRANZLER, C. D., MAYER, G. R., DYER, C. O., and MUNZER, P. T. "Counseling with Elementary School Children: An Experimental Study," *The Personnel and Guidance Journal,* Vol. 44 (1966), pp. 944–49.

KRUMBOLTZ, JOHN D. "Behavioral Counseling: Rationale and Research," *Personnel and Guidance Journal,* Vol. 44 (1966a), pp. 376–82.

———. "Promoting Adaptive Behavior: New Answers to Familiar Questions," in *Revolution in Counseling* (ed. JOHN D. KRUMBOLTZ). Boston: Houghton Mifflin Company, 1966b.

LUCHINS, A. S. *Group Therapy: A Guide.* New York: Random House, Inc., 1964.

LUCHINS, A. S., AUMACH, L., and DICKMAN, H. *A Manual in Group Psychotherapy.* Roseburg, Ore.: V.A. Hospital, 1960.

McCANN, W. H., and ALMADA, A. A. "Round-Table Psychotherapy," *Journal of Consulting Psychology,* Vol. 14 (1950), pp. 431–35.

MAHLER, C. A. *Group Counseling in the Schools.* Boston: Houghton Mifflin Company, 1969.

MAHLER, C. A. and CALDWELL, E. *Group Counseling in Secondary Schools.* Chicago: Science Research Associates, 1961.

MAYER, G. R. "Elementary Counseling and Classroom Interpersonal Relationships." Ph.D. dissertation, University of Indiana, 1966.

MAYER, G. R., and BAKER, P. "Group Counseling with Elementary School Children: A Look at Group Size," *Elementary School Guidance and Counseling,* Vol. 1, No. 2 (March, 1967) pp. 140–45.

MAYER, G. R., KRANZLER, G. D., MATTHES, W. A. "Elementary School Counseling and Peer Relations," *Personnel and Guidance Journal,* Vol. 46 (1967), pp. 360–65.

MORENO, JACOB L., and KIPPER, D. A. "Group Psychodrama and Community-Centered Counseling," in *Basic Approaches to Group Psychotherapy and Group Counseling* (ed. GEORGE M. GAZDA). Springfield, Ill.: Charles C Thomas, Publisher, 1968.

MURO, JAMES J. "Some Aspects of the Group-Counseling Practicum," *Counselor Education and Supervision,* Vol. 7 (1968), pp. 371–378.

MURO, JAMES J., and DINKMEYER, DON C. "Counseling Process as a Function of Counselor Lead," *Elementary School Guidance and Counseling,* Vol. 5, No. 3 (March, 1971).

MURO, JAMES J., and FREEMAN, S. L. *Readings in Group Counseling.* Scranton, Pa.: International Textbook Company, 1968.

MURO, JAMES J., and REVELLO, E. A. "Counselor–Student Perceptions of the Extent of Performance of Guidance Services," *School Counselor* (1970), pp. 17, 193–99.

OHLSEN, MERLE M. *Guidance Services in the Modern School.* New York: Harcourt Brace Jovanovich, Inc., 1964.

————. *Group Counseling.* New York: Holt, Rinehart and Winston, Inc., 1970.

OTTO, HERBERT A. *Group Methods Designed to Actualize Human Potential.* Chicago: Stone-Brandel Center, 1967.

PATTERSON, G., SCHWARTZ, R., and VAN DERWART, E. "The Integration of Group and Individual Therapy," *American Journal of Orthopsychiatry,* No. 26 (1956), pp. 618–29.

REDL, F. *When We Deal with Children.* London: The Free Press, Collier-MacMillan Limited, 1966.

SHERIF, M. "Competition, Communicating, and Conformity," in *Conformity and Deviation* (eds. I. A. BERG, and B. M. BASS). New York: Harper and Row, Publishers, 1961.

SLAVSON, S. R. "Group Psychotherapies," in *Six Approaches to Psychotherapy* (ed. J. L. McCARY). New York: Dryden, 1955.

THOMAS, E. J., and FINK, F. C. "Effects of Group Size," in *Readings in Group Counseling* (eds. JAMES J. MURO, and S. L. FREEMAN). Scranton, Pa.: International Textbook Company, 1968.

THOMBS, M. R. "The Effects of Group Counseling using Play Media and Group Counseling using Verbal Techniques on Peer Relationships of Second Grade Isolates." Master's thesis, University of Maine, 1970.

VAN HOOSE, W., PETERS, M., and LEONARD, G. E. *The Elementary School Counselor.* Detroit: Wayne State University Press, 1967.

WARTERS, J. *Group Guidance: Principles and Practices.* New York: McGraw-Hill Book Company, 1960.

WHITAKER, D. S., and LIEBERMAN, M. A. *Psychotherapy through the Group Process.* New York: Atherton Press, Inc., 1964.

WOLBERG, L. R. *The Technique of Psychotherapy.* New York: Grune and Stratton, Inc., 1954.

ZELENY, L. D. "Validity of a Sociometric Hypothesis: The Function of Creativity in Interpersonal and Group Relations," *Sociometry,* Vol. 18, (1956), pp. 439–49.

CHAPTER 7

Establishing and Maintaining the Group

GETTING STARTED

Regardless of how well prospective group members have been oriented to group counseling, the initial session of a group is likely to produce a degree of anxiety in the counselor and the group members. In the search for structure in a novel situation, the early stages of group process will be punctuated with awkward pauses, hesitant statements, nervous laughter, polite talk, and a preoccupation with self as opposed to group concerns. These behavioral patterns need not be of serious concern to the counselor for several reasons. First of all, nonpersonal discussions and a rather high level of anxiety are a model operating pattern for most newly formed groups. Some anxiety, of course, stems from the fact that the members are not a true group in a psychological sense, but a collection of individuals who are seeking individual identity in ways they perceive to be socially acceptable. Talk is rapid, and a host of topics may be introduced, examined briefly, and discarded. In one sense, each member is somewhat like the professional boxer who is unsure of his status and must feel out the opponent to discover the most comfortable and effective way of functioning.

The initial goal of such behavior is to reduce the anxiety level of the group to a level wherein the individual feels comfortable. It is the rare group member who does not fear discussing himself in front of others, and such fears are compounded in a situation where trust has not yet developed (Johnson, 1963).

A counselor must be aware of this phenomenon and be prepared to deal with the uneasiness that exists. In his efforts to establish rapport and cohesion, he should be essentially supportive and keep his remarks group oriented. When the opportunity presents itself, the counselor should bring these fears into the open where members may deal with them. In fact, it may not be harmful for the counselor to express his own uneasiness, if such exists. When the counselor can be perceived as human with human uncertainties, he will discover that group members themselves can become more open. In fact, Otto (1967) feels very strongly that the leader's way of sharing himself "sets the tone and establishes the depth of experience in a group" (p. 5). While no counselor should utilize the group to work on his own concerns, his willingness to share some of himself is a strong catalyst to assist others to do the same. The counselor, through his behavior, thus becomes a model and a teacher of how the group can function. Not only does the counselor present a model of openness and authenticity, he also serves as an example of one who is able to empathize, clarify, and reflect. Group members who observe such behavior in counselors can learn by example to become more effective group members and helpers through the utilization of effective counseling techniques. For example:

> COUNSELOR: Mary, you seem to be saying that nobody understands you and that you often feel unwanted in school.
> SUE: Yes, I sense that in Mary, too, and I also feel that John, too, is feeling unwanted. Is it possible that you don't feel understood very often, too, John?

In this case, Sue, by listening to the counselor's verbalization, learned to phrase her own response in an empathic manner. Seldom does the group leader's behavior go unnoticed by participants, and his actions are the data that help determine the modes and mores of small group life.

Once the counselor is aware that the initial sessions of counseling groups tend to be superficial and nongroup oriented, he has several options. He may, if he chooses, allow the group to develop along natural lines and deal with the responses of the group members. He may, however, wish to introduce certain warm-up exercises to assist the group members in their efforts to get started. As with other aspects of group life, the use of warm-up techniques is not an either-or proposition. Some counselors and some groups seem to function effectively without programmed exercises, while others do not. Timing and a sense of how the group may react are crucial in either instance.

To illustrate briefly an initial group session where programs or warm-ups were not used, a sample protocol from a group of college freshmen is represented here. The reader should note the superficial level of functioning.

Dialogue Analysis

Dialogue
Analysis

COUNSELOR: I know I spoke to each of you individually about our group sessions, but I wonder if we could review some of the things we discussed. (He repeats meeting dates, times, etc.) Is there anything I left out?

MARY: Yeh — you said there would be four boys and four girls. Did a girl quit already?

Mary expressed her own anxiety about what may happen in the group.

COUNSELOR: No, she called. She'll be here next week.

HELEN: Will we meet next week? That's prelim time [exams], you know.

JOE: Who cares; I won't pass anyhow! (loud laughter followed by silence)

HELEN: Well, maybe, but I need to study.

ANDY: Who's the other girl?

Note the rapid, clipped dialogue. It is also possible that Andy and Pete are really feeling critical of the group.

COUNSELOR: Sue. She lives in Oxford (a dorm).

HELEN: That's a crummy dorm.

ANDY: I'll say. They should rip it down, but we never rip anything down in Maine. Look at this so-called building!

PETE: My uncle is a contractor. He says the state won't pay for good buildings at the university.

ANN: Ours is nice; it's new though.

MARY: So is Hilltop. I'm moving there next semester — thank goodness. I want to cut out on my roommate.

Superficial discussion reduces anxiety.

In these sessions, as previously noted, the counselor should be supportive and group oriented. If the group lapses into silence, he may choose
to repeat the last comment made by a member prior to the silence. He
should follow the theme of the discussion and call it to the group's
attention. For example, in the above example if the discussion continues, he could note that: "We've had a lot of conversation about the
buildings here. I wonder why we're focusing on the buildings?" This
causes the group to focus on what they are doing and perhaps will lead
to a discussion of the purposes of the group. The counselor should also
support group members and ignore penetrating observations or interpretations. Frequently, some members will ask: "Are you a doctor—or
a psychiatrist? Do you shrink heads?" This could represent some anger
toward the group leader. It is not uncommon for naïve students to
wonder who the counselor is and what he may do to them. Joking is a
common way to approach this subject. The counselor may wish to
respond with: "Several of you seem to wonder about what I'm going to
do in this group. Do any of you have any thoughts about me in this
session today?" Regardless of who made the observation, the counselor
should respond to the group as a whole. Usually, members will not
respond in a negative way, but the counselor's request for them to
respond to him encourages the group to examine their feelings toward
him. This also is an encouragement on the part of the counselor for
members to examine their relationships to one another (Johnson, 1963).

Some counselors, however, prefer to initiate counseling in a more
direct way via a warm-up program or exercise. Some of the following
procedures for warm-ups may prove helpful.

1. WHAT I'M AFRAID OF. As previously noted, most people enter
the group with at least a small amount of apprehension. Instead of
letting this be a drawback to group development, the counselor can
utilize this anxiety to good advantage. Since the fear of the group is
present, the counselor should attempt to get each member to express
those aspects of the current situation that he may find frightening or
perhaps those elements in the situation that would make it difficult for
the individual to express himself (Finney, 1969). The tension level at
initial sessions is usually sufficient to insure the success of this technique.

2. EXPECTATIONS. Each member is provided with a small pad and
pencil and asked to introduce himself to the group. When each member
has introduced himself, the counselor then says: "I'm going to ask each
of you, even at this initial meeting, to write down some of the things
you might expect from other group members." Participants are then
asked to share their thoughts (Munzer, 1964).

3.   PARTNER INTRODUCTIONS.   The counselor asks members to choose a partner from the group to work with. Each member is then provided with a brief period of time (three to six minutes) to complete the task of learning as much about his partner as he can. He is instructed to find out the really important things about him for the purposes of introducing him to the group. Each person in the dyad is given an equal amount of time to ask questions of the other. The counselor then asks for volunteers to introduce members for the group. After all introductions have been made, the group discusses whether or not the introductions were trivial or contained really important information (Explorations Institute Exercises, 1969).

4.   DRAWING MYSELF.   Each group member receives a large sheet of paper and a box of crayons and is asked to draw a picture to respond to the question: "Who am I?" Pictures may be abstract or representational. The leader may then ask members to write a description of the drawing. Group members can show their pictures and read their descriptions, followed by a discussion (Explorations Institute, 1969).

5.   WHO I AM.   Members are asked to close their eyes and ask themselves the following question: "Who am I?" Each then shows what happened with the group (Explorations Institute, 1969).

6.   STIMULUS FILMS.   The counselor selects a film that tends to produce effective responses in individuals. Group members view the film and share their thoughts about it in terms of their own lives. Many films would serve this purpose. *Some Personal Learnings about Interpersonal Relations*[5] is an excellent stimulus film to promote early group interaction.

7.   DEPTH-UNFOLDMENT EXPERIENCE.   Otto suggests a technique labeled the *depth-unfoldment experience* to assist groups to break down interpersonal estrangement. The leader informs the group that one of its first tasks is to get to know each other better. Members are then told that the group will have ten minutes to suggest methods that would assist in helping to know each other better.

After actively encouraging the group to contribute ideas, the leader summarizes the contributions and introduces the DUE method. He suggests to the group that this is a very effective approach but that it

---

[5] Academic Communications Facility, University of California at Los Angeles. *Some Personal Learnings about Interpersonal Relationships.* Berkeley, Calif.: University of California Extension Media Center.

requires courage and a deeper sharing of self. In addition, he notes that it does produce tension but that it is worthwhile. Finally, the counselor states that the approach will be employed only if consensus is reached.

The method itself utilizes an egg timer. Each individual has six minutes (timed on the egg timer) to share himself. Five of the six minutes are utilized for the sharing of key experiences in his life that the individual feels made him the person that he is. The final minute is used by the individual to describe the happiest moment of his life. If a group member does not use all his allotted time, other participants may ask questions. Otto notes that the leader's way of sharing sets the tone for the group and establishes the depth of experience (Otto, 1967, pp. 4–5).

8. WHY I'M HERE. Mahler, in suggesting that the counselor assure the involvement of all members in the group, advocates that one good approach to initiating the group interaction is to clarify the purposes of the group. In this technique, the counselor would say: "I am aware of some of the reasons you wished to get a group started, but it may be helpful to review our purposes for beginning such a group. Who would like to begin by telling us why he is here?" (Mahler, 1969, p. 68)

9. WHAT I WORRY ABOUT. Mahler further suggests a technique for obtaining involvement through the use of a three-by-five card. Group members are asked to write down one thing they worry about. Each member then reads his response to the group, and members select a topic for discussion (Mahler, 1969, p. 95).

10. PICTURE SHUFFLE (children's groups). Prior to the initial group session, the counselor, through the use of a Polaroid camera, takes a picture of each child. When the group convenes, each child is handed his picture and asked to look at it and tell the group all he can about what he sees in the picture. Other members may ask questions when he is finished. Following each individual introduction, the pictures are gathered, shuffled, and placed face down on the table. The counselor flips a coin, and the child on his immediate right and left calls "heads" or "tails." The winner of the toss selects one of the face-down pictures and attempts to reintroduce the child whose picture he has selected.[6]

11. CIRCULAR METHOD (children's groups). Each member offers an idea, experience, or question at his turn. The member is allowed to speak, pass, or call for five seconds of silence when his turn arrives (Schmidt, no date).

---

[6] Yearly elementary school photos are also a good source for pictures of children.

12. GUESS WHO (children's groups). Each member, in turn, draws the name of another group member from a hat. He then proceeds to describe a recent event in the life of the individual whose name he has drawn. The description may be either written or oral (Schmidt, no date).

13. THE MICROLAB: Each group is divided into two subgroups for the purposes of this exercise. Subgroup composition will remain the same for the duration of the exercise. Subgroups will be labeled A and B. To begin the exercise, Group A will meet for five minutes responding to an assignment given them by the trainer (see below). While Group A is meeting in a small circle, Group B will sit outside that circle observing the members of Group A. Each member of Group A will have a feedback partner in Group B, this being determined by the schedule below. After Group A has met for five minutes, it will break for a two-minute feedback session during which each individual in Group A will receive feedback on his five minutes of behavior from his partner in Group B. When the feedback session has concluded, Group B meets in the small circle while Group A observes. When five minutes of activity is terminated, the two-minute feedback session again occurs, with individuals in Group A giving feedback to the same individuals in Group B who had initially given them feedback. At this point, the members change partners according to the schedule below. Always change partners at the point where the members have both given each other feedback. At this point, a round is completed. After the partners have changed, the process indicated above continues. Before beginning the first meeting, a timekeeper is selected in each subgroup. The subgroup on the outside times the inside group for the five- and two-minute periods.

Assignments. The trainer gives the assignment to each group, indicating that they shall follow the assignment until otherwise instructed. The microlab can be conducted on assignment or a structure of changing assignments at end of each round. The authors have tried: the following assignments (1) Become a group; (2) Make yourself known to each other; (3) Talk about your own subgroup; and (4) Talk about your feedback. If a series of assignments is used, it is suggested that one try assignments one through four in that order.

The use of programs, of course, is a matter of preference. Some writers, most notably Stoller (1969), feel that the casual or unexpected nature of group sessions is essential to the goals of the group. Therefore, interaction must be spontaneous and unprogrammed. Others, such as Schutz(1969) and Malamud and Machover (1965), regularly employ

Table 2.

Participant Structure.

Round	Subgroup	10 Participants					11 Participants						9 Participants					8 Participants				Round
I	A	1	2	3	4	5	1	2	3	4	5	x*	1	2	3	4	x	1	2	3	4	I
	B	6	7	8	9	10	6	7	8	9	10	11	5	6	7	8	9	5	6	7	8	
II	A	1	2	3	4	5	1	2	3	4	5	x*	1	2	3	4	x	1	2	3	4	II
	B	10	6	7	8	9	11	6	7	8	9	10	9	5	6	7	8	8	5	6	7	
III	A	1	2	3	4	5	1	2	3	4	5	x	1	2	3	4	x	1	2	3	4	III
	B	9	10	6	7	8	10	11	6	7	8	9	8	9	5	6	7	7	8	5	6	
IV	A	1	2	3	4	5	1	2	3	4	5	x	1	2	3	4	x	1	2	3	4	IV
	B	8	9	10	6	7	9	10	11	6	7	8	7	8	9	5	6	6	7	8	5	
V	A	1	2	3	4	5	1	2	3	4	5	x	1	2	3	4	x	1	2	3	4	V
	B	7	8	9	10	6	8	9	10	11	6	7	6	7	8	9	5	5	6	7	8	

Rounds VI through X are the same as I through V. *An x indicates that for that particular round, the person paired with x does not have a partner. This only occurs in odd-numbered groups.

program concepts. At any rate, they are listed here for those who would prefer to employ them in initial meetings.

SOME EARLY PITFALLS

Perhaps the most common error of the neophyte group counselor is his tendency to expect individuals who may be together for the first time to engage in deep work levels of confrontation and speculation. Thus a counselor who prematurely probes in early sessions may destroy a group.

If he is not employing a program, he should slowly attempt to teach members of the group the ways that they should interact for maximum benefit. Teaching, in the sense, is not a didactic-lecture mode of behaving, but rather one of modeling wherein group members learn to interact through observation of the counselor as model. For example, if honesty is desired, it can best be obtained by the counselor being honest; if feedback is important, the counselor can promote it by giving feedback (Stoller, 1969). In a group, the counselor who wants to promote feedback might respond as follows:

> TOM: I really felt Joe did a good job last week. I was impressed.
>
> JACK: Me, too.
>
> COUNSELOR: I can sense what you're saying. You're really pleased with Joe. His actions affected you very positively. I'm also pleased with you, Tom, and with Joel and Jack. I feel good that you were able to tell him that he is doing so well. Your warmness to them affects me very positively.

A second common pitfall for the counselor during early sessions is to fall into the authority trap or to become the expert who has the answers to all problems and concerns. In initial sessions, group members will often direct their verbalizations to the counselor in such terms as: "What do you think?" or "How can I get along better?" This dynamic is powerful and difficult to resist in that the role of group leader is "heady stuff" and requests or pseudo requests for help are difficult to turn down. In adult groups, at least, the structure is essentially one of a peer group in which everyone gradually serves in the leadership capacity that his skill and background permit. The counselor should, therefore, try to assist the group to move from unshared individual behavior to a climate of interdependence.

A third area that the counselor must try to avoid is his own tendency to react to certain group members in a way that might be labeled *countertransference* (Bach, 1954). The group, since it represents a small community, may well contain members who arouse powerful feelings of love or dislike in the counselor. If such feelings are not recognized, the counselor may lose his potential effectiveness by behaving in ways that retard group development and destroy rapport. Therefore, the counselor must be aware of his motives so that his effect on the group may be predetermined.

Group members, and sometimes counselors, will also frequently try to keep the anxiety level low by engaging in long conversations with another group member. For the counselor, this may satisfy his felt need to get something going or his perceived role as leader. Group members use this approach to relieve anxiety in that they need to be involved with only one other member at a time. Through the years, the authors have observed numerous one-to-one discussions in early group meetings. The counselor must be alert for such behaviors and look for ways to involve more members in the process. In subsequent sessions when rapport and cohesiveness have developed, he may point out such behaviors to the group (Johnson, 1963).

The inability to detect and deal with group themes is another factor that can cause disruption and lack of member commitment to the process. All groups have themes, and it is the job of the counselor to recognize them and explore them with members. For example, Muro and Denton (1968) identified such themes as self-perception, self-analysis, and relationships with parents in a study of college students in groups, while Bates (1966) found such themes as outwitting the adults, problem parents, and my brother the brat to be common in adolescent groups. The counselor can and often should use such themes in a tentative analysis to help the group members gain insight into their own behavior. For example:

> COUNSELOR: We've been talking for quite a while about our younger brothers and sisters and how they bug us. Is it possible that some of us feel that they get more attention from mom and dad than we do?

Even in early sessions, the search for a group theme is important even as members jump from topic to topic.

Finally, the counselor must be aware of pseudo conformity in the group. This phenomenon is most commonly expressed by members who ostensibly agree with or closely follow the directions of the counselor—as if they are afraid to disagree or challenge him on any measure. In so doing, they may well confront each other but react either passively or cooperatively with the counselor. In children's groups, this trait may be observed in those individuals who feel that they must ask the counselor to use certain play media, be extra polite with peers, and refrain from disruptive activities. In order for groups to develop therapeutic cohesiveness, this underlying hostility and passivity needs to be recognized, dealt with, and cleared away (Johnson, 1963). Thus sooner or later, the group leader will become a target or person they focus on and must be prepared to deal with this aggression if the group is to move to new levels of growth.

GROUP TENSIONS

Group tensions may be the result of either leader or member behaviors and are a part of group life. In fact, a certain amount of tension is mandatory for optimal group functioning.

The group leader is a potential source of tension in several ways. In early sessions, this may be a result of his behaving in ways that are unexpected by group members. This seems to be particularly true in school groups where children have a stereotyped view of the adult teacher and transfer his stereotype to the group leader. When the group leader does not respond in a stereotyped fashion to a member set up for support and information, his action serves to raise the tension level in the group. Thus at some time in the life of the group, the leader will become a target or focal point for the group. He must be prepared to deal with feelings of aggression, warmth, and indifference if the group is to move to new levels of growth. Bach notes that group tension always rises when the leader refuses to lead actively since the group encounters difficulty in maintaining its equilibrium in socially expected (leader-active, member-passive) ways. Thus the tendency of the beginning group to seek out the counselor for advice and support will result in a degree of group tension if the counselor behaves contrary to member expectations.

Tensions may also be caused by the leader operating unwillingly within the context of extremes of some philosophical position. For example, the counselor who is too client centered, too directive, or too group centered, emotional tension may run high (Bach, 1954). Groups which do not get the leadership they seek thus turn to other group members to fill the role of the leader. The authors feel that the counselor does have responsibility for group leadership, of helping the group find ways to move toward greater growth, and that complete passivity is inappropriate for the group leader. On the other hand, complete dominance of the group may be equally poor in that the therapeutic power inherent in the group is seriously curtailed by one-man leadership. Counseling groups function best when the leader operates as a balance wheel—he is active when activity is necessary, he is keenly observant and silent when the purposes of the group are best served through the leadership of a member. For example, there may be times when the group or at least some group members are directing their verbalizations to a scapegoat. It is entirely appropriate in such cases for the counselor to ask: "What are we doing now?" or "What seems to be happening in the group?" or "Is it possible we have some reason for directing all of our talk toward John?" At other times, the counselor will not want to intervene at all. When a given group member is speculating about his impact on another, the counselor should observe, note the interaction but remain silent. We refer to situations such as the following:

> JOE: John, every time I say something to you, you seem to frown. Maybe I'm wrong, but I have a feeling you never agree with me! What do you object to—what I say or the way I say it?
> JOHN: It's just that every time you speak you bombard the whole group. I guess you're right; I get a little annoyed with you.

In this case, the first speaker, Joe, is speculating about his impact on John. He is actively seeking self-understanding. John has provided direct feedback. The counselor should note the interaction, perhaps provide a tentative interpretation or clarification at a later time in the life of the group, but for the moment he should not interrupt the process.

Bach has also noted that tension and anxiety in the group can arise from the nature and quality of subgrouping, which in turn creates isolates. Since it is not uncommon for group members to be socially attracted to one another, it is not uncommon for group members to isolate one or several members. A close study of communication patterns in the group is an effective way for the counselor to determine who holds rank and prestige in the group and who does not. However, the group members themselves will eventually discover the subgroups of the popular and less popular and in one way or another let their feelings be known. In a recent group led by one of the authors, the female members began to complain that the men were dominating the group. This observation created a good deal of group tension and for a period of time threatened the cohesion and functioning of the group. In this particular case, the group size—fifteen—was overly large and rather poorly balanced in terms of passive and aggressive members. It was not until the group leader recognized the subgrouping patterns and brought them to the group's attention that members were able to cope with the subgroups in an open manner.

Any counselor who has operated under the open-group point of view has experienced the phenomenon of new-member tension. Bach vividly describes the entrance of the newcomer into the group:

> An established group may be likened to a fairly calm lake. The introduction of a newcomer or newcomers may be likened to the dropping of a stone into the water. It is interesting to observe in more detail how the splash that the newcomer makes gradually calms down, how he is integrated into the group structure. [Bach, 1954, p. 386]

Because of prior interaction, group cohesiveness and a sense of trust, the newcomer to a group disrupts an established culture. Like others in the group, he will seek an identity within the structure. Behaviorally, he may be shy, aggressive, dominating, friendly, or in whatever way he feels that he can obtain desired group identity. Established members may isolate him, attack him, but generally they will accept him in the initial role he wishes to portray. Gradually, however, through group interaction, the member will become a part of the group structure through his natural, spontaneous behavior. In relatively short-term counseling groups of a verbal nature in contrast to those working with play media, the newcomer can represent a threat to the group, especially if the group does not continue long enough to incorporate him into the fold.

RULES IN GROUP COUNSELING

Group counselors and therapists differ with respect to the use of rules (or perhaps limits) in the group situation. Johnson (1963) outlines a procedure that he likes for a group contract wherein the goals and plans for treatment are discussed; Bach (1954) presents prospective group members with a typewritten sheet that defines certain boundaries; and Luchins (1964) advocates that rules be presented either during initial sessions or during the life of the group so long as they are not seen as limitations of behavior. Others, such as Gibb (1969) and Stoller (1969), suggest that boundaries and rules are restrictive of the creativity and growth potential of the group and are dysfunctional in terms of group-learning experiences.

Gendlin in assuming the position of Bach, Luchins, and others has developed what he describes as an informal constitution that is a useful guide for those counselors who feel a need to impose a degree of structure in the process. It is presented in abbreviated form here:

1. Everyone who is here belongs here—just because he is here and for no other reason.
2. For each person what is true is determined by what is in him, what he directly feels and finds making sense in himself, the way he lives inside himself.
3. Our first purpose is to make contact with each other. Everything else we might want or need comes second.
4. We try to be as honest as possible and to express ourselves as we really are and really feel—just as much as we can.
5. We listen for the person inside living and feeling.
6. Everyone is listened to.
7. The group leader is responsible for two things only: he protects the belonging of every member, and he protects their being heard if this is getting lost.
8. Realism—if things are a certain way, we do not pretend they are not that way.
9. What we say here is confidential. That means no one will repeat anything said here outside the group unless it concerns only himself. This applies not just to obviously private things but to everything. After all, if the individual concerned wants others to know something, he can always tell them himself.
10. Decisions made by the group need everyone taking part in some way.
11. New members become members because they walk in. Whoever is here belongs. We look at a new person with a feeling of "I want to sense who you are" (perhaps we say something of the sort). We cannot tell new people what we do and engage them. [Gendlin and Beebe, 1968]

In a similar vein, Demos presents a set of rules that he provides for members just prior to their involvement in marathon (24–72 continuous hours of contact) groups:

1. Everyone will remain together in the same place during the 24-hour group experience. However, free movement within the group is encouraged.
2. Subgrouping is not allowed during the marathon. Full involvement with the total group is encouraged.
3. Decisions regarding such things as meals, exercise, napping, etc. are made in accordance with the wishes of the group.
4. No alcohol or drugs are allowed during the 24-hour session.
5. The group leaders consider themselves full participants in the marathon and are bound by the same rules as everyone else. (It is desirable to have two group leaders, if possible.)
6. All expressions of physical violence are outlawed. Full license is given to verbal expression of feelings, however.
7. Everyone has the full responsibility of involving himself in the group. There are no observers—only active participants.
8. Since this is a basic encounter group, the here and now or present is stressed and discussion of past personal life experiences other than brief references are considered irrelevant.
9. While nothing is sacred within the group, the information expressed during the marathon is confidential.
10. You are responsible for yourself. What you get out of the group depends upon the extent to which you are transparent, open, and candid with the other participants. The group offers you an opportunity to "be the self which you truly are." [Demos, 1969, p. 4]

Some structure may also be necessary in children's groups. Ginott feels that limits are necessary to direct catharsis into symbolic channels, to enable the therapist to maintain attitudes of acceptance and regard for the child, to insure the physical safety of children, to strengthen ego controls, and for considerations of law, ethics, social acceptability, and budgetary considerations (Ginott, 1961, pp. 103–105). With this rationale, he employs time limits, limits against physical attacks on the therapist and other children, and limits against the removal of toys from the playroom.

The authors also feel that some limits (structure) may be helpful with children in verbal group counseling. Such rules should not be presented as ironclad do's and don'ts but rather as general guides. Generally, the authors have found it most effective to present a set of rules to children prior to the first meeting or at an early point during the initial session. In so doing, the counselor might say: "In other groups like this, some boys and girls have found it helpful to decide how we will do things here —you know, sort of make a few rules so that everybody will get more out of our meetings. Does anyone have any suggestions as to how we should do things in the group?"

The counselor should then allow time for the group to discuss and contribute any suggestions that they might have for the group. He should note on a little card what each has said and summarize the suggestions of the group members. After the group has completed this process, the counselor might say: "I have a list of some things that other boys and girls have also found useful in groups like these. I have them with me today since I thought you might be interested in them. Would you like to see them and talk about them for a little while?"

If the group agrees, the counselor should provide each child with a mimeographed list of ground rules. A sample of one list is presented here:

> *Rules for our Group*
> 1. What we say here is just among us. We say what we want in the group, but we do not repeat what we say here outside our group.
> 2. We listen to everyone. Everybody has a right to say what he thinks.
> 3. We will try to trust each other so that we can work together better.
> 4. We should talk when we have something to say. It's help-ful to find out that we may not be alone in the way we feel.
> 5. We try to help each other not hurt each other.
> 6. We don't have to always agree on what we say—we're here to explore together.

As can be seen from a review of the rules suggested by Demos, Gendlin, and the authors, those who advocate the use of regulations as a premeeting device do not intend to hinder interaction and cohesive-ness, but instead attempt to foster it. There is little research available to support the use or absence of any set of rules. Suffice for the counselor to note that some practitioners do utilize rules for certain purposes. As a general rule of thumb, rules become more useful as the counselor begins to work with younger children. Ohlsen (no date) has noted that children's groups generally need more structure, and Ginott (1961) states that limits (rules) help tie the process into reality. Again, it is not a question, in the authors' opinions, of whether or not to use rules but rather a decision of how rules or lack of them will affect the purposes of the group.

GROUP DISORGANIZATION

Anyone who counsels groups over a period of time will experience the disorganized session. In some cases, the group members may ramble from topic to topic, in others they may appear preoccupied, and in still others they may utilize group time to clown and joke. Disorganization can occur at any time in group life and generally it is short lived. Luchins (1964) recommends that the counselor might ask if the total group is aware of the disorganization or is it only the counselor? What does it mean to the counselor and the group? The counselor can, if he chooses, ask the group about such behavior in terms of possible hidden meanings. For example, he might say: "We've been doing a lot of laughing today. Is it possible that we really have some other things we'd like to discuss and are having trouble getting started?" By calling the group's attention to their behavior and alluding to the possible reasons for the laughter, the counselor may open avenues that will lead members into more productive discussions.

The counselor can, of course, ignore disorganization or perhaps call it to the attention of the group. If video equipment is utilized for the purposes of focused feedback, the counselor may want to replay certain segments of the tape (audio or video) to bring the group's attention to the problem. Or, as Luchins suggests, the counselor may simply cut in, note that the group has wandered off the point, describe the behavioral level on which the group is operating and contrast it with what they should be doing (p. 138). The authors agree with Luchins, however, in his view that an occasional disorganized session is not a serious matter since there are times when groups simply do not want a focal point. When this occurs, the counselor may well decide to go with the superficial flow of the group.

GROUP DEVELOPMENT

Hill (no date) has noted that from an extensive search of the literature on small groups, he was able to discover over one hundred separate theories of group development. He further contends that since group development is closely related to such factors as leader style and group composition that all groups do not go through the same process of development. Therefore, it would seem that general theory of group development that would apply to all groups is not possible at this time. However, when one reviews some of the theoretical models proposed for the development of groups, he discovers that there are common trends if not identical elements in the life of a counseling or a therapy group. While a review of all theories of group development is beyond the scope of this book, the authors have selected some of the thoughts of Martin and Hill (1957), Geller (1962), Rogers (1969), and Bonney (1969). The first three were selected because they provide some elements of group-therapy development and the latter because it has been formulated from a counseling base. None of them is presented in its entirety since the authors agree with Hill that a specific theory is not possible at this time. We hope to describe in general terms what may happen in group therapy, encounter groups, and group counseling. While any given group may deviate from the process described here, the authors feel that this general guide, based upon personal experience and the thinking of several scholars in the group field, is a representative guide to movement in the group. We have labeled the various stages *phases,* and while we would seem to be presenting them as separate and isolated stages through which all groups go, such is obviously not the case. Each phase can and does overlap; some groups may seem to skip one or more of these phases, and the time each group spends in a certain period of development may quite likely vary. Weekend encounter groups, for example, quite probably develop much more rapidly than once-a-week counseling sessions, while some therapy groups take months to reach a certain work level. With these cautions in mind, what can the counselor expect as he works with a group?

PHASE I: THE PSEUDO GROUP

There is consensual agreement that the initial phase of group development is one characterized by minimal group involvement. The individual does not have a sense of we-ness or groupness, and the other group members though physically present do not represent important individuals in his life. His behavior, therefore, is a manifestation of his perception of the group situation. There is an element of social isolation wherein members estimate each other's potential and gain some advantage in the group. The group leader is the central figure and often the target of group hostility, even though attempts are made to become dependent upon him. Members are likely to be uncertain, hesitant, and anxious, much of which is an attempt to provide structure. Silences are common, and while members seek support and approval, there is much milling-around behavior and resistance to personal exploration.

Groups move through periods of transition when they become dissatisfied with the present level of functioning. When members tire of the superficial levels of Phase-I development, they move sometimes rapidly, sometimes gradually, into Phase II. Bonney writes that the transition is motivated because the group begins to realize that it is not pursuing the agreed-upon goals, while Martin and Hill write that members' statements seem to trigger reactions in a chain-like sequence. Verbalizations, however, still tend to be personal, a thought shared by Rogers who has noted that the initial feelings that seem to emerge from the group are expressed in terms of past happenings although they may be those that are currently part of the individual. Geller however writes that the transition is assisted by the development of cohesion.

PHASE II: THE NEGATIVE–AGGRESSIVE STAGE

Both Rogers and Geller agree that the first significant feelings that may emerge are likely to be negative and aggressive. Geller in describing this stage notes that the individuals seek to set rules, goals, and provide structure. He uses the terms sarcastic, critical interpretations, member-to-member accusations, and petty anger to describe the group. Rogers simply notes that the feelings are likely to be negative, and Bonney characterizes the group movement as tentative and with conflict in this experimentation phase. Martin and Hill in their six-stage description of group development note that individuals are reacting in terms of fixed stereotypes rather than viewing other members as individuals in their own right. The group leader is frequently stereotyped in a negative fashion. Rogers writes that the expression of negative feelings is a way for members to test the group, to see if the members can be trusted. Once the group discovers that negative feelings may be stated openly and without undue harm, more significant levels of functioning are possible.

The expression of negative feelings thus provides a vehicle into a third phase of group operation, described by Martin and Hill as an exploration of interpersonal potential, by Geller as a regressive period, and by Bonney as an operational stage. Bonney notes, however, that movement from level two to level three may be accompanied by regressive behaviors and that those conflicts must be resolved if further group work is to be achieved.

PHASE III: INTRAPERSONAL FUNCTIONING

For perhaps the first time, all members are functioning as a task level. The individual comes to realize that the group is in part his, and his expressions of feeling become immediate. These feelings are sometimes positive or sometimes negative, but the growing cohesiveness in the group allows the group to function in a healing capacity. There is evidence of self-acceptance and the beginning of change. The interaction is likely to be characterized by the exploration of individual personalities and is accompanied by much emotion. Members may tend to flatter each other, reject each other, and perhaps move into a number of subgroups.

While this does not constitute the final phase of group life, many groups do not progress much beyond this point (Martin and Hill, 1957). As previously noted, the pairings or subgroupings may be common. The early and perhaps exciting aspects of group life begin to wear thin as the members repeat earlier observations. The repetition may be a vehicle for a new mode of operation. In Martin and Hill's 1957 six-stage description of development, they note that the group leader may have to point the new area of relationships. In fact, the forming of subgroups and the awareness of these within the group constitute a separation of group development for Hill and Martin who also note that a group observer may be helpful to point these patterns out to the group.

PHASE IV: THE CREATIVE ENCOUNTER

Both Bonney and Geller stress that at this point in group life there is open and direct communication. A creative use of ideas is now possible, and leader dependency is minimal. Rogers writes that the group at this point would become impatient with façades as the group moves toward a deeper encounter. Individuals receive both positive and negative feedback and member-to-member confrontation is common.

In the authors' experience, this four-phase process, as described by Bonney and Geller, is a fairly accurate expectation level for most counseling groups. While Rogers has described group process in a series of steps rather than through a complete theory, his conceptualization of the development of groups is a highly accurate portrayal of group process. While many groups can and do deviate from the outline presented here, the reader can be reasonably assured that in general at least there is a fairly ordered sequence in the life of a counseling group.

DEVELOPMENT IN CHILDREN'S GROUPS

Ginott (1961) writes that the process of play therapy has never been subjected to a large-scale investigation, and the studies that have been completed are unfortunately based on small samples. At the present time, to the knowledge of the authors, no investigation has been made of the process in counseling groups, especially in school situations. As a result, our knowledge of group process with children is minimal. Nevertheless, the work of Moustakas provides at least some hypotheses if not complete data of what the counselor who works with normal children might expect:

> *First Level.*   Undifferentiated and ill-defined positive and negative feelings prominent.
> *Second Level.*   Emergence of focused positive and negative feelings in response to parents, siblings, and other people.
> *Third Level.*   Ambivalent feelings distinctive.
> *Fourth Level.*   Negative feelings in primary focus, sometimes specific.
> *Fifth Level.*   Ambivalent positive and negative attitudes prominent.
> *Sixth Level.*   Positive feelings predominate and appear as organized attitudes. Negative attitudes also present. Both positive and negative attitudes differentiated, focused, direct, and generally in line with reality.   [Moustakas, 1955, p. 79]

Much work needs to be done in the area of group development. The lack of available, empirically derived data is especially apparent in children's groups. The authors feel that the theories reviewed here should be considered trends in group life rather than formal theories. What is important for the counselor however is the knowledge that groups develop over time (even marathons). He must be sensitive to those points in group life wherein members seem to be seeking new and perhaps deeper levels of personal exploration. Group development is a process, and as the word implies, the group moves—sometimes slowly and haltingly—toward its goals. The art of the group counselor, combined with his careful observations of movement in the group, is essential for promoting maximum interpersonal experiences.

SUMMARY

One of the most difficult tasks for the neophyte group counselor is that of starting a group. While some group counselors prefer to have groups develop along natural or unstructured lines, others feel that programs or warm-ups are effective tools to get groups started. Some suggested warm-up exercises fall under the following headings: (1) what I'm afraid of; (2) expectations; (3) partner introductions; (4) drawing myself; (5) who I am; (6) stimulus films; (7) the Depth-Unfoldment Experience (Otto, 1967); (8) why I'm here; (9) what I worry about; (10) picture shuffle; (11) circular approaches; (12) guess who; and (13) the microlab.

Some early pitfalls in the life of a counseling group include the counselor's unrealistic expectations from members; his tendency to remain as an authority; countertransference problems; inability to deal with group themes; long unproductive conversations; and pseudo conformity among group members.

All group work involves a certain amount of tension, some of which is leader evoked and some that arises from the very nature of the group process. An understanding of the causes of group tension is vital to the group counselor.

Some counselors have found it useful to provide specific rules or codes of expected group behavior to prospective members of groups. Most experienced counselors would agree that some structures or limits are necessary with children's groups, although not all would agree with the concept of providing the children with a prepared list of rules. Gendlin and Beebe (1968) and Demos (1969), however, have prepared specific lists for adult group sessions. At times, however, in spite of rules and effective skills, many groups will seem disorganized at least temporarily.

Most experienced counselors agree that groups move through certain developmental phases, yet a specific theory of group development is probably not possible at this time. The authors have, however, attempted to provide the reader with a tentative outline of group development based on some of the concepts of Martin and Hill (1957), Geller (1962), Rogers (1969), and Bonney (1969). The four-stage outline is described as the (1) pseudo group; (2) negative–aggressive stage; (3) interpersonal functioning; and (4) the creative encounter. Counselors who work in elementary schools should also be aware of the developmental phases of children's groups as suggested by Moustakas (1955).

REFERENCES

BACH, GEORGE R. *Intensive Group Psychotherapy.* New York: The Ronald Press Company, 1954.

BATES, MARILYN. "Themes in Group Counseling with Adolescents," *Personnel and Guidance Journal,* Vol. 44 (1966), pp. 568–75.

BONNEY, W. C. "Group Counseling and Developmental Process," in *Theories and Methods of Group Counseling in the Schools* (ed. GEORGE M. GAZDA). Springfield, Ill.: Charles C Thomas, Publisher, 1969.

DEMOS, G. D. *Marathon Therapy: A New Psychotherapeutic Modality.* Berkeley, Calif.: Explorations Institute, Vol. 2, No. 4 (1969).

EXPLORATIONS INSTITUTE. *The Group Leader's Workshop: Exercises.* Berkeley, Calif.: 1969.

FINNEY, B. C. *The Group Leaders' Workshop: Peer Groups.* Berkeley, Calif.: Explorations Institute, 1969.

GELLER, J. J. "Parataxic Distortions in the Initial Stages of Group Relationships," *International Journal of Group Psychotherapy,* Vol. 12, No. 1 (1962), pp. 27–34.

GENDLIN, EUGENE, and BEEBE, JOHN. "Experiential Groups: Instructions for Groups" in *Innovations to Group Psychotherapy* (ed. GEORGE GAZDA), pp. 192–206, Springfield, Ill.: Charles C Thomas Publishers, (1968).

GIBB, JACK R., and GIBB, LORRAINE, M. "Role Freedom in a TORI Group," in *Encounter* (ed. A. BURTON). San Francisco, Calif.: Jossey-Bass, Inc., Publishers, 1969.

GINOTT, H. G. *Group Psychotherapy with Children.* New York: McGraw-Hill Book Company, 1961.

HILL, WILLIAM F. *Group Development.* Filmed lecture. Los Angeles, Calif.: University of Southern California, Youth Studies Center (no date).

JOHNSON, J. A. *Group Therapy: A Practical Approach.* New York: McGraw-Hill Book Company, 1963.

LUCHINS, A. S. *Group Therapy: A Guide.* New York: Random House, Inc., 1964.

MAHLER, C. A. *Group Counseling in the Schools.* New York: Houghton Mifflin Company, 1969.

MALAMUD, D. I., and MACHOVER, S. *Toward Self-understanding: Group Techniques in Self-Confrontation.* Springfield, Ill.: Charles C Thomas, Publisher, 1965.

MARTIN, E. A., and HILL, WILLIAM F. "Toward a Theory of Group Development," *International Journal of Group Psychotherapy,* Vol. 1 (1957), pp. 20–30.

MOUSTAKAS, C. E. "Emotional Adjustment and the Play-Therapy Process," *Journal of Genetic Psychology,* Vol. 86 (1955), pp. 79–99.

MUNZER, JEAN. "The Effect on Analytic Therapy Groups of the Experimental Introduction of Special Warm-Up Procedures during the First Five Sessions," *International Journal of Group Psychotherapy,* Vol. 14, No. 1 (1964), pp. 60–71.

MURO, JAMES J., and DENTON, GORDON M. "Expressed Concerns of Teacher-Education Students· in Counseling Groups," *Journal of Teacher Education,* Vol. 19 (1968), pp. 465–70.

OHLSEN, MERLE M. "Counseling Children in Groups," in *Elementary School Guidance in Illinois* (ed. RAY PAGE). Springfield, Ill.: (no date).

OTTO, HERBERT A. *Group Methods Designed to Actualize Human Potential: A Handbook.* Chicago: Stone-Brandel Center, 1967.

ROGERS, CARL R. "The T-Group Comes of Age," *Psychology Today,* Vol. 3 (1969), pp. 27–31, 58, 60, 61.

SCHMIDT, W. I. "Group Guidance in the Elementary School," in *Elementary School Guidance in Illinois* (ed. R. PAGE). Springfield, Ill.: Office of the Superintendent of Public Instruction (no date).

SCHUTZ, WILLIAM C. *Joy: Expanding Human Awareness.* New York: Grove Press, Inc., 1969.

STOLLER, F. H. "A Stage for Trust," in *Encounter* (ed. A. BURTON). San Francisco, Calif.: Jossey-Bass, Inc., Publishers, 1969.

CHAPTER 8

Special Problems in Groups

EVEN EXPERIENCED group counselors encounter occasional difficulty in attempting to comprehend the numerous situations that occur in the life of a group. Why, for example, does a group seem to interact well one week and fall silent the next? Why do certain members remain in the group and still seem to resist the attempts of others to help them? Why does John constantly monopolize the conversation? Why is attendance dropping off? In reality, most of the problem areas suggested in these questions do not occur in isolation. Absences from a group meeting as well as member tardiness for the start of a session for example could be resistance to the process. So, too, could group silence be considered resistance, but it may also be the result of an emotion that has overwhelmed the members. Therefore, while certain group problems will be treated in isolation in this chapter, the reader should bear in mind that they are presented this way for organizational purposes only.

SILENCE IN THE GROUP

The silent group or perhaps the silent group member can be a frustrating experience for counselors. The authors can recall experiences in their training wherein the apparent success of the counselor seemed to correlate directly with how long he was able to hold a silence. Anything over two minutes was considered remarkable, and there were unconfirmed reports that student X at Hallowed University had lasted for over thirty-five minutes! In reality, a silence that is warm and accepting is a way of pacing an interview, of giving an individual time to think, and of allowing him to bring forth that material that is important to him. For the neophyte counselor, the ability to utilize silence in a constructive manner is a learned clinical skill. When appropriately utilized, it is a significant part of counseling, either with individuals or in groups.

Hinkley and Herman write that silence in the group may have a number of meanings:[7]

1. Silence may be a deliberate holding back of self in order to punish the therapist or group members.
2. Silence often is the way in which patients run away from that turmoil: it is an escape from the reality of conflict.
3. Not infrequently, silence is the shelter behind which patients do conduct a dream life.
4. Sometimes silence indicates suspicions and fears of the reactions of others in the group.
5. Silence can mean a particular patient's inability to formulate his reactions because he never acquired the habit of articulating strong feelings.
6. Silence may conceal ambivalence.
7. Silence may have positive aspects, often overlooked by the therapist. Silence may be a means to an end. In this privacy, patients remove outward defenses and cast about for satisfying and acceptable substitutes. [Hinkley and Herman, 1951, pp. 76–78]

Johnson (1963) writes that silence in groups is due to the anxiety that members experience in meetings and occurs most frequently in the initial stages of group life (See Chapter 7 section on group development). In his view, silence may also result from a fear of discussing something that may be displeasing to the leader, or hostility toward him or one of the members.

Lifton in discussing group-centered counseling writes that silence in a group signifies a need for group members to think through what they wish to say. In his view, this type of silence reflects group communication of the need to change behaviors. Silence, however, can also communicate shock (following a hostile outburst) or support (Lifton, 1968, pp. 240–41).

In counseling groups, silence can occur for other reasons. For example, if orientation to the group has been poor, some members may be surprised by the personal mode of interactions and remain quiet. Others feel that their contributions may not be worthwhile and fear that

---

[7]NOTE: Since they discuss therapy groups, the term *patient* is used.

ridicule will follow their verbalizations. Still others find that some sub-groups dominate the discussion and that they have difficulty getting in even when they try. In children's groups, the counselor's clumsy at-tempts to set limits are often followed by periods of silence.

There is no single way for the group leader to handle silence nor should he feel that he must always keep the group moving. Luchins suggests that the counselor should:

1. Ask himself why he is disturbed by the silence.
2. Is the group disturbed by it?
3. Is the member (or are the members) really not participat-ing because he (they) is silent?
4. What does the silent member mean to the group?
5. Are there nonverbal activities that may be dealt with? [Luchins, 1964, pp. 141–42]

Hinkley and Herman (1951) suggest that silence of individual mem-bers may be handled by a friendly intervention directed to the group member. When the entire group becomes silent, they recommend sup-port and clarification from the counselor with responses like: "Silence is sometimes uncomfortable? Can you think of why this happens?"

Johnson however states that a group should not be allowed to remain silent for more than a few moments. The group leader, in his thinking, has several possible techniques open to him with regard to silence: (1) he can ask the group about their thoughts on silence—they may or may not deal with it; (2) he could ask what thoughts are being experienced about the silence; or (3) he can change the subject to one that is more comfortable. It is important for the group leader to assess properly the anxiety level of the group prior to making an intervention. He further suggests that leaders ask questions such as: "We have a couple of mem-bers who are not talking. Do you have any idea why they are quiet?" Silent members should never be mentioned by name and observations should be general and directed toward the group (Johnson, 1963, pp. 167, 169, 170).

Silence is generally not a problem in children's groups. In fact, the counselor may encounter difficulty if he, for some reasons, would find a silence desirable. His main job may be one of keeping the children from all verbalizing at once. When play media are utilized, there may be times when all four or five children become busily engrossed in a toy, and the group becomes silent. After a while, the children will sense this and perhaps look to the counselor for an explanation. In such instances, the counselor should simply smile or nod to convey to the child that the silence is acceptable.

Because of the rapid-fire tempo of some group sessions, the counselor may lose some of the nonverbal cues that could be indicators for counselor or group interpretation. A technique suggested by Pile has been useful to the authors in their attempts to determine the thoughts of silent and talkative members alike. After each session, members are requested to complete a three-by-five index card summarizing the main things that occurred during the session. The procedure accomplishes five purposes:

1. The thoughts of nonverbal participants can be determined.
2. The amount of content and its parts which seemed important to the clients and the counselor can be determined.
3. The degree and kind of individual selectivity in reporting content are revealed.
4. An indication of the amount of material assimilated by the group is available.
5. Intrapersonal perceptions are revealed. [Pile, 1958, pp. 10–11]

The cards may then be utilized as a continuing record of group proceedings. In addition, they provide the counselor with changes in member perceptions and are an indication of group development (Muro, 1968).

Of interest to the counselor is Lifton's (1968) well-conceptualized discussion of how the silent client communicates. After listing all the nonverbal cues he could think of, he found that such cues could be categorized under three labels: (1) cues that reflected avoidance behavior such as lack of eye contact, a mouthful of gum or chewing a pencil, or the movement of an individual's chair away from the group; (2) cues that reflected emotions of pleasure or anger including a smile, frown, clenched fist, and upraised hand; and (3) cues that had symbolic meaning within a cultural context such as the girl who flutters an eyelash or playfully rolls her eyes. Lifton suggests that since the major role of the group leader is to facilitate group awareness, he might respond to such nonverbal cues with statements like: "John and Mary have said they favor the plan, but Jim and Betty seem to be shaking their heads in disagreement" (Lifton, 1968, pp. 240–44).

TALK AS AN AVOIDANCE

The group leader who feels pressured to keep the group going may well be delighted with the member who takes up group slack with a long and sometimes highly personal discussion of himself or a pet topic. While with some members this may represent an approach to seeking group help, it may be at best a rather indirect way of indicating a need. Even when an individual is revealing what appears to be significant aspects of self, he may be either *consciously or unconsciously trying to control the group's potential impact on him.* As long as an individual is speaking, he holds the group's attention, prevents interaction, and minimizes the probability of being confronted by another group member. Since the discussion is personal, he runs little risk of evoking negative comments from others; since he may be speaking with considerable affect, he can probably elicit feelings of support, advice, and positive feelings from others. In a way, this behavior is similar to that of a child who fears some unpleasant task (going to school), so he discusses a hurt or illness designed to evoke sympathy from his parents and siblings. The child, in a sense, is setting up the adult for the desired emotional response. This same child is likely to emerge in later years in the person of an adult member of a counseling group.

The counselor will also encounter other individuals who employ talk as an avoidance–resistance device. In addition to the emotional set up, the counselor will encounter Mr. Topic or the individual who searches for topics to discuss. He is characterized by such statements as: "What about the war?" or "Do you think the President is doing a good job?" When such nongroup topics are discussed, the individual can avoid personal interaction.

In graduate student groups, Mr. Co-counselor is a frequent member. This is the individual who tends to follow the counselor's cues, repeat his interpretations, and perform a host of other group chores. While it is desirable as the group develops to share leadership, Mr. Co-counselor uses leadership techniques to minimize his involvement. Mr. Co-counselor also may appear as Junior Freud or King Solomon. Other group members avoid personal involvement through joking, acting as a protector of others, and functioning as housekeeper—the individual who goes after missing chairs, opens windows, etc.

The counselor must be alert to these avoidance techniques, and gradually the group members will also understand the goals of such behavior. The leader's role with the talking avoider should be one of helping him understand why his overt behavior is really in opposition to his ultimate goals. Like other members, he most probably desires feedback and help, and he wants to become liked and accepted in the group. Yet, he may fear the group, its leader, and may be overly anxious that verbalizations directed toward him will be more negative than he can bear. When rapport has developed and group cohesion exists, the counselor might note that: "Some of us seem to want to talk all the time

—almost as if we were a little hesitant to come into the group. Does anyone have any thoughts about this?" or "We joined this group to get a better idea of how we effect each other. I wonder if everybody is really trying to do that." As with the silent member, the group-oriented question is preferable at least as a starting point with those who use talk as an avoidance device.

THE CHRONIC MONOPOLIST

Like the individual who uses talk as an avoidance device, the chronic monopolist is the type of person who must hold the group's attention and becomes anxious when the focal point shifts to another member (Warters, 1960, p. 176). Bach (1954) feels that individuals who attempt to monopolize the group proceedings are employing in reality a defensive overreaction to the fear of attack or isolation from the group. In general, most individuals who work with groups are in agreement that the individual who persists in remaining as the center of the group's attention should not be a part of a counseling group. Obviously, it is far better for the counselor to know beforehand that an individual tends to draw the group's attention to him constantly and with such knowledge he may exclude the individual from the group. Warters (1960) suggests that an individual who is monopolizing an ongoing group be offered individual counseling until he can function more appropriately in groups.

ACTING-OUT OR HOSTILE BEHAVIOR

The acting-out group member is perhaps as much of a concern to the beginning counselor as the discipline problem is to the student teacher. Often the behavior erupts suddenly and catches both the leader and the group unaware. For example, a graduate student in a group-counseling practicum supervised by one of the authors tells how one individual tested his freedom atmosphere by jumping up on the table and asking the counselor how he liked that little show? Johnson (1963) writes that acting-out behavior can be observed in patterns of lateness, absences, alcoholic indulgences, and overt forms of hostility between members (pp. 171–72). Luchins (1964) feels that in some cases the disruptive patient can actually be a benefit to the group in that the members tend to bring certain problems to the conscious attention of the other members (p. 139).

Johnson notes that a frequent cause of acting-out behavior is the negative feelings individuals have toward the group leader that cannot be expressed. It is important, therefore, that the counselor not react defensively to the hostility of the members since this encourages further acting out.

No single solution is available for dealing with disruptive persons, although Luchins (1964) advocates that the group leader discuss the disturbing individual's role in the group and perhaps what the other members think of him. Luchins also suggests that the extremely agitated person be allowed to take a break until the session is over and engage in a conference with the group leader following the session.

Johnson (1963) finds that the design and structure of the group also provide certain safeguards and limitations against acting-out behavior and that the leader's skill in helping the group recognize the work through hostile feelings is a significant part of the group process.

Some child therapists (and counselors) have found that constructive use can be made of disruptive behavior through the techniques of limit setting. Ginott (1961) advocates that the leader in a helpful and nonpunitive way can utilize the limits to promote growth. He suggests the following sequence: (1) recognize the child's feelings or wishes and help him to verbalize them as they are; (2) clearly state the limit on a specific act; (3) point out other channels through which the feelings or wishes can be expressed; and (4) help the child to bring out the feelings of resentment that are bound to arise when restrictions are revoked (p. 107).

An example of this in a counseling session might be:

CHILD: I'm going to throw this clay at you.
COUNSELOR: Um-hum—You really want to hit me, but you know people are not to be hit. Maybe you would like to throw the clay at that toy soldier.
CHILD: I want to hit somebody.
COUNSELOR: Yes, you wish you could hit me—you would like it better if we could hit people.

Such incidents can and do happen in sessions where play media are utilized, and aggressive children feel the need to attack physically either the counselor or one of the other children. Ginott's suggested sequence is a very effective way to deal with aggression in young children.

SCAPEGOATING

In some counseling groups, an individual member is sometimes consciously or unconsciously identified as the individual who personifies all that is or could be wrong inside or outside the group. Thus when someone seems to be blocking the process, when the group wants to identify the too-silent or too-disruptive member, one or perhaps two individuals may be singled out to bear the brunt of the group's animosity. Such individuals become the group scapegoats.

The use of a scapegoat is a convenient way for the group members to reduce individual and group anxiety by making the assumption that one or a few individuals are the sole possessors of undesirable traits, mannerisms, or behaviors. Thus an ongoing member may accuse the scapegoat of excessive anger or the nonparticipant may find that he participates more than the scapegoat. It is an interesting group phenomenon to notice how some individuals will attempt to solve their own problems through the use of elaborate advice and direction to the scapegoat. "Harry, if you would keep your voice down a little, we would hear you better" is an example of a loud individual solving a problem for another. Another way in which scapegoating is used is through the mechanisms of displacement. Individuals direct statements that may have negative consequences toward a scapegoat instead of toward the actual target of their displeasure (Whitaker and Lieberman, 1964, pp. 288–89).

Since scapegoating is obviously a growth-hindering aspect of group life, the counselor must be alert for signs of an individual being singled out for this purpose. A question like: "We all seem to be blaming one or two individuals for our failure to progress—I wonder what is happening in the group?" will generally serve to call the group's attention to what is happening. If this fails, the counselor may have to make a more direct interpretation or confrontation: "Mary, you're saying that Joe really bugs you, but is it possible that much of what you find annoying comes from John?"

ABSENCES

Although absences from group sessions can occur because of reality situations (illness), they may also be the result of increased group anxiety (Johnson, 1963). As a group develops and members sense that subsequent interaction may penetrate into areas that are frightening or potentially harmful, some may become absent. Other factors, of course, can and do influence absenteeism. Members may not be meeting individual needs, the size of the group may be too large to insure participation, or subgrouping and insensitive group leadership may have prevented cohesion. On college campuses where counselors work with normals, the demands on student time are excessive; hence, the group may rank low on the student's list of priorities. For the group to be successful, it must be a significant aspect of the student's life—it must not be a casual discussion that may either be attended or left alone. For these and other reasons, the orientation to group life, the clarification of goals, and skillful leadership are essential.

While absenteeism is frequently regarded as a form of resistance in groups, Hinkley and Herman (1951) feel that a member's absence is his way of testing the limits of acceptance in the group, although they do note that absenteeism can represent resentment (p. 75).

It is interesting to note that groups in the early minutes of sessions often take roll and seek out who is absent and why. Although there is not always open resentment about the absent member, there may be considerable discussion about him—what we did to him at the last meeting, or perhaps his lack of commitment. Discussions of the absent member provide the group with a focal point, delay the work at home, and allow some individuals to verbalize what they may not be able to when the absent member is in the group (Johnson, 1963).

Perhaps the most effective approach the counselor can take with regard to member absences is to deal with problem directly. He may ask: "How do you feel when others are absent?" or "How does it affect the group when someone isn't here?" While the group may deny any feelings about the absences during early meetings, they may become quite hostile as the group progresses in that they feel that some members are deliberately avoiding the group and slowing its progress (Johnson, 1963, pp. 148–49).

In a pragmatic sense, the counselor should make a direct effort to contact absent members, especially in the early stages of group life. Members need to know that their presence is desired and that they have been missed. A personal letter or phone call from the counselor can effectively communicate to the absent individual that he does have an important identity in the group (Luchins, 1964).

THE MANIPULATOR

It is not uncommon for the group counselor to encounter manipulative members within the group. Such individuals tend to steer the group interaction to meet their own ends. For example, a group member may try to put the heat on a certain individual that he dislikes, or he may joke or clown if the process is touching close to an area that he does not wish to deal with. He may also try to manipulate the counselor into recognizing him as a favorite son or one whose behaviors and verbalizations in the group are recognized and rewarded. Some counselors unwittingly fall prey to the manipulator's plans in that their goal to get the group moving may be supported by the subtle manipulation of one or more members. In some cases, this takes the form of revealing some personal thought, not for the purpose of achieving self-understanding or some other agreed-upon goal but for the purpose of gaining group or counselor attention. The manipulator may carefully choose what he says, revealing only enough to steer the group toward whatever response he wishes. Once he feels he has succeeded in his purpose, he may become relatively silent to observe the fruits of his efforts.

Manipulation may be used by the counselor as a basis for discussion in the group. He could note "that some individuals seem to be taking advantage of others in the group—has anyone else been aware of this?" Again, he should not use the individual's name directly but should introduce the topic to assist the group to develop insights into the ways individuals seem to be utilizing the group.

DO-GOODERS

Luchins notes that there may be individuals in the group who perform in socially proper ways in the group and are still disruptive. Members who fill this category are labeled do-gooders. The do-gooder's behavior is usually evident through his desire to give advice to others, to help members plan what they should do, and through exaggerated assistance in helping another member to achieve. Luchins feels that members who are such givers may be repeating manipulative behavior patterns that led them to earlier difficulties or that they may become gods to the takers or the receivers of such help who then fail to make needed gains for themselves. Such behaviors may be used for discussion of the behaviors of givers and takers in that members should gain awareness of their personal motives and the social and practical implications of what they do (Luchins, 1964, p. 145).

RESISTANCE

In a sense, member behaviors listed in this chapter can be considered forms of individual resistance. The silent member, the member who singles out a scapegoat, the do-gooder and others may in one way or another be attempting to block or impede the group's process because of personal fears that they in some way will be subjected to unpleasant experiences in the group. In fact, the press, television, and popular magazines show a distorted picture of people under great stress in a therapy group. It is not surprising, therefore, that the popular image of the counseling or therapy group is a place where members are brutally and systematically analyzed because of incapacitating personal problems. Individuals who receive such misinformation frequently shy away from such groups, or if they do become members, their resistances to the group process may be unusually high.

Hinkley and Herman (1951) discuss five different dimensions of resistance. In their view, resistance may mean: (1) protection of the ego and an attempt to adjust to social demands; (2) an attempt on the part of an individual to escape the uncertainties and fears he may be asked to explore; (3) a means to keep those unpleasantries about self from recognition; (4) anger toward self for having revealed his inadequacies; and (5) a means for stating that he cannot utilize the help offered (pp. 63–64). Mahler (1969) feels that a basic sense of trust and member involvement is necessary for a group to progress satisfactorily toward the working stage or one wherein members will bring their problems to the group for assistance in making decisions and understanding dilemmas (p. 139).

As might be expected, resistance to personal exploration is most common during early sessions where individual unshared behavior is high and cohesiveness and trust are minimal. The group experience may be novel to most participants and the fear of the unknown is to be expected. As the group develops and trust and cohesiveness emerge, the initial fears tend to dissipate and resistance will become less of a problem. The important thing for the counselor to remember is that early and sharp probing will tend to increase resistance and perhaps destroy the group. Groups need time to develop and grow, and unnecessary haste accompanied by didactic lectures or unwarranted interpretations can destroy the group and cause individual harm.

Foulkes (1951) describes what he calls a leadership-by-default technique in which the group leader responds to initial tensions in the group by turning back questions. Since, in his thinking, initial questions are authority ridden and reflect members' wishes to be led, the group leader simply invites the speaker to give his own answer in a warm but firm reply—"Let me hear what you think about this" (p. 319). Bach (1954) notes that this approach is effective in helping group members become aware that they must handle their own problems.

Davis and Robinson in an early study discovered that counselors employ a number of secondary or resistance-reducing techniques in individual counseling. A few of these that some counselors have found useful in groups will be briefly described in the following summary–adaptation:

> *Assurance.* The counselor expresses approval or agreement
> to the group or to an individual member. The approval is

usually intended to encourage the group or individual member.

Humor.   The counselor eases tension with a humorous remark. This may be done when, in the counselor's opinion, the group tension is too high for optimal functioning.

Objective Materials.   The counselor uses materials—a story or a poem—to promote discussion. This technique is probably more effective with children's groups.

Personal Reference.   Personal references are a means for the counselor to insert his own personality into the group—"I feel that; I think; It seems to me."

Nonpersonal Anecdote.   The use of the experience of another person to illustrate a point.

Member Responses as Springboards.   The counselor follows a group member's lead and uses it to involve other group members in the discussion—"Joan says she's still not sure what we're to do here. I wonder if others are unsure too?" [Davis and Robinson, 1949, pp. 297–306]

Like other techniques, none of these produce instant magic. Yet if timed properly, they are useful during the early stages of group life.

ETHICS

The rapid rise in the popularity of the encounter group, sensitivity group, weekend marathon and other forms of group training has been a cause of concern to many who feel that while the group has potential for promoting personal growth, it also has the potential for great harm. Shostrom vividly describes the experience of a teacher who joined a group of therapeutically sophisticated participants who cruelly probed the painful segments of her life. As a result, this woman eventually took her own life. While most counselors are or at least should be aware of the dangers involved in joining groups, Shostrom's suggestions are worth reprinting here:

1.   Never respond to a newspaper ad. Groups run by trained professionals or honestly supervised by them are forbidden by ethical considerations to advertise directly.

2.   Never participate in a group of fewer than a half dozen members. The necessary and valuable candor generated by an effective group cannot be dissipated, shared and examined by too small a group, and scapegoating or purely vicious ganging up can develop. Conversely, a

group with more than sixteen members generally cannot effectively be monitored by anyone, however well trained or well assisted.

3. Never join an encounter group on impulse—as a fling, binge, or surrender to the unplanned.
4. Never participate in a group encounter with close associates, persons with whom you have professional or competitive social relations.
5. Never be overly impressed by beautiful or otherwise close-signaled surroundings or participants.
6. Never stay with a group that has a behavioral ax to grind —a group that seems to insist that everybody be a Renaissance *mensch* or a devotee of *cinéma vérité*–or a rightest or leftest, or a cultural, intellectual, or sexual specialist.
7. Never participate in a group that lacks formal connection with a professional on whom you can check. [Shostrom, 1969, pp. 38–39]

Birnbaum in writing of the potential benefits of sensitivity training also issues a warning and calls for group organizers and leaders to make their purposes clear:

Each of these varied approaches to sensitivity training is designed to serve specific purposes. Undoubtedly, each can be immensely beneficial to certain individuals—and provide little help or have negative results for others. What must be made clear is the purpose to be achieved and the kind of training best designed to serve that purpose. [Birnbaum, 1969, pp. 83, 96]

He further notes:

The most serious threat to sensitivity training comes first from its enthusiastic but frequently unsophisticated supporters, and second from a host of newly hatched trainers long on enthusiasm or extrepreneurial expertise but short on professional experience, skill, and wisdom. [p. 97]

Larkin (1969) in an excellent review of the ethical issues in sensitivity training points out that while the therapist's mandate is "to provide a corrective experience to someone who presents himself as psychologically impaired, the trainer's mandate is relatively ambiguous. There is no way for an individual who joins a sensitivity group to know in advance or appraise the intentions of trainers, process of groups, or its effects on him." (p. 924). More psychologically disturbed individuals seem to be attracted to training groups with a growing number of ill-trained or poorly prepared leaders. Screening is minimal and some leaders do not seem to be concerned with their limitations. In the process of training groups, some leaders have influenced participants to behave in certain (sometimes aggressive and/or affectionate behaviors) by modeling them—when opportunity is not provided for working through the emotional effects of such experiences. Moreover, while the participant may be encouraged to express strong emotions, the trainer's function in promoting these is often obscured (pp. 124-25). Further issues involve the participant who comes into a sensitivity group under threat of evaluation and that confidentiality is difficult to insure when participants are related, classmates, or members of the same company. Finally, Larkin notes that participants frequently find an experience so gratifying that they seek to do training themselves (Larkin, 1969, pp. 923-28).

While none of these writers were speaking directly to the group counselor *per se,* their thoughts must be carefully considered by all those who lead groups whether they are labeled *encounter, sensitivity, counseling,* or something else. Some guidelines for the counselor with regard to ethics might include the following:

1.   Be thoroughly familiar with and be guided by the Code of Ethics of the American Personnel and Guidance Association. This includes the responsibility of the counselor to be aware of his own limitations and to refer individuals that need assistance beyond his capabilities to appropriate agencies.

2.   Have a good basic knowledge of small-group life and its possible benefits and potentials for him. Special preparation in group counseling including a supervised practicum is vital.

3.   When a counselor is uncertain with respect to whether or not an individual should be a member of a group, he should discuss the case with his colleagues or with other competent professional authorities. If such help is not available, he should not have the individual in the counseling group. Screening for group counseling is essential (Larkin, 1969).

4.   The counselor must be certain to make his goals and purposes clear to group members. Prospective group members must be clear with regard to the purposes of the group (Larkin, 1969).

5.   The confidentiality of the group must be insured in the same

manner as the confidentiality of individual sessions. The APGA Code of Ethics provides guidelines for the counselor with regard to confidentiality.

6. Group counseling is more than a set of techniques; therefore, the large number of suggested group techniques must be carefully evaluated by the counselor and utilized for specific purposes of the group. The injudicious use of random group techniques without regard to their probable impact is a dangerous practice (Larkin, 1969).

7. The counselor should not misrepresent himself by describing himself as a *T-Group leader, group therapist,* or by some other label that implies that he has the specialized training and qualifications of institutions and agencies that prepare specialized group leaders (Larkin, 1969; Birnbaum, 1969).

8. The impact of the counselor on the group is potent. His leadership style and goals will set the tenor of his group. Therefore, he must thoroughly understand his own dynamics and his impact on others. Experiences designed to help him understand himself should be a vital part of his training.

While the American Psychological Association has been studying ethical issues in group procedures (Larkin, 1969), counselors as a group, to the knowledge of the authors, have yet to deal with ethics as they relate specifically to counseling groups. For the present, it would appear that the APGA Code of Ethics should be utilized as the practitioner's guide. As the interest in group counseling grows, it seems probable that the guidance professionals will wish to review closely the special ethical problems that may occur in groups.

SUMMARY

Even experienced group counselors encounter certain special problems in groups. These include group silence and the silent group member, the use of talk as an avoidance technique, the chronic monopolist, the acting-out group member, scapegoating, absenteeism, the manipulator, do-gooders, and general problems of resistance. Suggestions are provided by the authors for dealing with these problems.

Of special concern to those interested in group work are problems of an ethical nature. The rapid use of groups under a host of labels and approaches has become a matter of concern to those who feel the unqualified or unsophisticated group leader can organize groups that are a source of potential harm to members. A counselor who would organize counseling groups should be thoroughly familiar with the APGA Code of Ethics, have a basic knowledge and background of group work, employ proper screening procedures, and not misrepresent professional qualifications or work with groups beyond his level of competence. Self-understanding is essential for the group counselor since his probable impact on the group can be extremely potent. Counselors have yet to come fully to grips with ethical group concerns, and for the present, the APGA Code of Ethics must serve as a general guide to counselor behavior in group work.

REFERENCES

BACH, GEORGE R. *Intensive Group Psychotherapy.* New York: The Ronald Press Company, 1954.

BIRNBAUM, M. "Sense and Nonsense about Sensitivity Training," *Saturday Review* (November 15, 1969), pp. 82, 83, 96, 97.

DAVIS, S. E., and ROBINSON, F. P. "A Study of the Use of Certain Techniques for Reducing Resistance during the Counseling Interview," *Educational and Psychological Measurement,* Vol. 9 (1949), pp. 297–306.

FOULKES, S. H. "Concerning Group Leadership in Group Analytic Psychotherapy," *International Journal of Group Psychotherapy,* Vol. 1 (1951), p. 319.

GINOTT, H. G. *Group Psychotherapy with Children.* New York: McGraw-Hill Book Company, 1961.

HINKLEY, R. G., and HERMAN, L. *Group Treatment in Psychotherapy.* Minneapolis, Minn.: University of Minnesota Press, 1951.

JOHNSON, J. A. *Group Therapy: A Practical Approach.* New York: McGraw-Hill Book Company, 1963.

LARKIN, M. "Some Ethical Issues in Sensitivity Training," *American Psychologist,* Vol. 24 (1969), pp. 923–28.

LIFTON, WALTER M. "Group-Centered Counseling," in *Basic Approaches to Group Psychotherapy and Group Counseling* (ed. GEORGE M. GAZDA). Springfield, Ill.: Charles C Thomas, Publisher, 1968.

MAHLER, C. A. *Group Counseling in the Schools.* Boston: Houghton Mifflin Company, 1969.

MURO, JAMES J. "Some Aspects of the Group-Counseling Practicum," *Counselor Education and Supervision,* Vol. 7 (1968), pp. 371–78.

PILE, E. "A Note on a Technique to Aid in Studying the Process of Group Psychotherapy," *Group Psychotherapy,* Vol. XI, No. 3 (1958), pp. 211, 212.

SHOSTROM, E. L. "Group Therapy: Let the Buyer Beware," *Psychology Today,* Vol. 2, No. 12 (1969), pp. 36–40.

WARTERS, JANE. *Group Guidance: Principles and Practices.* New York: McGraw-Hill Book Company, 1960.

WHITAKER, D. S., and LIEBERMAN, M. A. *Psychotherapy through the Group Process.* New York: Atherton Press, Inc., 1964.

CHAPTER 9

Group Counseling with Children

THROUGHOUT THIS TEXT, the authors, when appropriate, have referred to the use of group procedures with the preadolescent. However, because of the current interest in elementary school guidance and counseling, a special section on children's groups is presented here.

Group counseling with children is an exercise in interpersonal relationships. Developmental group counseling with children is understood as part of the educational process. It is concerned with the needs of children who have typical developmental problems.

The group is a particularly effective approach with children because the child is a social being and is generally interested in interaction. Children like to be part of a group and the group can be a most effective process to assist in the learning of developmental tasks (Dinkmeyer, 1970). As a group counselor of children, you may be the first adult with whom the child has had a meaningful relationship. You and the group become a part of a social laboratory in which the child tries new patterns of relating aggression, anger, love, and tests reality. As Thomas notes: "People are like porcupines with sharp quills who repel each other as they try in their own fumbling way to get close. They attack and defend, they soliloquize or remain silently in a shell. They vie with each other for attention or control" (Thomas, 1969, p. 74). So it is with the child—he, too, wants to get close, and thus the group is an appropriate learning situation with considerable opportunity for personal growth.

One needs only to review the socioteleological approach to human behavior to understand the vital place of the group in the life of the child. The fact that behavior for children is indeed goal directed and purposive, that belonging is a basic need and that one needs to understand better how an individual utilizes what he possesses are just some of the tenets of this model (Dinkmeyer, 1968).

Taken from a pragmatic viewpoint, groups are a way of life for an elementary school child. He is taught in groups, plays and eats in groups, and his worth or lack of it is often expressed in terms of how well he meets the local or national norms on some standardized achievement measure. The fact that school groups are inevitable does not mean that they are organized so individuals derive the same benefits from them. The transition from home to school requires that the child actively seek approval from peers and teachers perhaps for the first time in his life. In the years preceding school entrance, he may have found that love and acceptance are predicated on what he does (Mussen, *et al.,* 1963). In schools we tend to value the product rather than the child. A child who exhibits traits we like is duly rewarded; one who does not receives little positive feedback.

In the group, the child may explore his hopes, fears, and impact on others in an atmosphere where external evaluation is minimal. He must still seek acceptance, but the criteria for earning approval are quite different than those required in the classroom or on the athletic playground. For a fleeting period of time, at least, each child in the group gets some individual attention. Learning to delay gratification, controlling emotional reactions, dealing with abstractions, formulating values and giving of himself to others characterize children's groups (Havinghurst, 1953). While these developmental tasks are not always discussed *per se,* they provide realistic guidelines for counseling practice.

The group is also a place for dealing with children's problems. The child learns that he is not alone in his concerns, that his turn to be helped will eventually come. His capacity for altruism and social interest is certainly increased. Add to this the possibilities for gaining self-understanding and the fact that the child truly can empathize with another and the reasons for group work with children become clearer. Finally, the possibilities for immediate feedback and the fact that a group is indeed a rehearsal area for new behaviors make the desirability of groups more evident. An analysis of children who referred themselves for counseling in twenty Maine elementary schools revealed the fact that over 65 per cent of these individuals expressed an interest or concern with peer and adult acceptance. What better place for the child to discover such acceptance than in the exciting world of the counseling group?

SOME MECHANICS OF CHILDREN'S GROUPS

1. PERMISSIVENESS — THE PLACE OF LIMITS IN GROUPS. Some counselors seem to feel that the use of any limit or structure in working with children (and adults) is akin to raising the ghost of Haxley. As Shaw (1966) notes, helping people must try to rid themselves of any guilt they may feel because they control children. In a large sense, the counselor does control, firstly because he is an adult and secondly because he sets certain conditions including the relationship. As Hayakawa (1967) has written, therapeutic permissiveness is a great idea, but it never has meant that Joey should be allowed to pour hot soup on Mary. He further points out that children should be allowed to do what they want up to the point of harming others—a concept similar to Glasser's (1965) ideas on individual responsibility.

What is important for the group counselor, however, is that the child be able to verbalize how he feels, and in the group he is allowed to do so within certain limits. With some children, the authors have utilized printed ground rules (*See* Chapter 7), but with those up to about the third grade, we have found in general that prepared rules have little impact on group life. Thus, we have found Ginott's limits useful:

1. No toys are taken from the room.
2. No physical attacks on the counselor or on other children.
3. No leaving the room.
4. Limits on time. [Ginott, 1961, pp. 109–13]

The technique of limit setting, described in some detail by Ginott, has also been useful. He suggests that the counselor pick up the feeling underlying the act, state the limit, help the child channel the energy into an appropriate outlet, and help him express any resentment he may feel because of the limit (Ginott, 1961, pp. 106–8). For example, suppose Joey, a third grade boy, announces that he is going to smack Sue with some clay. The dialogue could go as follows:

COUNSELOR: Joe, I know you're upset because Sue took the • truck, but Sue is not for hitting. If you want to, you can hit Bobo the clown over there all you want.
CHILD: Aw—I—OK. (perhaps a glare at counselor)
COUNSELOR: You're a little angry at me, aren't you?

This technique, suggested by Ginott is very effective in dealing with children in groups.

2. PLAYFULNESS. Playfulness is an important part of child counsel-

ing, and counseling with children in groups is no exception. Being a
little playful, whether you use toys or not, helps you enter the world of
the child. As a normal human, the counselor can expect to feel positive,
negative, and even a little angry toward some children. As Shaw (1966)
states, the counselor must bear in mind that he is in constant interaction
with other people's children who by definition have been reared in
quite the wrong ways! The counselor, however, must not become just
another child. The reader will note that the authors suggest that the
counselor get used to playfulness, but this does not mean that the
counselor laugh at the group member's descriptions of how they bug
a given teacher (and thus reinforce them). He listens, smiles if amused,
and expects the group to engage in play. He need not, however,
become the reinforcer of negative and perhaps distorted descriptions
of individuals in the school and home.

3.   ORIENTATION.   The counselor has a clear responsibility to make
the purposes for forming a group clear to the children. In a sense, it
could be considered unethical to tell a child that he may join a group
to discuss anything he wishes and then push the group into a discussion
of academic achievement. The child must be aware that he is to discuss
himself and his personal relationships if this is indeed a projected part
of the group process. The authors have found two approaches to be very
successful in orienting children to group counseling. The first of these
is the use of a portable stage and hand puppets to tell the counseling
story, and the second is the use of prepared slides and a tape recording
in which the nature of groups is discussed.

4.   GETTING STARTED.   Any group of children, together for the first
time, may be preoccupied with their expectations from each other and
from the counselor (Johnson, 1963). Some anxiety is natural and talk
may be rapid and superficial. Subjects will change rapidly, and there
will be little evidence of group focus. Much of the discussion will be
punctuated with giggles, laughter, and general horseplay. After all,
most children haven't read the counseling texts that tell them how to
behave! In general, the counselor should be supportive and keep a
group focus. Gradually, the children will learn to interact with their
peers and with the counselor as an adult. The counselor, however,
should expect initial confusion and try-out behavior. For example:

JOE: Do we have to raise our hand to talk?	Joe tries out the situation. Does he mean what he says? Can I say what I want?
COUNSELOR: In here, you can talk when you want to.	

SUE: I have a new dog!

MARY: Harry looks like a dog.
(Laughter)

HELEN: Will you tell our teacher   More try-out
what we say?   behavior to test
                                           situation.

SUE: Mr._____, tell Joe to stop
pushing my chair.

JOE: I'm not; I just moved my foot!

This type of interaction should not disturb the counselor. It is often a necessary phase of the process in working with children's groups.

Several programs or prepared techniques are also available for counselor use and have been discussed in detail in Chapter 7. Recently, Dinkmeyer (1970) has suggested the use of a short story or an unfinished story to stimulate discussion. This technique is part of a more inclusive guidance approach entitled *Developing Understanding of Self and Others* published by the American Guidance Service in Circle Pines, Minnesota.

5. COMPOSING CHILDREN'S GROUPS.   Group composition, as we have noted in Chapter 6, may be a crucial factor for counseling success. Few children will remain unaffected by the group experience. Because of this, children's groups should not be randomly composed. As Ginott notes, the children in the group should have a developmental or remedial effect on each other. The group should be balanced so that shy children interact with more social ones, immature with more mature, and so on (Ginott, 1961, p. 30).

Several approaches are available to help the counselor in his approaches to grouping. Ginott and Harries have suggested inclusion and exclusion lists as aids to grouping. A summary of their thinking is presented here:

Good group conditions—inclusion list

1. Compulsive children
2. Effeminate boys
3. Restricted children
4. Constant do-gooders—children with pseudo assets
5. Children with specific fears (tests, etc.)
6. Conduct problems. [Harries, 1969; Ginott, 1961, pp. 15–28]

They have also suggested an exclusion list of those children the counselor might exclude. The authors feel, however, that some of the types of children may be able to be helped in the groups and advocate this list as a tentative approach:

1. Children who have experienced a severe trauma—death, divorce
2. Severe sibling rivalry
3. Children who steal
4. Children who seem to have little conscience, low affect, poor sense of right and wrong by any dimension. (Ginott, 1961, pp. 15–28; Harries, 1969).

In addition to the lists presented here, groups may be formed along other dimensions. The following may be of use to the counselor:

a. *Incomplete Sentences* (Harries, 1969). The child is asked to complete the following sentences: I am————. Other members in school think I am————. The counselor may employ any number of incomplete sentences to obtain the information he desires. The chief value of this approach lies in the fact that it provides a quick estimate of the child's self-concept.

b. *Children's Drawings* (Harries, 1969). The child is asked to draw a picture of himself. From the picture, the counselor may be able to determine how the child sees himself. For example, does he draw a happy child, a sad one, a large one, or a small one? Does he include other children in the picture? This approach, too, provides a quick, if somewhat unreliable, estimate of the child's self-concept.

c. *Gesell Tests.* The Gesell Behavioral Examination has been discussed in more detail in Chapter 6. As an illustration of how two children who are chronologically the same age may differ markedly in developmental patterns, two sections of the exam—the copy signs test and the incomplete man test are presented here. The child's work shown on page 220 has an assessed developmental age of four and one-half years, the one on page 219 , a developmental age of five and one-half. Both children are chronologically six years of age.

d. *Teacher Observation* (Harries, 1969). Teachers may be used to help the counselor form groups. Because of their constant interaction with a given class, they can be excellent judges of the shy child, the immature one, the acting-out boy, and so on. By discussing the proposed group members with the teacher and using the exclusion–inclusion lists previously presented, the counselor can make a reasonable assessment of how a proposed group may be balanced for counseling purposes.

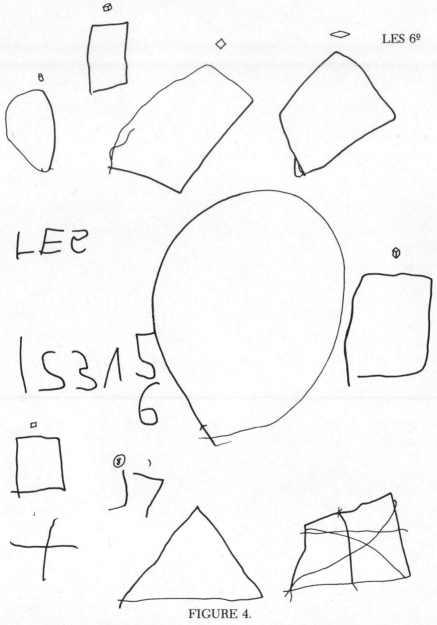

FIGURE 4.

CHILD IS 6 YEARS OF AGE. DEVELOPMENTAL AGE 5-1/2.

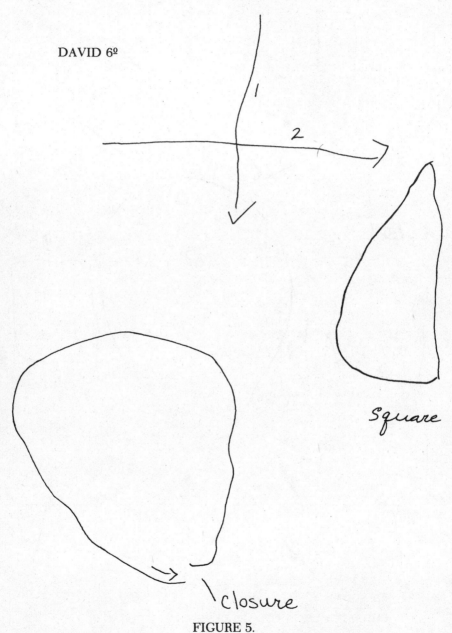

DAVID 6º

FIGURE 5.

CHILD IS 6 YEARS OF AGE. DEVELOPMENTAL AGE 4-1/2.

Reprinted by permission of the Gesell Institute of Child Development, New Haven, Connecticut.

LES 6º

FIGURE 6.

CHILD IS 6 YEARS OF AGE. DEVELOPMENTAL AGE 5-1/2.

DAVID 6º

FIGURE 7.

CHILD IS 6 YEARS OF AGE. DEVELOPMENTAL AGE 4-1/2.

Reprinted by permission of the Gesell Institute of Child Development, New Haven, Connecticut.

e. *Thomas Self-Concept Scale.*   One of the most useful and effective self-concept inventories developed in recent years is the Thomas Self-Concept Scale, developed by Walter Thomas and available from the Educational Service Company of Grand Rapids, Michigan. The instrument, designed for assessing the self-image values of preprimary- and primary-aged children, is based on the theoretical guidelines of Mead and Sullivan along with Thomas's theoretical basis for values. In a unique approach to testing, the examiner takes a Polaroid snapshot of the youngster. The photo is then placed before the child, and his attention is directed to it in terms of fourteen bipolar adjective items that constitute the representative value system in which the child reports his self-perceptions and his perceptions of how significant others view him. Improving self-images has long been a goal of counseling, and the authors feel that this instrument is a highly promising way to assess the self-image of the child.

f. *Perception of Parents Scale:*   Harries (1971)[1] and other researchers have developed an approach to composing children's groups based upon the child's perceptions of his parents. Utilizing an instrument labeled the *Perception of Parents Scale,* groups of children may be placed together on the basis of their perceptions of the specific roles and reactions of their father and mother in the home environment. Various group compositions are possible through use of this instrument. For example, a counselor could form a group of children who came from homes where the parents are perceived as accepting, rejecting, indifferent, and so on. Groups may also be formed on the basis of "balance" wherein a number of children who perceive their parents as punative might be put in a group with the children who perceive their parents as loving.

The scale has three forms: F (father), M (mother), and O (other). There are also separate level inventories for use in the primary grades, middle school, and junior and senior high school. According to Harries, the original concepts of this approach have been examined at the State University of New York at Buffalo, Syracuse University, University of Rochester, and the University of Maryland.

g. *Age Range and Sex Composition.*   The research and recommendations here are not definitive. Ginott indicates that only one chronological year should separate the members if the children are at the latency age (Ginott, 1961). Slavson (1950), however, indicates that children can differ in age by a maximum of two years and still function effectively in the group.

---

[1]Personal Communication

Redl (1966) is more concerned with developmental stages than chronological distinctions. He believes that maturational congruence is a necessity if all members are to hold similar advantages in a group concerned with their adult relationships, sexual interests, verbal skills, and security needs.

Ohlsen (1968) and Ginott believe that group participants should be of the same sex during latency. Ohlsen and Gazda (1965) found that in their group girls were more mature, had more interest in boys than boys in girls, were more verbal, and tended to dominate discussion. However, after grade six, we would tend to favor having boys and girls in the same group. It is an excellent media for them to learn to relate with each other more effectively.

6. LENGTH OF SESSIONS AND DURATION OF GROUP AS A UNIT. The ideal amount of time will vary with the type of group and the interest of the members. Often school regulations will influence the time spent, and a group will meet for one or two periods of the school day, from thirty to sixty minutes. Younger children usually will not benefit from lengthy sessions. The factor of a set time helps the group become more readily involved in the work of the group.

While the group may meet many needs and provide much support, it also must terminate. We suggest that you indicate to developmental groups that they will meet for eight to ten weeks. The limited time stimulates some to greater involvement.

7. MODELING. Since the peer group can serve as a strong social reinforcer, the counselor can choose to include in the group a child who possesses certain desirable traits. For example, an outgoing child might serve as a model in a group of shy children or a good student might be included in a group where several members were bright under-achievers. Through interaction, the children may imitate the pattern of the model child or children in working toward agreed upon group goals. In fact, Hansen, Niland and Zani (1969) found that models in group counseling tend to strengthen learning about social behavior.

8. GROUP SIZE. The size of counseling groups for children has been a matter of concern for some group counselors, and like other areas in group counseling, the research evidence is not conclusive. The authors agree with Mayer and Baker (1967) who after extensively reviewing the literature related to group counseling concluded that the actual size of the group should probably vary with the age and maturity level of the counselees. As a general guide, however, they note that optimal size should probably not exceed five or six members, and group size of less than five is appropriate for very young elementary school children.

9. PLAY MEDIA FOR CHILDREN'S GROUPS. Some counselors find the use of media to be helpful. While play media in counseling is still an issue in the field (Nelson, 1967), it is safe to hypothesize that a number of counselors are now using some type of play media with very young elementary school children. At any rate, the authors have found that a list of media prepared by Meeks provides workable guidelines for those counselors who wish to experiment with its use in counseling groups:

Use of Toys in Elementary Guidance—*Minimum Essentials*
1. *Open shelves* to which the child has free access so that he can choose his own medium of expression. (A wide range of material is necessary to deal with children of all ages and grades of ability.)
2. *Real-life toys* to play out life situations and to help the child express his feelings toward the world in which he lives.
   a. *Doll house.*
   b. *Doll furniture* (As nearly life-like as possible) in appropriate sizes for dolls; plus washers, sewing machines or other equipment.
   c. *Dolls* (jointed) representing mother, father, boy, girl, baby, grandparents, and trades people; plus authority figures such as policemen, doctors, nurses, soldiers; other community figures such as postmen, firemen.
   d. *Animals.*—farm and zoo, with cages, trucks, and train for hauling.
   e. *Medical kit.*—suitable for doctor or nurse.
   f. *Traffic set-ups.*—cars, tricycles, motor bikes, dump trucks, wrecker truck, ambulance, etc. plus building blocks.
   g. *Puppets.*—family and authority figures.
   h. *Money.*—paper and coin; bank, cash register
   i. *Telephone.*
   j. *Schoolroom toys* with desks, children, teacher, etc., to help a child express his feeling toward school, authority figures, and peers.
3. *Toys for release of aggression.*—bop-bag, guns and holsters, animal puppets, soldiers, tanks, ambulance, and fire truck; peg-pounding board; toss games; dolls sturdy enough to hit and pound; clay and play dough.
4. *Toys for enhancement of self-concept.*—toys, which can be manipulated or erected, requiring some thinking-

through procedure to provide problem-solving situations
in which the child can figure out things for himself: erec-
tor set, Lincoln logs, puzzles, automatic fire truck.

All media are arranged on open shelves, and the child upon entering
the counselor's office or playroom is permitted to select any of the toys
or games that catch his attention. The media then become the child's
manner of expression. The toys are his words.

Several theoretical approaches to use with media are possible, and
there is little evidence to show that one approach is necessarily more
effective or better than another. The approach that has proved most
effective for the authors, however, is essentially that labeled *relationship theory* wherein the child makes certain types of behavioral and
attitudinal changes in exchange for acceptance by the counselor and
the group. Guidelines for the process are outlined in detail by Ginott
(1961), Axline (1947), and Moustakas (1959). In essence, the counselor
accepts the child, allows him to express his feelings, and waits for the
child to come to terms with himself. The process is a gradual one, and
the child slowly comes to grips with himself and his concerns. What is
important for the counselor to note, however, is that he must be very
cautious in not going beyond his capabilities in making interpretations
about the child's use of media. In this context, the counselor would
never say "You really hate your father," to a child who may be vigor-
ously attacking a doll that could represent the child's parent. Instead,
the counselor stays with the child's feelings and the *what* of his actions.
For example, the counselor could say "You're feeling a little angry—
you're giving that doll a good hit!" Unjudicious and gross interpretation
(or misinterpretation) could, after all, convince a child that he does
indeed hate his father when the counselor has no evidence for such an
interpretation. Play media in counseling is essentially a communications approach based on relationship theory. The counselor who uses
play media in groups should, therefore, observe the child, try and determine what feeling he is communicating, and stay with the here and now
of group life rather than probe into the past experiences of the child.
For example, in a group of four second grade boys, the following dialogue took place. Joe, an aggressive youngster, was joined by Jimmy
who was also somewhat aggressive in a game they described as *set up
the meanies.* The boys proceeded to set up a group of toy soldiers, then
each picked up a puppet—in this case a bear and wolf.

JOE: I'm going to eat those meanies—I'll tear them up with
my teeth—Grr!

JIMMY: Me, too—I'm going to eat 'em up—they're nasty and mean.
COUNSELOR: Uh-hum—You're angry at those meanies there —you're going to get them.
JOE: Yeh, here I go.
JIMMY: Get 'em—get 'em.

Both boys mentioned here were considered behavior problems by the teacher and had been subjected to several disciplinary measures. In addition, Jimmy came from a home with a punitive father. The counselor, knowing these things, could have interpreted the boy's attack on the soldiers as an attack on the teacher or a parent. Instead, he wisely chose to stay with the feeling the boys seemed to be expressing and with the reality of the current group situation.

One final note on the use of media is appropriate here. As a general guideline, the counselor might expect that children in groups will generally play with toys that help them release aggression in the early stages of group counseling and gradually move into real-life toys and toys that enhance the self-image as counseling progresses (Moustakas, 1959).

ASSISTING CHILDREN TO BECOME GROUP MEMBERS

Ohlsen (no date) has noted that younger children need more structure than adolescents to work effectively in groups, and the authors are in agreement with this premise. In some fashion, each group counselor teaches children the ways to operate in a group. For example, the counselor can promote member-to-member interaction with such comments as: "Joe, you said you really like the way Harry helps others— what other things do you like about him?" This approach to teaching stems from a natural flow of group interaction wherein the children learn to function as group members through observation of and interaction with the counselor.

There are, however, several other more direct approaches to helping children learn to be group members. Harries (1969) has suggested that the counselor use audio and video tapes in which children role play the desired way of operating in a group. The authors have also found McCarty's book, *It All Has To Do With Identity,* with bright fifth and sixth grade children creates a set for group counseling. Based on the Hill Interaction Matrix, it is designed to induce more member-originated behavior, increase the frequency of member participation and the number of children who participate. The booklet goes through each cell on the Hill Matrix in a humorous and informative way that enables the child to understand the nature of group life. Its only drawback is the fact that it can take from five to seven sessions to cover the material and requires that the child grasp some rather difficult abstractions. Yet, it might be an effective group-guidance approach and an excellent orientation to group counseling for children from the fifth grade on. An example of McCarty's approach to teaching children about group operation is presented here. Note how he uses examples to illustrate the relationship–confrontive mode of group interaction.

REORIENTATION THROUGH GROUP COUNSELING

Earlier, the authors made a case for developmental groups—those that emphasize growth and development instead of cure. Thus, the school counselor would not be as interested in the basic personality change advocated by Ginott (1961) as he would in smaller or less profound goals since he does, after all, deal with essentially normal children.

Thus, it seems to the authors that after a period of time the group must be utilized in creative ways to assist the child. Once the child has identified a value (better acceptance by others), the counselor and the group can help him examine his way of life or life-style. In what ways is he achieving his goals? What is he doing to meet his needs as he sees them? Together the group and the counselor help the child describe his behavior and make judgments about whether it is effective or not. For example, a child who states that he desires peer acceptance and relates that he picks on kids a lot might be asked: "How is this helping you?" If it appears that the child accepts his behavior as ineffective, he and the group should develop a specific and realistic plan to help him meet his needs in more responsible ways (Glasser, 1965). This may be accomplished through behavioral or developmental contracts (Keirsey, 1969; Dinkmeyer, 1964–65). Once the child has decided what he hopes to accomplish outside the group, the contract is used for discussion. If the child did not complete his contract, the process should be repeated, with the counselor and the group focusing on the *what* of the child's behavior to include an assessment by the child of the effectiveness of what he did. The group and counselor provide support and encouragement for all effort, and while the child may offer excuses for not fulfilling his commitment to the group, his failure is played down in favor of encouraging him to try again, perhaps at a level that will insure success (Glasser, 1965). A sample of a group contract completed by a fifth grade group is presented on page 230.

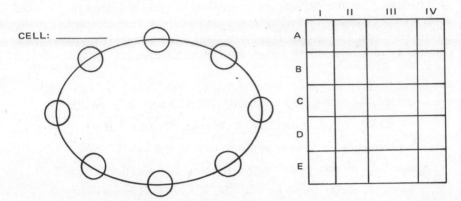

CELL: _____

START:
In this cell, a member talks about a RELATIONSHIP in a CONFRONTIVE way. He does this by calling the group's attention to one of two things: (1) The way one member reacts to another member (or members) (2) The way he, himself, reacts to another member (or members). Then he supports his point by giving examples of things that have actually happened in the group. The examples serve as a "test" to see if others see things the same way. One goal is honesty, and another is a true desire to help — not simply be heard.

EXAMPLES:
*Jim, whenever I ask you a question, you act like you're mad at me. Do I say things that rub you the wrong way?
*I don't know why, but I feel uneasy around you most of the time. It's like you're always trying to please me.

(1.)
ONLY A;
b is
mild,
but it
is a
real
way of
showing
that
the
speaker
does
under-
stand.

1.   Which are not IV E?

a.   This group bores me! Everybody's an expert, and no-body knows anything!

b.   You say you want us to understand you. What do we do different when you are talking about yourself than when John is talking about himself?

c.   Betty, you are doing what makes me so angry at you. A minute ago you agreed with Jim. Now you're agreeing with me, and I'm saying the exact opposite of what Jim was saying. How can you agree with both of us? People can't know you and trust you if you don't say what you really mean. Don't be afraid to disagree.

d.   Al, whenever we try to get you to talk about how you feel about Jim, you make a joke out of it and won't say. Do you think he needs you to protect him, or what?

FIGURE 8.

The use of such contracts is effective in helping children make small behavioral changes toward agreed-upon goals. It is important that the counselor and the group reinforce and support each member who makes a commitment for some change he desires.

CONTRACT BETWEEN GROUP AND   Mike Smith
_____

     Mike   has stated that he would like to try the following things between now and our next group meeting. We, the members of this group, agree to help him do the things he wants. We also agree to talk about how well he is doing at the next meeting.

1. Mike wants more friends on the playground.

2. He agrees to not pick on anybody for the next two days as a start.

3. All group members will help Mike on the playground for the next two days.

SIGNED: Mike Smith
(Group   _____
Members) Joe Headlin
              _____
              Otto Belle
              _____
              Harry Murchley
              _____
              Steve Scott
              _____
              Mr. Marks
              _____

AN EXAMPLE OF GROUP COUNSELING WITH THIRD GRADE CHILDREN

1. MW: When we left last time, it seems to me that we were going to start with something today. Do you remember what it was?

1–9. Introduction of topic previously decided to be discussed at last meeting.

2. JAME: I think I thought of it —
   oh, yeah, reading.

3. MW: It has to do with it, you're
   right there, Jame. What about it?

4. JAME: Oh, yeah. Listening to
   other people and — uh— uh—
   listening to what they have
   to say about good reading and
   stuff.

5. MW: Do you remember that?

6. BOYS: (Silence)

7. MW: Remember just before we
   left last time we talked about
   what we'd learned and someone
   said that Mark had given Jame
   some pretty good ideas about
   how to be a better reader, and
   Jame had said 'he guessed he'd
   tuned Mark out when he was
   telling him those ideas?

8. TIM: Oh, yeah!

9. MW: What do we mean when
   we say we tune people out?

10. MARK: Oh, not really listening to   10. Seek to clarify definition of
    it, they go on and do something   topic.
    else.

11. MW: Who would have an idea   11. Seek to get them to clarify.
    as to why a fellow would tune
    out somebody who is trying to
    help him?

12. BOYS: (Long silence)

13. MW: What would be some of
    the reasons?

14. BOYS: (Long silence)

15. JAME: Well, he wouldn't want to take the time and bother — he'd rather do something else . . . than just listen to his black spots.

15. Jame's reason for tuning people out.

16. MW: What do you mean?

17. MARK: Well, listening to the things he can't do well, and then he thinks he can't do it as well as any other person, and you get sorta mad at somebody else telling you some things better to do.

17. Mark supports and adds to Jame's reasoning.

18. MW: I think that's an interesting idea; does anyone else have another idea?

19. BOYS: (Rather long silence)

20. MW: All right then. If I understand what you're saying, it's kind of hard when you know there's something that you can't do real well, and then it's kind of hard when there's somebody who does it well — to hear somebody who does it well tell you how to do it — is that what you mean?

20. Clarification of reasons.

21. MARK: Uh huh — unless it's an older kid or somebody.

21. Probable exception to accepting advice.

22. MW: Does that make a difference?

23. BOYS: (Silence)

24. MW: When somebody older says it?

25. MARK: Not really. You still feel sort of stupid — and — uh— things like that, but it's — not your fault.

25. Negates probable exception — supports Jame's reading problem, but tells him it's not his fault.

26. JAME: Most people don't really expect you to know everything . . . you get confused — (he breaks off and there is a great silence. The boys grow uncomfortable and wiggle in their chairs. Tim giggles and Tom wipes his brow). It's hard; I can't think of what I want to say.

26. Jame admits he's somewhat confused.

27. MW: Well, sometimes it takes time to think of something, doesn't it, boys?

28. TIM: Gee, Tommy looks like he's really thinkin'.

28. Tim points up fact that Tom has been quiet.

29. MW: Can you think of any reason why it might be to a fellow's advantage NOT to listen to what the other guy is telling you when he's giving you some good tips? Would there be any reason or would you have any idea why you wouldn't really want to hear it?

29. Why wouldn't a person want to hear advice?

30. TIM: Well, maybe 'cause — maybe you want to be alone sometimes.

30. Sometimes you want to be alone with your troubles.

31. MARK: Well, maybe they feel they will learn it all some other time; they'd rather play or some other things — uh, I'd rather learn it NOW, but — well, I guess they'd really like to learn it now.

31. Kids feel they'll learn some other time BUT Mark feels they'd really want to learn now.

32. MW: When do you fellows think it would be the easiest to learn it?

33. JAME: When you're home.

33. Jame wants to take learning out of school.

34. MW: Well, that's a place, but when do you think it would be easiest to learn? (pause) Now or next year?

35. MARK: Now.

35. Mark says it's easiest to learn now.

36. MW: Why?

37. JAME: Well, um, maybe when you're out of school would be a good time — maybe when you have more time and stuff.

37. Jame thinks you'd have more time to learn out of school.

38. MW: Why?

39. JAME: Well, when you're in school you don't have much time and stuff and when you get home, you have more time.

39. Shows he feels pressured to learn faster than he's able.

40. MW: Do you have the things at home, boys, that would make it easier to learn?

40– Jame tries to get off subject
49. of reading.

41. JAME: Yeah.

42. MW: Really?

43. JAME: Yeah.

44. MW: Like what?

45. JAME: Models.

46. MW: Models? Does this help you to read?

47. JAME: They don't really help you to read but you learn how to do stuff.

48. MW. Making models is important, right?

49. JAME: Sorta.

50. MW: But you said you weren't so bothered about making models; you said you were bothered about not being able to read.

   50. Refocus back to reading.

51. JAME: But my hobby's models.

   51– Discussion of model
   63. making.

52. MW: That's a good one, too, isn't it? Do you have to read to make a model?

53. JAME: Yeah . . . sometimes.

54. MW: Do you have trouble making the models?

55. JAME: Yeah, sometimes.

56. MW: How do you get over the trouble when you're making the model?

57. JAME: Well, I don't need the directions; I can pretty well figure out how to put the parts together and stuff.

58. MW: Does it take longer to figure out than it does to read it?

59. MARK: Not really.

60. MW: Not really?

61. TIM: I never put a motor in my model.

62. MW: Why?

63. TIM: Cause it's so hard to make.

64. MW: Tommy, you're a little older than these boys are. Tell

   64. Attempt to draw Tom into discussion.

me it is easier to learn — uh —
when is it easier to learn — now
as you're going through it, or
later on?

65. TOM: Um — um — now.

65– Usual hesitation by Tom to
73. contribute idea and conver-
    sation in the group. Yet, his
    contributions are always
    helpful.

66. MW: Why?

67. TOM: Well — well — 'cause later
on you might want to do something else.

68. MW: Like what?

69. TOM: Well, play or scouts . . .

70. MW: After school you mean —
are you saying it's easier to learn
in school now so that after school
you can do the things you like to
do after school?

71. TOM: Yeah.

72. MW: I see. . . . Is it easier to
learn reading in first or second
grade than it is, say, to try to
learn it in the third grade?

73. TOM: Oh, yes!

73– Boys support
75. Tom's idea.

74. MARK: Yes.

75. TIM: Oh, yeah. That's even
harder than writing. It's hard to
learn to use your pencil, but it
would be harder in third. And
in third you gotta learn to write
real fast. Boy!

76. MW: Why do you think things wouldn't be so hard to learn in first or second than they'd be in third?

77. JAME: Well, ya know ya gotta write and then you get in there and ya can't write.

77. Jame attempts to get the boys to give support to his idea of putting off learning until later on.

78. JAME: So — well — so I was thinkin' that if you do have vacation you haven't got time to play around — you have got lots of time to play around and to do your work — you can all do your work together. Like if you're going into third grade you wanted to learn some more about reading and try to read better, you could, um, stay home, and don't go out with your friends a lot, you'll get it pretty good and then go out and play 'cause you've got all the time in the world, like — uh — go on vacations.

79. MW: You know this might be an interesting idea — do you think it is? It is to me, but I don't want to put my ideas in your head — but it does interest me because, if I understand you, Jame, you're saying you would rather learn in vacation time 'cause you think you have more time — what do you think about that idea?

79. Leader shows interest in idea; asks boys' opinion.

80. MARK: I think it's a pretty good one cause —

80. Mark shows some support.

81. JAME: 'cause some people don't do it as fast as other people — they need more time.

81. Jame reveals more concern about trying to keep up with others.

82. MW: How would it work if everybody came to school and didn't learn and then did it all at vacation time?

82. Leader poses idea as it would relate to all children in school.

83. TIM: Not good.

83– Tim and Mark don't like
84. idea.

84. MARK: I don't think it would work so good.

85. MW: You don't think it would work so good?

86. JAME: But if you've got papers at home and things, and you've missed out you can learn them at home during vacation so you know 'em and stuff.

86. Jame again attempts to take learning out of school to where he feels he can learn at his own speed.

87. MARK: But you got to do your regular work in school.

87. Mark tries to turn him back. Good to let children attempt to have this effect on each other.

88. MW: Well, what about the idea — you know — and everything's pretty well scheduled out for you, right? Well, if you don't use that time to good advantage — I'm not talking to you, Jame, I'm talking about all of us because I'm sure we all waste a lot of good time in school that we could put to much better advantage — but how do you think you would operate if you don't use the time that's set for you to learn these things, how in the world would you set it up at vacation time when you don't have a schedule or anything?

88. Leader wonders if you can keep on a schedule at home even if you can't do it at school.

89. JAME: Hmm. Well, I really don't get that. You'd have to make your own schedule or something.

89– Jame suggests making own
90. schedule and Tim supports that.

90. TIM: Yeah.

91. MW: Do you think there's a chance that a person could — could stick to one schedule at vacation time if he couldn't stick to a schedule in school time?

92. BOYS: (Long pause)

93. JAME: It'd be possible, I think (pause). It just came into my mind — I think you should do most of your stuff at school — well, like on Saturdays or Sundays you should enjoy yourself, play or read or something — like maybe for eight or ten days you should enjoy yourself, you learn a lot of stuff — go to country clubs and stuff.

93. Jame again tries to avoid the issue but finally faces the issue that it's better to work at work time so he'd have some free time to play.

94. MW: In other words, are you saying — are you telling us that you think it's better to do the job in school so you're free when the last school bell rings because when you are free you don't have to think about it again?

94. Leader clarifies Jame's statement.

95. JAME: Yep.

96. MW: What do you think about that?

96. Leader asks support from the group.

97. TOM: Yeah.

97– Group supports Jame's
111. statement.

98. MARK: I think it's a pretty good idea.

99. MW: Are you snowing me?

100: TIM: What?

101. MW: Are you snowing me? You know what I mean by that, don't you?

102. MARK: What?

103. MW: Well, are you just telling me something that you think I want to hear or do you really think that's true?

104. TIM: I think it is.

105. TOM: I think it is.

106. BOYS: (Very long silence)

107. MARK: I think it is.

108. MW: Do you really think that's a good idea?

109. JAME: Yeah, because you put your mind on things.

110. MARK: Yeah. When you're in school, you put your mind on school things and then like after school you want to do other things you put your mind on that and then you can come here or go there and you don't have to work and read all the time.

111. MW: Well, Jame, did we help you with something today?

111. Leader asks Jame if the group has helped him.

112. JAME: Yeah.

112. Jame says it has.

113. MW: Do you really think so?

114. JAME: Yeah.

115. TIM: Me, too.

115. Tim says he was helped too.

116. MW: Good. You know, I kind of have a hunch we all have these problems. You're in school, and we teachers are in school much of the time and I'm sure we could all use our time better, so we'd have more time to do more of the things we like to do. So thank you, Mark and Jame, Tim and Tom for helping us to work around to that point. Last week when we met here was another point that was pretty interesting. Who remembers what it was? We started to talk about it and then we jumped to something else.

116. Leader poses another question for discussion.

117. Boys: (Silence)

117. Boys show hesitation to discuss it.

118. MW: What was happening in our group last week?

119. Boys: (Silence)

120. MW: I remember, Timmy, that you just sat in your seat and you wiggled and you squirmed and you shrugged your shoulders a couple of times.

121. TIM: Oh, yeah, I remember! (Warning). Mark kept on talking and nobody ever — he never let anybody in, and he was talking and talking and nobody wanted to butt in — and Tommy was thinkin'.

121. Tim, who was most frustrated when the incident occurred in a previous session, now remembers and eagerly discusses his version.

122. MW: And what did we say? What did we say was happening — what did we feel was happening?

123. Tom: We didn't want to talk.

124. Tim: That's right! We didn't want to talk when Mark was taking all the talk away from us!

125. MW: Well, what else did we say might be happening?

126. Boys: (Silence)

126– Boys like Mark and hesitate
131. criticizing his behavior, i.e. monopolizing time.

127. MW: Remember?

128. Boys: (Silence)

129. MW: Remember?

130. Boys (Long silence)

131. Mark: Ah-h-h — I was talking too much.

131. Mark breaks silence, states incident as he remembers boys' feelings about last session.

132. MW: Well, that's what they tried to say wasn't it — that YOU were talking too much. But do you remember after we got to talking about it what finally started to come out of it?

133. Mark: Uh huh.

134. MW: What?

135. Jame: Well, even when Mark was just keeping his mouth shut nobody was saying a thing.

136. MW: If I remember right — and be sure to change me if I'm wrong — but if I remember right, we decided that Mark was doing all the talking because Tom and Jame weren't coming in and talking — they were letting Mark do all the talking.

136. Leader clarifies previous discussion.

137. TIM: I wasn't. I was trying to think of something.

137. Tim disagrees.

138. MW: Were you? What was it you wanted to say?

138. Leader gives Tim opportunity to start new discussion.

139. TIM: Well, I — I — I've forgotten now but, well, Mark got tricky or something. When I'd start to talk, he'd start talking again.

139. Tim avoids leading discussion, turns back to criticism of Mark.

140. MW: Aw, look at the time! We have to go at two o'clock. I told you that Monday would be kind of short, didn't I? Well, what did we learn today?

140. Leader begins to bring session to a close — looks for summary.

141. JAME: Well, that we should learn about things and study on it.

142. MW: Is that what we learned?

143. MARK: Well, we thought of different times and different places to do the work when you should do it.

144. MW: Okay. Have you an idea of what you'd like to talk about Thursday?

145. JAME: Yeah, sports!

146. MARK: Huh uh — no. Something about the people who want to belong to things, but they're not in — in — being left out.

147. TIM: Yeah! Being left out.

148. MW: All right, I'll do some thinking about that. Will you?

149. BOYS: Yeah, yeah!

SUMMARY

Group counseling with children like group counseling with adults is an exercise in interpersonal relationships. Developmental group counseling with children is a part of the educational process concerned with the needs of children who have typical developmental problems.

Because the child is a social being who learns and grows in the context of groups, counseling through this approach is quite natural for children. Important factors for the counselor to consider in working with children include limits, playfulness, orientation to counseling, and the special problems involved in composing and initiating children's groups. In addition, special consideration should be given to the length of group sessions with children, the size of groups, and the possible usefulness of play media. The authors believe that in general children's groups need more structure than adult groups and that children in developmental groups are provided excellent opportunities to meet individual needs within the context of group structure.

REFERENCES

AXLINE, VIRGINIA M. *Play Therapy*. Boston: Houghton Mifflin Company, 1947.

———. "Developmental Group Counseling," *Elementary School Guidance and Counseling Journal*, Vol. 4, No. 4 (1970).

———. "Theory and Practice of Group Counseling in the Elementary School," in *Readings in Group Counseling* (eds. JAMES J. MURO, and S. L. FREEMAN).

DINKMEYER, DON C. *Towards a Theory of Child Counseling at the Elementary School Level*. Morovia, N.Y.: Chronicle Guidance Publications, 1964–65.

GINOTT, H. G. *Group Psychotherapy with Children*. New York: McGraw-Hill Book Company, 1961.

GLASSER, WILLIAM. *Reality Therapy*. New York: Harper and Row, Publishers, 1965.

HANSEN, J., NILAND, T. M., and ZANI, L. "Model Reinforcement in Group Counseling with Elementary School Children," *Personnel and Guidance Journal*, Vol. 47, No. 8 (1969), pp. 741–44.

HARRIES, F. *Presentation at ASCA Workshop in Group Procedures*. Pembroke, N.H.: Dec. 12–14, 1969.

HAVINGHURST, R. J. *Human Development and Education*. New York: Longmans Green, 1953.

HAYAKAWA, S. I. "Communicating with One's Children," *Psychology Today*, Vol. 1 (1967), pp. 48–53, 74, 76, 77.

JOHNSON, J. A. *Group Therapy: A Practical Approach*. New York: McGraw-Hill Book Company, 1963.

KEIRSEY, D. W. "Systematic Exclusion: Eliminating Chronic Classroom Disruption," in *Behavioral Counseling* (eds. J. D. KRUMBOLTZ, and C. E. THORESEN), pp. 89–114. New York: Holt, Rinehart and Winston, Inc., 1969.

McCarty, T. M. *It All Has to do with Identity.* Salt Lake City, Utah: Institute for the Study of Interaction Systems, 1969.

Mayer, G. R., and Baker, P. "Group Counseling with Elementary School Children: A Look at Group Size," *Elementary School Guidance and Counseling Journal,* Vol. 1 (1967), pp. 140–45.

Moustakas, C. E. *Psychotherapy with Children: The Living Relationship.* New York: Harper and Row, Publishers, 1959.

Mussen, P. H., Conger, J. J., and Kagan, J. *Child Development and Personality.* New York: Harper and Row, Publishers, 1963.

Nelson, R. C. "Pros and Cons of Using Play Media in Counseling," *Elementary School Guidance and Counseling Journal,* Vol. 2 (1967), pp. 143–47.

Ohlsen, Merle M. "Counseling Children in Groups," in *Elementary School Guidance in Illinois* (ed. Ray Page), pp. 83–96. Springfield, Ill.: (no date).

———. "Counseling Children in Groups," *The School Counselor,* Vol. 15 (1968), pp. 343–49.

Ohlsen, Merle M., and Gazda, George M. "Counseling Underachieving Bright Pupils," *Education,* Vol. 86 (1965), pp. 78–81.

Redl, F. *When We Deal with Children.* London: The Free Press, Collier-Macmillan, Limited, 1966.

Shaw, C. R. *The Psychiatric Disorders of Childhood.* New York: Appleton-Century-Crofts, 1966.

Slavson, S. R. *Analytic Group Psychotherapy.* New York: Columbia University Press (1950), pp. 246–47.

Thomas, H. F. "Encounter: The Game of No Game," in *Encounter* (ed A. Burton). San Francisco, Calif.: Jossey-Bass, Inc., Publishers, 1969.

CHAPTER 10

Group Dynamics in the Classroom: The Teacher as Group Leader

RATIONALE

Colleges of education and in-service training for teachers have emphasized the teacher's role as a child-development specialist and a purveyor of the culture. Much emphasis has been given to understanding her role in dealing with individual differences, variances in rates of learning and other important educational procedures. These functions are certainly vital for the classroom teacher. However, little consideration is given to her major role as a group facilitator.

It is our contention that the teacher is a leader of a group, even though she is typically not trained in group dynamics and group leadership. Her very presence in the classroom requires some knowledge of group procedures. She seldom works with children on a one-to-one basis, and as a result, she must be concerned with all of the group activities that occur within the classroom. It is apparent that group procedures appear to be among the most effective methods for dealing with classroom organization, discipline, and the general instructional aspects of guidance. Group work is often the best procedure for working with children who have inadequate concepts of self and self-defeating patterns of behavior insofar as it provides the corrective and encouraging efforts of the peers. It obviously is also effective in working with children who have problems in social relationships.

The power of the psychological group is always present in the school classroom. The consideration is whether the teacher is aware of its presence and is able to utilize it to promote maximum development for both individuals and the group, or whether she operates in a vacuum regarding the dynamics of the group. Some teachers even misunderstand the use of sociometrics and identify the leaders in order to control and suppress them. However, it is usually best to work with those who have the social power.

The group does have an effect upon the behavior of the total classroom and the individuals in it. The values and norms established and accepted by the group set the classroom and individual standards almost regardless of the standards and values held by the teacher. It is fundamental to recognize the norm-and value-establishing functions of the group in order to maximize cohesiveness.

Formerly, the autocratic approach to classroom management was considered efficient. It was believed that all one had to do was to impress children with the fact that you were in charge, more powerful, and able to control through a system of punishment and reward. However, the current literature and experiences with student teachers and full-time teaching professionals indicate that the spirit of the times is such that the autocrat has little chance to function effectively in the classroom. The teacher who tries to dominate and lead through authoritarian procedures will only produce rebellion and resistance, both active and passive. If the teacher is going to succeed in developing a cooperative effort among the members of the class, she must be acquainted with group procedures. It is her responsibility to develop a cohesiveness and to recognize both the individual and group needs of her students. If she refuses to deal with these needs, then she becomes a victim of the power of the group and its negative action towards her. Student unrest and rebellion are rampant not only in colleges, but on the public school campus and at all levels of instruction.

Some teachers have coped with the problem through withdrawal. They have tried to avoid the issue of group dynamics. They have maintained an unsure, almost detached approach to classroom interaction. They have attempted to make all the rules and decisions themselves. As a result, they have suffered from the tyranny of the group.

Thus, we are suggesting that the teacher needs to become acquainted with the procedures that are described in this book. Some of the group procedures will not be appropriate for the classroom. However, an acquaintance with the theories of group work, group dynamics, and the way in which groups influence behavior, sets a background for a more effective relationship with children. At the same time, acquaintance with group-counseling procedures and ways of adapting them to groups led by classroom teachers will be valuable.

ANALYSIS OF CLASSROOM GROUPS

It will be important for the teacher to develop skills in formally and informally observing social transactions. The classroom is a dynamic, changing society. Sociometrics provide a systematic way of identifying, evaluating, and eventually implementing the interaction patterns of the classroom. Persons are constantly involved in making choices. The use of sociometrics makes it possible to study the pattern of social choices.

Social and emotional development are crucial for academic development. Studies continue to indicate that if a child is to do well intellectually, he must be socially secure. In order for the child to achieve well in school, the teacher must be aware of the importance of peer relations and the child's view of self in relation to others. Until he is able to cope with social and self problems—often best solved through group-guidance classroom discussions or group counseling—he may not be able to cope with the sources of underachievement.

The science of sociometrics was orginally the work of Moreno. He discovered the procedure of working with delinquents (Moreno and Jennings, 1944).

It is not the purpose of this chapter to present a detailed description of how to conduct sociometric studies. Those interested in more details of how to construct questionnaires and analyze and tabulate the data of sociometrics should refer to Dinkmeyer and Caldwell (1970).

It will be equally important that the teacher become aware of the social nature of human behavior. Once she conceptualizes man as a social being, this should place an emphasis upon the significance of the social transactions in the classroom. This can be seen best by analysis of three factors:

(a) *The action.* The behavior of either the teacher or the child, for example, most of the children are sitting down in the classroom while one is still standing.

(b) *The responding behavior of the teacher.* What does she do? For example, the teacher reminds him to sit down.

(c) *The consequence.* The result of the teacher's action, does the child respond to a request to sit down or does he remain standing? How does the teacher feel and behave at this point?

This ABC procedure enables the teacher who keeps anecdotal records to begin to analyze what it is that reinforces this behavior. The anecdotes provide an ongoing observational record of the social behavior in the classroom. To help in understanding the current situation and the child's personal interpretation of his experience, teachers can begin to comprehend life through the child's eyes by their observations and records of behavior. The anecdotes would describe the setting, the actions, the reactions and the responses of those involved. It would supply questions and mood cues whenever possible. Details related to anecdote-recording can be found in Chapter Three of Dinkmeyer (1965).

METHODS OF SOLVING GROUP PROBLEMS

The significance of group dynamics for the teacher stems from our awareness that man is a social being and that all of his social transactions and social movements express his personality, character and style of life (Dreikurs, 1958). The teacher must become able to understand the pattern of psychological movement. She becomes cognizant of the social purpose and consequences of behavior. The democratic society has made it a necessity that teachers understand the group, peer relations, and sociometric patterns. The power to demand conformity and to influence children autocratically is rapidly diminishing. Any teacher will testify that children do not respond instantly to authoritarian requests and that new procedures are necessary.

Jennings (1951) and a number of others have found that children are influenced more by the opinions of peers than the approval of teachers as they grow older. The group has the therapeutic potential to exert corrective influence once the teacher comprehends her role as a group leader. The group will either aid the development of the individual and the total class or become an impediment. While we would not minimize the importance of the individual, it is apparent that far too little attention has been directed towards assisting the teacher in her role as a group leader. It is our position that the classroom teacher would benefit from a special course in group dynamics that would help her understand her role as a leader, while developing skills in sociometric analysis, group leadership, observation, and analysis of social transactions, role playing, sociodrama, group-discussion leadership, and acquainting herself with programs in developmental group guidance.

The group can be utilized to motivate learning by facilitating the development of attitudes and norms which foster positive attitudes toward learning and stress cooperation and competition. An emphasis is placed on the ability to develop cohesive groups. The teacher's effectiveness is often determined by the capacity to unite the class by establishing mutually derived goals and purposes.

Dreikurs developed a formula for solving group problems. His democratic approach contains the following steps:

1. THE RELATIONSHIP. The emphasis is upon mutual respect and mutual trust in which the participants neither fight nor give in. They are kind and firm in their approach to the problem. This characterizes their concern for others as well as for themselves. They have social interest and are willing to see the other person's point of view.

2. PROBLEM IDENTIFICATION. Members identify the problems and establish a hierarchy or set of priorities in a relationship of complete equality. Thus, administration and staff, teacher and student, president and employee, parent and child—each comes with the same rights and responsibilities for identifying and solving the problem. It is critical to pinpoint the real problems and issues—i.e. on the surface problems between people often appear to be over a specific decision about how to accomplish a task, etc., when the real issue is often one of who has superior status and power and who can force the other to comply.

3. CHANGING THE AGREEMENT. There is recognition that in order to solve the problem you must reach an agreement since you can change others and the transaction only if you change yourself; change must begin with your own attitudes, values, and perceptions. Once we are aware of our power to change our approach to life and our tacit agreement regarding relationships, then we have the capacity to change. We must accept the blame for our actions and be responsible for our own behavior without seeking to place the blame outside of self. We ask, "What can I do differently?"

4. FULL PARTICIPATION IN DECISION MAKING. This step recognizes that authorities alone can no longer dominate and require submission. Decision making now requires full participation and democratic leadership; when all are responsible to decide, then they all are responsible to cooperate.

GROUP-DISCUSSION PROCEDURES

Many teachers are not aware of the value of group discussion. They have been trained to focus on eliciting facts and to be concerned with the cognitive elements of a discussion. However, if we are to influence human behavior, attitudes, and values, a regularly established set of discussion procedures conducted during a specified period will be required. In many instances the teachers feel ill-prepared and inadequate to lead these discussions. Some are concerned with whether discussions are a proper utilization of school time. However, if they look at the general objectives of human development and classroom guidance, it is apparent that these objectives can be best accomplished through the group discussion. It will be important for the teacher to be aware of the relationship between feelings of adequacy, self-concept, and adequate academic functioning. The evidence indicates that students who feel adequate function more effectively academically (Combs and Soper, 1963; Sears and Sherman, 1964).

Group procedures, then, can perhaps be our most powerful tool to motivate and influence behavior. The teacher has before her an opportunity to develop a productive discussion. The goals of group discussion are:

1. To develop a self-understanding.
2. To develop awareness of self and others.
3. To develop a new perception of human relationships.

These require discussions in which the leader avoids lecturing, sermonizing, and moralizing. In contrast, she shares the responsibility for direction with the members of the group. She encourages open, congruent expression of what the children really feel and experience.

This type of group leadership requires that the teacher be alert to all of the social transactions occurring in the classroom. She needs to investigate with the students what is happening in the here and now, and what they think about it. They explore how they feel about others, what they experience in themselves, and what they will do about their feelings and experiences. The discussions are designed to help stimulate better relationships and new goals for the group. The discussions may involve human relationships and a new understanding of the purposes of behavior.

It is evident that if the teacher is to serve as a leader of group discussion, she will need to have all of the typical counseling procedures at her command. She must be able to reflect, clarify, and confront what is happening between the members of the group and the leader.

COMPETENCIES FOR GROUP DISCUSSION

In our training of group-discussion leaders, it became apparent that we needed to establish specific competencies which could serve as goals for those learning, and yardsticks for those evaluating and instructing them. The following material is given to students to provide direction and to become the basis for their self-evaluation and the instruction and evaluation of their group-discussion leadership skills.

1.   Show the group you care and are concerned with developing a relationship of mutual respect. Demonstrate your interest, concern, and kindness, but be committed to meaningful discussion and do not hesitate to be firm, showing respect for yourself as well as the children. Help the children comprehend how the teacher hears by reflective

listening to each input. Be sure to hear not only the words, but the meanings and the feelings of what is said.

2. Structure the group so the members understand the purpose of the group discussion and establish their own limits. Members must be ready to share their concerns and willing to listen closely to others. A spirit of give-and-take and honest, open feedback should pervade.

3. Sense the group atmosphere and be willing to discuss it. Be sensitive to the feelings of the individual in the group and help him feel understood—i.e. "I am getting a message that you are unhappy," or "I feel you really care!"

4. Link the thoughts and feelings of group members. Point out the similarities and differences in the concepts, attitudes and feelings being discussed. The leader especially must be able to show the relationship between what two children are talking about to help them recognize common problems, and clarify differences and commonalities.

5. Encourage silent members to participate when they feel ready. This usually involves being aware of nonverbal clues such as a facial gesture, glance, or halting attempt to enter the group.

6. The children are learning a new process of cooperation in contrast to competition. The leader must observe any tendencies of children to be empathic or to link or supply alternative solutions to problems. These attempts should be immediately encouraged and reinforced.

7. Group discussion can take a negative turn if the leader is not perceptive of the interaction. We are interested in fostering personal development, hence the interaction should be concerned with topics which permit interpersonal exploration. Group members should be assisted to see both the strengths and assets in individuals. Emphasis is placed on positive as well as negative feedback. The leader helps the group see the value of feedback by modeling it and encouraging its utilization.

8. The leader must be alert to detect feelings and attitudes which are implied but not expressed. He helps the group develop tentative analyses of the purpose of behavior. He might say, "Is it possible"or "Could it be?" and state his hunch about the purpose in a tentative manner. He helps the group learn to formulate hypotheses and make guesses about the purposes of each other's behavior.

9. The effective group leader is able to help the children express more clearly their thoughts, feelings, and attitudes. He does this through clarifying, restating, and summarizing.

10. The leader helps the members summarize and evaluate what they have learned. About five minutes before the close of the session

he asks, "What do you think you learned about yourself and others today?" He tries to involve each child in considering his personal learning. Helping the group consider what is happening accelerates and facilitates the group process.

Children should be encouraged to formulate their own limits. However, the leader should help them consider some of the following procedures which promote effective discussion:

a.   The discussion goes best when we trust each other and have mutual respect. We have to be concerned enough to listen and want to help others.

b.   Really listen to what others say. Are you able to state what he has said and felt when he finishes?

c.   Be honest and open. Say what you really feel. Speak whenever you feel you have something to say which will help you or the group.

d.   In giving feedback, consider how it will help the others for you to say this.

When certain individuals or the group become negative, or pick on an individual, the mature leader can use this as an opportunity to discuss the purpose of getting special attention or power through this behavior. The leader can also use puppetry and role playing to help increase sensitivity to negative remarks.

The potential in group discussion is tremendous and teachers will find it a most rewarding experience as their skills develop.

LEARNING THROUGH DISCUSSION

Although the democratic way of life is generally endorsed, our educational procedures have not been characterized by democratic interaction. Instead, we have relied upon authoritarian practices and uninspiring lectures to transmit knowledge and acquaint students with the dreams of equality, involvement, and purposefulness.

William Hill (1969) has developed a systematic procedure whereby one can acquire knowledge for use through group discussion. This is in direct contrast to mere acquisition of facts and memorization. The purpose of group discussion is to bring about the interaction between students who understand or who do not understand a specific topic so that they might increase their understanding through attempting to clarify and explain to each other.

While the discussion groups are subject to the laws of group dynamics, the focus of the group is upon increasing communication for the purpose of enhancing the potential of the members and learning the course material. These group discussions are developed in an orderly sequence and an agreed-upon method of procedures is utilized.

Hill has the group proceed through nine steps called the group cognitive map.

Group Cognitive Map

Step One.   Definition of terms and concepts.
Step Two.   General statement of author's message.
Step Three. Identification of major themes or subtopics.
Step Four. Allocation of time.
Step Five. Discussion of major themes and subtopics.
Step Six.   Integration of material with other knowledge.
Step Seven. Application of the material.
Step Eight. Evaluation of author's presentation.
Step Nine. Evaluation of group and individual performance. [Hill, 1969, p. 23]

Hill's booklet describes these steps in detail.

In order to transverse the steps of the group cognitive map effectively, members must have the interpersonal skills necessary to perform certain group roles—the roles facilitate group maintenance and task accomplishment. While the leader must have skills in these roles, members must also assume the responsibility for taking on several of these roles.

The roles have been categorized by Hill as follows:

Group Roles and Member Skills

A.   Sequence of task roles specific to discussion of a topic.
    1. Initiating.
    2. Giving and asking for information.
    3. Giving and asking for reactions.
    4. Restating and giving examples.
    5. Confronting and reality testing.
    6. Clarifying, synthesizing, and summarizing.
B.   Overall task roles required in *Learning Through Discussion* method.
    7. Gatekeeping and expediting.
    8. Timekeeping.
    9. Evaluating and diagnosing.
    10. Standard setting.
C.   Group maintenance roles required in *Learning Through Discussion* method.

11. Sponsoring and encouraging.
12. Group tension relieving. [Hill, 1969, p. 33]

The process requires that a member help the group initiate or get down to work. Then there must be a sharing of understandings and perceptions. This cannot be accomplished ritualistically, such as in the typical recitation–rotation process where one member states his understanding and passes it on to the next who gives his understanding of the next topic, but without really hearing each other or interacting. There must be reactions and feedback if there is to be maximum benefit. Instead, in this process members are asked to restate what others have said and to provide feedback. Misinformation is not allowed to pass and confrontation is an important procedure. Members develop skills in clarifying, synthesizing, and summarizing. The gatekeeping function attempts to spread participation by involving those who have not said anything. The timekeeping function involves awareness of the clock so that the group paces itself and budgets time for the topic. Evaluation and diagnosis can be handled by assigning a group member to be the process observer. The group also needs members who are capable of encouraging and relieving group tension.

The group must develop criteria applicable to a good group learning situation. Here is Hill's list of criteria:

List of Criteria

1. Prevalence of a warm, accepting, nonthreatening group climate.
2. Learning is approached as a cooperative enterprise.
3. Learning is accepted as the *raison d'être* of the group.
4. Everyone participates and interacts.
5. Leadership functions are distributed.
6. Group sessions and the learning task are enjoyable.
7. The material is adequately and efficiently covered.
8. Evaluation is accepted as an integral part of the group operation.
9. Members attend regularly and come prepared. [Hill, 1969, p. 41]

The role of the instructor in *Learning through Discussion* is one of a resource expert. He demonstrates and circulates between the groups, and serves as the group trainer. He acquaints the students with the mechanics of the group cognitive map, group role and member skills, and the list of criteria. He observes groups and feeds back his observations to the group and the class as a whole.

In introducing the class to the method, the thirty-minute film, "Learning through Discussion," by Hill and Stoller is very valuable. This film features a classroom presentation. This can be followed by a demonstration group led by the instructor. Then the class can be divided into small groups led by a designated leader from the group who assumes responsibility for getting the group to follow the *Learning through Discussion* method.

The role of the student in the *LTD* method necessitates internalizing the group cognitive map and playing most of the group roles. There are five critical interaction behaviors which he should practice:

1. Restate in his own words what others have said.
2. Sponsor other members.
3. Give encouragement and approval.
4. Formulate and cite examples.
5. Ask questions. [Hill, 1969, p. 50]

Hill also says:

It is perhaps instructive to think of *LTD* as a technological tool similar to programmed instruction and teaching machines. Personally, we do not feel threatened by these devices, but do feel that programmed instruction and teaching machines very effectively impart to an individual facts and rote memory learnings of impersonal matter. The relevance and personal significance of these learnings are best explored through group discussion. [Hill, 1969, p. 60]

This section serves as an overview of the *LTD* method and those interested in developing this essential skill will benefit from the book. *Learning through Discussion* by William F. Hill.

THE LARGE GROUP DISCUSSION

William Glasser has made extensive efforts in recent years to popularize large group meetings. He suggests that the classroom is the setting for a variety of meetings concerned with social behavior, intellectually important subjects, and a diagnosis of the progress being made in school. The social-problem solving meeting is one in which focus is placed on solving the individual and group educational problems of the class and the school. The meeting recognizes and emphasizes the fact that each student has individual and group responsibility. This responsibility for learning and behaving is shared by the entire group. Glasser suggests that the children not only learn how to solve their problems through the meeting, but they gain in scholastic achievement. He refers to a report by Edmund Gordon (1967) indicating that the extent to which a pupil feels he has control over his own destiny is strongly related to achievement.

Glasser gives a number of examples of ways in which he works with classroom groups. He begins by applying the principles of reality therapy in suggesting that to change behavior you must become involved. He then permits a thorough and open discussion of whatever concerns the children. This is what he calls exposing the problem for open, honest discussion. It is conducted in such a way that the children feel free to examine the total problem and all of its aspects.

He tries to get a commitment from the students to do something about the problem. The discussion is always directed toward some solution just as long as the solution does not include punishment or fault finding. The meetings are conducted with all the students seated in a tight circle. Glasser believes this element is critical for getting total involvement. He suggests that the group should be utilized for the essential purpose of attempting to solve the individual and group educational problems of the class and the school (Glasser, 1969, p. 122). The process stems from the basic philosophical premise that the school class is a working problem-solving unit in which each child has both individual and group possibilities. Thus, responsibility for learning and behaving becomes a shared concept between the group leader and the class. Topics are many and varied, but the essence of the process suggested by Glasser stems from the principles he formulated in his earlier text, *Reality Therapy* (1965). The child seeking a basic identity must be helped to discover behavioral pathways that will provide him with identity and responsible behavior. To be responsible in Glasserian terms is to be able to meet the basic needs of love and worth without interfering with another's right to meet the same needs. Applied to the large group meetings, the group leader works with his groups along certain inflexible guidelines:

1.   All problems relative to the class as a group and to any individual in the class are eligible for discussion.
2.   The discussion itself should always be directed toward solving the problem; the solution should never include punishment or fault finding.
3.   Meetings should always be conducted with the teacher and students seated in a tight circle. [Glasser, 1969, pp. 128, 129, 132]

To add relevance to education, Glasser suggests open-ended meetings wherein the leader does not look for factual answers but attempts to stimulate children to think and to relate their knowledge to any given topic under discussion.

The actual leader role necessary to initiate and maintain class meetings has been outlined by Glasser in his book *Schools Without Failure,* and the reader is referred to this book for a more complete discussion. The essence of the leader's role advocated by Glasser is as follows:

1.   The philosophy of the leader [taken from *Schools Without Failure*] is discussed with the school faculty.

2.   If possible, someone who has had experience in the types of meetings advocated by Glasser demonstrates techniques.

3.   Groups are arranged in large circles with the leader and the class sitting in a single circle.

4.   The leader sits in a different place in the circle each day.

5.   Leaders should team lead whenever possible.

6.   Topics for discussion may be introduced by the leader [programmed] or by the class.

7.   Meetings concerning discipline should not be repetitive. To discuss continually one child with problems does more harm than good.

8.   Time and length of meetings should depend on the age and meeting experience of the class.

9.   Children seem to respond best if they are given an opportunity to raise their hands.

10.   A leader never interrupts a child to correct bad grammar, bad usage, or mild profanity.

11.   Children will often become very personal, talking about subjects that ordinarily are considered private. [Glasser, 1969, pp. 155–161]

Glasser advocates such meetings on a daily basis for all age groups, and it would appear that teachers who could accept and follow the guidelines he presents would be making great strides toward the concept of guidance for all children. The stimulating questions he suggests in *Schools Without Failure* should be carefully read by teachers at all levels.

Role playing is another procedure readily adaptable for classroom use. This informal dramatization of a situation presented by the leader or developed by the class provides an opportunity for students to take on various roles and thereby find out how others think, feel, and behave. Role playing should be done so that the child who is acting comes to comprehend how the other person thinks, feels, experiences. The purpose is to get a better understanding of self and others in order to cope with the tasks of life. It is learning through participation—learning by doing—and the opportunity to assume the role of others and react to various situations, that develop a better understanding of one's behavior patterns as well as those of others.

The critical factors in role playing which produce changes are empathy (the ability to experience how others feel) and choice. These are used as agents to change attitudes and behavior. Role playing provides the opportunity to transfer a concept into action and provides the milieu for practice of behavioral changes that are beneficial for an individual's development. Role playing, of course, should be accomplished in a creative and spontaneous manner. When it is practiced in this way it is bound to increase spontaneity.

While role playing has certain therapeutic effects one should not overlook its diagnostic value. Often, under the guise of being someone else, the student may say or do things that he really desires to do. In the role of teacher, brother, or father, he reveals his perceptions about his world, how he believes these people think, and how they feel about human relationships. Thus, access to his style of life becomes available through the role-playing activity.

While the role playing is going on, the leader encourages all the members of the class to become observant of the purposes and causes of behavior. They learn to anticipate the results of their behavior and to analyze situations and human relationships.

Role playing really enables us to deal with the whole person. While humans always act, think, and feel simultaneously in their responses, in the school situation teachers more often behave as if they were not concerned with the holistic response. They take a part of the response and consider the child's thoughts, feelings, or what it is he is doing, failing to comprehend the fact that they are inextricably interrelated. The role-playing situation permits the child to utilize all these processes when he tries on a new behavior.

In initiating role playing in a group, it is important to begin with volunteers and preferably sociable children who will do well in the role-playing activity. In any instance, one should be certain to make some positive, encouraging remarks about certain aspects of the role playing.

Another system which uses improved communication techniques to enhance the self is titled *Self-Enhancing Education.* Norma Randolph and William Howe have been particularly active in developing training manuals and institutes for teachers in these processes. The *Self-Enhancing Education* procedure is one that teaches communication techniques directly to students and teachers. It is concerned with developing more fully functioning individuals through awareness of both verbal and nonverbal messages. It regards each person as a unique resource of his feelings and perceptions and thus provides regularly scheduled as well as on-demand opportunities for children, teachers, and parents to be such resources. It is the thesis of the technique that this is the most effective way to foster feelings of acceptance and worth. From this process the reflective image automatically becomes "I count, I am important, I have worth, I am heard, somebody cares about how I feel and perceive." (Randolph and Howe, 1968).

The two primary communication techniques involve exercises in reflective listening and congruent sending. The leaders provide training in developing transactions with others so that the quality of the perception will enhance the relationship rather than alienate it. Their manual details methods whereby these communication processes can be taught.

Bessell and Palomares (1967) have developed a procedure whereby the teacher becomes the facilitator of a modified encounter group. They provide a manual and an Institute in Training in Awareness of Classroom Behavior. The system is based upon some of the original constructs of Karen Horney and Alfred Adler. They suggest that the basic drives to achieve mastery and to gain social approval are the foundations of motivational development. The focal motivational problem in life then becomes the person's view of self. If one feels loved and self-confident he is free to pursue the urge to be capable in gaining approval.

Bessell and Palomares have developed a curriculum for the prevention of poor self-concept and inadequate motivational situations. It centers around cultivating awareness of self and others, developing self-acceptance, and a healthy self-image. It deals with one's feelings, thoughts, and behavior. The human-development program includes a large number of specific exercises and lesson plans. The magic-circle groups aim to dispel any feelings of uniqueness and in the circles children who feel uncertain and afraid begin to recognize that there are others like them (universalization). The sessions are so scheduled that success is provided in every session, and while the tasks are challenging, the program is set up to encourage positive behavior and reinforce confidence. The program uses group therapy and group-encounter techniques which have as their goal the development of greater awareness and a higher level of functioning. At the same time, it is designed to be within the range of children's understanding.

The curriculum is usually divided into units of six weeks each. Through a number of games such as *You Can Make Him Feel Bad or Good* and *Can You Guess What Makes Me Mad?* the group members begin to understand the cause-and-effect relationship between behavior and feelings.

A comprehensive multimedia program titled *Developing Understanding of Self and Others* (DUSO) is available from American Guidance Service, Circle Pines, Minnesota 55014. This program provides a planned sequential curriculum for use by the classroom teacher. Activities include open-ended stories designed to stimulate group discussion, role playing and puppetry activity lessons, and pictures to stimulate discussion. The materials are currently developed for use in the primary grades.

The DUSO program has also been used by counselors to stimulate more meaningful and purposeful group counseling with primary school children. The short, open-ended stories focus the children's attention on a particular concept or problem. It facilitates more purposeful discussion by directing their attention to a particular concern which can become a common problem. The role-playing activity is another procedure for getting the children involved in meaningful interaction with each other; it involves learning through doing.

Pictures which illustrate children coping with certain basic developmental tasks become an excellent avenue to open up particular areas of concern. It has been demonstrated that classroom teachers can conduct productive group discussions provided thay are supplied with adequate directions and materials which stimulate interaction.

It is apparent that the teacher must become competent in group leadership. Now there are a number of programs available which provide specific assistance for teachers in group discussions.

SUMMARY

Consideration is given to the teacher's role as a group facilitator in the classroom. The rationale for group approaches is based upon the nature of the child and the setting. An ABC procedure for analyzing transactions with the child is presented. The goals of group-discussion procedures and specific competencies for group-discussion leadership are set forth.

Learning Through Discussion by Hill, a systematic procedure for acquiring knowledge, is included. This procedure includes a group cognitive map, group roles and member skills, and criteria for a good group learning situation.

The large group discussion procedures of William Glasser are an application of his reality therapy in the classroom. This approach is concerned with developing identity and responsible behavior in the child.

Role playing is another group procedure directed at developing a better understanding of self and others through assuming the role of others. Other methods for improving communication include: self-enhancing education, the Bessell and Palomares human-development materials, and the DUSO program.

REFERENCES

BESSELL, HAROLD, and PALOMARES, UVALDO. *Methods in Human Development.* San Diego, Calif.: Human Development Training Institute, 1967.

COMBS, ARTHUR W., and SOPER, DANIEL. *The Relationship of Child Perceptions to Achievement and Behavior in the Early School Years.* Gainesville, Fla.: University of Florida, 1963. U.S. Office of Education Cooperative Research Project No. 814.

DINKMEYER, DON C. *Child Development: The Emerging Self.* Englewood Cliffs, N.J.: Prentice-Hall, Inc., 1965.

DINKMEYER, DON C. *Developing Understanding of Self and Others* (DUSO), Circle Pines, Minnesota, American Guidance Service.

DINKMEYER, DON C., and CALDWELL, EDSON. *Developmental Counseling and Guidance: A Comprehensive School Approach.* New York: McGraw-Hill Book Company, 1970.

DREIKURS, RUDOLF. "Group Dynamics in the Classroom," *Group Psychotherapy and Group Approaches.* Chicago: The Alfred Adler Institute, 1960. 13th Congress of International Association of Applied Psychology.

GLASSER, WILLIAM. *Reality Therapy.* New York: Harper and Row, Publishers, 1965.

———. *Schools Without Failure.* New York: Harper and Row, Publishers, 1969.

GORDON, EDMUND. *JACD Bulletin.* Vol. 3, No. 5 (November, 1967). New York: Yeshiva University, Ferkauf Graduate School.

HILL, WILLIAM F. *Learning through Discussion.* Beverly Hills, Calif.: Sage Publications, Inc., 1969.

JENNINGS, HELEN H. *Sociometry in Group Relations.* Washington, D.C.: American Council, 1951.

MORENO, JACOB L., and JENNINGS, HELEN H. "Sociometric Methods of Grouping and Regrouping," *Sociometry,* Vol. 7 (November, 1944), pp. 397–411.

RANDOLPH, NORMA, and HOWE, WILLIAM. "Self-Enhancing Education," *Communication Techniques and Processes that Enhance Training Manual* (1968), p. 50. Cupertino, Calif.: Cupertino Union School District.

SEARS, PAULINE, and SHERMAN, VIVIAN. *In Pursuit of Self-Esteem.* San Francisco, Calif.: Wadsworth Publishing Company, Inc., 1964.

CHAPTER 11

Group Counseling and Consulting with Teachers

THE GROUP procedures we have outlined have considerable potential and value in a variety of situations. They can be used effectively in the classroom, with parent groups, and also have many implications for teacher education and teacher development. The procedures and processes involved in group counseling need to be applied on a broader base if school counselors are to have a developmental emphasis and if the maximum gain is to accrue to children, parents, and teachers. Skill in utilizing the group process, once developed, can be applied to many areas. In the ensuing chapters, specific application to teachers, the classroom, and parents will be presented.

In preparation for work with groups of teachers, the counselor would certainly want to be acquainted with the implications of group-dynamics research for the classroom. He would recognize that many of the group-dynamic factors mentioned in Chapter 2 have implications for a teacher group. Certainly, pressures to uniformity, power, motivational processes in groups, and an understanding of the therapeutic forces in a group are critical to effective functioning. One of the theoretical orientations that has given particular attention to group procedures is the Adlerian. Group work with children, teachers, and parents is outlined in detail in the book by Sonstegard and Dreikurs (1967). These groups have been conducted throughout the nation, particularly in Oregon, California, Arizona, Illinois, and West Virginia.

Sonstegard and Dreikurs suggest that seminars with teachers should be developed in collaboration with school administrators. The principal provides his support and encouragement for the meetings which are

conducted by the counselor. It is important to have the school administrator introduce the first meeting and thereby provide official sanction.
'If he is able to join the teachers as a participating member and become
aware of the reactions and attitudes of the group, this can be of considerable value. However, it is important he divest himself of the role
of administrator or he will be a liability (Sonstegard and Dreikurs, 1967).

The leader becomes part of the group and does not function in a
manner that gives the impression he is a lecturer or instructor. There
is considerable evidence from observation that didactic seminars on
discipline, understanding the child, and other equally suitable topics
will probably not produce change in the teacher or the child. The
didactic lecture usually reaches only the cognitive domain, but does not
involve the feelings of the teacher, nor does it expect her to translate
beliefs into action or practice new behavior. No commitment to change
is extracted, little is expected, and little is accomplished. Efficacious
in-service work must involve the whole teacher, her beliefs, feelings,
values, attitudes, and behavior.

An atmosphere of mutual trust and mutual respect is basic for the
effective teacher group. "No teacher, regardless of competency, will
relate the baffling problems with which she struggles in the classroom
if there is any possibility that the method she has used to attempt to
correct the situation might be pointed out as wrong and as a reflection
of her ability" (Sonstegard and Dreikurs, 1967, p. 73).

These sessions do not discuss child behavior in the abstract, or bury
the teacher in generalities and educational terminology. Instead, they
focus on the specific behavior of a child and produce definite recommendations for action. In the teleoanalytic procedure the counselor
checks out the purpose of the child's behavior by looking at the way the
child responds to the teacher's corrections, and the feelings which the
child's behavior produces in the teacher. The book by Sonstegard and
Dreikurs provides typescript examples of teacher seminars.

Other theories have also been interested in working with teachers in
group settings. Albert Ellis has done considerable work with teachers
to help them think more logically in regard to their faulty assumptions
about life and the child's behavior. Glasser has also spent considerable
time in educating teachers in the utilization of reality-therapy concepts
in classroom sessions (Glasser, 1969). The transactional approach with
teachers is well represented in the Harris's work *I'm OK; You're OK*
and has made a major impact in work with teachers.

A group procedure that has devoted particular attention to teachers
involves the work of the National Training Laboratories (NTL). NTL
has developed a rather extensive set of workshops to develop self-

understanding. The Achievement Motivation Seminars sponsored by the Stone-Brandel Foundation in Chicago have also made a significant impact on teachers. These seminars focus on helping the teacher become aware of her personal assets and strengths. They also emphasize utilizing encouragement and positive approaches with children.

RATIONALE

One might ask, why work with teachers in groups? Some brief attention to the validity of working with teachers in a group setting in contrast to one-to-one is probably valuable and necessary at this point.

The authors have chosen to counsel with teachers in groups because of some fundamental theoretical beliefs about the nature of man and human behavior. We recognize that most problems are interpersonal and social. Problems originate in the group and in relationship to others, and they can best be solved in a group setting. Actions have a social purpose. All the behavior and meanings in the group have a purpose whether they be verbal or nonverbal. We need to deal with the meanings that are occurring in the social transactions between the members of the group. The group provides the opportunity to see the life-style, faulty assumptions and mistaken ideas of both the teacher and the child. It is a holistic approach, taking into consideration the intellect, feelings, and behavior of both the teacher and the child. It creates an opportunity for the teacher to enter an atmosphere which is loving, caring, and support providing. At the same time the atmosphere processes considerable feedback to the teacher about her behavior, feelings, and attitudes. The group obviously provides a broader mirror of the teacher's behavior than any individual consultation permits. The group provides an opportunity for give and take. Most important, the opportunity to give some assistance to another teacher is critical in the development of the teacher who provides the help. She has the chance to feel needed, accepted, and that she contributed.

This type of group provides a new medium and mode for communication between professionals. Education and the schools have lacked a channel whereby experienced and beginning teachers might share insights and approaches to understanding the child. This group provides the setting for dynamic interaction between concerned educators. It has the potential to stimulate professional and personal development and to promote cohesion of the teaching staff. The teacher has at her disposal all the corrective influences that are available in a well-structured group. The group deals with both the external units (the child and his problems) and the internal units (self-concept and attitudes of the

teacher). Behavior is always understood in terms of its social consequences. The teachers soon learn to analyze not only what the child
does, but what it is they are doing that is reinforcing or encouraging this
behavior. The teacher group is encouraged to look at the ABCs of
behavior. The ABCs involve:

> A: the antecedent, or the event that stimulates behavior by
> another, i.e. in teacher–child reactions the antecedent may
> be an action by the child or the teacher which stimulates a
> response.
> B: the behavior in response to the antecedent event, the
> action of the other party.
> C: the consequence of the interaction, the action which is
> taken by the originator of the interaction.

The teacher is encouraged to keep anecdotal records which provide
her and the consultant with insight into the purpose of the behavior. An
anecdotal example illustrates the procedure:

> TEACHER: John, why are you walking around the room?
> JOHN: I don't know!
> TEACHER: Get to your seat.
> JOHN: (He moves slowly while Bill and Carl grin and he
> finally sits down smiling. Some time passes and John is still
> not working.)
> TEACHER: John, what are you doing?
> JOHN: I don't understand the problem.
> TEACHER: Did you listen when I explained it?
> JOHN: Yes, but I just can't do it.
> TEACHER: Well, try, or I'll send you out of the room.
> JOHN: (He makes feeble effort.)
> TEACHER: All right, I'll show you how. (She comes to the
> desk and does the problem for him.)

This interaction shows us how John learns to control the teacher,
receives social reinforcement and encouragement from his peers for his
resistance, and gets special service by playing inadequate.

The purpose of teacher groups is to facilitate the development of
teachers by helping them recognize the relationship between the cognitive and affective domains—between their ideas, attitudes, and beliefs about children, and their own feelings and self-percepts. It is based
on a contention that we can reach more individuals and help more

children by working with the teachers who have an opportunity to work 1,000 hours a year with an individual child. Teachers have access to the child's life space and milieu and can observe his approach to the work tasks of life.

This approach, then, is directed at integrating the guidance process and the educative process in order to affect the learning climate.

WHO LEADS TEACHER GROUPS?

We are suggesting that the leader of the teacher group most logically is the new developmental counselor. This is the counselor who serves as a consultant–counselor, an agent of change, a catalyst, a stimulator of ideas, thoughts, an investigator of feelings and of attitudes, and a motivating force who helps teachers change their behavior. In the group he has the opportunity to investigate the purposes of behavior, create insight into alternatives, enable group members to experience reality testing, to benefit from spectator therapy (learning through listening to others) and finally, to make a commitment to change.

This developmental counselor requires a special type of professional preparation. His training will be directed at developing a person with special skills in human relations and group work. He will have all of the typical counselor-education training but he will also have specific courses designed to prepare him for leading teacher groups. These courses include: seminars in developmental and adolescent psychology, the teacher and classroom guidance procedures, guidance consulting, developmental appraisal, group processes in guidance, and group consulting.

In his professional training he has been in a didactic experiential practicum in which he has had specific instruction in group leadership and has also experienced the benefit of the group process. He will have had not only classroom lectures and discussions, but experiences as a client in a learning, efficiency-process experience where he as a member of a group became aware of self and others.

We are also suggesting that this counselor needs more than the typical master's degree training. He needs advanced training to conceive of and practice his role as a human-relations specialist. He needs to comprehend curriculum development and ways to improve conditions for learning. He will have had advanced group dynamics, advanced group counseling, theory and practice, and certainly sufficient practicum and supervision experiences. Preferably, he will have a supervised internship accompanied by advanced training in sociology, psychology, and anthropology. We are describing the developmental counselor who can and will make a difference in the school milieu.

The counselor will accomplish this first by enlisting administrative support. He will be certain that both administration and staff understand the nature of his work and the direction in which his skills in group procedures will take the staff. This consultant must be an expert in human relationships and human behavior. It is essential that he understand the necessary conditions for developing an effective communications system with administration. He must have procedures through which he translates the specific milieu of the school and the psychological relationships among staff, administration, and pupils into a more meaningful pattern which helps administration clarify the direction it must go.

The counselor would not accept a position in a school system until he was certain the administration understood what he meant by developmental counseling and what it was he hoped to facilitate through teacher groups. This type of person is one who is able to deal with both human relationships and the necessary details of organization and administration. He will establish communication with the staff regarding the possibilities and availability of group counseling and consulting. Through contact with the administration he helps encourage development of a schedule which makes it possible for him to meet with teachers during the professional day. In his contact with teachers he will make it clear that he is available for either individual or group consultation.

The counselor recognizes that the administrator's support is essential to the development of teacher groups. He spends considerable time helping the administrator clarify how the teacher groups will improve teaching efficiency and staff morale. Once the administrator is convinced of the value, he becomes the force which introduces the idea and makes available time, space, and resources to facilitate teacher groups.

The counselor in his personal contacts with teachers clarifies the potential of the C-Group. He finds several teachers who he believes would make an effective group and suggests the possibility of their working together. It is important that the first group be composed of some staff members who are considered leaders. The group should be composed of staff members who are capable of helping each other and who are committed to improvement and change.

The counselor that we are describing will be more than the product of an educational system and a series of graduate courses. During his graduate study, he will have experiences which make him aware of his personal beliefs and feelings and their influence upon his effectiveness as a counselor. The training will direct him to become the kind of person who is empathic and able to relate with both children and adults. He must be able to develop a mutual trust relationship which is more than rapport and which facilitates mutual goal alignment. He recognizes that he must be both sensitive and active in his relationships and certainly able to comprehend psychological movement and the transactions that go on between people in formal and informal groups. He will be accepting of individuality and uniqueness, but also able to understand and diagnose what is happening in the here and now. The leader needs to be poised, free from anxiety, perceptive, imaginative, creative, and spontaneous. Above all, he must be desirous of helping other people.

Groups such as we are suggesting have been carried on in a number of settings. Muro and Denton report that undergraduates both need and want help with their personal concerns and decisions (1968). It became apparent through groups led at the University of Maine that the teaching of facts did not seem sufficient to produce a change in teacher behavior. We cannot just tell teachers to become warm, empathic, and understanding. They need to experience these traits and eventually to internalize them and become aware of their own interpersonal needs.

The relationship within the teacher group is very similar to any other type of group. There must be a mutual respect and a desire to collaborate in reaching goals of mutual interest. The counselor lends his expertise in human relationships and group dynamics. He is not the expert who solves all the problems; he is the one who serves as a catalyst to create interaction as the teachers develop psychological solutions. It is apparent that he is a co-worker in the group, a facilitator who considers the affective and cognitive elements, the external (child) and internal (teacher self-concept and attitudes) elements in bringing about change. The goals of teacher groups include:

1. Development of an understanding of the practical applications of the dynamics of human behavior. Development of hypotheses regarding behavior and specific recommendations.
2. Acquisition of an understanding of self and awareness of the teacher's role in teacher-child conflict.
3. Developing acquaintance with new ideas and procedures and the values which come from group thinking.

GROUP CONSULTING—THE C-GROUP

Group consulting with teachers is designed to develop in the teacher an awareness of her strengths and assets for coping with the tasks of teaching. It is closely related to some of the principles of Achievement Motivation Seminars in its focus on strengths of each individual and the desire to help them develop meaningful personal goals (Sharp, 1968).

Experience with teachers' in-service education groups caused us to observe that telling teachers more effective ways to handle disciplinary or motivational problems was not effective. They might become acquainted with new approaches such as encouragement, reinforcement procedures, or group discussion, and they might even agree that the approaches had much potential. However, upon later observation, it was apparent that basically they had not changed their approach. They had learned about a procedure, but it had not led them to become involved in changing their behavior, ideas, or attitudes.

In order to assist a person to change, you must have access to the affective as well as the cognitive domain. This is obviously just as important in work with teachers as with children and adolescents. It became necessary to develop a procedure whereby we could get at values and attitudes. This is best accomplished by combining the didactic material which talks about a different way to handle students, with an experience which enables the teacher to understand what keeps her from adopting the new procedure. This can be facilitated through a group experience where one becomes aware of the effect of self upon behavior. The new approach was labeled *C-Group* because many of the factors which make it effective begin with a C: collaborating, consulting, clarifying, confronting, concern, confidentiality, caring, and commitment. It is not to be confused with a T-Group in that it goes beyond consideration of the process and self to examination of the transaction between teacher and child and the application of specific procedures. It also confronts the teacher with the ways in which her attitudes and feelings may keep her from changing. A process which combines the didactic and experiential approach is thereby achieved.

The specific factors which are components of the C-Group include:

1. The group collaborates, works together on mutual concerns.
2. The group consults. The interaction within the group helps the members develop new approaches to relationships with children.
3. The group clarifies for each member what it is he really believes and how congruent or incongruent his behavior is with what he believes.
4. The group confronts. The group expects each individual to see

himself, his purposes, attitudes, and be willing to confront other members of the group.

5. The group is concerned and cares. It shows that it is involved with both children and group members.

6. The group is confidential insofar as personal material discussed in the group is not carried out of the group.

7. The group develops a commitment to change. Participants in the group are concerned with recognizing that they can really only change themselves. They are expected to develop a specific commitment which involves an action they will take before the next C-Group to change their approach to a problem.

The group is usually developed from teachers who share similar concerns or who work with the same children. However, it can be formed from any group of teachers willing to work together. The fundamental criterion is that teachers in the C-Group are concerned with enabling each other to get a new perception of children and self—to truly SEE transactions.

The teacher group is usually confined to four to six members in order to secure maximum participation and involvement. They may meet during the school day when the schedules have been adequately planned. This type of scheduling is feasible when the staff has elicited administrative support. It has been demonstrated that administrators are generally cooperative in supplying time when they meet with teacher enthusiasm for this program. Otherwise, teacher groups meet during lunch hours, on released time, or after the school day. As the counselor starts to develop these groups, he is encouraged to help administration and staff see the value of these groups so that appropriate times are scheduled within the school day. The group would always meet in pleasant surroundings which permit maximum confidential interaction. The arrangements should be such that comfort, the ability to meet in a circular setting, and the opportunity to relate in a relaxed, pleasant, open and honest manner are considered basic to the conduct of the group.

It has been our experience that in the beginning there is a tendency for much generalization to occur. The members of the group, as in any other group, are anxious, concerned, frustrated, even confused. They are seeking perhaps an identity for themselves in the group. They are really asking, "What is supposed to happen here?" The leader will recognize that it is his job to become active and deal with these generalizations and to help direct the discussion to specific incidents and reactions. He will be concerned with getting at the personal meanings that exist within the group. He will recognize that the therapeutic forces mentioned in Chapter 4 also exist in this group. He must facilitate the group's development from negative to positive forces.

In many instances he will begin with a specific child that a teacher has presented. In discussing this child, he will determine if this child represents a mutual concern. In many instances this can be done most readily by going around the group to have them talk about the kind of child that concerns them most. The ability to universalize a problem will always assist in the development of a cohesive group. The group should try to deal with common problems. This will then permit other mechanisms to occur, such as the feeling of acceptance, altruism, and the willingness to give as well as to receive help. These mechanisms must be stimulated by the leader if the C-Group is to grow and develop its full potential.

This group, then, presents the opportunity for reality testing, a chance to test ideas, and alternative approaches among professional colleagues.

The group processes blend new approaches to working with children with the teacher's current beliefs, attitudes, and values. This cannot be accomplished by anything less than a holistic approach which combines the teacher's cognitive and affective domains. Little will be accomplished by telling her what to do. The specific behavior of a child is discussed, i.e. Johnny does not complete assignments. The teacher and the group focus on a particular incident. They might choose to employ logical consequences, a behavior-modification procedure, or advice on a way to individualize the assignment. However, past experience shows that mere advice will not change the teacher's behavior. In many instances she will even be aware of the new approach, but has never tried it. The group helps the teacher explore her feelings about the child. The members help her consider the impact of her beliefs and attitudes upon the child. It is the teacher who makes a commitment to change what she has been doing by developing a new perception of the relationship with the child and the alternatives available.

Insight in and of itself is not enough. Through these sessions, clarification and reflection of the teacher's feelings and attitudes must be experienced so that each member becomes aware of his own reactions. As the teacher becomes aware of her own response to the child, she can start to see alternative ways to function.

Thus, the original focus is on the external unit (the child). However, as the group develops mutual trust, the leader will help the members confront and clarify their own feelings, attitudes, and beliefs. The purpose of this group is not group therapy, nor is it merely studying a child.

Instead, it focuses upon the transactions between the teacher and the child and their meanings for both the teacher and the child. This is a holistic approach to the treatment of the purposes, values, attitudes, beliefs, and behavior of both children and teachers.

The following is an excerpt from a beginning session led by a counselor in training. It provides some acquaintance with the type of things which might occur and the teacher's feelings about the experience:

COUNSELOR: Today we've come together to talk about problems we have in our classrooms and to help each other understand them, and hopefully solve them. Let's begin by giving your name and the grade level you teach and briefly state a problem or concern of yours.

TEACHER$_1$: My name is Denise. I teach third year students. My problem is Richard who doesn't finish his work.

TEACHER$_2$: My name is Alice. I teach second year students. I have a student who is chronologically two years ahead of my class and I still have a problem challenging her academically.

TEACHER$_3$: My name is Mary Ann. I teach first year students. I also have a problem with a girl, Susan, who doesn't finish her work.

COUNSELOR: Since two of you mentioned having problems with getting children to finish their work, maybe this would be a good place to start.

TEACHER$_2$: I had Richard last year and I had the same problem with him.

COUNSELOR: Good, then we all have experienced the same type of problem. Mary Ann, what does Susan do instead of finishing her work?

TEACHER$_3$: Susan sits and daydreams, walks around the room, looks at the other kids doing their work.

COUNSELOR: What do you do then?

TEACHER$_3$: I usually keep reminding her to do her work, which I probably shouldn't do.

COUNSELOR: Is it effective?

TEACHER$_3$: No, nothing I've done so far has worked.

COUNSELOR: What else have you done?

TEACHER$_3$: Well, I've kept her after school to finish. It doesn't seem to make any difference to her.

COUNSELOR: Does she ever complete her work?

TEACHER$_3$: Oh yes, and she does it well when she does it so she *can* do it.

COUNSELOR: What do you do then?

TEACHER$_3$: I always compliment her and make a fuss over it.

COUNSELOR: What do you suppose she gets out of not completing her work at times?

TEACHER$_3$: She gets a lot of attention. I call over to her from the other reading group if I'm not working directly with her. It's not positive attention, but she does get a lot from me. I know she needs attention. The kids don't talk to her. I don't think she has any friends. Just recently she's been hurrying through her work, scribbling and doing it carelessly, turning it in so it looks like she's completed it. Then she goes to the back of the room with a few girls to work on a puzzle or play a game with them.

COUNSELOR: You said she had no friends. Could it be she wants them so badly she sacrifices her work to be with them?

TEACHER$_3$: Oh, I'm sure it is.

COUNSELOR: How do you feel about this?

TEACHER$_3$: Well, I want her to have friends, but I also want her to do the work.

COUNSELOR: Perhaps you need to decide which is benefiting her more, particularly now that it is so close to the end of the year. Maybe she could benefit more from working with these girls since you said she didn't finish her work before anyway.

TEACHER$_3$: Yes, I tend to feel that way, too.

COUNSELOR: Also, could you try asking her how many times she needs you to remind her to finish her work. Then maybe you could just say "Susan, 1, 2, 3, etc., instead of giving the attention she desires."

TEACHER$_3$: That's a good idea. I'll try that.

COUNSELOR: How do the rest of you feel?

TEACHER$_1$: Well, Richard doesn't finish his work for attention, I don't think. I stopped giving him the attention long ago. It didn't do any good. I've kept him after school too, and he'd stay until 5:00 if I let him.

TEACHER$_2$: I know because I had Richard last year. We've been ineffective with him for three years now. He's smart enough to get the work without doing the seat work. Some people say not to require the written work then, but I don't go along with that. I think he needs to develop the responsibility of doing it. Otherwise, when the work gets more difficult in the upper grades, and he does need to do it, he won't be in the habit of being responsible about his written work.

TEACHER₁: I think we need to think of some more resourceful ways for Richard to utilize his time, something he's interested in.

COUNSELOR: What do you think?

TEACHER₂: I never could figure out what he was interested in, though.

COUNSELOR: Does he have the responsibility of any chores in the room?

TEACHER₁: Yes, and he does them. That he thinks is fun. He doesn't have any responsibilities at home so that might be part of it.

TEACHER₂: Could you give him any responsibilities connected with the work, like helping someone else?

TEACHER₁: That might work. It might also be an incentive for him to finish.

COUNSELOR: Time is almost up today. Do you think you learned anything?

TEACHER₁: I think just talking like this helps. It seems the only time we get to talk is to complain. This is a good, constructive outlet.

TEACHER₂: I agree. We never seem to have time to do this or we just go in circles because our training didn't prepare us for the children of today. We don't have the answers to so many of our problems. We try, but it's like shooting in the dark.

TEACHER₃: We were taught so differently than what these children need. The way we were taught just doesn't work. I really feel a need for something like this.

FUNCTIONS AND RESPONSIBILITIES OF THE LEADER

All of the aforementioned principles of group leadership obviously apply to the leadership of the C-Group. However, some functions are more important in facilitating effective teacher group consulting. Leadership functions we have found crucial include:

1. Structuring the group from the very beginning so the purpose and focus are apparent. We are not only dealing with children and child study, nor are we involved in group therapy. We are involved in a meshing of child problems and teacher attitudes to make the greatest progress through the teacher in order that she may facilitate the development of the child.

2.   The leader is sensitive to affect and feelings, what is said and not said. He is observant of voice, facial expression, and nonverbal cues. He is not afraid to deal with feelings just because it is a teacher group. When something is being expressed which indicates strong feelings of either great love, anger, or anxiety, the leader deals with the affect in terms of its meaning for relating with the child, or the classroom group.

3.   He focuses on how the ideas of members are related. He utilizes the linking function and thereby underlines similar problems. These attempts to universalize bring about a more cohesive group as each member recognizes how his problems are similar to those of others in the group.

4.   He must be patient, to enable quiet members to participate verbally as well as through more passive listening. He believes in the mechanism of spectator therapy and permits it to be practiced.

5.   He is always concerned with helping the group focus on what is happening here and now as well as what is happening in their classroom. He deals with the data from the present as well as the past.

6.   He is very concerned with focusing on assets and strengths to develop feelings of adequacy. He helps each person acquire an asset inventory of his particular strengths in working with teachers, children, and other staff personnel. This can be done formally through the DUE experience of Herbert Otto (*See* Chap. 5) and multiple-strength perception (*See* Chapter 4).

7.   The counselor helps clarify the basic problem and find alternative solutions. He understands the purposive nature of behavior and is able to help in generating tentative hypotheses.

8.   He enables teachers to make specific commitments to action. He does not permit irresponsibility. He never encourages "Oh, Johnny's just like that, nothing can be done" or any other statement which reflects discouragement or unwillingness to cope with the problem.

The C-Group is a consideration of both the child and the teacher's situation and perception of life. In order to comprehend the classroom interaction, the use of anecdotes is suggested (Dinkmeyer, 1965). This anecdotal procedure gives teachers a specific method for observing their own behavior and analyzing their reactions. The anecdote includes a discussion of the child's behavior, the child's feelings and attitudes, the teacher's response or behavior, the teacher's feelings and attitudes, the consequences of the interaction. Some C-Groups eventually move from consideration of child situations to more intensive focus on their own attitudes, beliefs, and behavior, and how they influence their interaction with children.

The sessions are organized so that a definite set of commitments and actions are agreed upon. It is the development of a commitment by the teacher that enables the insight and the attitudes to become operationalized. Thus, after each discussion of a specific child, the teacher is asked what she plans to do differently next week. She selects an idea or recommendation with which she is comfortable. The ensuing week provides the opportunity to discuss how it went and to analyze progress.

COUNSELING OR CONSULTING?

Specialists in the area of school counseling will be asking themselves if the C-Group is counseling or consulting, child study or group therapy, or some mixture of these processes. The purpose of this process is to improve communication between teacher and child, between staff members, between counselors and members of the staff. The approach enables the counselor and teacher to focus originally on units that are external or outside of the teacher, but at the same time to recognize that her behavior is a result of her own internal unit (her person), style of life, and self-concept. The teacher must become part of a relationship which enables her to be more aware of herself, her unique needs, defenses, anxieties, and traditional approaches in relating with others. This awareness of the interpersonal relationships with children and her own psychological structure makes it possible to relate more honestly and effectively with children. The assumption is that the improved learning climate in the teacher group frees the teachers to learn about themselves and their procedures and that this understanding and climate are eventually transferred to the classroom.

Frequently, teacher education in the universities and in in-service education in the school system functions as if we could change educational practice by lectures. We seem to assume that information alone will change basic attitudes. However, all that we know about human beings and human behavior indicates that this approach cannot be effective. There must be an opportunity to understand ourselves and what keeps us from utilizing this knowledge, and then to experience a learning climate which exemplifies the best conditions for changing attitudes.

This C-Group serves an in-service purpose by increasing the development of skills and knowledge related to human behavior while making available a service that will increase the capacity of the teacher to communicate and relate with the children. The counselor needs to establish a counseling relationship based on mutual trust, mutual respect, and mutual goal alignment. He recognizes that teachers' anxieties, concerns, and fears cause them to experience emotional pain and distress; and that it is only as we deal with the whole person that more effective human relations and learning climates can be developed.

ACHIEVEMENT MOTIVATION SEMINARS

Another procedure which has been found to be very effective in facilitating the development of teachers and more positive learning environments is the Achievement Motivation Seminars sponsored by the W. Clement Stone Foundation in Chicago. The Achievement Motivation Seminars are founded on a simple premise that if we focus on an individual's strengths and assets, we will produce more development than if we focus on what is wrong with him and his liabilities. Achievement Motivation Seminars are concerned with establishing positive feelings about self in order that life goals may be developed. Billy Sharp indicates the goals must be:

> conceivable
> believable
> achievable
> measurable
> and stated with no alternatives—something a person wants
>   to do. [Sharp, 1968]

The focus of the Achievement Motivation Seminars is on self-discovery and encouragement (Dinkmeyer and Dreikurs, 1963). A number of basic procedures and exercises originally developed by Herbert Otto are utilized. Principle techniques include: strength bombardment and success bombardment, including a thorough discussion and analysis of personal values and goal setting. The procedures are comparatively simple in the hands of a well-trained leader. In strength bombardment the student tells the group what he sees as his personal strength. He then asks the group to indicate what other strengths they may see in him. He is encouraged as the group is able to elicit a list of strengths. After this part is concluded the group member will ask, "What do you see that is preventing me from using my strengths?" In this setting, which is definitely oriented towards positive reinforcement and encouragement of assets, the group members help the individual understand how he can more effectively use his strengths.

Following strength bombardment, another procedure is success bombardment. In this, the member tells of his principal success experiences. The success patterns are identified, analyzed, and encouraged. They then are again reinforced. This is followed by the establishment of goals which are articulated in the group situation followed by a public commitment to carry out these commitments prior to the next session.

Teacher groups have considerable promise. They operate on the premise that we need to affect a total milieu and that we begin by working with teachers in order to maximize their strengths and thereby assist the pupils. The teacher group or C-Group requires the capacity to combine general group-leadership skills with some understanding of the dynamics of human behavior and some capacity to assist in developing ideas about how to relate and work more effectively with children. The leader must conceptualize not only what it is that the member is thinking and feeling, but what it is that goes on in his relationship with the child that concerns him. The preliminary results from utilization of C-Groups in university and in-service settings indicate there is much potential for affecting the educational process through the C-Group.

SUMMARY

Group procedures can be a potent tool in working with teachers. This chapter presents a rationale and format for group consulting with teachers. Detailed procedures for development of teacher groups by counselors are presented.

The C-Group, a unique approach which combines the affective and cognitive, the didactic and experiential approaches, is described. The C-Group label was developed because the crucial features of this group all begin with a C. They include: collaborate, consult, clarify, confront, concern, care, confidential, commitment, and change. These teacher groups begin by considering external units, the children, but also include the critical internal components, their feelings and attitudes, and how they influence the transactions between teacher and child. Excerpts from actual C-Groups are included.

The unique functions and responsibilities of the C-Group leader are detailed. Achievement Motivation Seminars and a description of their strength bombardment procedure are included.

REFERENCES

DINKMEYER, DON C. *Child Development: The Emerging Self.* Englewood Cliffs, N.J.: Prentice-Hall, Inc., 1965.

DINKMEYER, DON C., and DREIKURS, RUDOLF. *Encouraging Children to Learn: The Encouragement Process.* Englewood Cliffs, N.J.: Prentice-Hall, Inc., 1963.

GLASSER, WILLIAM. *Schools without Failure.* New York: Harper and Row, Publishers, 1969.

HARRIS, THOMAS. *I'm OK; You're OK.* New York: Harper and Row, Publishers, 1967.

MURO, JAMES J., and DENTON, GORDON. "Expressed Concerns of Teacher-Education
    Students in Counseling Groups," *Journal of Teacher Education,* Vol. 19,
    No. 4 (Winter, 1968).
SHARP, BILLY. "Within Every Student is a Gifted Student?" Chicago: W. Clement
    and Jessie V. Stone Foundation, 1968, Achievement Motivation Seminars.
SONSTEGARD, MANFORD, and DREIKURS, RUDOLF. *The Teleoanalytic Approach to
    Group Counseling.* Chicago: Alfred Adler Institute, 1967.

CHAPTER 12

Parent and Family Group Counseling–Consultation

RATIONALE

The group process is effective in a number of settings. In this chapter we shall discuss some unique applications of group procedures to work with parents.

A number of pioneers have worked with the family in groups, particularly Fullmer and Bernard (1968) and Satir (1967). The unique type of family group counseling or parent C-Groups advocated here is an outgrowth of professional contacts with Dreikurs (1959) and Fullmer (1968). However, the method is unique insofar as it utilizes the best elements of dealing with both the cognitive and affective elements involved in family-group procedures.

It is apparent that the family is the most significant single influence on the development of the child. It is the primary environmental influence and the most pervasive of all life influences. In addition, the family structure provides the climate in which the child learns to trust, to accept, to love, and to self-actualize. If the family is not healthy, the child obviously learns to fear and his growth process is inhibited.

It is in the family that the first meanings about life are derived—the meanings of love, acceptance, rejection, and adequacy, for example. The family provides the opportunity not only to receive love, but also to give and to provide love and acceptance. The family is perhaps our most significant factor in the development of personality, because it is here that the culture and the beliefs of society are handed down to the individual.

It is within the family that the child observes certain beliefs, customs, and myths, and internalizes certain values of the parents. The family provides the scene for his struggles with feelings of adequacy and inadequacy. It is in the family that he forms his opinion of self as a social, working, and sexual being. It is here that he develops his basic identification with people.

The family serves as the first socializing agent. It is with the parents and the siblings that the child begins to develop identity and learns what is expected of him. Thus, the family should never be underrated as a first learning atmosphere for the child.

It is in the family that the first basic education of the child in emotional and social matters occurs. One of our major societal problems involves the fact that parents almost never have adequate experiences, training and educational background to enable them to function effectively in child training. As a result, many parents who are really largely unequipped play the most significant role in the development of society.

Parents are often handicapped by their own attitudes, ideas, and interrelationships. In many instances they are still struggling for freedom from their own autocratic backgrounds and permissive patterns which does not assist the parents in their attempts to find a democratic approach for working more effectively with their children. It is increasingly apparent that parents must learn democratic procedures because the pressure of the schools, society, and the peers necessitates that they treat their children with mutual trust and mutual respect. The learning of new methods to manage children in this democratic era is no longer a choice; it is a critical necessity.

The fact that our nation is undergoing a rapid social change to a democratic society makes it crucial that we develop new principles for training and educating children. The standards must be consistent with the culture and democratic methods. There have been a number of attempts to develop this type of democratic approach to family life. Many practicing school counselors have taken the initiative by developing new approaches to the problem of family education. Some of these have been described by Stormer (1967) and Hillman (1968).

It seems apparent that the coming of the new developmental counselor brings us to a new era of family and child-study groups. The counselor who is concerned with the total development of the child will recognize the necessity of working with the significant adults and the total milieu.

Parents in the past have been hesitant about bringing their real problems to the school. They have not had effective relationships with school personnel. When the child was difficult, too often the school shifted the problem back to the parents, indicating that Susie or Johnny was a difficult child, so Mother and Father, original precursors of the problem, were supposed to correct the situation. The parents were provided with criticism, not ideas.

Unfortunately parents have also been influenced by newspaper columns, journalists, magazine articles, psychological novelists, and a number of other authorities. To put it simply, they have been thoroughly confused by a variety of procedures labeled *best.* They are already tremendously concerned about the do's and don'ts, and thus the motivation for parent groups is tremendous.

It is the experience of the authors working with public school personnel that when the school counselor makes his services available to lead parent groups there is almost always an overwhelming enthusiastic response. Parent organizations in the past have attempted to approach the problem through occasional meetings, but there has been little provision for groups of parents to get together and dialogue their concerns, their feelings, and their attitudes. It is no longer conceivable that these demands and needs can be met through individual counseling or teacher conferences. The only possible way is through the parent group, more accurately called *parent education.* These groups are formed to help those assembled learn to work with their specific child.

It has been the experience of the authors that parents really seek these kinds of experiences, that regardless of socioeconomic standing, they are not too stupid to learn, especially if we provide them with an effective vehicle for learning to understand themselves and their children and the meaning of the transactions between them.

Thus, the parent group provides many advantages. It helps them find a mutual source of support. It enables them to face their actions, their attitudes, their feelings, and to recognize that the problems the parents have are universal. They are not alone in their fears, helplessness and discouragement. The group then provides an opportunity to increase communication skills between parents and between parents and children.

GOALS AND OBJECTIVES

Parent groups provide a direct service to parents and an indirect service to the child. They are a procedure which enables the counselor to expand his clientele by servicing parents, and at the same time enables him to deal with a very basic problem—the family milieu. Some objectives of this type of service are:

1. To help the parent–child relationship become more effective, more growth promoting.

2. To help the parents understand the significance of the transactions they have with their children.

3. To help the parents develop communication skills which enable them to understand the meanings of the messages that they send and to recognize the meaning that they impart to the messages they receive.

4. To coordinate school and home efforts in child training.

5. To share information, ideas, and develop within the parents some awareness of their significant role in the child's development and ways in which they can be of mutual assistance.

THE FAMILY: A BASIC LEARNING MODEL

The family presents the first learning model for socialization and cultural transmission. We must become much more aware of what is communicated from the significant adults in the life of the child. It is apparent that almost all cultures in the world today use the family as the basic small group which provides the first interpersonal situation for learning and socializing. The problem is that whereas the family at one time provided sufficient stability and an emotional climate to support development present families are often ineffective and insufficient to create and develop human potential.

Inadequate families are not limited to poverty or culturally disadvantaged situations. Just as many problems occur in terms of communication between parents and child in the wealthy as among the poor. The family needs to receive additional help. On the other hand, the school traditionally has provided no assistance in helping the family create and establish policies and principles related to human behavior. It is only in recent years that there have been attempts to enlist parents in a partnership with the schools.

One of the functions of the parent-education or parent-consultation groups is to help parents become aware of how the family influences human development. The activities and communication within the family set the pattern for the development of human behavior. The child learns to cope with emotional, social, and personal problems as he observes others and as he notices feedback from his transactions. The effective group will help each parent become aware of the effect and meaning of his transactions upon the child. The family meeting provides a real interpersonal situation where one can discuss more effective ways of relating to children, and at the same time deal with the personality characteristics of the individual which prevent healthy development. The focus is on dealing with parents as persons, to help them become more adequate people and hence more adequate mothers and fathers. The focus is on assisting them to become effective in their response patterns with children. This is done by helping them toward awareness of the messages and meanings that they send within the family. Basically, the roles, traditions, and loyalties established within the family produce stability or instability. Family consultations should provide the opportunity for a systematic observation of the social transactions and the messages which are transmitted verbally and nonverbally. This approach takes the position of recognizing the interpersonal nature of all human problems. It helps the parents become more conscious of self and their communications.

One of the basic types of help provided is guiding parents toward better awareness of both verbal and nonverbal communication. It helps them see what it is they communicate to children, what they expect, and how the children interpret their behavior and intentions. The focus is on helping both the receivers and senders of messages become more functional instead of dysfunctional communicators. It should be constructed to open up the feedback system so they can clarify what they intend and send more complete messages.

THERAPEUTIC FORCES AND PARENT GROUPS

The parent group provides a unique opportunity for all involved to become more aware of the parent–child relationship and to experience feedback regarding the effect that their parent practices have upon their children. This is derived through feedback from other parents about their procedures. The opportunity for mutual therapeutic effect is constantly available. At the same time, there is the opportunity to create a strong interdependence which takes advantage of the universal problems that confront parents. There is an opportunity for parents to contribute to each other and to develop new approaches to parent–child relationships. The corrective process of feedback from contemporaries has tremendous effect upon the group dynamics.

The counselor who runs the parent groups must be careful not to organize the group as if its intention were to transmit information or to deal only with cognitive ideas. This is not a lecture, it is not a group discussion; it is truly parent group counseling. This necessitates that the group mechanisms and dynamic processes occurring in any well-organized therapeutic group be utilized. The leader must always be aware of the potential that exists in the group setting.

Some of the group mechanisms which are particularly pertinent to group work include the following:

1. Group identification or a communal feeling. The idea that we are all concerned about a common problem—relating more effectively with our children.
2. Opportunity to recognize the universal nature of child training problems.
3. Opportunities not only to receive help but to give assistance, help and love to others.
4. The opportunity to develop cooperation and mutual help, to give encouragement and support.
5. The opportunity to listen which not only provides support, but in many instances provides spectator therapy. Someone else's idea may enable the parents to start a new approach to transactions with their child.
6. One of the basic values involved in the mechanism of feedback—the individual gains from listening to and observing others, but he particularly gains as he becomes able to experience feedback about his own actions, beliefs, and ideas. [Dinkmeyer, 1969]

THE PARENT CHILD-STUDY GROUP

The counselor uses his training in group procedures to help parents develop more effective relationships with their children. He does this because he realizes that frequently parents have common problems which can be discussed in the group setting. The group setting provides the opportunity for the parents to recognize that they are not alone. The universal nature of certain kinds of parent relationships provides the real setting for experiencing the growth that comes from group process. The experience depends on both interactional processes and didactic information.

Often the individual has difficulty helping a parent see a new way to relate, but the group almost invariably increases the parents' receptiveness to different ideas. Parents begin to think, "Oh, I see you are doing it," or "If you can do it, then I can certainly do it." The example of parents who try certain procedures, investigate them thoroughly, make adaptations, and make them work, is much more convincing than any pontifical pronouncement of a professional. Parents are always highly influenced by ideas that work. The group transaction also allows the parent to integrate ideas that may have been previously unacceptable to his point of view. Child study, when conducted in the C-Group setting, evokes mutual help and presents the chance for parents to participate.

It is basic to recognize that parent groups can only be functional insofar as they develop ideas related to practical problems. The group is never to degenerate into a group discussion, merely talking about certain theoretical points, unless the points can be applied to specific individuals. Principles are never discussed in the abstract, always in the concrete. The leader must make it clear that this is not a theoretical course, but is concerned with helping human beings develop more effective interaction. He always insists that they go back to applying the principles to specific children.

ADMINISTRATIVE DETAIL

Groups can be organized in a number of ways. It is usually advisable to start with parents whose children are at a given age or grade level. The teacher may originate the contact or the counselor may present the idea through a PTA. In any instance, the possibility of dynamic sessions for parents is announced at a general meeting which specifies a certain grade level. Then notices are sent through the mail and some preregistration is received. It is always desirable to keep the groups at a maximum of ten if one hopes to have some type of effective interaction. Thus, the response will dictate the number of groups that any given counselor can handle.

Once the number of participants has been selected, a time, location, and length of meeting will be established. In school settings, it is considered desirable if groups can meet during a school day. The group should preferably meet for one to one and a half hours. The program should allow from six to ten sessions, dependent upon the number of groups it will be necessary to conduct within a given school district.

The sessions are always conducted in a setting which permits the parents to face each other comfortably in circular form. The leader becomes a part of the group, a facilitator who helps in the development of understanding.

While the emphasis is upon group discussion and group transaction, it has been found that some printed material often stimulates discussion. Some groups that one of the authors has lead have used *The ABC's of Guiding the Child* by Rudolf Dreikurs and Margaret Goldman (1964). This material is used to provide a starting point and to keep transactions from degenerating into complaints or mere sharing of limited ideas and concepts. The ABC's are open to discussion, dialogue, and clarification. They are not learned, they are discussed until they can be internalized to specific situations. The leader uses this material to expand the group thinking, never to distract the group from practical problems, and never to limit dealing with real human transactions.

The *ABC's of Guiding the Child* includes a number of principles and statements which can be the basis for dialogue. Some typical statements include:

"Don't discourage the child by having too high standards and being overambitious for him."

"Reward and punishment are outdated."

"Acting instead of talking is more effective in conflict situations."

The leader can begin a group by discussing the implications of such a statement, and then throwing it out to the group for discussion. These statements obviously are intended to serve as a catalyst for discussion. The leader helps the group members see the intent of the principle, but directs them to see how this applies to their personal concerns.

The early sessions are used to clarify the purpose of the group. It is made certain that parents do not misunderstand that this is group therapy. At the same time it is made clear that this is not a discussion about theoretical children, but *their* children and *real* concerns. The focus then is on real children and on the transactions which parents have with them. The leader does not pose as a psychological expert or authority. He makes it clear that members are expected to participate in presenting problems, developing suggestions, and assisting each other. It is vital to develop a basic contract about the purpose of the group early in the group's life. Those who participate learn to focus on how they can change their behavior rather than how they can change their child or their spouse. They soon learn that as they change themselves they change the transactions and interactions with the child.

The developmental counselor recognizes that his long-term goal is to expand child study so that as many parents as possible can be reached. He does this by closely watching for people in his group who have potential leadership. Once several groups have developed, he then starts to work with persons who desire to become discussion leaders. These people are acquainted with leadership procedures and group dynamics. At the same time, they are given some opportunity to serve as co-leaders. The co-leaders eventually develop their own groups.

Vicki Soltz (1967) has developed an excellent manual to accompany *Children: The Challenge* by Dreikurs and Soltz (1964). The manual establishes the goals for parent groups and delineates the leader's responsibilities and limitations. Indicating that the leader is not to lecture, counsel, or give advice, the manual makes specific suggestions regarding qualities and skills which must be developed.

The manual goes into specific traits such as width of vision, contact with the whole group, sense of humor, use of group pressure, and encouragement. Since the group frequently has individuals who present a specific challenge, a section is devoted to dealing with problem members. The challenger, the resister, the chatterbox, the bored one, and the reluctant spouse are some of the types discussed.

One of the most useful sections for leaders who use *Children: The Challenge* is entitled "Discussion-Promoting Questions and Supplementary Material." This section includes detailed questions on each chapter—actually more than could be used in a single session—and can be used as a homework assignment for parents. The manual includes a wealth of material to increase the leader's understanding of this approach.

The group counselor could use this material with a course in the fundamentals of group procedures to develop a strong core of parent leaders. The background information acquired in the study groups would accelerate the learning in parent group counseling.

A MODEL FOR PARENT GROUP COUNSELING

The following serves as a set of guidelines and fundamentals for this type of parent group counseling.

1. Size of the group. It is important that the group be kept small; any number between six and ten is desirable. The emphasis is on a size that is small enough to permit active participation by all concerned. The counselor tries to get each parent involved each time in presenting a concern, reporting on progress, or in helping others. This cannot be accomplished in a large group.

2. Focus on normal parents and normal developmental problems. Make it clear from the beginning that this group is dealing with average parents who have normal developmental problems with their children. It will be important in beginning the group to give examples of typical kinds of difficulties that occur. State, for example, "We will be concerned with children who don't eat as we wish they would, who neither get up easily nor willingly go to bed, who leave their clothing and toys around the house, and who refuse to come when called or cooperate on simple requests. In other words, we will be talking about our children. We have just been deluded into believing this behavior is normal and must be accepted." Be explicit in having them recognize that this group deals with the common problems that they all have. This awareness of

the phenomenon of universalization—that they all have similar problems—will provide great strength for this group and will enable all to participate productively. Universalization is a basic mechanism for promoting cohesiveness, and so from the start it is important to help them see how their concerns, feelings, and attitudes are similar.

3.   Integrate the group. The leader should work to help the group become cohesive as quickly as possible. The leader does this by introducing the members to each other. The very first day he has name tags available so they get acquainted on a first-name basis. In the early introductions each person tells something about himself and the names and ages of his children. It would be important in the early stages for them also to talk about some good experiences that they have had in interaction with their children. This enables the group to develop some fellowship and awareness of their individual situations and recognition that they all have some assets and strengths to work effectively with children. A good exercise in the beginning is to go around once asking each parent to tell about the good part of their relationship with their child. Have them state their strengths in child management and the child's assets. Then go around and have them talk about their concerns and specific problems.

4.   At a first setting the leader may begin briefly by discussing some theoretical principle that he advocates strongly. This might involve a principle such as encouragement, logical consequences, setting of limits, or any other topic which he can illustrate vividly. The discussion would be brief and serve as an opportunity to acquaint the members with a theoretical point, and with the leader's point of view. After this very brief introductory presentation, never to last over five minutes, the leader gets someone to begin to discuss a problem that he has. When the person begins to describe the problem, it is important that the leader focus on having him present the problem in specific terms. This means he will indicate what the child does, how the parents respond, and how the child reacts to the parents' response. After he has had an opportunity to survey the group and the kinds of problems that concern them most, the leader then begins to work with problems which are common concerns. This permits the greatest amount of participation and at the same time utilizes the mechanism of universalization, which brings cohesiveness.

5.   As the group starts to explore specific problems, members of the group are strongly encouraged to provide each other with ideas. The counselor is considered an additional resource. In the early sessions he will need to provide tentative hypotheses and tentative solutions. However, the counselor must be aware immediately that if he takes on the

role of authority he will not get the kind of group dynamics, group expression, and group cohesiveness that is vital. From the start, the counselor should serve as a facilitator and model the behavior he expects of group members. He teaches the group members how to listen, understand feelings, clarify for each other, and begin to offer tentative hypotheses.

6.   Seek maximum participation. The counselor attempts to involve each participant during each meeting in discussing some things of primary concern to him and his family. If the group is to serve the purpose of providing help, not merely talk, it is important to provide an opportunity for all to become involved. The counselor tries to schedule the time so that no one becomes dominant and all are invited to raise their concerns.

7.   During each session, the counselor has made an opportunity to get maximum involvement. He also tries to develop some tentative hypotheses and solutions for each parent. At the end of the session, the group members are asked to summarize what they have learned. This is a very significant part of the group since it permits the members to say what they have really experienced and perceived. It also gives them an opportunity to verbalize and utilize their new information. It is during the session or at this point that the counselor attempts to elicit a public commitment from each member to something that the parents will do about their situation. It also provides some opportunity to correct any faulty impression that parents may have about recommendations that have been developed by the counselor or other members of the group. A brief demonstration of this type of group counseling is included.

The following case as led by Don Dinkmeyer and Jon Carlson demonstrates this process:

Five mothers of fifth and sixth grade children met with the counselors during the first sessions. After a short introduction about the purpose of parent groups, the mothers introduced themselves and gave the names and ages of their children. The counselors then asked who would like to begin. After a specific incident was related by one of the mothers, the counselor inserted the following statement in an attempt to universalize the problem. "How many of you other mothers have this same or a similar problem?" This tended to increase the active involvement of the group.

From here, the group moved from incident to incident on topics such as waking children in the morning, children not wanting to eat their breakfast, not wanting to brush their teeth, not doing their chores, or not coming to dinner when called. During the summary session the counselor helped each member of the group develop new approaches to try before the next session. At this time, he also gave each participant a copy of *The ABC's of Guiding the Child* by Dreikurs (1964). They were asked to read it and consider some of the ideas that were presented.

The next session began as follows:

> COUNSELOR: What did you get from our meeting last week? (General discussion and identification of new concepts by the group.)
> MOTHER$_1$: Well, she is still Sally.
> COUNSELOR: But are you still Mother? Did you do anything different? (The emphasis in this consultation is on recognition that mothers can only change their behavior and hope that this will change the interaction with their children.)

After a short discussion the mother reported that she had not tried anything different. Another mother asked if she would try some of the things that were suggested to her last week and she replied that she was not sure how to go about it.

> COUNSELOR: What would you like to change? Take one specific thing.
> MOTHER$_1$: Her attitude in general.
> COUNSELOR: We need something more specific and tangible.
> MOTHER$_1$: How about when I try to wake her in the morning. I say "It is time to get up," and she says "Try and make me."

The power contest between the mother and daughter was by this time evident to the group. After a short discussion, they recommended that she buy her daughter an alarm clock and let her be responsible for her own awakening. Thus, the mother would be extricating herself from the conflict and leaving her daughter without an opponent. Another mother volunteered.

> MOTHER$_2$: I already had success using what you said. My daughter tried to get my attention by playing the same song over and over. I used to rush in and tell her to stop it and then the battle would start. This time I shut the door to the kitchen and turned up the radio and went about my housework. She soon stopped and began to play another song.
> COUNSELOR: Very good. In other words, you removed the

wind from your daughter's sail. Did anyone else have any other results this past week? (One mother began to talk about the difficulty she was having with her son swearing and other mothers voiced similar dilemmas.) What could you do about something like this?

MOTHER$_3$: You could ignore it.

MOTHER$_5$: Ignore it; depending on the word. I might tell him this is not very nice.

COUNSELOR: What about the logical consequences of the situation?

MOTHER$_4$: Well, if they swear, I won't take them someplace that they want to go.

COUNSELOR: Wouldn't that be more of a punishment?

MOTHER$_4$: Yes, I guess it would.

MOTHER$_1$: What about if I tell him that if he can't talk properly outside with people, he will have to come inside to his room where there are no people to hear him, until he feels that he can talk to others without swearing. (The entire group felt that this would be a very good way to handle this situation.)

At this time the discussion was shifted to *The ABC's of Guiding the Child.* The group talked about the principles set forth in this pamphlet and discussed similar topics. The members were depending more upon other members of the group for aid and solicited less and less assistance from the counselor. During the third session, the counselor passed out a copy of "Child's Mistaken Goals" (*See* Table 3). This helped clarify the previous materials and accelerated the progress of the group.

The final session opened with:

COUNSELOR: Did anybody try anything different this past week?

MOTHER$_1$: I've been trying things and I have become so critical of myself. I've been changing and now the entire house is running smoother. I really can understand how "good mothers are America's tragedy" (Dreikurs and Goldman, 1964).

MOTHER$_2$: Children can do a lot more than we let them do. We do too much for them. As I have realized lately, children are quite capable of taking care of themselves. They really are very capable.

COUNSELOR: Could it be that you are saying we don't give children enough responsibility? (All the mothers agreed.)

When mothers can realize this fact and begin to do something about it, they have come a long way. With this in mind, the following was presented:

> COUNSELOR: I feel that you are in a position to take this procedure and these concepts and meet with other mothers, some of your neighbors, perhaps, over a cup of coffee, and talk about some of these same things that we have discussed. Concern yourself with normal problems that they might have with their children. It is time for you to help other parents understand the dynamics of their child's behavior while recognizing that their problems are much like the problems of other parents.
>
> MOTHER₁: The mothers who need this kind of help won't come to the school for a group of this kind.
>
> COUNSELOR: Might they come to your house for an informal meeting?
>
> MOTHER₂: Yes, we can work on a different population than you work on at school.
>
> MOTHER₃: Maybe we can help each other because our children play together and we can encourage them for the changes that they made.

Thus, a core group has been established that will help take the burden of parent education off the counselor's already overloaded work schedule. A group of mothers who has been exposed to new ideas can be leaders in the parent-education program of the community. Under the supervision of the counselor, what started out as five mothers might become twenty-five mothers (five times five new group members) and so on.

Another example of a first session of a small parent group led by the authors is included. You will note the emphasis on handling specific problems, diagnosing the purpose of the behavior, developing alternative approaches, and getting a commitment from the parent to change her behavior.

PARENT GROUP DIALOGUE

> COUNSELOR: Since this is our first meeting, I would like to explain what we are going to discuss and what we might hope to accomplish by these meetings. First, we are going to discuss normal types of problems that all parents have with their children—such things as behavior problems that arise

Child's Mistaken Goals

Parent Study Groups   Nancy Pearcy
Corvallis, Oregon 97330   Louise VanVliet

Goal of Misbehavior	What Child is Saying	How Parent Feels	Child's Reaction to Reprimand	Some Corrective Measures
Attention	I only count when I am being noticed or served.	Annoyed; wants to remind, coax; delighted with "good" child.	Temporarily stops disturbing action when given attention.	Ignore answer or do the unexpected; give attention at pleasant times.
Power	I only count when I am dominating, when you do what I want you to.	Provoked; generally wants power challenged; "I'll *make* him do it." "You can't get away with it."	Intensifies action when reprimanded; child wants to win, be boss.	Extricate self. Act, not talk; be friendly, establish equality, redirect child's efforts into constructive channels.
Revenge	I can't be liked. I don't have power, but I'll count if I can hurt others as I feel hurt by life.	Hurt; mad; "How could he do this to me?"	Wants to get even; makes self disliked.	Extricate self. Win child; maintain order with minimum restraint; avoid retaliations; take time and effort to help child.
Inadequacy	I can't do anything right so I won't try to do anything at all; I am no good.	Despair; "I give up."	No reprimand, therefore, no reaction; feels there is no use to try; passive.	Encouragement (may take long); faith in child's ability.

TABLE 3.
Child's Mistaken Goals

at mealtime or at waking up and going to bed, fighting, school difficulties, or any other thing that you can think of. One of the questions that I had asked you previously was, "Are you willing to help other people with their problems?" All of you agreed that you would try to help—that is the purpose of these discussions—to try to help each other. Before we go any further, I would like you to introduce yourself to the other members of the group and tell us the names and ages of your children.

PARENT A: Mrs. A. I have two children: Johnny, seven, and Joey, six.

PARENT B: My name is Mrs. B. and I have three children: Charles, fifteen, John, ten, and David, two.

PARENT C: My name is Mrs. C. I have a boy named Robert and he is seven years old.

PARENT D: My name is Mrs. D. I have five children: Bill, fourteen, Sue, twelve, Janet, eleven, Jerry, nine, and Sam, six.

COUNSELOR: I think that we are ready to begin now. Who would like to tell us something about a situation that concerns her?

PARENT A: Well, Joey gives me the most problems. He is always in trouble at school, he always fights, and he is naughty around the house. Now Johnny, his brother, is completely the opposite, he gets good grades in school, never fights, and he always helps around the house.

COUNSELOR: Since you cannot control Joey's behavior when he is at school or away from the house, tell me a little bit more about some of the problems you are having with Joey at home.

PARENT A: He doesn't like to work alone. Whenever he brings homework from school, I try to help him and show him how to do it. The minute I walk away, he stops doing it.

COUNSELOR: What do you do when he stops?

PARENT A: I shout at him and tell him to get busy.

COUNSELOR: Does he go back to work then?

PARENT A: For a little while.

COUNSELOR: And then what happens?

PARENT A: I shout again and tell him to finish his work or else he can't watch television.

COUNSELOR: Does he finish his work then?

PARENT A: Sometimes.

COUNSELOR: How do you feel when this is going on?

PARENT A: I am very annoyed and by now I guess I feel discouraged.

COUNSELOR: Does anyone have any ideas or suggestions to help Mrs. A. with Joey?

PARENT B: Is the homework too hard for him?

PARENT A: No, when I am with him he does it right.

COUNSELOR: Is it possible that Joey needs attention and wants you by him all the time?

PARENT A: Yes.

COUNSELOR: Well, since shouting at him and threatening to take television away from him have not been very effective, let's see if we can find some other ways of giving him attention. What are some of the things that Johnny does well by himself?

PARENT A: He likes to color and play card games.

COUNSELOR: Could you arrange to spend some time with him each day coloring and playing card games? Substitute positive for negative attention.

PARENT A: It would take time, but I think it might help.

PARENT C: I did something like that with Robert and it worked well.

COUNSELOR: Why don't you do that this week and then report back to the group next week.

PARENT A: Okay.

COUNSELOR: Mrs. B., can you tell us about the thing that concerns you most?

PARENT B: It's John. He's a complete mess at home. He refuses to cooperate with any requests and leaves his things all over the house.

PARENT D: I know what you mean; I have had that problem too.

COUNSELOR: Mrs. B., tell us about a specific time. Tell us what John does and what you do.

PARENT B: Just this afternoon I asked him to take the garbage out at least three times. Then he had to go to his Little League game and couldn't find his glove. We all had to search for it.

COUNSELOR: You seem very bothered by John.

PARENT B: Well, I always feel like he wins and gets me to do what he wants.

COUNSELOR: It seems like he must be the boss?

PARENT B: Exactly! And we are all the servants.

PARENT D: When Bill was younger we had a rule that any toy left out went into the mystery box and it was a mystery when it would come back.

PARENT B: Hmmm. You mean I could put the glove away and he'd have to accept the consequences.

COUNSELOR: You seem interested, why don't you do that this week and let us know how it works.

PRINCIPLES OF PARENT GROUP LEADERSHIP

1.   The type of parent group leadership that we are suggesting requires awareness of certain basic procedures and skills. The leader must be very cognizant of group process, group dynamics—the therapeutic forces which occur within the group. He works with the group in ways to enhance the development of group interaction and utilizes group mechanisms to foster human potential.

2.   He sees the program as a practical program. He is not interested in developing a series of lectures. He intensively avoids generalizations. He stresses specific situations and the application of the general principles to them.

3.   He is always interested in the application of theory to practice. Thus, he makes available to parents printed material which supplements the understandings which are developed through their discussion. He always makes certain that parents are able to apply the general principle in a variety of settings. He does not attempt to develop a limited approach.

4.   The leader must be careful to recognize that while he provides certain understandings regarding human behavior, he does not take on the role of the authority, the expert or the specialist. Thus, in all transactions he is quick to have people look at the meaning of the behavior that is being discussed. He does this in simple form. When one parent finishes describing a situation, he makes certain that the situation has been described specifically. Eventually he sees to it that other members of the group help the parent describe the situation in specific terms. Once it has been discussed, he may ask questions like "What did you think about that? What would you do if you were the parent? How have you handled similar situations?"

5.   He stresses the importance of group analysis of the problem, the tentative hypotheses regarding the purpose and nature of the behavior, and an analysis of the solution.

6.   He is very concerned with developing commitment. This is not to be just a discussion group. People are to lead the group and come up with solutions and ideas for a change.

7. He places emphasis on helping the group develop mutual help and mutual encouragement.

The parent group leader thus combines his knowledge of group procedures and his understanding of human behavior to help parents develop more effective relationships with their children. This is a holistic approach which engages the intellect and feelings of the parents while exacting a commitment to action. The potential good in parents sharing ideas under the guidance of an effective leader should be obvious.

SUMMARY

The application of group procedures to work with parents recognizes the fundamental importance of the family and the siblings in the development of the child. This chapter presents goals and objectives, a learning model for families, and discusses the relationship of therapeutic forces to parent groups.

Procedures for parent child–study groups including the purpose, administrative details, format, and special materials for parents and leaders are described.

Guidelines for a unique model of parent group counseling, similar to the C-Group model, are set forth. An overview of this model is illustrated through typescripts.

The principles of parent group leadership include an emphasis on the pragmatic, and a recognition that it is vital to secure group participation in analysis of the problem. Each parent presenting a problem is encouraged to make a commitment about some way in which he will change his behavior in relationship to his child.

REFERENCES

DINKMEYER, DON C. "Group Counseling: Theory and Techniques," *School Counselor,* Vol. 17, No. 2 (November, 1969).

DREIKURS, RUDOLF, CORSINI, RAYMOND, LOWE, RAYMOND, and SONSTEGARD, MANFORD. *Adlerian Family Counseling.* Eugene, Ore.: University of Oregon, The University Press, 1959.

DREIKURS, RUDOLF, and GOLDMAN, MARGARET. *The ABC's of Guiding the Child.* Chicago: Alfred Adler Institute, 1964.

DREIKURS, RUDOLF, and SOLTZ, VICKI. *Children: The Challenge.* New York: Meredith Corporation, 1964.

FULLMER, DANIEL. "An Evolving Model for Group Work in the Elementary School," *Elementary School Guidance and Counseling,* Vol. 3, No. 1 (October, 1968).

FULLMER, DANIEL, and BERNARD, HAROLD. *Family Consultations,* Guidance Mono-
graph Series. Boston: Houghton Mifflin Company, 1968.
HILLMAN, BILL W. "The Parent–Teacher Education Center: A Supplement to
Elementary School Counseling," *Elementary School Guidance and Coun-
seling,* Vol. 3, No. 2 (December, 1968).
SATIR, VIRGINIA. *Conjoint Family Therapy.* Rev. ed. Palo Alto, Calif.: Science and
Behavior Books, 1967.
SOLTZ, VICKI. *Study Group Leader's Manual.* Chicago: Alfred Adler Institute,
1967.
STORMER, G. EDWARD. "Milieu-Group Counseling in Elementary School Guid-
ance," *Elementary School Guidance and Counseling,* Vol. 1, No. 3 (June,
1967).

CHAPTER 13

Research in Group Counseling

WHILE A COMPLETE discussion of research and research methodology is beyond the scope and purposes of this text, the authors feel that the book would be less than complete unless some mention and some attention were given to the problems of research. In general terms, this text was written primarily for those who are or who will be practicing group counselors. It is perhaps safe to hypothesize that the practicing school counselor is more of a research consumer than he is a producer. Counselor educators, of course, regularly call for more research investigations by high school counselors, and while this is perhaps desirable, the work schedules of most counselors make the process difficult. However, for those readers who have research interests, this chapter may prove to be of some assistance.

RECENT HISTORY OF GROUP-COUNSELING RESEARCH

In reviewing group procedures from 1960 to 1963, E. Wayne Wright wrote that group counseling "by far received the greatest attention of all group-guidance activities" (p. 206). More recently, Anderson (1969) in a similar article wrote that the "rapid growth in the professional practice of group counseling has been accompanied by a proliferation of related research studies. Some 240 of the articles reviewed (covering the period from summer, 1965 to fall, 1968) were considered pertinent to this chapter" (p. 209). It is perhaps significant to note that Anderson entitled his article "Group Counseling," while Wright (1963) only six years earlier noted that many references were made to multiple counseling, and the terms *group counseling* and *multiple counseling* were used interchangeably. The general acceptance of the term and the relatively large number of studies reviewed by Anderson are perhaps indications that group counseling has come of age. Perhaps Mahler's (1969) comment that there "has been very little research in the field" may not be valid by 1975 and beyond. While the bulk of the investigations will probably still flow from master's and doctoral studies at the university level, the mere fact that more counselors are interested in this area will suffice to provide the field with more empirical data to guide practice.

REVIEWS OF GROUP-COUNSELING RESEARCH

While group-counseling research has become increasingly sophisticated since Wright's early review, the group-counseling researcher still encounters a number of problems. In 1966, Kagan called for counselors to spell out specific procedures and techniques in order that others could replicate their efforts and noted that most studies were small-scale unrelated efforts that provided bits of information. The lack of adequate group theory to guide group-counseling practice still hampers counselors (Anderson, 1969).

Gazda and Larsen (1968) in providing the group counselor with a comprehensive number of abstracts note that their study of over a hundred groups is inconclusive. Among the reasons for this state of affairs are the great variations in group size, length, duration or intensity of treatment, type and quality of treatment, sophistication of research design, instruments of evaluation, and test statistics (Gazda and Larsen, 1968, p. 64).

In the related field of group psychotherapy, Buchard, Michaels, and Katkov (1948) were proposing as early as 1948 that for the purposes of comparison, evaluation studies should provide data on seven factors: (1) therapists' frame of reference; (2) therapeutic goals and aims; (3) patient population; (4) role of the therapist; (5) the group; (6) the management of meetings; and (7) appraisal of results. Although these suggestions are still valid and current for group counseling, most of them have either been slighted or ignored in the majority of group studies reported in the literature.

More recently, professionals who are more closely associated with group counseling have been critical of the research results reported in this field. Gazda and Larsen (1968) note that one of the more serious problems in group-counseling research is that of defining experimental variables that are common to each group participant. They note that when data are grouped, gains made by certain subjects are cancelled out by other subjects who actually make progress by changing in the opposite direction of a given variable.

Zimpfer (1968) in an excellent discussion of the conceptual and research problems in group counseling notes that the assumptions that the goals of individual counseling are appropriate for group counseling and that groups need to focus on a common problem area are open to question. Like Anderson (1969), he too points out that there is no true theory of group counseling, thus causing problems for the researcher who utilizes several counselors or perhaps divergent philosophical positions in a given investigation. Counselors have also tended to employ a common evaluative instrument on all members of a group, thus causing an injustice to the potential of the group for altering "its course toward more significant personal experiences" (p. 328). Other conceptual problems include the use of too many labels for group counseling, different counselors conceiving of one counselor or more than one, groups ranging from three to thirty members, individual versus group focus, cognitive versus affective content, and disagreement on the most appropriate type of leadership (p. 329).

Mahler has also called the group researcher's attention to some of the serious methodological difficulties in the study of group interactions and outcomes. Six of the most serious in his opinion are: (1) lack of proper control groups; (2) use of immediate rather than long-term criterion measures; (3) use of too short a series of meetings to justify an expectation of change; (4) lack of experience and competence among group counselors; (5) not enough attention to members' reasons for joining a group—that is to their motivation for participating; and (6) use of a single group-counseling approach such as the client-centered method with diverse individual problems but with the expectation of similar outcomes (Mahler, 1969, pp. 208–9).

Researchers in group counseling like their counterparts in group therapy seem to have designed studies without awareness of other studies in the same area (Pattison, 1965). The recent efforts of Gazda and Larsen (1968), Anderson (1969), and Zimpfer (1970) are positive steps in bridging this communications gap.

EVALUATION STUDIES OF GROUP COUNSELING

1. BEHAVIORAL CRITERIA: Pattison (1965) in reviewing group-therapy research notes that the "most obvious behavioral measure is the overall clinical impression of the therapist." A step beyond this in his view is the use of evaluation by a mutual observer. However, in his view, the difficulty with clinical evaluative criteria is not their validity

but their reliability. The problems Pattison notes in group-therapy research are also concerns that plague the counselor. Although a number of group-counseling investigations have utilized mutual observers, the lack of specific criteria for judges and judging makes comparisons difficult. In addition, the clinical impressions of the counselor, unlike those of his therapist counterpart, are not as useful in school settings as they would be in a hospital ward. For example, the therapist who works with an individual who tends to distort reality to the extent that he needs institutional care can make a rather accurate assessment of any improvement by noting how accurately the patient seems to perceive reality. The counselor, on the other hand, since he generally works with a more normal population, would encounter more difficulty in determining just how far an individual has moved toward maximum use of his potential, an oft-stated counseling goal. Stated another way, counselors generally counsel for different outcomes in that their chief aim is generally not to restore psychological health or improve an individual to the point where he can be released from custodial care.

Counselors, however, have utilized specific behavioral criteria to evaluate a number of counseling studies. Bilovsky, *et al.,* (1953) attempted to determine if group counseling or individual counseling had any effect on the realism of vocational choice of twelfth grade boys. No significant differences were found between experimental groups that were individually counseled and those that were counseled in groups. However, approximately 58 percent of both groups made realistic choices—such choices were assessed as realistic by four counselor-psychologists. In a similar investigation, Hewer (1959) counseled students individually, in groups, and added a third experimental condition—a college class in vocations to determine if any of the experimental conditions had any effect on realism of vocational choice. No significant differences in treatments were noted and findings were considered questionable because of low inter-rater reliability.

Krumboltz and Thoresen (1964) studied the effects of several behavioral-counseling techniques in both individual and group-counseling approaches to determine treatment effects on educational and occupational information-seeking behavior of eleventh grade volunteers. An evaluation team reported that model reinforcement and reinforcement counseling significantly increased occupational and educational information-seeking behavior and that model-reinforcement counseling was more effective than individual counseling in significantly increasing occupational and educational information-seeking behavior.

Russell (1959) used judges' ratings to test the hypothesis that group counseling with mothers of boys retarded in reading would affect parental attitudes toward their children. Correlates between parent-attitude change and ready gain were significant, supporting the hypothesis that group counseling was effective in contributing to change in mothers' attitudes and sons' reading progress.

Runaway behavior, general institutional adjustment, attitudes toward parental–maternal figures and authority, and reality testing were among the specific outcomes judges' (cottage parents, teachers, and psychologists) rates in Friedland's (1960) investigation of delinquent and predelinquent boys. Significant improvement was noted in the experimental group in reality testing and frustration-tolerance ability.

Cohn and Sniffin (1962) combined teacher, counselor, and parent reports to learn more about acting-out pupils, to effect a change in attitudes, and to study techniques of group counseling. In a descriptive report, they state that subjects used the guidance office more frequently, requested referral to outside agencies, became more sensitive to others, showed more self-discipline, exhibited a higher standard of behavior, became less critical and more positive toward school and authority figures.

Goldburgh and Glanz (1962) studied the effectiveness of group counseling in helping students verbalize in class. Instructors used as judges reported that counseled students showed significant improvement following group counseling, although peers of the counseled students noted no significant differences in the way those who participated in groups verbalized in class.

Other investigators have used independent raters along with other outcome criteria to judge group-counseled students' improvement in academic achievement (McDaniel and Johnson, 1962; Ohlsen and Oelke, 1962; Garwood, 1964; Ohlsen and Gazda, 1965; while Smith (1963) used the group approach to counseling to see if this procedure would reduce college dropouts. While 24 percent of the control group withdrew from college, Smith reports that only 8 percent of those who attended group sessions made decisions to leave school.

Other specific attempts at behavioral change as a result of group counseling include Antenen's (1964) investigation of the relationship between content variables in group counseling and outcomes, Harshman's (1964) study of patients in a V.A. hospital, and the Lodato et al. (1964) study of the effects of group counseling on slow learners. Each of these studies used either clinical judgments or independent judges as part of their evaluation.

The behavior problem or acting-out child has been the target individual in several investigations (Webb, 1964; Blakeman, 1967; and Day, 1967). While each of these produced some positive results, Day's investigation is perhaps most interesting in that this is one of the few studies reported in the literature where a specific theoretical approach —that of activity-group counseling—was specified in the study.

2. PSYCHOMETRIC CRITERIA. Most of the researchers in the field of group counseling have utilized some form of psychological test to determine the effectiveness of group counseling. The MMPI has been used with some success (Lerner, 1953; DeWeese, 1960; Spielberger and Weitz, 1964; and Davis, 1967), but apparently the sophistication and training needed to utilize this instrument have prevented its wide use in group-counseling research. Slightly more popular has been the use of the Thematic Apperception Test (TAT) (Broedel, *et al.,* 1960; Gazda and Ohlsen, 1961; Reiser, 1961; Sawyer, 1965; and Gazda and Ohlsen, 1966) to measure group-counseling outcomes. Like the MMPI, the TAT requires special training and competence beyond that provided for most counselors. Furthermore, its use has produced mixed and inconclusive results.

In addition to the MMPI and TAT, a wide number of psychometric instruments have been employed by group researchers. Among the most common are the Mooney Problem Check List (Thurston, 1959; Landon, 1962; and Duncan, 1965); Brown–Holtzman Survey of Study Habits and Attitudes (Baymur and Patterson, 1960; Mink, 1964; and Chestnut, 1965); Allport–Vernon Study of Values (Mink, 1964; Duncan, 1965; Clements, 1966; and Davis, 1967).

Several standardized achievement tests and batteries have been used as part of studies in order to determine the effects of group counseling on scholastic performance. Generally, these have been employed in conjunction with student's grade-point average. Among such measures are: California Achievement Test (Broedel *et al.,* 1960); Cooperative English Test (DeWeese, 1960); and Iowa Test of Basic Skills (Spielberger and Weitz, 1962).

Changes in some aspect of self have perhaps been the favorite target of group-counseling researchers, and the self-concept of counseled subjects has been operationally defined in so many ways that one would encounter difficulty in trying to determine if group counseling actually affects the self-concept. A review of these self-studies indicates that the self seems to take on an entirely different meaning from investigation to investigation. Several common psychometric measures of self-concept, however, have appeared consistently in group-counseling studies. The Bills Index of Adjustment and Values has been used by Duncan (1962), Garwood (1964), Duncan (1965), Clements (1966), and Muro and Ohnmacht (1966) with generally poor results. The Tennessee Self-Concept Scale, a wider measure of self than the Bills, was used in research by Kuntz (1967) and Padgett (1967) and appears to have some promise for group investigations of self-concept. Of particular interest is Kuntz's study in which group counseling was effective in producing a more realistic self-concept for nonconforming high school students. His experimental counseled group of thirty-six students was also somewhat larger than many of the experimental groups used by other researchers.

A wide variety of other psychometric measures has been employed by group researchers to measure outcomes. Among them are the 16 Personality-Factor Questionnaire, Edwards Personal Preference Scale, California Psychological Inventory, Guilford–Zimmerman Temperament Survey, and California Test of Personality. None of these, however, have been used with any marked degree of consistency from study to study.

Numerous investigations have utilized a shotgun approach to assessing outcomes of group counseling by employing several (and at times rather diverse) psychometric instruments to determine whether or not the group-counseling process had any effect in a wide number of variables. It would almost appear that researchers are convinced that group counseling is effective in producing some kind of change but are seeking instruments to determine the exact nature of such change.

Like the common instruments used in group-therapy research, those used in group-counseling studies have generally produced disappointing results. Kraus (1959) has noted that the consistently negative reports in group therapy reflect the insensitivity and inappropriateness of these tests for group assessment. It would appear that his comments are also valid for group counseling. The inconclusive evidence produced by the use of psychometric measures in group counseling reflects their general inability to assess the workings of counseling groups.

3. CONSTRUCT CRITERIA. In addition to behavioral and psychometric criteria, a third approach has been to devise psychological constructs sensitive to personality change and suitable for measurement (Pattison, 1965, p. 386). Brodbeck (1963) notes that "in order to help explain certain manifest behavior, the scientist formulates concepts that name unobserved states of the organism or object exhibiting the observed criteria." Such inferred concepts are frequently labeled *constructs* (Brodbeck, 1963, p. 61).

Caplan (1957) used a Q-sort technique to measure the self-concept of boys twelve to fifteen years of age with records of long-term and frequent conflict with school authorities and regulations. Following ten weeks of group counseling, he reports that counseled subjects showed a significant random increase in congruence of self-ideal self. Q-sort approaches were also used by Baymur and Patterson (1960) to check adjustment of junior high underachievers, by Clements (1963) to measure the self-concept of able underachievers, by Zimpfer (1964) to test self-ideal self-congruence in a pretest–posttest design of high school students who displayed maladaptive behavior, and by Catron (1966) to measure changes in perception of self and others through educational–vocational group counseling. Zimpfer (1967) also used the Q-sort devised by Baymur and Patterson (1960) as part of his study to assess the relationship between changes in affective behavior of clients and counseling outcomes.

Two studies reported within the last decade—those by Waldman (1961) and Webb and Eikenberry (1964)—have utilized a semantic differential to evaluate counseling outcomes. Although Waldman reports generally nonsignificant results, counselors in Webb and Eikenberry's groups showed significant congruence of me-with-school-and-rules and me-with-mother-and-father scales.

Pattison in his discussion of construct criteria notes: "The problem which construct criteria *face* revolves around their relevance. To which patients and groups are such constructs relevant? Are these groups specific?" (Pattison, 1965, p. 387) The group-counseling researcher may well ask himself these same questions.

VARIABLES IN GROUP-COUNSELING EVALUATION

1. CLIENTS. In most of the studies reviewed by Gazda and Larsen (1968), those who were to receive group counseling represented a diverse and sometimes poorly defined population. Statements like "volunteers from an eleventh grade class" or "acting-out teen-agers" or "eight male and female students from X University" are frequently used to describe group members. In most cases, the total description of the student in group counseling consists of his grade level and score on psychometric measure, rating scale, or some construct. Thus duplications of studies by other researchers become increasingly difficult when one is faced with the task of matching samples with limited data. More inclusive and more specific descriptions of the clients in a given study would allow for easier and perhaps productive replication. This, of course, would be useful since many of the studies noted by Gazda and Larsen (1968) were conducted with relatively small numbers.

2. GROUP COUNSELING—WHAT IS IT? To paraphrase Leona Tyler (1961), *group counseling* is a term that everybody seems to understand but no two people seem to understand the same way. Again referring to Gazda and Larsen's (1968) review, group counseling seems to be free discussions, personology clubs, lectures, puppet plays, and numerous

other vague and varied descriptions. When one adds some of the newer terms such as *encounter groups* and *sensitivity groups,* the problem is even more complex. One finds it almost impossible to tell exactly what is meant by group counseling unless he carefully reads a description (frequently not given) of how a given researcher defines group counseling.

The other variable, of course, is the counselor himself. Who is he? Where was he prepared? By whom? One might envision, for example, quite different counselor approaches from a student of Krumboltz and from one prepared by Patterson. To the knowledge of the authors, no study similar to Fiedler's (1950) classic investigation has been done on group counselors, and perhaps we may well discover that experienced group counselors of different philosophical orientations behave in ways that are similar. Experience, not theoretical orientation, may be the factor that separates counselors, but until this has been determined, both the experience level and theoretical position of the counselor should be noted in reporting research.

3. COUNSELING CONTEXT. In what context has counseling taken place? Were the clients referred? Were they institutionalized? Were they volunteers? Were group members in some other experimental condition along with the group counseling? Researcher answers to these and similar queries would provide helpful information to those who would replicate promising research.

4. COUNSELING TIME AND GROUP DEVELOPMENT. Wide differences in the frequency of group-counseling meetings may be noted in the literature. Group counseling has been conducted for periods ranging from three weeks to well over a year. However, little is known about the optimal number of sessions necessary for productive results. Unfortunately, many of the studies reported seem designed to fit into some administrative framework (one semester, two quarters) rather than for purposes based upon theory or prior research. Although some of the principles derived from group-dynamics research would seem useful in providing guidelines for counselors, these have been largely ignored by most group-counseling researchers.

Most group counselors would generally agree that groups move through certain developmental phases (*see* Chapter 7). One must wonder, therefore, about the time or phase at which an evaluation was taken (Pattison, 1965). For example, would a group who had been in session for six weeks be at the same developmental phase as one that had been operating for a semester or longer? Would they reflect similar outcomes? These may be crucial questions and ones that need careful consideration in group-counseling research. The problems involved with respect to developmental phases include the relative lack of empirical knowledge with respect to group development and the probable notion that groups tend to develop unevenly. While one experimental group may move rapidly into therapeutic work levels, another conducted by the same counselor may spend weeks on superficial non-group topics.

5. RELEVANCE OF PARAMETERS. As Pattison (1965) notes, regardless of the criteria designed to measure group outcomes, "one is faced with two questions: (a) Is the measure a reflection of therapeutic change or just change alone? and (b) Does the measure reflect a unique group effect?" (Pattison, 1965, p. 389). Counselors, of course, are beset with the same problem—is the change really helpful? One could well imagine, for example, that participation in group counseling was indeed effective in assisting students to obtain improved grades, but suppose the student in striving harder for superior academic marks became increasingly more anxious as a result of his new behavior? The question of just *what* change is indeed helpful is a matter that must be considered by counselors, and if most of the published research is an indication of what counselors consider good for clients, there seems to be little agreement on which changes resulting from groups are most desirable. Pattison's (1965) second question—that of the results of any change reflecting a unique group experience—must also be considered by the group-counseling researcher.

6. INDIVIDUAL VERSUS GROUP EVALUATION. While the individual may not become lost or forgotten in the process of group counseling, it is possible that any change he has made will become lost in the final evaluation of a particular study. This may be especially true when one utilizes the balanced-group approach to group composition. Suppose, for example, a number of aggressive children are placed in a group of those who are shy. Theoretically, the members would have a remedial or developmental effect on one another. Following group counseling, one may find that by lumping outcome scores, both shy and aggressive children moved closer to a new (and perhaps group-influenced) norm that is to the center of these bipolar traits. By using group data alone, the individual change may be lost (Pattison, 1965).

DIRECTIONS FOR FUTURE RESEARCH

Cohn in an excellent APGA publication sets the tone for future group-counseling research in the following statement:

Before guidelines for future research can be drawn, there

must be an understanding of terms as well as general agreement about what group counseling is. While defining terms,
problems become evident in designing research projects capable of producing valid and reliable results. It became apparent that it would be necessary in the future for specialists
in several fields outside group counseling to combine their
efforts from the beginning of planning a research project.
[Cohn, 1967, p.38]

Using Cohn's statements as a guide, what are the areas of concern
that should be of interest to the group-counseling researcher? Some of
the most significant will be noted here.

1. WHAT IS GROUP COUNSELING? In over 95 percent of the 104
studies reviewed by Gazda and Larsen (1968), the independent variable was group counseling, and it would appear that group counseling
was operationally defined to be whatever the group counselor did in
that particular situation. This ranged from role playing to providing
educational–occupational information. When Cohn (1967) asks for a
clearer definition of terms, he is not making a casual statement. Small
wonder that we have encountered difficulty evaluating group counseling since we have had a great deal of difficulty defining it!

2. TREATMENT TECHNIQUES (Bender, 1970; and Cohn, 1967). Similar
to defining exactly what group counseling is, research efforts could be
enhanced with a knowledge of what group counselors *do* in the counseling sessions. In recent years, there has been a rapid increase in group
techniques ranging from nonverbal games to tape recordings that serve
as leaders and instruct members to do or say certain things. If programs
of specific group experiences are used by the group counselor, these
should be identified and communicated to the potential research consumer. If, however, the content of sessions is introduced by the group
members themselves, this fact also needs to be known.

3. THEORETICAL MODELS. In Chapter 3 of this text, the authors identified several theoretical models for counseling groups. While these
models generally have not been developed for group work *per se,*
numerous authors claim that their behavior is guided by the tenets of
some counseling theory. In this respect, the use of theoretical models
probably influences both the definition of group counseling and the
techniques utilized by the counselor. One might expect a different
approach or at least a different emphasis from a group led by a behav-
iorist than from one led by an existentialist. At any rate, if a counselor
does employ a theoretical model, this, like definitions of terms and
specific techniques, needs to be clearly identified.

4. GROUP GOALS AND INDIVIDUAL GOALS (Bender, 1970). What were the specific goals of this group? What objectives did the counselor have in mind? Were the counselor's goals the same as those of group members? If not, what specific objectives did the counselor have in mind in imposing external goals for members?

In this context, the authors would like to make a plea for individual goals for group members. As early as 1957, Walker and Peiffer noted that the outcomes selected for clients seem vague and general, and this critique has often been noted in subsequent articles dealing with group research. Recently, Ohlsen (1970) in noting Walker and Peiffer's critique called for counselors to identify specific idiosyncratic goals that may be stated in measurable terms.

For example, an individual who joins a group for the purpose of gaining self-understanding should be able to utilize the group process for smaller individualized goals. Why shouldn't an individual be allowed in a group because he is lonely and wants to use the group as a start in making new friends?

Another individual may have an important career decision to make and may well want to join a group to get assistance from others in making that decision. A third may join a group in order to learn new ways to understand herself, but she may also want help in dealing with her teen-aged son or daughter.

Thus, the counselor and group members must be open enough and free enough to permit idiosyncratic goals for all members regardless of whether or not the group was formed for the purposes of moving toward a general overall goal. In a similar vein, the group must be flexible enough to allow for an individual goal that may arise because of the group interaction. For example, a group member who listens intently to another relating how much night school has helped him in his job may wish to set a similar goal for himself. The group and the counselor could then assist him to examine himself, his hopes, ambitions and fears with respect to this new venture in his life. Prior to the group experience, the individual may not have had that goal, but the interaction in the setting may have helped him realign his plans in a way unique to him.

In sum, the authors are of the opinion that a group member should be afforded the opportunity to define and clarify those goals that are unique to him within the context of the group. Counseling after all is a process that seeks to help the individual make use of his potential and discuss topics of importance to him. Broad, external group goals should not and must not be so rigid that an individual is unable to work on matters that may indeed be external to the overall reason for the formation of the group. In a broad sense, individual counseling is possible within the group setting.

5. PROCESS AND OUTCOME MAY NEED TO BE STUDIED INDEPENDENTLY. Pattison (1965, p. 309) notes that though process and outcomes are obviously related, simultaneous research on both aspects seems too complex. Too often, discussions of group-therapy results turn out to be discussions of group process. The same situation is also true of group-counseling studies.

In summarizing the state of group-counseling research several individuals have made noteworthy concrete suggestions. Pattison notes that: (a) the use of specific construct criteria appears promising; (b) the global problem of assessment needs to be dissected into variables such as the type of patient population; (c) the types of group therapy; (d) the context of group therapy; (e) the effect of time; and (f) the phase effect of group process (p. 393).

Cohn in addition to some of the other suggestions noted in this chapter lists other important factors in group research that are needed for more refined investigations. These include: (a) groups with or without adjunctive individual counseling; (b) parallel, duo, and triplicate counseling groups (parent, teacher, pupils); (c) group size; (d) length of group sessions; (e) duration of counseling sessions; (f) composition of groups; and (g) follow-up evaluation (Cohn, 1967, pp. 39–41).

Finally, Anderson's comments are probably an accurate reflection of the needed direction in group-counseling research.

> Group counseling needs studies that specify concrete, measurable goals for individual clients, detailed analysis of verbal and non-verbal communication which constitutes the treatment, and a variety of appropriate criteria. The formulation of general principles about group counseling still awaits the use of identical treatment procedures in different settings with different clientele as well as multivariate approaches which compare several treatment procedures in similar settings with similar clientele. [Anderson, 1969, p. 203]

The group-caused researcher of the 70's and beyond could do much to advance our knowledge of group counseling if attention is given to the thoughts of Ohlsen (1970), Pattison (1965), Anderson (1969), and Cohn (1967).

CONDUCTING GROUP-COUNSELING RESEARCH

Although the counselor should refer to more complete books on research and research methodology to become fully competent in the area of group-counseling research, some basic concepts are presented here for practicing counselors who may wish to conduct experiments in local schools. In this spirit then a few essential concepts are presented to serve as guidelines for the neophyte group-counseling researcher.

CONTROL AND CONTROL GROUPS

An essential requirement of an experiment is the control of all except the independent variables—those that are to be studied. The purposes of control are to isolate the independent factors, to achieve change in magnitude, and to obtain quantitative evaluations (Bledsoe, 1963). Methods of control range from mechanical devices such as one-way screens to surgical approaches in which the researcher removes parts of the brain, glands, etc. The latter, of course, has not been of much interest to counselors (unless the authors have neglected to review some significant studies).

Of more interest to the group counselor are the means by which control may be achieved through use of statistical techniques. Among the most commonly employed are the analysis of variance, analysis of covariance, and partial correlation. Tables of random numbers and other similar approaches to selecting samples are also extremely useful to the counselor who is interested in research.

The concept of a control group in counseling research means that the counselor is employing two or more groups which are as nearly alike as possible along certain dimensions. Such groups are usually designated as *experimental* and *control* for the purposes of the study. For example, if a counselor wishes to compare students who had been counseled individually with those who had been counseled in groups, he might elect to have two experimental (counseled) groups, and a control group who received no treatment. Thus, if individuals who have been counseled show significantly greater gain along some dimensions than those who received no counseling, the researcher can conclude that the gains were made because of the process.

Although the concept of using a control group is simple, obtaining a truly equated control group is rather complex. Other than the use of identical twins (who seem to be hard to come by for counseling research), the counselor has the option of utilizing matched pairs of a randomized group technique. In the former, the counselor selects subjects with as nearly similar characteristics as possible and assigns one to the experimental and one to the control group until a sufficient number is obtained. The obvious disadvantage of this procedure is the difficulty in obtaining similar clients. Individuals who are similar in one trait or factor may be quite dissimilar in another.

Fortunately, the counselor can achieve control through the process of randomization. To use this approach, the counselor numbers the population for his study with two (or perhaps three, if the population from which the sample is to be selected is over 100) digit numbers:

01 Joe Jones
02 Sally Smith
03 Harry Adder
04 John DaLoure

He then goes to table of random numbers and begins to read in a given direction until he has a sample large enough for his study. For example, if the counselor were selecting an experimental group, he would read along the table of random numbers until he reached the first set of two digits that corresponded to his prepared list. If the number 04 was the first one to come up in the table, John DaLoure in the sample above would be the first individual selected for the experimental group. The tables noted here are designed in such a way that their proper use eliminates researcher bias in the conscious and unconscious selection of subjects. Most statistics books have tables of random numbers in their appendices.

Bledsoe also calls the researcher's attention to the possibility of studying groups as intact units. Although the counselor is not likely to experiment with intact groups as a teacher would in studying a classroom group, the possibility of achieving control through this approach is worth knowing. According to Bledsoe:

> If groups cannot be equalized before the experiment is underway, statistical techniques to achieve the necessary controls can be employed. Thus, original differences in a relevant factor may be observed and measured during the experiment and accounted for by statistical procedures when analyzing the results. The most frequently employed technique used in this procedure is the analysis of covariance. [Bledsoe, 1963, p. 72]

The analysis of covariance to which Bledsoe refers is a statistical procedure employed in group comparisons on one variable when the researcher has information on another variable that is correlated with it. The technique is essentially a combination of correlation and analysis of variance, and allows the researcher to make adjustments for the source of variation when the data is analyzed. Full discussions of analysis of variance, analysis of covariance, and other methods may be found in texts by Walker and Lev (1953), Garrett (1953), Lindquist (1953), Siegel (1956), and Popham (1967).

PRE- AND POST-EVALUATION

Meehel(1954) calls for counseling research to have pre- and post-evaluations which are either objective, or if judgmental, are uncontaminated. Objectivity of measurement is concerned with score values obtained from an instrument that is independent of the personal bias of the researcher. Even so-called *objective* measures are far from perfect for counseling purposes, and there are those who feel that more significant research may be conducted when the measuring devices are developed to the point where changes that may occur in counseling can be determined by the instrument. For the present, however, many have to be content with instruments that have less than satisfactory reliability and perhaps questionable validity. All devices used in counseling research, however, should be thoroughly examined by the researcher with respect to reliability, validity, norms, and practicality. The well-known *Mental Measurements Yearbooks,* edited by Buros, are valuable tools for the counselor in reviewing measuring instruments.

The problem of eliminating observer bias is difficult in any research, and there is no simple way to be certain that the individual making observations is not biased. Studies in the field of perception tell us that humans tend to observe what they want to see and hear what they want to hear. Because of this, the possibilities for error are a constant problem. Moreover, if the subjects are aware of the fact that they're being observed, other problems occur. The well-known studies conducted at the Hawthorne Plant of Western Electric provide us with evidence that individuals who are aware that they are part of an experiment may react in ways to alter their performances, thus invalidating an experiment. Therefore, the counselor who uses judges' ratings as pre- and post-measures to determine group-counseling outcomes must be aware of possibilities of bias. The criteria for valid observation as listed by Bledsoe would seem to be a must for the researcher who wishes to use judges' ratings.

Criteria for Valid Observations

1. Observation is specific, relevant, pertinent, not diffused and distracted. Careful planning and purpose are evident. The observer knows what he is looking for.
2. Observation is systematic, not haphazard. It may involve

a time sampling of the frequency of observable forms of behavior during a number of definite time intervals that are systematically spaced.

3. Observation is objective. The observer is aware of possible biases and attempts to minimize or eliminate their effect upon his perceptions.

4. Observations are promptly recorded by expert and careful means. Mechanical devices such as tape recorders or motion pictures are used whenever possible.

5. Observations are checked and verified by repetition, by additional independent observation, or by repeating the study.

6. Observation employs quantitative means wherever possible, rather than employing vague nebulous terminology which varies in content and meaning from one person to another.

7. Observation carefully distinguishes the facts from the opinions and interpretations. Interpretations are permitted only after sufficient facts have been obtained to warrant such inferences of inductions.

8. The observer is aware of the *Gestalt* or wholeness of the observation. While he is sensitive to details, he is aware of the fact that the details are only a part of the entire configuration, and he considers events in their proper perspective, not in isolation.

9. The records of observations are kept confidential. [Bledsoe, 1963, p. 97]

FOLLOW-UP

Follow-up studies undertaken some time after clients experienced individual or group counseling are rare indeed. The very nature of gathering data in a follow-up approach makes it somewhat unpalatable to many researchers. In many cases, the students involved in the counseling process have graduated, dropped out, or moved away from the school or agency where the experiment has taken place. Counselors are then confronted with the task of locating the students and obtaining needed information to determine if the effects of counseling were permanent or at least lasting in nature. For example, a counselor may well discover that counselees become more self-accepting following a period of group counseling. He may wish to determine the permanence of such change, and if the individuals are not readily available, it may be impossible to obtain this data since many instruments require controlled test procedure. As a result, much research is reported with data gathered and analyzed immediately after counseling, but few studies have concerned themselves with the condition of the client at some designated time—six months to a year after counseling is completed.

Follow-up research is badly needed, even if only to see whether or not we would get better results after the effects of counseling have had time to sink in. Unfortunately, the bulk of the research is done by master's and doctoral students who work under time limits and are not willing to risk losing data in order to complete degree requirements. Hopefully, more school counselors will engage in research, and the sophomore-sample investigations will be replaced with more studies done in school settings.

OVERALL SUGGESTIONS FOR CONDUCTING GROUP-COUNSELING RESEARCH

Muro and Freeman suggested a six-step procedure for the counselor researcher to utilize in group-counseling investigations: (1) a careful definition of the problem to include the objectives of the study and the expected outcomes; (2) the assessment of the need for the investigation, to include the probability of shedding a new light or a different perspective with the obtained results; (3) an appropriate selection of a sample; (4) the selection of a statistical technique prior to the start of the study; (5) a listing of assumptions and limitations in the study; and (6) a definition of terms that are meaningful and perhaps unique to the research (Muro and Freeman, 1968, pp. 243–48). All of these steps are necessary for good research and for enabling the counselor to organize his data in such a way that communication with other counselors will be enhanced. Any good basic text on educational research will provide the reader with more elaborate data on the areas suggested in this section; however, they are mentioned here as guides for the individual who is perhaps contemplating an initial investigation in group counseling.

EXPERIMENTAL DESIGNS

Gazda and Larsen in surveying group-counseling research note four major models that have been commonly utilized in group-counseling research. These are described briefly here:

1. PRE-EXPERIMENTAL DESIGNS. In this category fall the one-shot case study, the one group pre-test, post-test design and the static group comparison. In the case-study approach, a single instance is compared

with remembered or observed events and inferences are made on the expectations of what behavior could have occurred if the treatment had not taken place. A control group and post-test observations are not utilized. The one group pre-test, post-test includes a pre- and post-assessment of treatment but does not include a control group. In the static-group comparison, only post-test observations are employed and the treatment group is compared to a group which has not had the experimental treatment in an effort to establish the effect of treatment.

2. TRUE EXPERIMENTAL DESIGNS. In the category labeled *true experimental design*, Gazda and Larsen note three models which include the pre-test, post-test control-group approach, the Solomon four-group design, and the post-test only control-group design.

In the classical pre-test, post-test control-group model, equivalent groups are randomly selected and many experimental variations are possible. All sources of internal validity are controlled and so are some, but not all, sources of external validity. The Solomon four-group design did not occur in the studies reviewed by Gazda and Larsen, but they refer those interested in this model to Campbell and Stanley (1963) for a complete description of the technique.

The researcher employing the post-test only control-group design utilizes group randomization and "controls for testing as the main affect but does not yield a measure of these effects" (Gazda and Larsen, 1968, p. 63).

3. QUASI-EXPERIMENTAL DESIGNS. Gazda and Larsen list three approaches in this category. The first, called the *equivalent-materials design,* is one wherein groups that have received equivalent treatments and are purported to have lasting effects are compared with groups receiving different treatments. Necessary to this design is the sampling of materials for the purposes of validity and proof of treatment.

In the *nonequivalent control-group design,* both experimental and control groups are administered a pre-test and post-test. Pre-experimental sampling equivalence is not employed. This design is employed with natural groups such as classes or seminars, and the treatment is randomly assigned by the researcher.

The final quasi-experimental design listed by Gazda and Larsen is the *separate sample pre-test, post-test model* where a control group is not employed. Its main usage is for those situations where random separation of subgroups is impossible for the purposes of experimental treatments. Control is possible through a random assessment of the time that subjects are to be observed.

In addition to the designs listed here, Gazda and Larsen also note that some researchers have employed a descriptive *one group pre-test, post-*

test approach where verbal description rather than statistical techniques is utilized to report observed differences in subjects. In addition, some studies use a *descriptive simple survey* wherein a subject's response and reactions are reported immediately after exposure to treatment, and the *process study* or a verbal description of the proceedings of the treatment. For a more complete discussion of experimental designs, the reader is referred to Gazda and Larsen's (1968) excellent article and to Campbell and Stanley's thorough treatment in Gage's (1963) *Handbook on Research in Teaching.*

SUMMARY

Although research studies in group counseling have shown a marked increase in recent years, much needs to be done in this area. Reviewers have generally been critical of both conceptual approaches to group counseling and of research designs used in investigations. Evaluation studies in group counseling as well as group therapy have been measured in terms of behavioral criteria, psychometric criteria, and construct criteria. Important variables in evaluating group counseling include the clients, the nature of group counseling, the counseling content, counseling time and group development, the relevance of parameters, and individual versus total group development. Future research in this area requires: (1) more precise definition of terms; (2) a statement of the counselor's theoretical orientation and techniques; (3) closer attention to individual goals; and (4) a separation of process and outcome studies. Refinement in group research should include more and better designed studies in comparisons of group versus individual counseling, parallel, duo, and triplicate counseling, group size, length and duration of group sessions, group composition, and follow-up evaluations (Cohn, 1967).

REFERENCES

ANDERSON, A. R. "Group Counseling," in *Review of Educational Research* (ed. C. E. THORESEN), Vol. 39, No. 2 (1969), pp. 209–26.

ANTENEN, W. W. "Change in Topic and Affect during Group Counseling: Its Relationship to Outcomes of Group Counseling," *Dissertation Abstracts,* Vol. 24, No. 12 (1964), p. 5185.

BAYMUR, FERIHA, and PATTERSON, C. H. "Three Methods of Assisting Underachieving High School Students," *Journal of Counseling Psychology,* Vol. 7 (1960), pp. 83–89.

BENDER, R. L. "Group Psychotherapy Research Variables," *International Journal of Group Psychotherapy,* Vol. 20, No. 2 (1970), pp. 146–52.

BILOVSKY, D., MCMASTERS, W., SHORR, J. E., and SINGER, S. L. "Individual and

Group Counseling," *Personnel and Guidance Journal,* Vol. 31 (1953), pp. 363–65.

BLAKEMAN, J. D. "The Effects of Activity-Group Counseling on the Self-Evaluation and Classroom Behavior of Adolescent Behavior-Problem Boys." Ph.D. dissertation, University of Georgia, 1967.

BLEDSOE, J. *Essentials of Educational Research.* Ann Arbor, Mich.: Edwards Brothers, 1963.

BRODBECK, MAY. "Logic and Scientific Method in Research on Teaching," in *Handbook of Research in Teaching* (ed., N. L. GAGE). Chicago: Rand McNally and Company, 1963.

BROEDEL, J., OHLSEN, M., PROFF, F. and SOUTHARD, C. "The Effects of Group Counseling on Gifted Underachieving Adolescents," *Journal of Counseling Psychology;* Vol. 7 (1960), pp. 163–70.

BUCHARD, E., MICHAELS, J. J., and KATOV, B. "Criteria for Evaluation of Group Therapy," *Psychoson. Med.,* Vol. 10 (1948), pp. 257–74.

CAMPBELL, D. T., and STANLEY, J. C. "Experimental and Quasi-experimental Designs for Research," in *Handbook of Research and Teaching* (ed. N. L. GAGE). Chicago: Rand McNally and Company, 1963.

CAPLAN, S. W. "Effect of Group Counseling on Junior High School Boys' Concepts of Themselves in School," *Journal of Counseling Psychology,* Vol. 4 (1957), pp. 124–28.

CATRON, D. W. "Educational–Vocational Group Counseling: The Effects on Perception of Self and Others," *Journal of Counseling Psychology,* Vol. 13 (1966), pp. 202–7.

CHESTNUT, W. J. "The Effects of Structured and Unstructured Group Counseling on Male College Students' Underachievement," *Journal of Counseling Psychology,* Vol. 24 (1965), pp. 388–94.

CLEMENTS, B. E. "Transitional Adolescents, Anxiety and Group Counseling," *Personnel and Guidance Journal,* Vol. 45 (1966), pp. 67–71.

CLEMENTS, T. H. "A Study to Compare the Effectiveness of Individual and Group-Counseling Approaches with Able Underachievers when Counselor Time Is Held Constant," *Dissertation Abstracts,* Vol. 23 (1963), p. 1919.

COHN, B. (ed.). *Guidelines for Future Research in the Public School Setting.* Washington, D.C.: American Personnel and Guidance Association, 1967.

COHN, B., and SNIFFIN, A. M. "A School Report on Group Counseling," *Personnel and Guidance Journal,* Vol. 41 (1962), pp. 133–38.

DAVIS, KATHLEEN L. "The Sensitivity of Selected Instruments to Personality Changes Produced by Group Counseling." Ph.D. dissertation, University of Georgia, 1967.

DAY, S. R. "The Effects of Activity-Group Counseling on Selected Behavior Characteristics of Culturally Disadvantaged Negro Boys." Ph.D. dissertation, University of Georgia, 1967.

DEWEESE, H. L. "The Extent to which Group Counseling Influences the Academic Achievement, Academic Potential, and Personal Adjustment of

Predicted Low-Achieving First Semester College Freshmen," *Dissertation Abstracts,* Vol. 20 (1960), pp. 3192–93.

DUNCAN, D. R. "Effects of Required Group Counseling with College Students in Academic Difficulty," *Dissertation Abstracts,* Vol. 23 (1962), p. 3772.

DUNCAN, J. A. "The Effects of Short-Term Group Counseling on Selected Characteristics of Culturally Deprived Ninth Grade Students." Ph.D. dissertation, University of Georgia, 1965.

FIEDLER, J. C. "The Concept of an Ideal Therapeutic Relationship," *Journal of Counseling Psychology,* Vol. 14 (1950), pp. 239–45.

FRIEDLAND, D. M. "Group Counseling as a Factor in Reducing Runaway Behavior from an Open Treatment Institution for Delinquent and Predelinquent Boys: The Evaluation of Changes in Frustration, Tolerance, Self-Concept, Attitude toward Maternal Figures, Attitude toward Paternal Figures, Attitude toward Other Authority and Reality Testing of Runaway Delinquent Boys," *Dissertation Abstracts,* Vol. 21 (1960), pp. 237–38.

GAGE, N. L. *Handbook of Research in Teaching.* Chicago: Rand McNally and Company, 1963.

GARRETT, H. E. *Statistics in Psychology and Education.* Boston: Houghton Mifflin Company, 1953.

LINDQUIST, E. F. *Design and analysis of experiments in psychology and education.* Boston: Houghton-Mifflin, 1953.

LODATO F. J., SOKOLOFF, M. A., and SCHWARTZ, L. J. "Group Counseling as a Method of Modifying Attitudes in Slow Learners," *School Counselor,* Vol. 12 (1964), pp. 27–29.

MAHLER, C. A. *Group Counseling in the Schools.* Boston: Houghton Mifflin Company, 1969.

McDANIEL, H., and JOHNSON, B. A. "Effects of Group Counseling on Achievers and Underachievers," *Journal of Secondary Education,* Vol. 37 (1962), pp. 136–39.

MEEHEL, P. F. *Clinical versus Statistical Prediction.* Minneapolis, Minn.: University of Minnesota Press, 1954.

MINK, O. G. "Multiple Counseling with Underachieving Junior High School Pupils of Bright, Normal, and Higher Ability," *Journal of Educational Research,* Vol. 58 (1964), pp. 31–34.

MURO, JAMES J., and FREEMAN, S. L. *Readings in Group Counseling.* Scranton, Pa.: International Textbook Company, 1968.

MURO, JAMES J., and OHNMACHT, F. W. "Effects of Group Counseling on Dimensions of Self-Acceptance, Dogmatism, and Preference for Complexity with Teacher-Education Students," *SPATE Journal,* Vol. 5, No. 2 (1966), pp. 25–30.

OHLSEN, MERLE M. *Group Counseling.* New York: Holt, Rinehart and Winston, Inc., 1970.

OHLSEN, MERLE M., and GAZDA, GEORGE M. "Counseling Underachieving Bright Pupils," *Education,* Vol. 86 (1965), pp. 78–81.

OHLSEN, MERLE M., and OELKE, M. C. "An Evaluation of Discussion Topics in Group Counseling," *Journal of Clinical Psychology*, Vol. 18 (1962), pp. 317–22.

PADGETT, H. G. "Effects of Group Guidance and Group Counseling on the Self-Concept and Professional Attitudes of Prospective Teachers." Ph.D. dissertation, University of Georgia, 1967.

PATTISON, E. M. "Evaluation Studies of Group Psychotherapy," *International Journal of Group Psychotherapy*, Vol. 15, No. 3 (1965), pp. 328–97.

POPHAM, W. J. *Educational Statistics*. New York: Harper and Row, Publishers, 1967.

REISER, M. "The Effects of Group Counseling on Interpersonal Relationships, Anxiety Level, Intellectual Functioning, and Certain Personality Characteristics in a Planned Workshop Experience," *Dissertation Abstracts*, Vol. 22 (1961), p. 325.

RUSSELL, M. "Effect of Group Counseling with Mothers on the Attitudes toward Children and on their Sons' Reading Disability: An Educational–Therapeutic Approach to Parent Attitudes and Reading Disability in a Clinic Situation," *Dissertation Abstracts*, Vol. 20, No. 2 (1959), p. 764.

SAWYER, W. G. "A Study of the Effect of Group Counseling on the Antisocial Behavior of Prison Inmates," *Dissertation Abstracts*, Vol. 25, No. 9 (1965), p. 5125.

SIEGEL, S. *Nonparametric Statistics for the Behavioral Sciences*. New York: McGraw-Hill Book Company, 1956.

SMITH, B. M. "Small Group Meetings of College Freshmen and Frequency of Withdrawals," *Journal of College Student Personnel*, Vol. 4 (1963), pp. 163–70.

SPIELBERGER, C. D., and WEITZ, H. "Improving the Academic Performance of Anxious College Freshmen: A Group-Counseling Approach to the Prevention of Underachievement," *Psychological Monographs: General and Applied*, Vol. 78, No. 590 (1964).

SPIELBERGER, C. D., WEITZ, H., and DENNY, J. P. "Group Counseling and the Academic Performances of Anxious College Freshmen," *Journal of Counseling Psychology*, Vol. 9 (1962), pp. 195–204.

THURSTON, A. S. "An Experimental Study of the Relative Effectiveness of Group Counseling and the Orientation Course in Assisting College Freshmen," *George Washington University Bulletin*, Vol. 59, No. 2 (1959), pp. 19–24.

TYLER, LEONA. *The Work of the Counselor*. New York: Appleton-Century-Crofts, Inc., 1961.

WALDMAN, M. "The Effects of Group Counseling in a Controlled Workshop Setting on Attitude, Manual Dexterity and Ability to Perceive Correct Spatial Relations," *Dissertation Abstracts*, Vo. 22 (1961), pp. 328–29.

WALKER, D. E., and PEIFFER, H. C. "The Goals of Counseling," *Journal of Counseling Psychology*, Vol. 3 (1957), pp. 204–9.

WALKER, H. M., and LEV, J. *Statistical Inference*. New York: Holt, Rinehart and Winston, Inc., 1953.

WEBB, A. P., and EIKENBERRY, J. "A Group-Counseling Approach to the Acting-Out Preadolescent," *Psychology in the Schools,* Vol. 1 (1964), pp. 395–400.

WRIGHT, E. WAYNE. "Group Procedures," *Review of Educational Research,* Vol. 33, No. 2 (1963), pp. 205–13.

ZIMPFER, D. G. "The Relationship of Self-Concept to Certain Affective Dimensions in Multiple Counseling," *Dissertation Abstracts,* Vol. 25 (1964), p. 3417.

————. "Expression of Feelings in Group Counseling," *Personnel and Guidance Journal,* Vol. 45 (1967), pp. 703–8.

————. "Some Conceptual and Research Problems in Group Counseling," *School Counselor,* Vol. 15, No. 5 (1968), pp. 326–33.

Appendix I

VISUAL AIDS

The visual aids listed below can be used to illustrate and supplement much of the material in this book. Since many of the films deal with various aspects of group work, we recommend that they be reviewed before use, in order to determine their suitability for particular groups of people or units of study.

Activity Group Therapy. Film Library, Yeshiva University, 526 W. 187 Street, New York, N.Y. (56 min.). This film is a condensation of several years of treatment of an actual group of latency-age boys. It illustrates an ego-level therapeutic process which is essentially experimental and noninterpretive. Restricted to clinical audiences.

The Actualization Group—Facing One's Self. Psychological Films, 205 W. 20th St., Santa Ana, Calif. 92706 (40 min.). Dr. Everett Shostrom demonstrates actualization therapy based on the concepts and theory of Dr. Abraham Maslow.

The Actualization Group. Psychological Films, 205 W. 20th St., Santa Ana, Calif. 92706 (B/W, 16 mm., 45 min. each).

Film #1 — General Theme: Risking Being Ourselves
      (1) Mr. Rabbit: The Nice Guy
      (2) Using Hurt to Cover Anger

(3) Top Dog vs. Under Dog
Film #2 — General Theme: Freedom and Actualization
(1) From Calculator to Trust and Letting Go
(2) Projection of the "Judge"
(3) Striving vs. Surrender
Film #3 — General Theme: Aggression and Actualization
(1) Fear of Aggression
(2) Violence about Violence
(3) The Emotional Pendulum
Film #4 — General Theme: Manipulation and Actualization
(1) Cleverness as Manipulation
(2) Judging as Manipulation
(3) Life as a Battle
Film #5 — General Theme: The Divorce from Parents
(1) The Mother-Blaming Game
(2) From Divorce to Appreciation of Mother
(3) From Fear of Being to Authenticity
Film #6 — General Theme: Self-Disclosure of the Therapist
(1) The Calculator: A Poker Player with Life
(2) The Calculator and the Clinging Vine
(3) Self-Disclosure of the Therapist
(4) A Magic Moment: A Peak Experience
Film #7 — General Theme: From Deadness to Aliveness
(1) From Deadness to Aliveness
(2) Breaking up the Family
(3) A Vision

Anatomy of a Group. Dynamics of Leadership Series. University of California Extension, Media Center, Berkeley ($9.00, 30 min.). This program illustrates the structure of a group, the goals to be achieved during meetings, participation patterns, the quality of communication, group standards, and group procedures. It asks and answers these questions: What is the difference between a collection of individuals and a group? How can a new group get off to a good start?

Behavior Theory in Practice. Appleton-Century-Crofts Film Library, 267 W. 25th Street, New York, N.Y. 10001 ($45.00 per week). One in a series of four twenty-minute films in which a number of species are presented under research conditions. Skinnerian behavior-theory basic research is described. Findings are extended beyond the laboratory. Designed for college classes in introductory psychology, experimental psychology, psychology of learning and educational psychology.

Belonging to the Group. Collaborator: Robert J. Havinghurst, Ph.D. The University of Chicago ($90.00). Stresses the importance of belonging to a group, whether in school, at work, or in the community. Two families gain acceptance in a new community by proving themselves capable in their work, by sharing the interests of their fellow students or fellow workers, and by understanding and respecting their established ways of doing things.

Broader Concept of Method—Part I, Developing Pupil Interest. Teaching Education Series. University of California Extension, Media Center, Berkeley ($4.00, 13 min.). This film contrasts the conventional teacher-dominated, lesson-hearing type of recitation with the informal group-discussion type of class session, and shows the effect of each method upon student attitudes.

The Circle—Parts I and II. McGraw-Hill Test Film Division, 330 W. 42nd St., New York, N.Y. ($345.00—rental available through universities and libraries). Traces therapy of drug addicts in Dayton, Staten Island, New York. A group-therapy center.

Developing Giftedness in the Educationally Disadvantaged. Bailey Films, Inc., 6509 DeLongpre Ave., Hollywood, Calif. 90028 ($15.00 for three days). Rafe is a gifted, educationally disadvantaged child portrayed in three environments: home, school, and neighborhood. The film is open-ended and is designed to lead its audience into discussion. The problem presented and the possible solutions suggested are intended to provide a stimulus for action toward establishing adequate programs to care for children like Rafe.

Diagnosing Group Operations. Dynamics of Leadership Series. University of California Extension, Media Center, Berkeley ($9.00, 30 min.). Through practical demonstrations and comments by Professor Knowles, this program looks into the causes of conflicts that arise in groups and tells how to identify symptoms of group problems.

Effective Leadership. Management Development Series. University of California Extension, Media Center, Berkeley ($9.00, 32 min.). Dr. Robert Tannenbaum defines and describes the characteristics of effective leadership in this filmed lecture.

Experimental Studies in the Social Climates of Groups. University of Maine, Orono, Me. 04473.

First Lessons. Drs. M. Ralph Kaufman, Ralph Ojemann, and Wilbur Miller. Iowa State Mental Health Authority ($105.00). Presents a detailed reenactment of a human-relations lesson in the classroom. The interaction of the pupils in Mrs. Deane's second grade class has produced a delicately balanced system which contributes to productivity and harmony under the understanding guidance of the teacher.

The Full Circle. New York University Film Library, 25 Washington Place New York, N.Y. 10003. Produced by the Mental Health Film

Board, the film illustrates the use of a group discussion by patients as well as individual interviews in a vocational rehabilitation program.

Getting Along with Others.   Coronet Instructional Films, Coronet Building, Chicago, Ill. 60601 (cost unknown, rental not available). Shows typical problems at school and at home. It is designed to help the child see what he can do to ease or solve such problems. One technique used in the film permits children in the audience to decide what they would do in a particular situation. For kindergarten and primary through third grade.

Getting Along with Parents.   Collaborator: Carl R. Rogers, Ph.D. The University of Chicago ($75.00). Explores some of the common problems that high school students face in their relations with their parents. Shows the conflict between six teenagers and their respective parents in a situation designed to provoke discussion. Emphasizes that each generation must recognize the other's differences in upbringing, thinking and feeling, and be willing to compromise on solutions to problems.

Going to School is Your Job.   Journal Films, Inc., 909 W. Diversey Parkway, Chicago, Ill. ($75.00 B/W, $150.00 Color). Available through University Rental Libraries, Boston University, Syracuse University, University of Illinois. Designed for use with kindergarten and primary-age children. Its purpose is to encourage positive attitudes toward school, and to show why rules are necessary, how they help us and benefit the group.

Group Needs.   Audio-Visual Center, Michigan State University, East Lansing, Mich.

Helping Students Understand Themselves.   Film #c-10. Dr. Art Glenn. Department of Education, Film Library, Harrisburg, Pa.

How to Use Encounter Groups.   Instructional Dynamics, Inc., 166 E. Superior Street, Chicago, Ill. 60611 (ten cassettes $69.95, playback unit $22.95). This is a series of half-hour cassettes in which Dr. Rogers talks about a variety of topics regarding encounter groups, including a discussion on his way of facilitating a group. The subscription can be for ten cassettes or twenty.

The Impact of Videotape Recording on Insight in Group Psychotherapy.   Ian Alger, M.D. and Peter Horgan, M.D., 500 E. 77th St., New York, N.Y. 10021. Portrays an actual adult group-therapy session in which a videotape recording is made of parts of it and is immediately played back to the members for their reactions to seeing and hearing themselves.

Journey into Self.   Psychological Cinema Register, 3 Pattee Library, Pennsylvania State University, University Park, Pa. (rental, $50.00).

This film, produced by W. H. McGraw, won an Academy Award for the best feature-length documentary film of 1969. Condensed into less than an hour, this is a film of the essence of a 16-hour weekend encounter group conducted by Carl Rogers and Richard Farson. It focuses especially on the experiences of four people during this highly intensive weekend.

Learning through Discussion (LTD).   Lecture by Dr. Hill on the use of the LTD technique for use of the discussion technique for learning course content. Introduction and continuity supplied by Dr. Stoller (B/W, sound, 16 mm.; also in 1/2 inch Sony video tape; 30 minutes, 1967).

Meeting in Session.   Columbia University.

Nineteen Trees.   ($125.00). The simple act of planting trees in one crowded city street starts a whole process of intergroup understanding and cooperation. Adult and secondary school levels.

Personality and Emotions.   Collaborator: Joseph McVickers Hunt, Ph.D. University of Illinois ($75.00). Designed for high school and college audiences studying personality development and mental health. Gives an overview of the development of emotions from infancy through early childhood, and implies that emotional maturity is a desirable goal in the development of personality.

Popularity Problems.   Consultant: Richmond Barbour, Ph.D., Guidance Director San Diego Schools. Answers many teenage questions. Shows teens how to get along with people of different temperaments and how to understand a teen's role in society. Several alternatives presented for each topic stimulate discussion and independent thinking.

Remotivation.   Service Section, Smith, Kline and French, 1500 Spring Garden St., Philadelphia, Pa. A new technique which has motivated chronic hospitalized patients. For the psychiatric aide to use with small groups of patients.

Roadblocks to Communication.   Dynamics of Leadership Series. University of California Extension, Media Center, Berkeley ($9.00, 30 min.). Professor Knowles examines some of the reasons for poor communication in group discussions and lecture presentations. Why do people misunderstand a message that seems perfectly clear? Why is it difficult for some people to listen? What can be done to develop better communications in a group? Professor Knowles explains a watchdog panel, a reaction panel, and an audience panel.

The Road to Reality.   Dr. Richard Abell, Tower Rd., Riverside, Conn. This film shows the dynamics of interaction within an adult psychotherapy group.

Role Playing in Human-Relations Training. University of California Extension, Media Center, Berkeley ($7.00, 25 min.). This film presents the technique of role playing in the study of human relations as demonstrated at a summer workshop of the National Training Laboratory in group development. The development of human-relations skills through reality practice is also shown.

Roots of Happiness. Drs. Juan A. Pons and Viola Bernard. Puerto Rico Department of Health ($115.00). Sheds light on the nature of family relationships, particularly the role of the father in building and maintaining a happy family environment. Set in Puerto Rico, it shows a family in which mutual love and respect provide the mortar to build a firm structure of self-respect, independence, and productivity. Despite the primitive living conditions, the warmth and maturity of the parents give the children the security they need to develop their capacities to the fullest.

A Session with College Students. Psychological Films, 205 W. Twentieth St., Santa Ana, Calif. 92706 ($15.00).

Sharing the Leadership. Dynamics of Leadership Series. University of California Extension, Media Center, Berkeley ($9.00, 30 min.). In this film members of the demonstration group get lost in the woods. They sit down then and discuss the best method to find their way home. The example is intended to show how leadership arises in a group, what is involved in the concept of leadership, and how group membership and leadership are related.

Target Five. Psychological Films, 205 W. 20th St., Santa Ana, Calif. 92706 (Color, 16 mm., Reel No. 1—26 min.). In this first section of the film series, Virginia Satir, family therapy, in cooperation with Dr. Everett L. Shostrom, Director of the Institute of Therapeutic Psychology, demonstrates the four manipulative-response forms. Each of the four forms is illustrated by a simulated family—Mrs. Satir describes the manipulative-response form and then it is demonstrated by a family situation. This film concludes with a family actualizing together which is described as "Target Five."

Reel No. 2—22 minutes. Satir and Shostrom combine to describe the three essential qualities of an actualizing relationship. The first of these is hearing and listening, the second, understanding, and the third is mutual meaning. Each of these three dimensions of the actualizing relationship is discussed in detail and then demonstrated on film. The development of the actualizing relationship, or "Target Five," is the key goal of this film.

Teaching the 3s, 4s, 5s—Part I, Guiding Behavior. Churchill Films,

662 Robertson Blvd., Los Angeles, Calif. 90069 (rental). Request rental sources from distributor.

Trouble in the Family. Indiana University Audio–Visual Center, Bloomington, Ind. (rental, $12.15). A middle-class New England family with emotional problems following the advice of a school guidance counselor decides to enter family therapy. Through use of the one-way mirror technique, cameras recorded the candid reactions of the family, and scenes from nine of the thirteen actual therapy sessions are included in the film.

Values for Teenagers—The Choice is Yours. Guidance Associates, P.O. Box 5, Pleasantville, N.Y. 10750 ($29.95, rental not available). A two-part sound filmstrip, based on live interviews, designed for use in group-guidance situations to stimulate discussion among young people about their developing values.

Appendix II

HIM-B TEST

1. I talk to people about my background, family, school, work, etc.
2. I tell other people specifically what kind of reactions I have toward them when they ask me.
3. I like to discuss psychology with people.
4. I side in with people who say they are getting a raw deal.
5. In a group I'd ask questions about how one member reacts to another.
6. I'm interested in what kind of things motivate people.
7. People need to be told off regularly.
8. When a group is having trouble operating, I figure out what's wrong with the group and propose solutions.
9. I ask for or give summaries and restatements of what's said.
10. I am sarcastic to people.
11. I try to support and encourage other people.
12. When people point out examples of my immature, irrational, or inadequate behavior I try to profit by this.
13. Even though my ideas are unpopular I tend to uphold them.
14. I side in with people who criticize the group.
15. I like to know something about the background of people.
16. I let people know what I think of them.
17. I offer suggestions as to how a group might improve its functioning.

Reprinted by permission of Dr. Wm. Fawcett Hill.

18. I'm willing to seek help from people for my personal problems.
19. I like people who initiate and plan group activities.
20. When groups try to solve people's problems, it's a case of the "blind leading the blind."
21. If conflicting goals are fouling up a group I will point this out.
22. Groups tend to get off the subject and wander all over.
23. I try to get people to honestly examine the kind of relationships they form with others.
24. I like to discuss current events.
25. I help plan a group's activities.
26. I like to chat with people.
27. I openly criticize the policies of those in charge or in positions of authority.
28. I try to integrate or synthesize and pull together divergent opinions or ideas expressed in a group.
29. I like to discuss what causes various kinds of emotional upsets and mental illnesses.
30. I compare the group I'm in with other groups I've known.
31. I try to help people with their personal problems.
32. I retaliate when people point out my weaknesses.
33. When people talk about their problems, I like to bring the discussion around to the principles or types of behavior that are illustrated by these problems.
34. I share with the group my observations of its function and it subsequent failures.
35. I point out discrepancies or contradictions between peoples' behavior and what they say they're like.
36. I like for others to help me understand myself.
37. I'm the one who asks what are the plans and procedures of the group.
38. I like to praise people.
39. I disagree with the way groups tend to operate.
40. I make fun of people.
41. I'm interested in people.
42. It is my responsibility to give group members an honest statement of how I react to them even if it may hurt their feelings.
43. I'm willing to share details of my private life with people.
44. When I tell people how I react to them, I try to do so—but in a way that doesn't hurt their feelings.
45. I try to clarify or pull out some conclusions for the group when it gets bogged down or confused when discussing a topic.
46. When a member's behavior prevents or inhibits a group's progress, I point out to the group the effect of his behavior.

47. I try to find out what kind of reactions my behavior produces on other individuals.
48. I like to exchange gossip.
49. I like to kid with people.
50. I try to get people to discuss the kinds of defenses and psychological principles that their behavior illustrates.
51. People have pretty foggy notions on most controversial issues.
52. I like to offer observations about the group's performance.
53. I like to get people to discuss how they feel about each other.
54. People need to know more about psychological and psychiatric terms and concepts.
55. I react negatively to suggestions implying that I change my personality.
56. I try to get people to deal with their problems which they avoid.
57. I like to argue with people.
58. I like to be close and personal with people.
59. People who talk about their troubles gripe me.
60. I share with the group how I think we're doing.
61. When people ask about how I react toward them I usually tell them something.
62. I try to find out how people actually see me and see my problems.
63. I like to socialize.
64. I'm interested in people.

Appendix III
GROUP METHODS AND PROCESSES IN
GUIDANCE AND COUNSELING
GOAL CARD   Name_____

There are 17 competencies expected in this course. Class activities and evaluations are organized around these goals. The goals are established to help the student see what is expected. They state what the student should be able to do as a result of the course.

Competencies	Unsatis-factory	Good	Exceptional Ability
1. Can develop a theory of group counseling which includes rationale, objectives, and a consideration of group dynamics and group processes	_____	_____	_____
2. Can describe and demonstrate the role of the group counselor as differentiated from the counseling of individuals	_____	_____	_____
3. Can describe the role of the group member and participate meaningfully in a group. Is sensitive and aware of self and others in the group setting; recognizes roles members play ...	_____	_____	_____
4. Can distinguish varied theoretical approaches to group process and group counseling such as the Adlerian, Group Centered, Behavioral, Transactional, and National Training Laboratories......	_____	_____	_____
5. Can describe the therapeutic forces and mechanisms of group counseling and understands their role in the unique social climate of group work	_____	_____	_____

(Appendix III continued)

Competencies	Unsatis-factory	Good	Exceptional Ability
6. Can structure the group, communicate the purpose of the group and set limits	_____	_____	_____
7. Is empathic and sensitive to affect, can reflect and clarify feelings	_____	_____	_____
8. Is aware of the potential effect of transactions between members upon specific members of the total group.......	_____	_____	_____
9. Can confront individuals and the group in terms of here-and-now behavior and the purpose of behavior	_____	_____	_____
10. Is able to convey links between members, similarities and differences, to facilitate group development.........	_____	_____	_____
11. Is able to encourage and increase a group member's feelings of self-esteem and worth	_____	_____	_____
12. Is able to promote interaction cohesiveness and the desire to work together among group members	_____	_____	_____
13. Can clarify, restate, summarize, and enable group members to evaluate what they have learned	_____	_____	_____
14. Has perceptions which are field dependent; influenced by the gestalt of the field	_____	_____	_____
15. Understands the place of programming in group development	_____	_____	_____
16. Can describe, discuss, and manage the special problems which develop in group work	_____	_____	_____
17. Is able to detect and make tentative analysis with respect to non verbal behavior .	_____	_____	_____

Appendix IV

GROUP OBSERVER'S FORM

Group-Guidance and Counseling Procedures

Today's Purposes: _____

A. Leadership:
   1. To what extent did we understand our purposes?
   2. What progress was made toward these goals?
   3. Was there evidence of group cohesion?
   4. Was there evidence of altruism in the group?
   5. Was the leadership democratic, autocratic, or laissez faire?

B. The General Atmosphere:
   1. Formal or informal?
   2. Permissive, inhibited, or overstructured?
   3. Cooperative or competitive?
   4. Friendly or hostile?

C. Contributions and Roles of Members:
1. Participation general or dominated? Was there a monopolist in the group?
2. Contributions pertinent or on too many tangents?
3. Did contributions indicate that contributors were listening carefully to what others in the group had to say?
4. Were contributions factual and problem centered or based upon preconceived notions and emotionally held points of view?
5. What were the main roles played in the group today?*

__Initiator	__Energizer	__Aggressor
__Info Seeker	__Encourager	__Blocker
__Opinion Seeker	__Observer	__Recognition
__Info Giver	__Recorder	Seeker
__Opinion Giver	__Follower	__Self-Confessor
__Elaborator	__Standard Setter	__Playboy
__Coordinator	__Expediter	__Dominator
__Orienter	__Compromiser	__Help Seeker
__Evaluator	__Harmonizer	__Special-Interest Pleador

*Adapted from Walter Lifton, *Working with Groups* (2nd ed.; New York: John Wiley and Sons, Inc., 1966,) pp. 20-21.

Appendix V

THE LOG

The log is a personal document which provides a chance to record feelings in writing which are perhaps still unshared verbally with others. It can provide an opportunity for self-evaluation while developing the courage through this rehearsal to become more congruent, honest, and open in expressing one's self later. It should permit one to understand what evokes his feelings, to recognize his personal psychological interaction and to become aware of his values, attitudes, perceptions, and style of life.

The group log might contain:
1. Observations regarding individual and group goals.
2. Changing attitudes in self and others.
3. An assessment of hypotheses regarding the group, its mechanisms, special problems, and strengths.
4. An assessment of your feelings, attitudes, and methods of operation.
5. Self-evaluation and personal progress.
6. An indication of the major themes and dynamics of the session. Each group meeting will have a number of major themes or topics (personal concerns, plans of individual members, etc). With the aid of your audio tape, you should be prepared to identify these themes. In addition, you should be able to respond to the dynamics relative to these themes. What forces were at work? What norms have emerged or are emerging?
7. Your group will develop or move through various stages. (See Chapter Seven on Group Development). For example, an initial stage of group development might be milling around or personal unshared behavior. Later stages might reveal different group and individual behavior. Your log should contain your impression of the developmental stage of the group.
8. To assist the counselor to understand the member's perceptions of a given session, the counselor may ask each member to respond to a simple question such as "What happened in the group today?" Members respond to this question on a 3″ by 5″ index card at the completion of each session.

NAME INDEX

SUBJECT INDEX